Microsoft Publisher Made Easy

About the Dover Pictorial Archive Series Clip Art Disk

Disk Contents: The disk contains 102 clip art illustrations from the Dover Pictorial Archive Series. Images that you can customize include stylized dingbats, Arabic designs, humorous office sketches, sports in action, seminar and educational promos, invitations and holiday motifs, and homestead and recreational clips. These images are in Computer Graphics Metafile (CGM) format and can be easily read into Microsoft Publisher using the Import Picture command.

System Requirements: IBM PC or 100 percent compatible with 900K of free disk space.

WARNING: BEFORE OPENING THE DISK PACKAGE, CAREFULLY READ THE TERMS AND CONDITIONS OF THE DISK WARRANTY ON THE BACK OF THIS PAGE.

Disk Warranty

This software is protected by both United States copyright law and international copyright treaty provision. You must treat this software just like a book, except that you may copy it into a computer to be used, and you may make archival copies of it for the sole purpose of backing up your software and protecting your investment from loss.

By saying, "just like a book," Osborne/McGraw-Hill means, for example, that this software may be used by any number of people and may be freely moved from one computer location to another, so long as there is no possibility of its being used at one location or on one computer while it is being used at another. Just as a book cannot be read by two different people in two different places at the same time, neither can the software be used by two different people in two different places at the same time (unless, of course, Osborne's copyright is being violated).

Limited Warranty

Osborne/McGraw-Hill warrants the physical diskette(s) enclosed herein to be free of defects in materials and workmanship for a period of 60 days from the purchase date. If Osborne/McGraw-Hill receives written notification within the warranty period of defects in materials or workmanship, and such notification is determined by Osborne/McGraw-Hill to be correct, Osborne/McGraw-Hill will replace the defective diskette(s).

The entire and exclusive liability and remedy for breach of this Limited Warranty shall be limited to replacement of defective diskette(s) and shall not include or extend to any claim for or right to cover any other damages, including but not limited to, loss of profit, data, or use of the software, or special, incidental, or consequential damages or other similar claims, even if Osborne/McGraw-Hill has been specifically advised of the possibility of such damages. In no event will Osborne/McGraw-Hill's liability for any damages to you or any other person ever exceed the lower of the suggested list price or actual price paid for the license to use the software, regardless of any form of the claim.

OSBORNE, A DIVISION OF McGRAW-HILL, INC., SPECIFICALLY DISCLAIMS ALL OTHER WARRANTIES, EXPRESS OR IMPLIED, INCLUDING BUT NOT LIMITED TO, ANY IMPLIED WARRANTY OF MERCHANTABILITY OR FITNESS FOR A PARTICULAR PURPOSE. Specifically, Osborne/McGraw-Hill makes no representation or warranty that the software is fit for any particular purpose and any implied warranty of merchantability is limited to the 60-day duration of the Limited Warranty covering the physical diskette(s) only (and not the software) and is otherwise expressly and specifically disclaimed.

This limited warranty gives you specific legal rights; you may have others which may vary from state to state. Some states do not allow the exclusion of incidental or consequential damages, or the limitation on how long an implied warranty lasts, so some of the above may not apply to you.

Microsoft Publisher
Made Easy

James Nadler

Osborne McGraw-Hill

Berkeley New York St. Louis San Francisco
Auckland Bogotá Hamburg London Madrid
Mexico City Milan Montreal New Delhi Panama City
Paris São Paulo Singapore Sydney
Tokyo Toronto

Osborne **McGraw-Hill**
2600 Tenth Street
Berkeley, California 94710
U.S.A.

For information on software, translations, or book distributors outside of the U.S.A., please write to Osborne **McGraw-Hill** at the above address.

Microsoft Publisher Made Easy

Copyright © 1992 by McGraw-Hill. All rights reserved. Printed in the United States of America. Except as permitted under the Copyright Act of 1976, no part of this publication may be reproduced or distributed in any form or by any means, or stored in a database or retrieval system, without the prior written permission of the publisher, with the exception that the program listings may be entered, stored, and executed in a computer system, but they may not be reproduced for publication.

Clip art copyright © Dover Publications 1992. The graphics in *Microsoft Publisher Made Easy* are used by special arrangement with Dover Publications and can be used only for desktop publishing purposes and applications. They cannot be duplicated, resyndicated, or resold as any other form of publishing, clip art, or graphic resource. Please refer all inquiries and questions directly to Dover Publications, Inc., 31 East 2nd Street, Mineola, NY 11501, Attention: Rights and Permissions.

1234567890 DOC 998765432

ISBN 0-07-881811-7

Information has been obtained by Osborne McGraw-Hill from sources believed to be reliable. However, because of the possibility of human or mechanical error by our sources, Osborne McGraw-Hill, or others, Osborne McGraw-Hill does not guarantee the accuracy, adequacy, or completeness of any information and is not responsible for any errors or omissions or the results obtained from use of such information.

To Lois

Publisher

Kenna S. Wood

Acquisitions Editor

Elizabeth Fisher

Associate Editor

Scott Rogers

Technical Editor

Nick Dimuria

Copy Editor

Paul Medoff

Proofreading Coordinator

Kelly Barr

Proofreaders

K.D. Sullivan
Audrey Johnson

Indexers

Phil Roberts
Peggy Bieber-Roberts

Computer Designer

J. E. Christgau

Typesetters

Marcela Hancik
Susie Kim
Marla Shelasky

Cover Design

Mason Fong

Contents

Acknowledgments .... *xv*
Introduction .... *xvii*

1 Putting Together a Publication 1
  Publishing Concepts 2
  Creating a Page Layout 3
  Adding Frames 7
  Filling Frames 8
  Customizing Frames 9
    Text Frames 9
    Picture Frames 10
    WordArt Frames 11
  Adding Spice with Graphics 12
  Inspecting Your Work 13
  Working Quickly: Templates and PageWizards 14
    Review 17

2 How Publisher Operates 19
  Using the Mouse 20
    Pointing 20
    Clicking 20
    Double-Clicking 21
    Dragging 22

	Working with Windows	23
	Parts of the Windows Screen	23
	Using Menus	25
	Using Dialog Boxes	27
	Getting Help	29
	Working with Publisher	34
	Publisher Window Features	34
	The Toolbar and Other Buttons	36
	Publisher Menus	38
	Using Publisher Dialog Boxes	42
	Correcting Mistakes (Undo)	43
	Printer Considerations	44
	Review	45

3 A Working Session 47
Starting Publisher 49
Selecting a Layout 51
Adding Text Frames 52
Undo 54
Working with Frames 54
Saving 56
Importing Text 58
Flowing Text 60
Entering and Formatting Text 61
Getting Help 66
Adding a Picture Frame 66
Resizing a Frame 69
Creating Borders 71
Using WordArt 71
Using PageWizards 74
Adding Graphics 77
Adding Pages 79
The Background Page 82
Printing 83

4 All About Frames 85
Creating Frames 86

	Centering Frames	91
	Squaring Frames	93
	Setting Frame Margins and Columns	95
Selecting Frames		97
	Selecting Multiple Frames	99
Moving Frames		103
	Moving a Group of Frames Between Pages	104
Cut, Paste, and Copy		107
	Duplicating Frames	109
Resizing Frames		112
Frame Graphics		115
	Review	119

5 All About Page Layout ... 121

Page Formatting		122
	Page Orientation and Paper Size	123
	Publication Type	127
	Page Size	135
	Page Margins and Layout Guides	136
Using Multiple Pages		143
	Inserting Pages	143
	Deleting Pages	146
	Paging	147
The Background Page		147
	Mirrored Guides and the Background Page	150
	Page Numbers	151
Working with the Publisher Screen		153
	Switching Views	153
	Working with Rulers	155
	Other Screen Display Options	159
	Review	160

6 Creating Text ... 161

Where Copy Fits in Your Work Flow		162
Getting the Word Around		164
	Entering and Editing Text	165
	Text and Other Applications	171

	Connecting Text	178
	Text Correction Tools	185
	Find and Replace	186
	Hyphenation	191
	Spelling	194
	Review	197
7	**Formatting Text**	**199**
	Formatting Characters	202
	Paragraph Formatting	211
	Selecting Paragraphs	212
	Indents, Alignment, and Spacing	213
	Leading	216
	Tabs	217
	Frame Formatting	222
	Review	226
8	**Working with WordArt**	**227**
	Entering and Editing WordArt	229
	Formatting WordArt	234
	Formatting Characters	235
	Formatting Paragraphs	244
	Formatting Frames	247
	Review	248
9	**Working with Images**	**249**
	Where Graphics Fit in Your Work Flow	250
	Creating Pictures	252
	Importing Images	252
	Pasting Images Between Windows Applications	256
	Inserting and Embedding Objects	258
	Editing and Formatting Pictures	265
	Cut, Copy, Paste, and Move	266
	Margins	266
	Repeating and Replacing Pictures	269
	Display Options for Pictures	269

	Scaling Pictures	270
	Cropping	274
	Review	279
10	**Line Art, BorderArt, and Shading**	**281**
	Line Art	283
	Solid Shapes	285
	Lines	287
	Switching the Visual Plane	287
	Shading, Shadows, and Colors	289
	Shading and Color	289
	Shadows	292
	Borders and BorderArt	293
	Simple Borders	293
	BorderArt	295
	Review	298
A	**Menu Reference**	**299**
	File Menu	300
	Create New Publication .	300
	Open Existing Publication	301
	Close Publication	303
	Save	304
	Save As	304
	Import Text	306
	Import Picture	308
	Print	310
	Print Setup	312
	Exit Publisher	315
	Edit Menu	315
	Undo	316
	Cut	317
	Copy	317
	Paste	318
	Paste Special	319
	Delete	321
	Delete Text Frame	321

Highlight Story	322
Edit WordArt Object	322
Insert Object	327
Find	328
Replace	331
Page Menu	**333**
Screen Views	333
Insert Pages	334
Delete Page	335
Insert Page Numbers	336
Ignore Background	338
Go to Background/Foreground	338
Page Setup	339
The Layout Menu	**343**
Layout Guides	343
Frame Columns and Margins	346
Send to Back/Bring to Front	348
Borders	348
Line	350
BorderArt	352
Shading	353
Shadow	356
Format Menu	**356**
Characters	356
Spacing Between Characters	359
Indents and Spacing	360
Tabs	362
Scale Picture	365
Crop Picture	367
Options Menu	**367**
Check Spelling	368
Hyphenate	370
Snap to Ruler Marks	372
Snap to Guides	372
Hide/Show Pictures	373
Hide/Show Rulers	373
Hide/Show Status Line	373

	Hide/Show Layout Guides	374
	Hide/Show Object Boundaries	374
	Settings	375
B	**Design Gallery**	**377**
	Lost Holdings	378
	Fifties	380
	Protection & Sense	382
	Places, Spaces, and Things	384
	Getting Started in Near East Philosophy	386
	Lingua Frenetica	388
	Leaving So Soon?	390
	Politics	392
	Family Focus	394
	Beyond the America's Cup	396
	Serious Authors	398
	Finance & Greed	400
	African Weaving	402
	Poetry & Literature	404
	Delphi	406
	RushWIND	408
C	**WordArt Fonts**	**413**
D	**Keyboard Shortcuts**	**419**
E	**PageWizards**	**421**
	How PageWizards Work	423
	Using the PageWizard Frame Tool	424
	Starting a Document from Scratch	426
	Modifying PageWizard Material	426
	Text	427
	Pictures	428
	WordArt, Line Art, BorderArt, and Shading	428

F	**Templates**	**429**
	How Templates Work	430
	Creating a Template of Your Own	431
	Modifying a Template	432
	Template Types	433
G	**Installing Dover Clip Art**	**435**
	Windows Installation	436
	Manual Installation	436
H	**Printers and Printing**	**437**
	Installing Other Printers	438
	Print Options	438
	Print Range	438
	Print Quality	439
	Copies	439
	Collate Copies	440
	Print to File	440
	Print Crop Marks	440
	Print Setup Options	441
	Printer	441
	Orientation	441
	Paper	442
	Options	442
	Index	**443**

Acknowledgments

Deborah Thomas provided the concepts, layout, and typography for all of the materials used to create the Design Gallery in Appendix B from her portfolio. Special thanks go to her for so generously sharing her talents and work as an art director with this writer.

Liz Fisher, the anchorwoman, did a terrific job managing the project in general, providing direction in times of duress, and making the entire process of creating this book more fun than I had anticipated.

Scott Rogers carried the ball through the details of editing, production, and the glitches that inevitably arise in getting to press. Although I seemed to be plugged in to a single two-month telephone conversation with him, he was always a pleasure to work with.

Thanks to Judith Brown and Paul Medoff for diligent and intelligent editing.

I am especially indebted to David Perry at Microsoft for his fortuitous inquiry in the summer of 1991. Without our initial dialogue and his support, I would not have had the opportunity to undertake this project.

Finally, my gratitude to John Mahon for tolerating and humoring me through my 5 o'clock mood swings.

Introduction

Simply put, Microsoft Publisher makes desktop publishing a breeze for anyone working in Windows. In addition, few programs for the IBM PC platform offer so much power with such a mild and brief learning curve. In this sense, Publisher's range is exceptional. Microsoft has included *canned applications* for so many common types and styles of publications—and made accessing them so simple—that beginners can often go to press with attractive-looking material on the same day that they begin working with the program. At the same time, Publisher supports the critical typographical functions necessary to produce sophisticated work. Even experienced users find it appropriate for all but the most demanding professional tasks.

Publisher incorporates the newest software technology from Microsoft. *WordArt*, for example, puts over 20 unique display-oriented typefaces in the hands of everyone, regardless of which printer they use. Similarly, *BorderArt* provides over 100 unusual and dynamically scalable border patterns, ranging in theme from the stately to the downright outrageous. *PageWizards* reduce the process of developing publications to a simple question and answer session with the program. Features such as object linking and embedding make working with Publisher in conjunction with the latest generation of products—Windows 3.1, Word for Windows 2.0, Excel 3.0, and so on—a virtually seamless process. Publisher applies to the desktop publishing arena the intuitive user interface that PC computing has promised for so long.

About This Book

It would be practically impossible to make Publisher's simpler features easier to use than they already are. As easy as it is to get started with this program, getting the most out of all of its features requires some additional explanation and practice. *Microsoft Publisher Made Easy* was written to provide both. The early chapters provide tutorials and explanations of the basic components you need to know about when undertaking page layout. The flow of chapters 5 through 10 mirrors the general sequence that you might follow in developing a publication. All of the material is presented in the context of the publishing process, and wherever appropriate, industry terminology and routines are explained. The discussion throughout contains numerous examples and exercises to help you hone your publishing skills.

While the chapters in the book examine the program in the context of publishing, the appendixes provide handy references. Included are design aids, command summaries, a Design Gallery, and WordArt Gallery. Considerable thought and effort went into selecting and presenting material that complements rather than repeats the information in the *Microsoft Publisher User's Guide*.

How This Book Is Organized

Chapter 1 gives you an overview of the steps needed to construct a publication and the tools that Publisher provides to help you do your work.

Chapter 2 describes the fundamentals of working with a mouse and basic Windows operations. You should feel comfortable with the topics in these sections before moving on to the remainder of the book. Chapter 2 also provides an overview of the Publisher menus and screens and some of their special characteristics.

Chapter 3 is a soup-to-nuts tutorial that demonstrates many of the major features in the program. The chapter contains explicit instructions for creating a sample application that leaves virtually nothing to chance. Depending on your level of Windows experience and overall familiarity with computers, the tutorial can be completed in as little as one hour. It is designed in modular fashion, so you can pause between sections if you don't have time to complete the entire tutorial in a single sitting.

Chapter 4 discusses the properties common to all types of frames and how to use them. While differences exist in the way frame types operate, the variations are small, and most features of all frame types behave in the same way. The sections in this chapter give you clear examples of all major aspects of working with frames. In addition, the steps of each procedure are listed separately in boxes throughout the chapter for easy reference.

Chapter 5 is meant to make you comfortable with designing a page layout. Having a sound design for layout is the key to a successful publication, and creating one is a primary skill for page designers.

Chapter 6 explains all of the ways you can enter, edit, and correct text in a publication. Even though Publisher is intended more for designing and formatting the appearance of pages, text creation and editing skills are critical to working effectively with the program.

Chapter 7 is all about text formatting. Formatting is one of the most powerful tools in desktop publishing. It opens up the world of typography, which, from size and legibility to the indirect influences it has on pictures and art, makes a dramatic impact on everything about a publication.

Chapter 8 explains WordArt—an alternative to text for displaying copy. There are countless design possibilities for WordArt fonts and styles. Almost any publication—from conservative to whimsical—can benefit from the powerful typographical effects available through this tool.

Chapter 9 explains how Publisher handles images. One of the distinguishing features of a publishing program is its ability to blend text and graphics smoothly. Publisher can include images from a variety of popular graphics programs for drawing, painting, and creating charts and spreadsheets. Once this material is in a publication, it can be resized to suit the needs of the piece.

Chapter 10 shows you how to manipulate graphic accents in Publisher. The drawing tools, frame backgrounds and patterns, and Publisher's extraordinary collection of BorderArt are all discussed, along with techniques for combining these tools to create additional special effects.

Appendix A explains each of the commands and associated dialog boxes that appear on all of the Publisher menus. While the chapters are organized around publishing tasks, this reference section is organized according to the menu structure of the program. Once you've become familiar with the program, it makes an excellent cross-reference for finding information about specific Publisher commands.

Appendix B is a Design Gallery of 16 original publications designed by an independent art director in the New York City area. They show outstanding examples of typography, page composition, and graphic accent using Microsoft Publisher. Next to the actual designs, the specifications and techniques used to create them are listed.

Appendix C is a WordArt Gallery. It displays all of the characters for the WordArt font sets in a standard (best fit) size. While examples of some of these characters exist in the *User's Guide*, you may find it helpful to browse through all of the possibilities when you're looking for a particular visual effect.

Appendix D contains a summary of keyboard equivalents (shortcuts) for commonly used commands.

Appendix E discusses PageWizards. They are so simple to use that they require very little documentation. On the other hand, PageWizards can be used for very powerful effects by even experienced publishers. This section explains how they operate, and offers a few tips about them.

Appendix F explains how to modify the Publisher templates and create new ones of your own. Templates are completed publications that contain preconfigured page layouts including frames and artwork. The templates are used as the basis for new publications used as examples in the main chapters of the book.

Appendix G explains how to install the files from the Dover Pictorial Archive Series on the disk that accompanies this book.

Appendix H discusses printing and printers. Most printing options and some of the important page setup and formatting options available in Publisher are printer-dependent. This section is intended to describe the basic print options available to you under Publisher.

About the Conventions Used in This Book

Microsoft Publisher Made Easy uses the following typographical conventions to make exercises and tutorials easy to understand.

Introduction

When you need to input characters from the keyboard, the instruction will be to "type" one or more characters, which will appear in bold. When you need to use any of the nonprinting keys on the keyboard, the instruction is "press," followed by the name of the key in small capital letters, for example:

Press F9 to zoom in on the new frame and type **winter 1991**.

Instructions for using the mouse to point, click, drag, and select are all used in the same way as described in the Microsoft manuals for Windows and Publisher.

Wherever possible the graphic icons that Publisher uses for the pointer to display its current activity are reproduced in the text for clarity. For example, the standard pointer ( ) can change to a crosshair (+) or a cropper ( ).

The Dover Disk

In addition to the clip art that comes with Publisher, the disk included with this book contains approximately 100 illustrations from the **Dover Publications Pictorial Archive Series**. The disk includes a varied selection of Dover clip art that is easy to load into your computer and place in your documents. Dover has been an outstanding name in clip art since long before the advent of desktop publishing, and is known throughout the fields of commercial graphics and art direction for the quality and scope of its material.

The illustrations on the disk were designed especially to work with Publisher. Images on the disk include stylized dingbats, Arabic designs, humorous office sketches, sports in action, seminar and educational promos, invitations and holiday motifs, and homestead and recreational clips. They use the same Computer Graphics Metafile (CGM) format as the clip art that comes with Publisher, and will work easily in a picture frame from any publication. Like all object-oriented files, they can be easily scaled without losing resolution. This variety of clip art will give you the extra tool you need to easily personalize your publications.

See Appendix G for explicit instructions on how to load the clip art onto your system.

1

Putting Together a Publication

Technology and personal computers are radically changing the way everyone communicates. Dramatic changes have occurred in the ways that professional-looking printed material is created, and in the people who create it. Many of the chores that you once found laborious and time-consuming on a typewriter are simple when accomplished on a word processor. When word processing programs first appeared on the market for personal computers (PCs), they looked and acted like their ancestors on larger, older computers. While these programs made writing and editing easy, they had limited features for changing the appearance of text. For example, putting together a letter was a simple matter, but formatting a table of numbers required the talents of a real pro. As the market for these products expanded, so did the power of the formatting features included in them. Complex tables, signature typefaces, and even sophisticated graphic effects can now be accomplished by almost anyone with a modern word processing program.

As word processing became more commonplace and more powerful for PCs, programs aimed at other specialized functions also evolved from older computing systems. Among them were programs designed to create professional-looking documents such as brochures, newsletters, business cards, and hundreds of other conventional publishing projects. The emergence of these programs along with the availability of cheaper, higher-quality printers gave birth to desktop publishing. As its name implies, *desktop publishing* brings the features and benefits once found in professional-level publishing to your desktop via the personal computer.

Where can you draw the line between modern word processing and desktop publishing? The documents you create with a publishing program, *publications,* differ from those created with a word processor in a number of ways. Publications usually have much greater integration of text and graphics, for example. From greeting cards to catalogs, words and pictures work together to convey a message. In addition, publications often accommodate more than a single source of text. Both of these differences are apparent in a newspaper, for example, which contains many stories and pictures on a single page.

The more powerful word processing programs available today are also capable of producing publications; however, creating publications with a program designed specifically to facilitate publishing chores is simpler and in many cases more effective. On the other hand, while a desktop publishing program is quite capable of creating letters and memos, it has fewer facilities for text manipulation than a good word processor.

Publishing Concepts

As you might imagine from its title, the purpose of Publisher is to create publications. The process of building a publication can be compared to constructing a house. Before you begin to build either, you must settle on an overall design for the project based on the purpose you want it to serve. Will the house be an elegant mansion or a simple bungalow; will it be for a large family or small? Will the publication contain a brief message, as in a business card or a party announcement, or is it meant to convey a lot of information as in a newsletter? Should it be formal or casual? Thinking about these questions doesn't require a computer, but helps to establish a clear theme.

Next you need to decide on some general construction parameters. How much space will the house occupy in total? Where will the primary living quarters be? How many levels will it have? In building a publication, comparable questions are a matter of page layout. *Page layout* lets you form a structural foundation on which further development can be built. General guidelines for where headlines or major titles will appear, the number of text columns per page, what paper size to use or the number of pages to include make putting the rest of the publication together easier and more consistent.

With the groundwork out of the way, you can create a blueprint for the interior. In a house this is a matter of making a floor plan. In Publisher, you add frames to your layout. *Frames* hold the information you place on a page in Publisher. Each frame holds a block of text or a picture, just as each room in a house is designed for a specific purpose. Visually, frames fit together on a page very much like the rooms and hallways in a blueprint.

Once the rooms are finished, you can decorate! In Publisher this means adding words and images to each of the frames, and then tailoring their appearance. After the house is furnished you can add some finishing touches. Similarly, to complete a publication, you can add graphic accents to highlight the information or message you have presented in the piece.

Publisher lets you control a publication through pages and objects. *Pages* form the foundation for a publication and provide the overall structure for its appearance. *Objects* let you manage the space within that structure and determine where text and graphics appear. Figure 1-1 shows you how objects fit on a page. Each of the sections in this chapter will give you an overview of the steps needed to construct a publication and the tools that Publisher provides to help you do your work. Later chapters will provide tutorials that help you create practice documents as well as advise you on how to best accomplish your own projects.

Creating a Page Layout

There is always room for modification in Publisher, but it's important to establish the basics before you proceed with a project. Otherwise it may become difficult to manage the project as it evolves, and work may have to be redone from scratch if the fundamental design changes. Page layout lets you decide on the broad parameters of a publication.

All of the pages in a publication have the same layout characteristics. For example, each page will have the same dimensions and have the same size

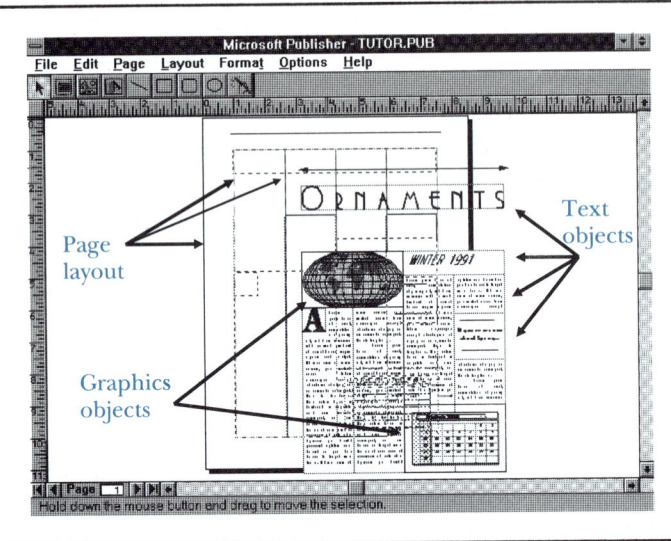

Figure 1-1.   *How objects fit on a page*

margins around the edge. *Margins* are the perimeter area between the edges of the paper and the point where printing starts. You can also establish a general structure for the number of columns and rows that you intend to use. *Columns* divide the page into vertical sections. This is a style typically found in newsletters or menus. *Rows* divide the page into horizontal sections of the type you find in a calendar. Figure 1-2 shows an example of a newsletter with columns. Figure 1-3 shows an example of a calendar divided into rows. Dividing a layout into columns and rows makes it easier to position objects later on.

If you would rather have Publisher do more of the design work, you can pick a layout from among dozens of templates that come with the program. *Templates* are preformatted pages, and all you need to do is add your own text and pictures. Publisher comes with templates that include the following types of publications:

Books
Greeting cards
Index and business cards

Chapter 1: *Putting Together a Publication* 5

Figure 1-2. Page divided into four columns

Figure 1-3. Page divided into six rows

Brochures
Business forms
Reports
Catalogs
Letterhead

Figure 1-4 shows samples of the layouts used in the templates. You can work with templates as they are or use any of the Publisher commands to modify them. Publisher provides default sizes for each of these shapes, but you can override these dimensions after a layout is selected.

It is always advisable to make choices that fit the most common design requirements of your publication. However, with the exception of the physical size of a page (you can't print in an area that doesn't exist), none of the choices that you make about layout is set in stone. For example, you can extend a caption into a margin area to call special attention to it, or you can place a picture in between two columns, as shown in Figure 1-5. In this sense, the settings for page layout are flexible. More details on how to work with page layout can be found in Chapter 5.

Figure 1-4. Layout options

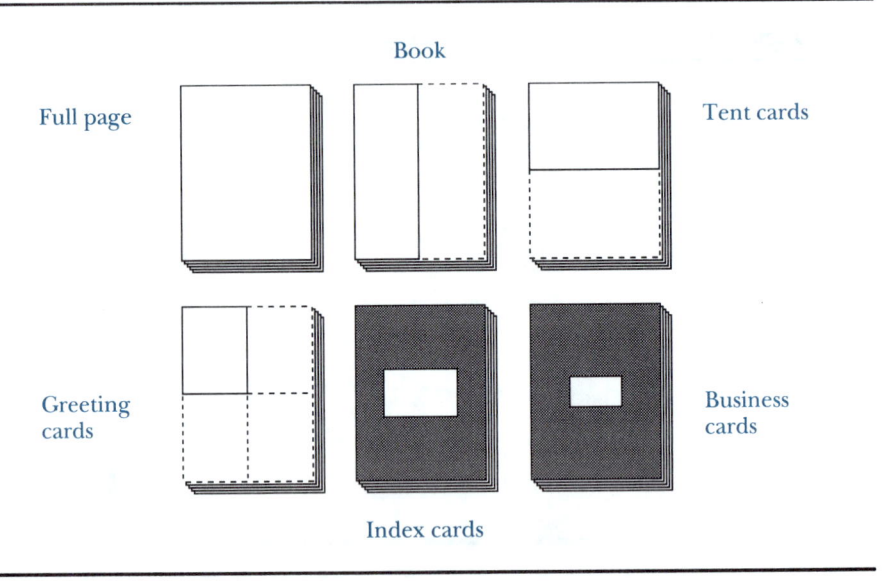

Chapter 1: *Putting Together a Publication* 7

Figure 1-5. *A picture placed between two columns makes the text "run around" the picture*

Adding Frames

After the layout is complete, you can start to manage the parts of the page that contain the publication's information. This is akin to adding the rooms to your house plan. Frames are the objects that let you manage text, pictures, and special effects. Each of the *frame tools* shown here lets you create one of these types of frames.

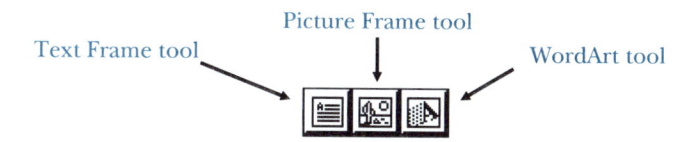

Text Frame tool — Picture Frame tool — WordArt tool

Frame tools let you design the shape, position, and interaction of frames. All frame tools create and modify frames in basically the same manner. Frames can be placed anywhere on the pages of a publication. They can exist side by side, overlap, and continue from one page to the next. They can also be resized, repositioned, or moved between pages, and Publisher will quickly reformat their content to adapt to the modification. Figure 1-6 shows a page with a number of frames added. Unlike pages, frames can differ substantially from one another in both shape and content, and can be easily modified while designing or redesigning a publication. In addition, frames may appear differently on each page of a publication. More information on working with frames can be found in Chapter 4.

Filling Frames

Frames are initially like the empty rooms in a house—they need some furnishings. In a publication, you will want to fill frames with text and graphics. These can come from a variety of sources including word processors, graphics programs, and material that you enter directly in Publisher. Remember, Publisher is designed for page designers, not for writers. Its text editing facilities are meant more to help you refine and tune the words in a publication than to create words from scratch.

With short blocks of text, such as headlines or picture captions, it is easy to type the words directly into a text frame. While you *can* enter lengthy blocks of text, it is much easier to do so with a program designed especially for

Figure 1-6.   *Frames added to the page*

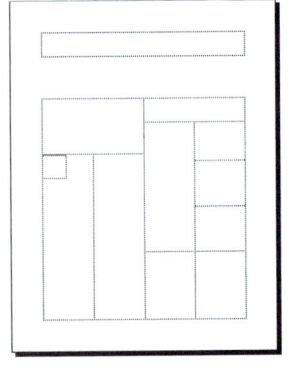

Chapter 1: *Putting Together a Publication* 9

editing, such as a word processor, because its editing capabilities are so much more powerful. You can then import its text files directly into Publisher. Similarly, while Publisher is capable of creating figures, complex graphics are best imported from a program designed specifically to work with pictures and drawings. Publisher's real power is meant to help you design pages. Wherever the material originates from, it is always displayed in one of the three types of frames.

Customizing Frames

Once you've added material to the frames in a publication, stylistic concerns for text and graphics can be addressed. Formatting the appearance of your material requires different techniques depending on the type of frame you are working with. Pictures may require background. Text may need to be enlarged in order to create a headline. Formatting brings out the decorator in you. The following discussion will give you a general sense of how you can use Publisher to format text and pictures in each of the different types of frames. By the time you've finished, the appearance of the publication will have developed considerably.

Text Frames

Text frames contain only text. They are used to display most of the words in a publication. Publisher lets you control the layout of a frame almost as though it were a separate page. You can decide on the number of columns that appear as well as the amount of margin. You can change the appearance of the characters in text dramatically by choosing from a variety of type styles and type sizes called *fonts*. Other more standard font modifications that you may recognize from word processing, such as italicizing and underlining, are also easy to implement. Some of these text formatting effects are shown in Figure 1-7.

The appearance of text within a frame can also be modified to display different alignments. *Alignment* determines the relationship of text to the edges of a frame. For example, the primary articles in a newsletter may be

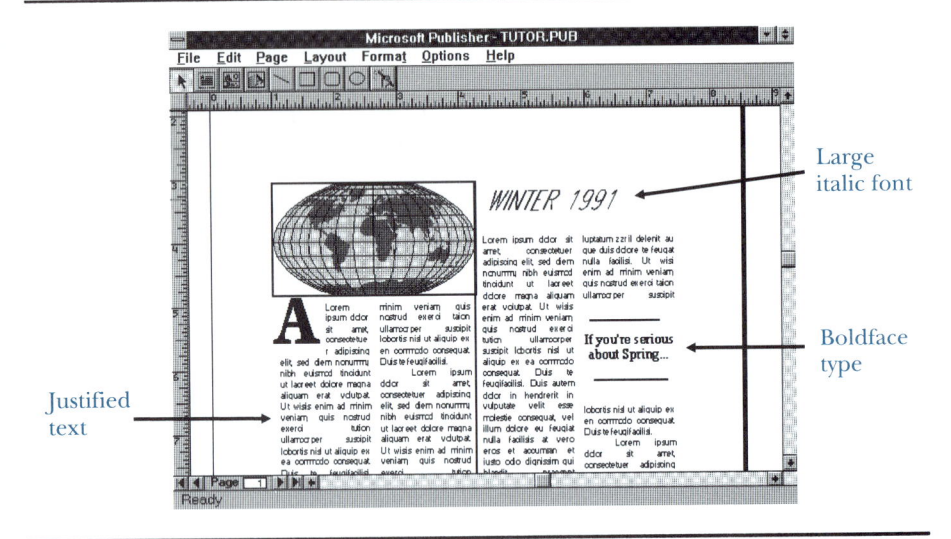

Figure 1-7. Applying different text formats to a page

flush on both sides as shown in Figure 1-7. This alignment is known as *justified*. On the other hand, a quotation from the article may be centered and double spaced to draw attention, as shown in the same figure. These are just some of the different effects that you can achieve with Publisher. You can find more details on formatting text in Chapter 7.

Picture Frames

Picture frames contain only pictures. They are primarily used to display images created using outside sources. Publisher is able to import images from a variety of popular graphics programs. As with text frames, Publisher provides formatting options for picture frames, and your design choices can differ substantially from one picture frame to the next. *Cropping* lets you cut down a picture so you can focus on the section your publication needs to get a message across. *Scaling* lets you reduce or enlarge your pictures to fit the available page space.

Chapter 1:   *Putting Together a Publication*   11

The options available for formatting pictures are not as extensive as those for text frames. If you need to modify your pictures further, you should do so in the application in which they were created. You can find more information on formatting images in Chapter 9.

Note

Publisher comes with a number of illustrations that are ready to use for any publishing project. This type of copyright-free artwork is known as clip art. In addition to the clip art that comes with Publisher, the supplementary disk included with this book contains approximately 100 illustrations from the Dover Publications Pictorial Archive Series. Dover has been a household word in clip art since long before the advent of desktop publishing. All of these illustrations are available to you in creating publications. Figure 1-8 shows samples of clip art.

WordArt Frames

WordArt frames contain text embellished with special effects. These can be easily blended with text or picture frames or used on their own for certain applications. Examples of WordArt appear in Figure 1-9. WordArt frames

Figure 1-8.   Clip art samples

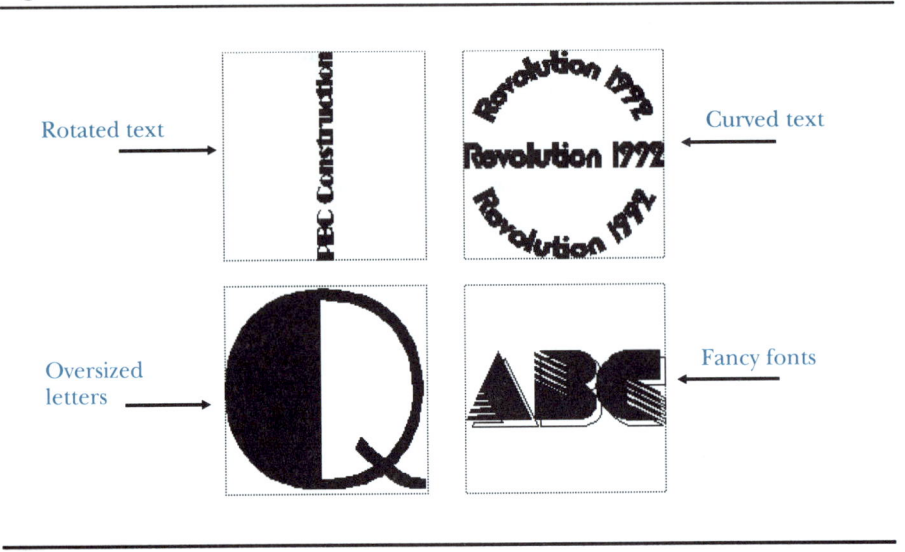

Figure 1-9.   Samples of WordArt

contain options for formatting that are not found in text frames. For example, the selection of fonts available for WordArt contains variations that are geared to attracting attention. In addition, these characters can be sized to any proportion in relation to a WordArt frame, from extremely small to almost 14 inches in height.

The text in a WordArt frame uses special characteristics not available in other frame tools. It can even be inverted, rotated, slanted, arched, rounded, stretched vertically and/or horizontally to fill the entire area of a frame, or given a drop shadow to make the characters appear to have depth. A rich variety of visual effects can be achieved. You can find more details on formatting WordArt in Chapter 8.

Adding Spice with Graphics

Once the major frames for your publication are in place, you may want to add graphic touches in order to highlight parts of the piece. Publisher makes decorating easy. Each of the *drawing tools* shown here lets you create one of the four types of geometric objects available in the program: lines, boxes, rounded boxes, and ovals.

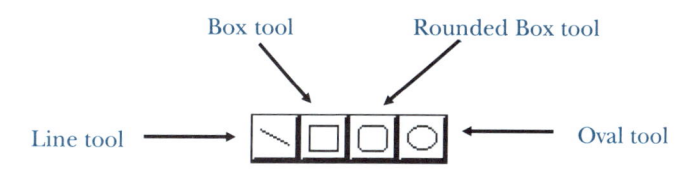

Box tool   Rounded Box tool

Line tool → [\ □ □ ○] ← Oval tool

These objects can be placed anywhere in a publication or combined to create more complex figures. They are typically used to separate sections of the text on a page. For example, you can use solid lines called *rules* to delineate columns or to create other attention-getters.

Publisher also contains a powerful set of options for creating borders around any of your frames. The program comes with a large library of decorative frames—over 100—called BorderArt. In addition, simple line-oriented borders of varying thicknesses can be ascribed to any frame. Publisher lets you add other graphic accents to frames as well. They can be embellished with patterns, shading, and colors. Figure 1-10 shows several samples of Publisher's BorderArt. Between Publisher's drawing tools and border options, you're almost certain to find something to work graphically with any publication, short of the most demanding professional applications. More details on how to work with drawing tools and BorderArt can be found in Chapter 10.

Inspecting Your Work

As noted earlier, Publisher is not meant to be a text processing program. However, two important text processing utilities normally found in word processors—spell checking and automatic hyphenation—are available for working with the text in frames. If you've added or deleted text, text alignment in the frame may benefit from hyphenation, or you may just want to check the spelling of a word you've added. Global search and replace functions are also on hand for last minute changes.

Figure 1-10.   Samples of border art

Working Quickly: Templates and PageWizards

If you're in a hurry to get something out or are just hungry for some new ideas, Publisher has two features that make the program especially easy and fast to work with. As mentioned earlier, templates are completed publications that contain preconfigured page layouts. In addition to layouts they also contain frames and artwork. In short, templates have everything— except your particular text and pictures—for creating many common applications. They are useful both for starting applications quickly and for learning more about the way Publisher puts things together. In cases where expediency is paramount, you can load a template and simply substitute the text and graphics from your own application for those in the template. You can practically go straight to press. This is particularly effective with simple projects such as price lists or product rosters. In such applications unique or innovative design may not be of the greatest importance, but detailed work is required to create and position a large number of frames. A sample template provided in Publisher is shown in Figure 1-11.

Figure 1-11. *Template for a price list*

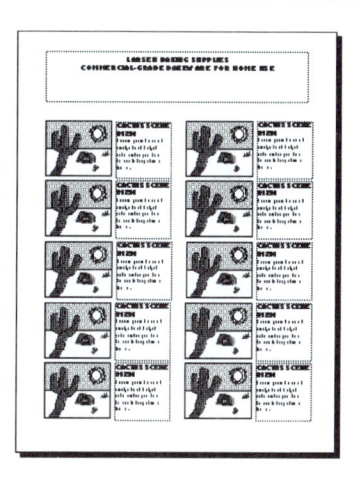

It's also easy to learn some of Publisher's more sophisticated capabilities and effects by seeing how they were put together by someone else. Fancy first letters, shadowed text, and unusual border effects are best taught using templates as models. You can use any of the tools you've already learned about to modify a template and then save it as a new publication. Templates **give you a great head start in getting your work off the ground.**

PageWizards form an interactive process for creating original publications or parts of publications from stock material. They are completely unique to Publisher. You can choose to begin a publication by using a PageWizard or select the PageWizard tool, shown here, from the Toolbar.

With PageWizards you can create advertisements, calendars, coupons, tables, greeting cards, and other applications in Publisher almost instantly.

Once you select the type of PageWizard you want to use, Publisher asks you questions about different aspects of the project and how you would like them developed. These might include how many folds you want in a greeting card or brochure, what style the layout should be, and whether pictures should be included. A sample PageWizard questionnaire is shown in Figure 1-12. After you've answered all of PageWizard's questions, it uses your responses to create a publication with the standard Publisher tools and options discussed in this chapter.

As it executes the job, PageWizard displays a dialog box at the bottom of the screen explaining exactly which Publisher commands it is using to build the publication as it goes along. You can even adjust the speed of the process to your learning level. Once the job is complete, you are left with a finished publication that meets the specifications you indicated on the PageWizard questionnaire. You can then substitute different text and graphics and use the completed publication as-is, or use any of the Publisher tools to make further modifications.

PageWizards make creating simple, original material fast and fun. They are also terrific teaching tools for learning Microsoft Publisher. PageWizards may seem a little baffling at first, but they're actually very easy to use and understand. More details on how to work with PageWizards can be found in Appendix E, as well as in the tutorial in Chapter 3.

Figure 1-12.   *Sample page from a PageWizard questionnaire*

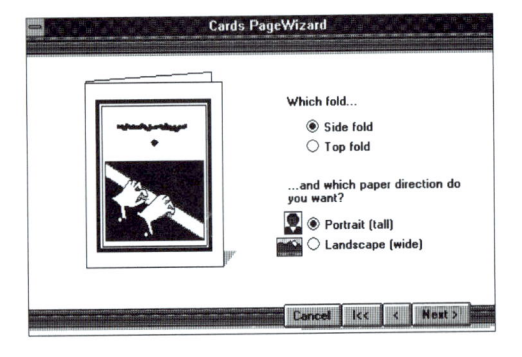

Review

The process outlined in this chapter—creating a layout, adding frames, loading and formatting material, and then adding graphics—is, of course, very simplified. In practice, these procedures will probably not occur in this exact sequence and may repeat in various stages of a publication's creation. Your own style of using Publisher's tools will develop as you become more familiar with the program. This discussion should have given you a sense of the major options available to you.

- Pages let you create the layout for a publication and determine its major design elements.
- There are two types of objects that you can create—seven objects in all—to fill the publication with text and visual information. Three of the objects are frames for displaying text and pictures. Four of the objects are drawing tools for creating simple graphic shapes.
- Text and pictures can be created in Publisher or brought in from other sources.
- There is plenty of ready-to-use art (clip art) on hand if you need to include an illustration.
- Spell checking and hyphenation facilities are available for proofing your work.
- PageWizards and templates can greatly reduce development time and help you to learn more about how Publisher puts together a tight-looking publication.

Any questions? Of course there are, but you'll find that Publisher is easy to learn and easy to work with. If you're familiar with Windows and feeling adventurous, go straight to the tutorial in Chapter 3 for a hands-on demonstration of the topics discussed here. If you need a little more orientation before beginning and are not familiar with Windows, read the material in Chapter 2.

2

How Publisher Operates

To operate Publisher you need to understand certain basics about Windows and about Publisher itself. This chapter is divided into the following three sections:

- Using the Mouse
- Working with Windows
- Working with Publisher

If you're new to Windows you'll need to acquire a few basic skills, but you should catch on very quickly. The first two sections address fundamentals, including how to get help from Publisher while you're working. You should feel comfortable with the topics in these sections before moving on to the last section in this chapter or the tutorial in the next chapter. If you're an experienced Windows user, you'll find that Publisher behaves very similarly to Windows and other applications that run under Windows. You can probably skip directly to the final section, "Working with Publisher." It reviews the Publisher menus and screens and some of their special characteristics.

Using the Mouse

As you read this section it's helpful to be seated at the computer with Windows running and the Program Manager window open. The examples assume that this is the case. There's no substitute for hands-on practice, especially with basic skills. The subjects covered are rudimentary and essential. If you're feeling timid, roll up your sleeves and give these activities a try now. There are four main actions you can take with a mouse.

Pointing

Pointing means moving the pointer (▶) to a specific location on the screen by moving the mouse on your desk or mouse pad. When you move the mouse, the pointer on the screen moves correspondingly. When you are pointing to something, the pointer actually appears directly over the object to which you are pointing. For example, in the following illustration, you would be pointing to the Microsoft SolutionSeries icon in the Program Manager window.

Note

Your screen may differ from the figures and illustrations shown in this section depending on what Windows applications you have installed. If you are working with Publisher, however, you will have both the Microsoft SolutionSeries and the Program Manager available in your Windows environment. These are the only two applications that the exercises in this section depend on. Don't worry about other differences between your screen and the sample screens you see in this section.

Clicking

Clicking means pressing and then releasing the left mouse button. You've got to be pointing to something before you can click on it. Clicking has different effects depending on what you're pointing to. For example, you can

Chapter 2: *How Publisher Operates*

click on an icon to display a menu. Try clicking on one of the icons in the Program Manager window.

1. Point to the Microsoft SolutionSeries icon.
2. Click the left mouse button.

The menu for the SolutionSeries pops up.

Note

Clicking and double-clicking always refer to the left button unless stated otherwise. There are some rare instances where you can use the right button, but these are always explicitly confirmed in the text.

Double-Clicking

Double-clicking means pressing and then releasing the mouse button twice in rapid succession. Double-clicking has the effect of executing two commands in succession. For example, you can double-click on an icon to display a window.

1. Point to the Microsoft SolutionSeries icon.
2. Double-click the mouse button.

The Microsoft SolutionSeries application window appears, as shown here:

In this example, the first click opened the menu, and the second displayed the window.

Dragging

Dragging means pointing to an initial location (object) on the screen, pressing and holding the left mouse button, moving to a second location, and releasing the button. It's called dragging because the object you first point to moves along with the pointer. Dragging is a fast and easy way to move things around. For example, you can move windows to new locations on the screen.

1. Point to the title of the Microsoft SolutionSeries window.
2. Press and hold the mouse button.
3. Move to a new location in the window.
4. Release the button. The SolutionSeries window has moved to the new location, as shown in Figure 2-1.

Figure 2-1.   Dragging a window

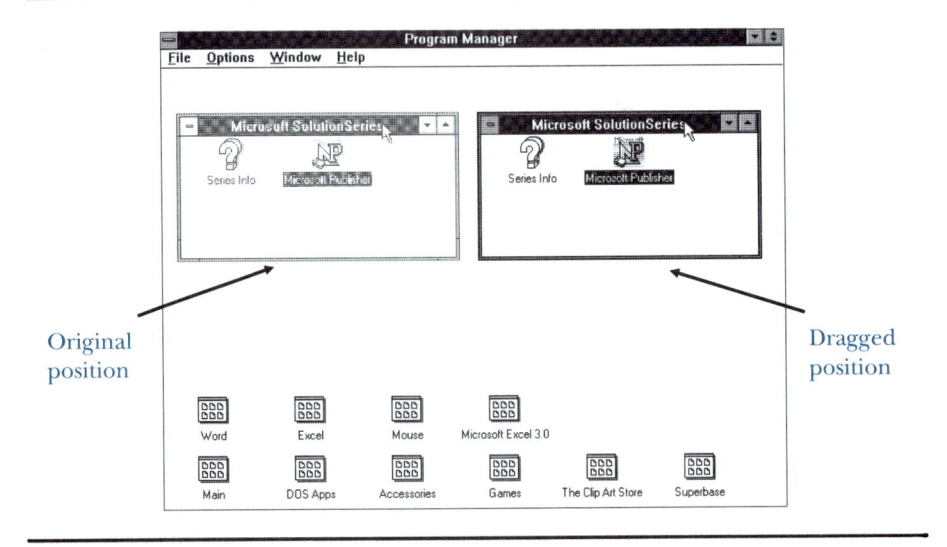

Chapter 2: *How Publisher Operates*

Working with the mouse is easy and fun. It's also essential to working effectively with Windows and Publisher. Most of the commands available in the program can be executed by either the keyboard or a mouse. However, manipulating frames in Publisher—an essential skill—*requires* the use of a mouse, and many commands are much easier to carry out that way. If you feel unsure about working with a mouse, review some of the mouse-related material and the exercises that come with Windows. In the long run, you'll be happier working with Publisher if you are comfortable with the mouse.

Working with Windows

This section is for users who are unfamiliar with the basics of working in a Windows environment. If you don't fall into this category, you are almost certainly fluent in all of the topics discussed here and can skip ahead to the section on working with Publisher.

Parts of the Windows Screen

The parts of the Windows screen shown in Figure 2-2 and explained here are also present during a Publisher session.

Note

Your screen may differ from the figures and illustrations shown in this section depending on what Windows applications you have installed. If you are working with Windows, however, you must have the Program Manager available in your Windows environment. This is the only application that the exercises in this section depend on. Don't worry about other differences between your screen and the sample screens you see in this section.

Desktop   This is the primary Windows background. All windows and application icons in your environment appear on the desktop.

Application Icons   These are the small pictures that represent the programs you can run.

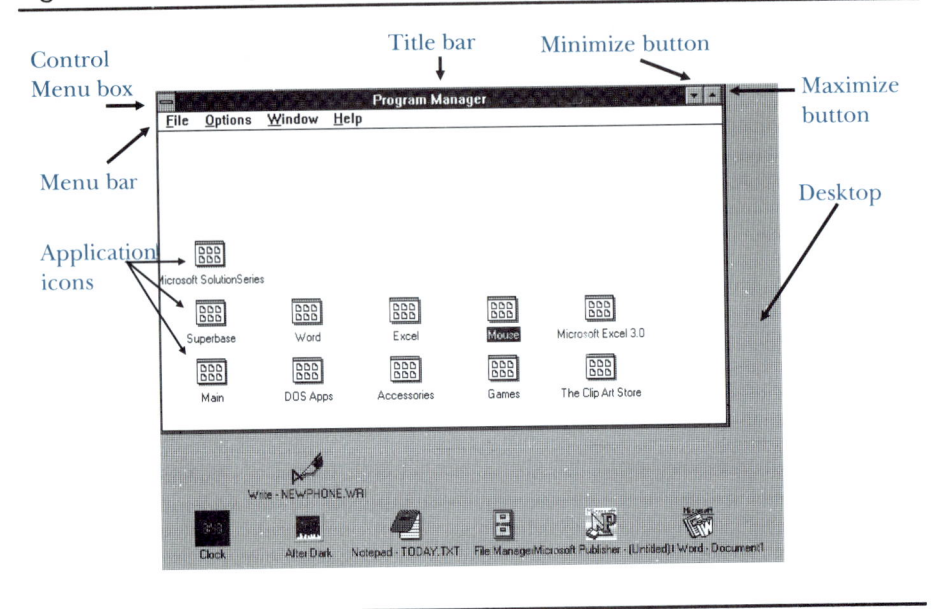

Figure 2-2. **Basic parts of the Windows screen**

Title Bar   This shows you the name of the application program that you are currently working on. In Figure 2-2, the application is Program Manager. You can drag on the Title bar to move a window, as described in the previous section on using a mouse.

Control Menu Box   Clicking here activates a menu called the Control menu with Windows commands for the active window, as shown here:

The Switch To option on the Control menu is useful for moving between different Windows applications. It displays the other applications that are

Chapter 2: *How Publisher Operates* 25

currently running in the Task List shown in the following illustration (these also depend on your installation and may differ from those you see here). Double-clicking on the Control Menu box closes an application.

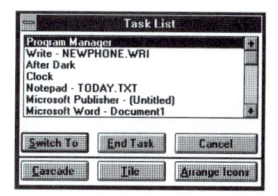

Minimize/Maximize Buttons These let you shrink Publisher down to an icon on the Windows desktop (▼) or enlarge it to a full screen (▲).

Menu Bar The Main menu options available for the application you're working on appear on the Menu bar. Figure 2-2 shows the commands for Program Manager.

Using Menus

Menus operate in the same way whether you're using Windows or Publisher. The menu options that are available for each program, however, are different.

- To select a command from the Main menu, click on it. When you select one of the commands, a submenu appears. Figure 2-3 shows the File menu from Program Manager. Try clicking on the Main menu options. Each displays a different submenu.

- To cancel a command on the menu, click on another menu option or click on the desktop.

The commands on submenus come in three flavors. Options that execute immediately upon selection appear in boldface. Open and Delete on the File menu are examples of this type of option. You can select these just as you would commands on the Main menu. Click on the option to execute it. *Inactive*

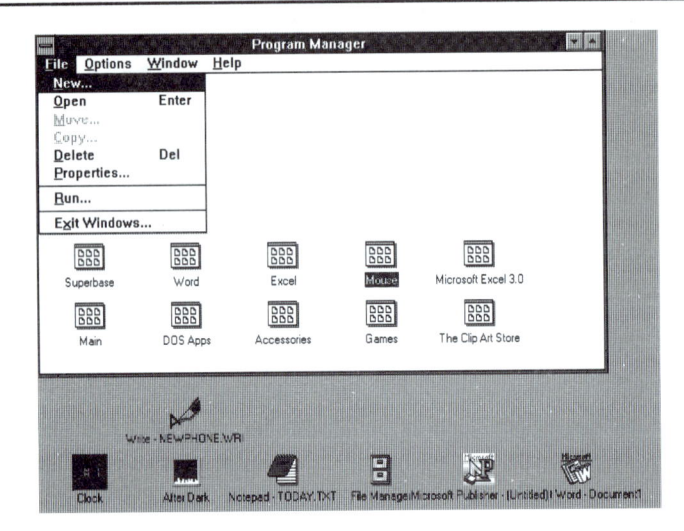

Figure 2-3.   File menu in the Program Manager

commands—those shaded in grey such as Move or Copy in Figure 2-3—cannot be selected at the current time. They become active or inactive because of other choices you make during a working session. If the command you want to execute is inactive, you may need to return to another menu or make other changes in order to activate it.

Options such as Run that appear in boldface followed by ellipsis marks (...) present a list of additional choices in a dialog box. Figure 2-4 shows the

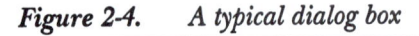

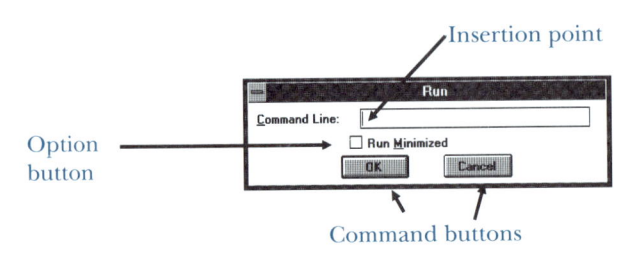

Figure 2-4.   A typical dialog box

Chapter 2: *How Publisher Operates*　　　　　　　　　　　　　　　　　　　　　　　27

dialog box for the Run command. *Dialog boxes* let you make several choices from a single screen about how a particular command will be executed.

Using Dialog Boxes

Dialog boxes usually ask for several pieces of information. In Figure 2-4, you can enter a name for the program you want to run, and select how it will run. You can modify your choices in the dialog box as much as necessary before continuing. Dialog boxes often request information in different ways. You can enter information in them using fields, buttons, and lists.

Fields

Fields are locations on the screen where you can enter or edit information directly from the keyboard, for example, the Command Line field in Figure 2-4.

1. Click on the Command Line field.
   If a field is empty, you can click anywhere in the field and then begin typing. A vertical bar called the *insertion point* appears in the field, as shown in Figure 2-4. The insertion point is a text cursor. It shows you where characters you type will appear next. This exercise will show you some different ways to edit a field.
2. Type **sample**.
   If a field already has data in it, you can click on a character that you want to modify.
3. Click between the letters *a* and *m* in the Command Line field.

The insertion point appears as shown here:

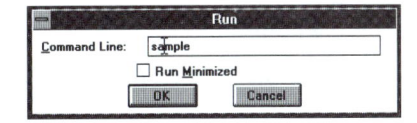

4. Use (BACKSPACE) to erase the letters *a* and *s*. Use (DEL) to erase the letter *m*.

5. Type **ap**. Congratulations! You've just changed "sample" to "apple."

When you want to edit the characters in a field, use (BACKSPACE) and (DEL) to remove characters, and then type new ones to replace them.

Tip

When a field is completely selected, as shown in the following illustration, any character you type will clear the field so you can begin typing a new entry from scratch. To select an entire field quickly, double-click on it.

Buttons

Think of a *button* as a switch. To select a button, click on it. The Run Minimized button in Figure 2-4 toggles a setting for whether this command will display as an icon or run in a window while it executes. Clicking on this button turns it either on or off, but you can't see the results of selecting the button until the command executes. Try clicking on this button several times to see the effect on the screen. It displays an X in order to indicate the button's current state. Buttons of this kind are called *option buttons*.

Any buttons that alter the display of the dialog box itself appear on a large grey background. These are called *command buttons*. These are like switches too, but they make things happen immediately. In Figure 2-4, OK and Cancel are command buttons. They both cause the dialog box to close. Command buttons also let you *complete* a dialog box. After you complete your choices in a dialog box, you can execute the command or cancel it.

- To complete a command from a dialog box, click the OK button.
- To cancel the command, click the Cancel button.

Chapter 2: *How Publisher Operates*

Click Cancel now to make sure that you close the dialog box for the Run command before continuing.

Lists

Lists are windows in a dialog box that contain a restricted selection of entries for you to pick from. Lists appear differently on the screen than fields because of the arrow (▼) at the right of the list window. Here is a sample of a list field.

To open this window, follow these steps:

1. Double-click on the Microsoft SolutionSeries icon.
2. Click on the File menu in the Program Manager.
3. Click on the Copy option from the File menu.
4. Click on the arrow to the right of the To Group field.
5. Click on one of the options in the window, or click on one of the scroll arrows in the window to display more options.
6. After you make a selection from a list window, the window closes. You must still complete the dialog box by clicking on the OK or Cancel button. Click Cancel.

Getting Help

Publisher and Windows were designed by Microsoft, so the help systems for both products operate identically. Help can be a terrific time saver if you need the answer to a technical question quickly. It contains much of the material from the *User's Guide,* and is especially handy for hard-to-remember commands.

These systems are *indexed* and *context sensitive*. If you want help on a particular subject, you can always display an index of help topics and select the one you need. You can also ask for help in the middle of executing a command—in context—and the system does its best to display a help screen about the command you are trying to run.

If, for example, you want to brush up on using menus, rather than reach for the manual, you can get most of the answers you need more quickly by using Help.

1. Click on the Help option in the Menu bar of the Program Manager.
2. Click on Index from the Help menu.

Tip

When the help system first appears, its window is only partially maximized. Click the Maximize button to run Help in a full screen–it's easier to read.

Help topics that you can find more information on are underlined. Further help is available from this screen on either Program Manager or Windows. When you point to a help topic, the pointer changes to a hand with an extended index finger (as shown in the following illustration) to let you know that there is more information available on that topic.

3. Click on Windows Help Index as shown here:

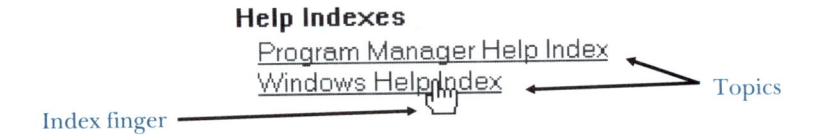

Help Indexes
Program Manager Help Index
Windows Help Index

Index finger

Topics

The main index for Windows appears. Within the index shown in Figure 2-5, category titles appear in boldface. Within each category topics are listed alphabetically.

4. Scroll down the list of topics until you see Selecting and Canceling Menus (it's near the bottom). To scroll, click on the scroll arrows or drag the scroll box to move down the list.
5. Click on Selecting and Canceling Menus. The help screen on selecting menus appears.

Chapter 2: *How Publisher Operates* 31

Figure 2-5. **Main Windows Help Index**

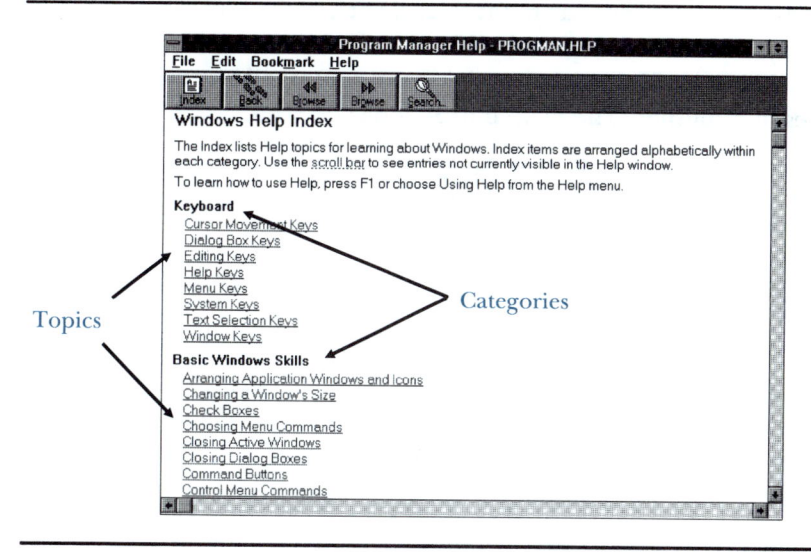

After you've finished reading this screen, you can go on to look at information on other topics, or close the help window.

6. To close the help window, double-click on the Control Menu box or click on the Minimize button.

Help Buttons

When you first select Help from the Main menu, it contains options for accessing Help in different ways, as shown here:

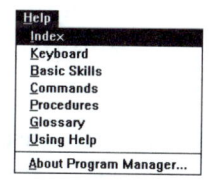

Each option on the Help menu begins with an index, and getting help is as easy as selecting a topic from the index. Each of the topics that you can access is always underlined, and underlined text is always a topic. That makes a topic difficult to miss! Help is also available as a command button from most dialog boxes in Publisher. The Help button looks like this:

Tip

You can display a help window at any time by pressing F1, *even in the process of executing a command.*

At first the help system may seem complicated. However, the buttons at the top of the help screen make it hard to get lost. The buttons shown here can be clicked at any time during a help session:

Index Button   Index displays the main index to the help system. Details on how to use the index have already been discussed.

Back Button   Back displays the previous screen in the help system. From the help screen on Selecting and Canceling Menus, try the following procedure.

1. Click the Back button. The Index screen appears.
2. Click Back again. The initial help screen appears.

Back walks you backward through the entire sequence of help screens you have used during the current help session. Back has a pretty long memory. If you continue to press it, progressively earlier screens appear in the order in which they were viewed.

Browse Buttons   Browse (back/forward) displays the previous or next topic in the help index, based on the screen you are currently viewing. These

Chapter 2: *How Publisher Operates* 33

screens are usually about a closely related subject. For example, if you followed the procedure described in this section to display the help screen on Selecting and Canceling Menus, click on Browse forward. Publisher displays a help screen on Choosing Menu Commands.

Search Button   Search uses a dialog box to let you enter a help topic, or pick from a list of topics. Locating specific information is sometimes faster using Search because you can enter your own words rather than looking through the index. It also contains some topics that aren't in the index. If you're looking at a help screen now, try the following steps.

1. Click Search. The Search dialog box, shown in Figure 2-6, appears.
2. Type **menus** and then press (ENTER).
   As you type the letters of the word, a list of keywords that begin with letters that match your entry appears in the keyword window. After you press (ENTER), a list of topics related to the keywords appears in the topic window. Whenever the Search dialog box is in view, several options are open to you. You can type entries as you have in this exercise. You can also double-click on any keyword in the keyword window to display a list of related topics. Finally, you

Figure 2-6.   *Search dialog box from the help system*

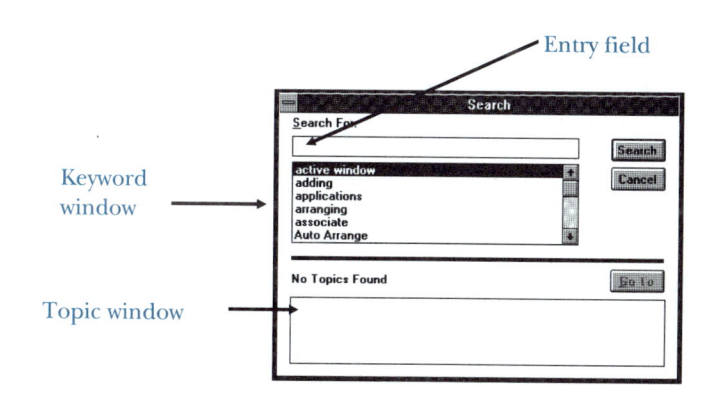

can double-click on any topic in the topic window to display the related help screen.

3. Double-click on Selecting and Canceling Menus in the bottom window. The appropriate help window appears.

Continue to experiment with Help until you feel at home and confident that you won't get lost. It can save you a lot of time when you're working with Publisher, but you need to feel comfortable using it. Once you've finished with Help, close or minimize the help window.

Working with Publisher

You may find it useful to load Publisher before reading through this section. That way, you can experiment with some of the features described here.

1. Double-click on the Microsoft SolutionSeries icon in the Program Manager window.
2. Double-click on the Microsoft Publisher icon in the SolutionSeries application window.

The Publisher screen has a familiar Windows look and feel. The Title bar, Control Menu box, Menu bar and Minimize/Maximize buttons all appear as they do in a standard Windows application, such as Program Manager.

Publisher Window Features

In addition to standard Windows features, the Publisher window, as shown in Figure 2-7, has the following unique parts.

Page Area   This area is a visual outline of the current publication page. Information that is in the page area will be included when the publication is printed.

Vertical and Horizontal Scroll Bars   These indicate which portion of the current page you are viewing. The scroll boxes and arrows let you change

Chapter 2: *How Publisher Operates* 35

Figure 2-7. Publisher's screen

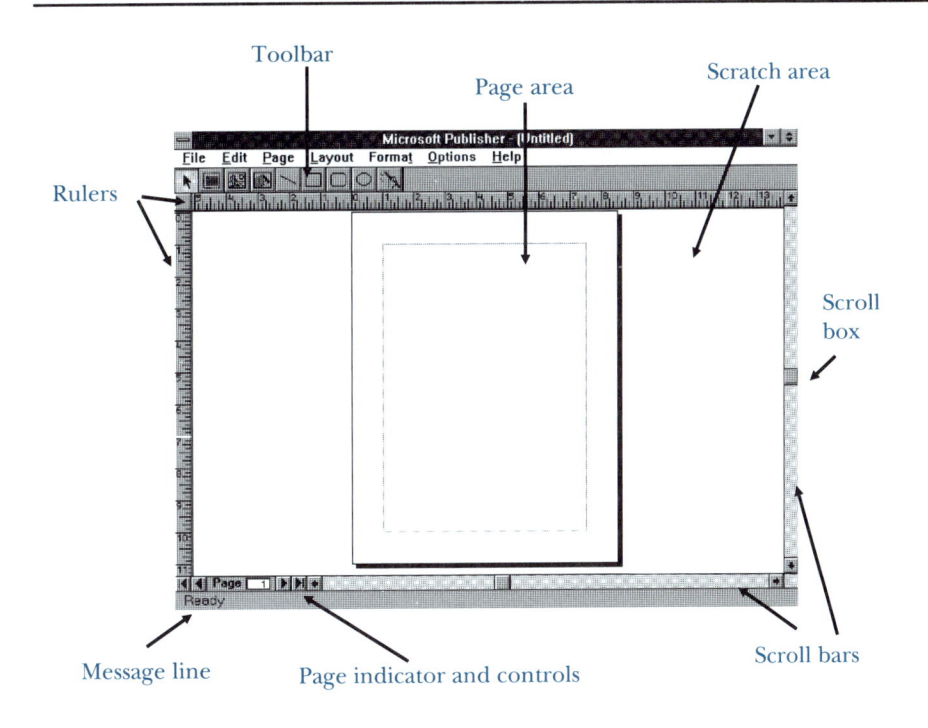

[Figure: Publisher's screen with labeled callouts — Toolbar, Page area, Scratch area, Rulers, Scroll box, Scroll bars, Message line, Page indicator and controls]

your current position on the page. Try dragging either of the scroll boxes or clicking on any of the scroll arrows to change the current view.

Scratch Area   This area is a temporary storage space for material that you are working with in the current publication. Information that is in the scratch area will not be included when the publication is printed. The scratch area extends above and below the page beyond what you initially see on the screen. You can use the scroll bars to display more of it.

Rulers   These guides let you measure distances horizontally and vertically across the page. You can move the rulers to convenient locations, and change their unit of measure depending on your project. Rulers are invaluable when you want to place objects with precision.

Page Indicator and Controls   The Page Indicator displays the number of the page you are viewing in the current publication. You can also use it to turn directly to a specific page. The Page Control buttons let you browse forward and backward through the publication.

Message Line   This line may display a comment or error message concerning the command or procedure that you executed.

Toolbar   The Toolbar contains all of the frame and drawing tools. Each of these appears as a button labeled with an icon to show what it's for. The Text Frame tool, for example, contains the icon of a paragraph.

The Toolbar and Other Buttons

When you select one of the buttons on the Toolbar, the right side of the Toolbar changes to display additional buttons.

- To select a button, just click on it.

Try clicking on the Text Frame tool. The options you see on the Toolbar are the most commonly used for the tool you select. Other formatting options for tools are usually available from one of the menus. When you first select *any* of the frame tools, Publisher displays the following options on the right of the Toolbar.

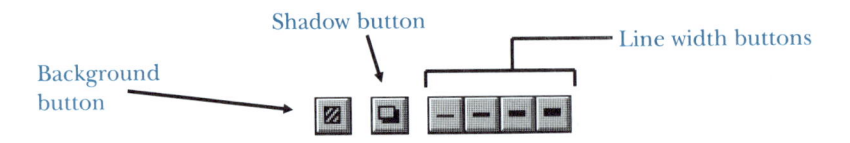

You can select any of these to change the characteristics of the frame.

Background Button   The Background button lets you select patterns and colors for the frame.

Shadow Button   The Shadow button lets you add a drop shadow to the frame.

Chapter 2: *How Publisher Operates*

Line Width Buttons   The Line Width buttons let you add borders or alter the line thickness of the border that surrounds a frame.

After you create a text frame, the Toolbar changes to display different options for formatting text.

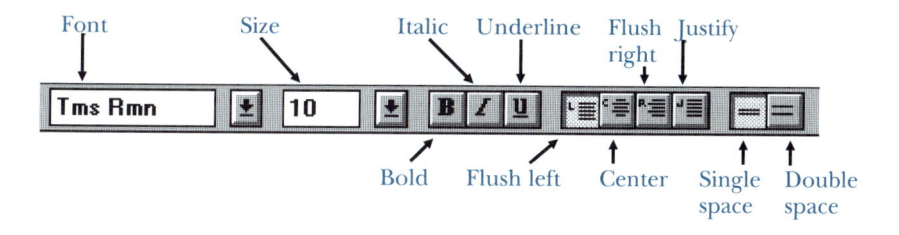

```
          Font          Size         Italic  Underline   Flush  Justify
            ↓             ↓            ↓        ↓        right
                                                           ↓      ↓
         [Tms Rmn  ▼]  [10 ▼]      [B] [I] [U]  [≡][≡][≡][≡]  [=][=]
                                     ↗      ↗        ↑       ↑     ↑
                                   Bold  Flush left  Center Single Double
                                                            space  space
```

Some of these are option buttons. Others operate as lists. Each has a distinct effect on the appearance of paragraphs and characters in a text frame.

Font Window   The Font window displays a list of typefaces.

Size Window   The Size window displays a list of sizes for each font.

Type Style Buttons   The Bold, Italic, and Underline buttons control their respective typographic characteristic.

Alignment and Spacing Buttons   The Flush Left, Center, Flush Right, Justify, Single Space, and Double Space buttons control the alignment and spacing of paragraphs.

Crop Button   If you create a picture frame, the Toolbar displays the following button as well:

The Crop button lets you trim the image in a picture frame.

Line Buttons   If you draw a line using the Line tool, Publisher displays the following buttons for changing the appearance of the line:

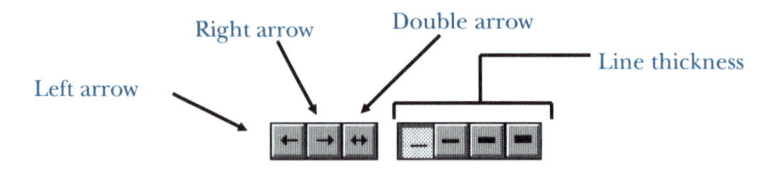

Right arrow — Double arrow — Line thickness
Left arrow

Left Arrow, Right Arrow, Double Arrow, and the Line Thickness buttons each change the type of line you can draw.

Publisher Menus

Publisher menus give you access to all of the commands in the program except frame creation. Many of the commands described in the Toolbar section, for example, shading or line thickness, can also be executed from menus. This section outlines the general capabilities available from each of the Publisher submenus.

File Menu   File menu commands open, close, or save publications to disk. You can also import external text and graphics files, control all printing options, and exit Publisher from this menu.

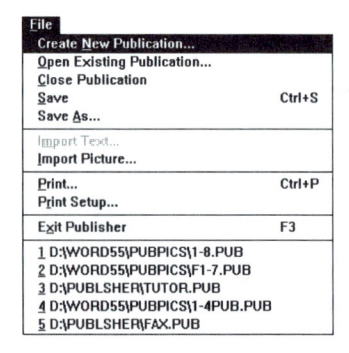

Chapter 2: How Publisher Operates

Edit Menu   Whole frames can be cut or copied, and then pasted within or between publications from this menu. You can edit text, invoke search and replace options, move text and graphics to and from the Windows Clipboard, and undo your last command.

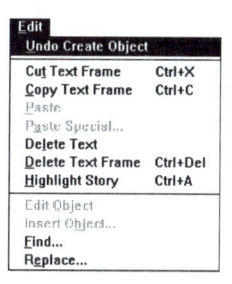

```
Edit
  Undo Create Object
  Cut Text Frame      Ctrl+X
  Copy Text Frame     Ctrl+C
  Paste
  Paste Special...
  Delete Text
  Delete Text Frame   Ctrl+Del
  Highlight Story     Ctrl+A
  Edit Object
  Insert Object...
  Find...
  Replace...
```

Page Menu   The basic page layout and the number of pages are determined from this menu. You can insert and delete pages. This menu also gives you access to the background page for creating objects that repeat on every page in a publication. In addition you can select views of the screen with different levels of magnification.

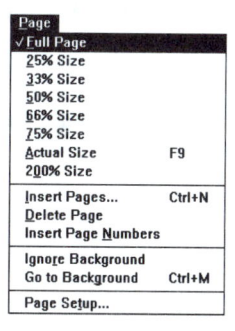

```
Page
  √ Full Page
    25% Size
    33% Size
    50% Size
    66% Size
    75% Size
    Actual Size        F9
    200% Size
    Insert Pages...    Ctrl+N
    Delete Page
    Insert Page Numbers
    Ignore Background
    Go to Background   Ctrl+M
    Page Setup...
```

Layout Menu   The page layout can be further refined, and frames can be individually formatted from this menu. You can bring objects to the front (on top of other objects) or send them to the back (behind other objects). You can also control graphic options for borders, border art, shading, and shadow.

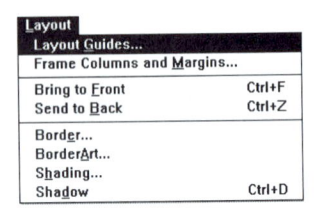

```
Layout
  Layout Guides...
  Frame Columns and Margins...
  Bring to Front              Ctrl+F
  Send to Back                Ctrl+Z
  Border...
  BorderArt...
  Shading...
  Shadow                      Ctrl+D
```

Format Menu   The Format menu commands control the appearance of text, including font selection, paragraph alignment, and tab stop settings. You can also control the formatting of graphic images through scaling and cropping.

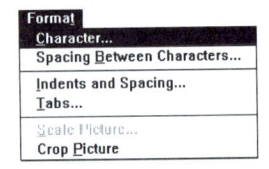

```
Format
  Character...
  Spacing Between Characters...
  Indents and Spacing...
  Tabs...
  Scale Picture...
  Crop Picture
```

Options Menu   A number of toggles for screen appearance and program interaction can be customized from this menu. You can display or hide pictures, rulers, the Status line, layout guides, and object boundaries here. You can also run text utilities for spell checking and hyphenation.

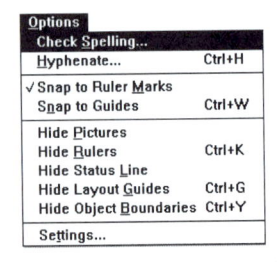

```
Options
  Check Spelling...
  Hyphenate...                Ctrl+H
  √ Snap to Ruler Marks
  Snap to Guides              Ctrl+W
  Hide Pictures
  Hide Rulers                 Ctrl+K
  Hide Status Line
  Hide Layout Guides          Ctrl+G
  Hide Object Boundaries      Ctrl+Y
  Settings...
```

Chapter 2: *How Publisher Operates*

Help Menu   Publisher's help system is accessed from here. In addition, you can run the tutorial program that comes with Publisher. The tutorial is a good refresher for some of the material covered here and in Chapter 1.

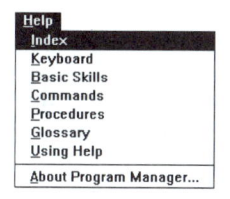

```
Help
Index
Keyboard
Basic Skills
Commands
Procedures
Glossary
Using Help
About Program Manager...
```

Keyboard Shortcuts

Publisher lets you execute menu commands using either a mouse or keystrokes. In general, you'll find it easier to explore and learn the basics of a Windows application such as Publisher using the menus and a mouse, even though there may be a sequence of keystrokes that takes less time to execute. These are called *keyboard equivalents* or *keyboard shortcuts*. Some commands are easier to execute in one way than another; there is no strict rule about which technique to use under what circumstances. Experimentation is the best path to understanding. Since the intention of this book is to make Publisher easy to use, it will rely primarily on mouse-driven instructions and only suggest keyboard shortcuts as tips.

When there is a keyboard shortcut available for a command, it appears on a menu next to the command name, for example:

```
Close Publication
Save                          Ctrl+S
Save As...
```

In this example, (CTRL)(S) (holding down the (CTRL) key and pressing the (S) key) executes the sequence for saving a file. These shortcuts can be executed directly during a Publisher session, and there is no need to activate any of the menus. A complete table of keyboard equivalents can be found in Appendix D.

Tip

All of the menus and many of the submenu options are accessible through keyboard shortcuts based on the (ALT) key followed by one or more letters indicated in the name of a menu or command. These letters always appear underlined on the menus, as shown in the previous example. To execute the Save As command, press (ALT)(F)(A).

ALT activates the Main menu. F is the key letter for File menu from the Main menu, and A is the key letter for Save As from the File menu.

Using Publisher Dialog Boxes

Publisher dialog boxes are like other Windows dialog boxes except the number of choices may be more extensive. For example, the Save As command in the File menu lets you save the current publication under a new name or in a new location. The Save As dialog box appears in Figure 2-8.

In this example, there are three command buttons, two option buttons, two list windows, and a directory tree. OK and Cancel respectively execute or ignore the current command, and then return to the Publisher screen. Help displays a help screen for the Save As command. Template and Backup are toggles for saving the file as a template or creating a running backup. The two list windows let you change the current drive and the criteria for the type of files that appear in the File window. Finally, the directory tree lets you change directories by clicking on one of the icons in the window just as you would in the Windows File Manager.

Figure 2-8. Save As dialog box

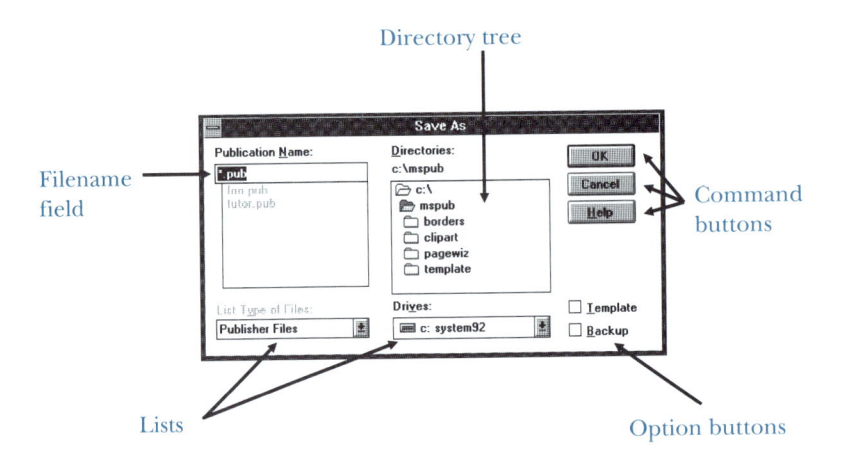

Sometimes several buttons are grouped together, as shown in the Print dialog box in Figure 2-9. Usually you must pick one of the buttons in the group. By selecting one of them, the others are automatically deselected. For example, within the Print Range group in the Print dialog box, the All and Pages choices are mutually exclusive in just this way. By selecting All, you decide to print an entire publication and cannot, therefore, enter a specific sequence of pages to print. If you were to select Pages, All would automatically deselect, and you could enter beginning and ending page numbers for the print job in the From and To fields.

Tip

Use TAB *or* SHIFT-TAB *as keyboard shortcuts to move between the fields and buttons in a dialog box.*

Correcting Mistakes (Undo)

As you become more proficient using Publisher, you'll develop your own techniques for correcting errors and editing your work. However, when you first begin to work with the program (and even after you become an expert) Publisher provides an invaluable tool for getting you out of trouble: the Undo command. Undo reverses the effects of the most recent action you took on a publication. For example, if you inadvertently delete some text or move a frame, Undo can correct the mistake. Undo will operate regardless of whether you execute an action using a mouse, the keyboard, a menu, or a button.

Figure 2-9.   Print dialog box

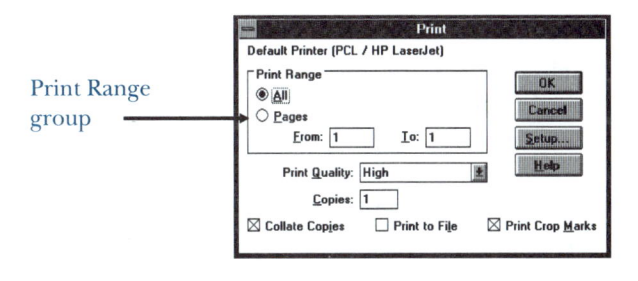

- Click on Edit from the Main menu.
- Click on Undo from the Edit menu.

Tip

The keyboard shortcut to undo an action is `ALT`-`BACKSPACE`.

Note

Undo can be a real life saver, but remember: it only affects your most recent action, not the one before, or the one before that. If you make an error, use Undo immediately; otherwise it may not undo what you had intended.

Printer Considerations

One last issue before you begin the hands-on tutorial in the next chapter—the primary objective of using Publisher is to create printed material. The capabilities of the printing device you are using significantly affect the results you'll get while working on a publication. For example, with certain laser printers the fonts available may be a direct function of cartridges or downloaded font sets. With other devices the selection of different page sizes may be limited. Observe the following guidelines before beginning to work with Publisher:

- Install your printer(s) correctly under Windows.
- Select the printer you want to use for a publication *before* starting the job.
- Don't use different printers for the same publication once it is underway.

Not observing the last of these cautions can have especially surprising results. If you switch printers for an existing publication, for example, headlines may appear in copy-sized type, and layouts can become distorted. Check your printer configuration once Publisher is running:

1. Click on File from the Menu bar.
2. Click on Printer Setup from the File menu.

3. If you want to change printers for the session, click on the Specific Printer button, and then click on the printer you want to use.
4. Click OK.

Review

You should now feel acquainted with the different parts of Publisher's screen and with its operational features such as lists and buttons. As you work through the tutorial in the next chapter, using each of these features will become more familiar.

- The mouse is essential for working with Publisher. Get acquainted with it before you do anything else!
- Lots of information is on the Publisher screen. The Title bar, Message line, page indicator, rulers, and scroll bars display information about what is currently going on in the publication, and what you are looking at.
- The scratch area provides you with a nonprinting work area.
- The Toolbar makes the most frequently used commands in Publisher easy to work with.
- Menus can be accessed using the mouse or through a variety of keyboard shortcuts. The mouse is usually the easiest way to learn, but the keyboard is often quicker to execute.
- The menus are organized in a logical fashion with commands grouped together by function.
- Publisher dialog boxes can contain an extensive number of options using a variety of selection methods.
- Undo can bail you out of serious trouble if you make a mistake, but you must remember to use it immediately.
- Printer configuration has a serious effect on how Publisher operates. You should take care to check it before beginning a Publisher session and be cautious about changing it for an existing publication.

3

A Working Session

If you want a good look at Microsoft Publisher before you begin to spend time building up your skills, this chapter is your best bet. It's a condensed look at many of the major features in the program. The chapter contains explicit instructions for creating a sample application that leaves virtually nothing to chance. In the process of creating the application, you'll see how Publisher accomplishes the following activities:

- Starting, exiting, and saving files
- Creating a layout
- Adding, moving, resizing, and connecting frames
- Importing text and graphics
- Formatting text
- Using borders, WordArt, PageWizards, and drawing tools
- Adding pages and using the background page

You'll get a taste for each of these subjects and a basis for learning more about them in the remainder of the book. Experienced Windows users should be able to complete the tutorial in under an hour. Newcomers may need a little more time. If you don't have time to complete the chapter in a single sitting, just save the publication at a convenient break point (one of the section breaks) and resume the session later. You should read through this chapter at the computer with Publisher up and running. Hands-on instructions show you how to create the newsletter shown in Figure 3-1 from scratch.

The flow of material is designed to simulate a working session that you might experience using Publisher: the order of steps you'll take in designing and modifying this sample publication is typical. To make them easy to locate, the section headings in the chapter are the main steps, and within each section instructions are numbered sequentially. In order to make following the steps clearer, the numbering sequence starts over for each section. However, in building the sample publication, each section depends on the completion of previous sections, so don't start in the middle of the tutorial unless you have already worked up to a particular section. Other suggestions for experimenting with Publisher appear in the text, but are not necessary to complete the

Figure 3-1.   Completed sample newsletter

publication. The measurements indicated for frame positions are approximate for creating the sample newsletter. Don't waste too much time trying to make them exact.

Remember that configuring your printer can affect the options available in Publisher and the appearance of publications dramatically. Be sure that the printer you plan to use for this session has been properly installed under Publisher before continuing. See "Printer Considerations" in Chapter 2 or Appendix H, for details on printer configuration.

Starting Publisher

The following instructions assume that your computer is on, that Windows is running, and that Publisher has been properly installed. If you're an advanced user and have changed the way Publisher normally starts from Windows, this procedure may differ slightly.

1. Double-click on the Microsoft SolutionSeries icon in the Program Manager window.
2. Double-click on the Publisher icon in the SolutionSeries window. The Publisher Start Up screen appears, as shown in Figure 3-2.

The Start Up screen gives you four different ways to start a Publisher session: with a PageWizard, with a template, with a blank page, and by opening an existing file.

Publisher always starts with PageWizards. This is the *default* selection, the choice that's made if you don't pick another. The window below the startup selections displays all of the PageWizard alternatives for starting a publication. Try clicking on the other choices—Templates, Blank Page, or Open—at the top of the Start Up screen, and watch the choices in the window change. When there are more choices than will fit in the window, a scroll bar appears on the right so you can display the remainder of the list.

3. Double-click on Blank Page. The Publisher screen appears, as shown in Figure 3-3.

Figure 3-2.   Start Up screen

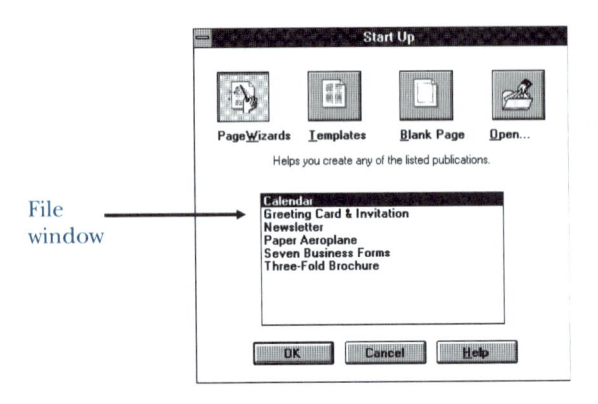

File window

Figure 3-3.   Publisher screen

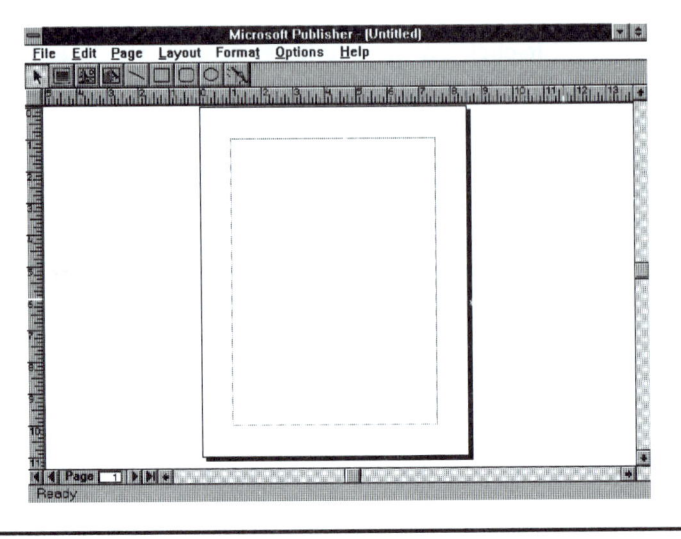

Selecting a Layout

The newsletter shown in Figure 3-1 has a predominantly four-column layout. While the headlines and illustrations stretch across columns, the bulk of the text conforms to this general appearance. Even after you select a layout in Publisher, you are free to insert frames that do not conform strictly to the layout. It is useful, however, to choose a layout that matches the most common columnar characteristics of the publication you want to design before you begin detailed work. This makes placing objects on the page easier later in the publication's development.

1. Click on Layout on the Menu bar and then on Layout Guides from the Layout menu.
2. Change the value in the Columns field to 4.
3. Change the value in the Top field to 0.75.

After you change the value for a field and move to another, the image of the page in the Preview window at the right of the dialog box changes to reflect your modifications. This is what the Preview window should look like after you make these entries:

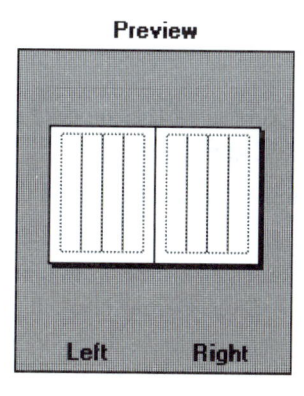

Preview

Left   Right

4. Click OK. The page area now appears with guides set for four columns and a reduced top margin.

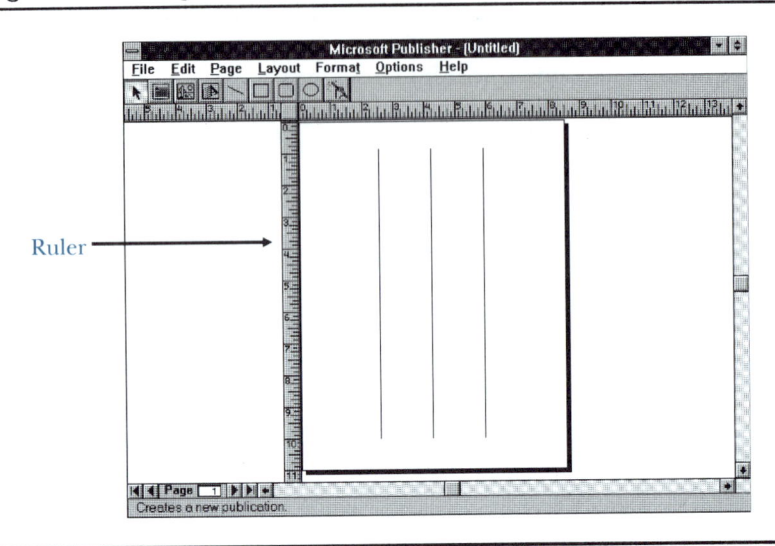

Figure 3-4.   Repositioned vertical ruler

Ruler

Adding Text Frames

You may find it easier to judge the measurements in this section if you move the vertical ruler closer to the edge of the page. Publisher lets you move either of the rulers anywhere on the page to help with measurements.

1. Point to the center of the vertical ruler until the cursor becomes a double-headed arrow (⇔).
2. Drag the ruler to the left edge of the page area, as shown in Figure 3-4.
3. Now you're ready to create Text frames for each of the four columns. Click on the Text Frame tool. The mouse pointer changes to a crosshair (+) to indicate that you're ready to create a frame.

Hairlines on each of the rulers track the path of the crosshair to indicate your vertical and horizontal position. As you can see in the following illustration, the hairlines make it easy to measure distances.

Chapter 3: *A Working Session* 53

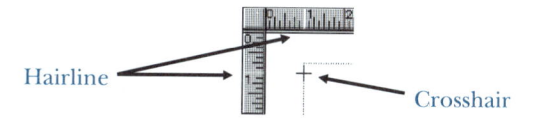

Hairline — Crosshair

4. Point to the layout guide for the left margin at approximately 3 inches on the vertical ruler line. Then drag the cursor across the width and length of the column. At the lower-right corner of the column, release the button.

The size and shape of the frame is determined as you drag the mouse. You can continue to shape and size the frame until you release the mouse button. At that point the frame is completed, and its handles and Connect button appear as shown in Figure 3-5. (You will learn more about handles and the Connect button in Chapter 4.) Many of the buttons on the Toolbar have now changed to formatting options for **Text** frames (formatting will be discussed later in this chapter).

Figure 3-5.   *Completed Text frame*

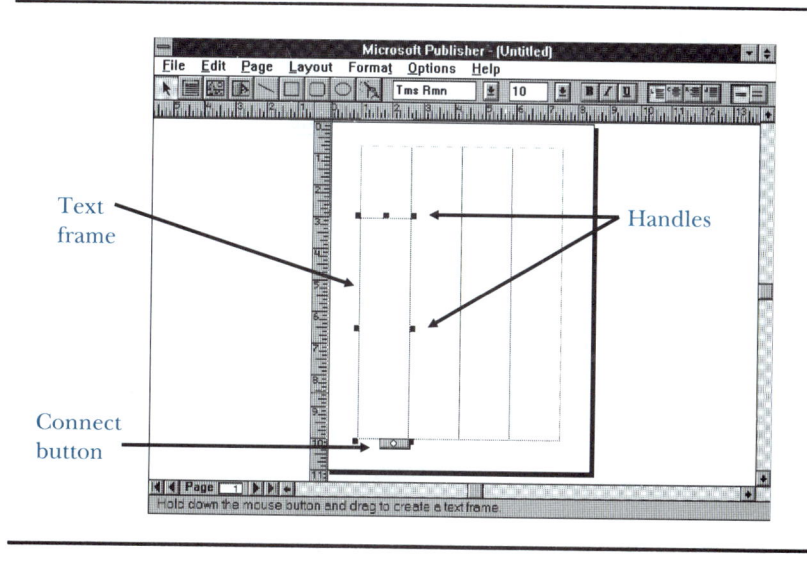

Publisher lets you actively work on only one frame at a time. The *active frame* is the one for which handles are visible. You can select the active frame by clicking anywhere within it (when you create a new frame, it is the active frame until you select another).

Note

You can deactivate a frame by clicking anywhere else on the page or scratch areas.

Undo

If you've made an error in creating the Text frame for any reason—it's poorly positioned or sized, for example—there are lots of ways to correct it. One of the easiest is to simply *undo* it. Undo is a very powerful command that will reverse the effect of practically any other command in Publisher. However, it will only affect the very last command you executed, so if you make an error and want to correct it using Undo, use it immediately! Now use Undo to cancel the creation of the Text frame.

1. Click on Edit on the Menu bar.
2. Click on Undo Create Object on the Edit menu. The Text frame disappears. The literal name of this option on the Edit menu will often change to reflect the last task, but the first option on the Edit menu is always Undo.

Tip

The keyboard shortcut for Undo is ALT-BACKSPACE.

Working with Frames

Publisher has several aids for freehand mouse work, such as creating frames. These make it easier to get your work properly aligned with ruler marks and *layout guides*, spots on the page you can designate as alignment points for frames to "snap" to.

Chapter 3: *A Working Session* 55

1. Click on Options on the Menu bar and then click on Snap to Guides. The check will appear, as shown here:

Snap to Ruler Marks	
✓ Snap to Guides	Ctrl+W
Hide Pictures	

When Snap to Guides is enabled, the crosshair "sticks" slightly when passing slowly over any of the layout guides to make positioning easier.

Note

When a menu selection has a check mark, it is currently enabled. Publisher has many design aids like this. They are called toggles. You turn them on or off alternately. For example, if you selected Snap to Guides again, you would disable it. The check mark would disappear.

Now, redraw the Text frame.

2. Click on the Text Frame tool.
3. Point to the leftmost layout guide at approximately 3 inches on the ruler line. Then drag the cursor across the width and length of the column. At the lower-right corner of the column, release the button.
4. Click on the Text Frame tool again and repeat the procedure described above to create a Text frame of the same height between the next two layout guides.

Tip

If you hold down CTRL *while you click on the Text Frame tool you can create several frames without reselecting the tool each time.*

5. Repeat the procedure in the previous step to create two more Text frames within the adjacent layout guides to the right. Your page should now look like Figure 3-6.

Remember that you can move the ruler across the page next to any of the layout guides for help in measuring your starting location. If the ruler is in your way, just move it back to the left edge of the screen into the scratch area.

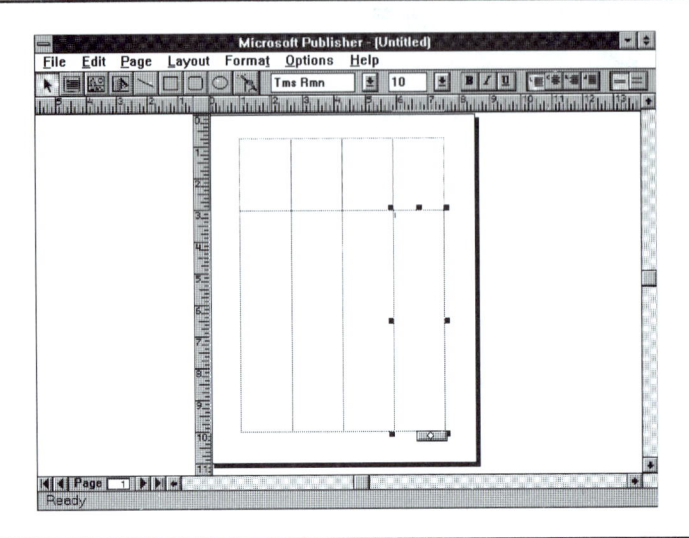

Figure 3-6.　*Publication after four Text frames have been added*

Saving

It's always prudent to save your work on a regular and frequent basis during the course of a session. This is especially important the first time you save a new publication, since it establishes the publication name and makes it easier to save material in the future.

1. Click File from the Menu bar and then click Save As from the File menu. The Save As dialog box, shown in Figure 3-7, appears.

Note

The volume name and drive letter that appear in the Drives list for your system will probably differ. Use a convenient location in your environment for storing this file.

The Save As option lets you save the current untitled publication under a name of your choice. For this tutorial, use TUTOR as the name of the publication. Thereafter you can simply use the Save option to update the disk.

Chapter 3: *A Working Session* 57

Figure 3-7.   *Save As dialog box*

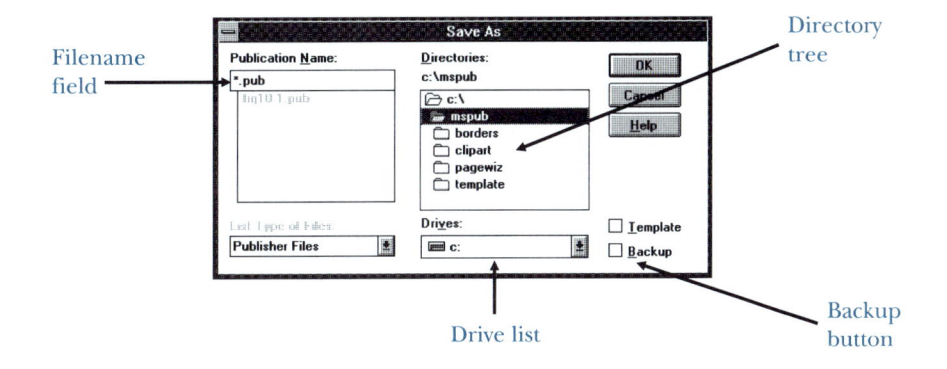

2. Type **TUTOR**. Remember that DOS is not case sensitive. You might see a name in lowercase letters in a file list and see the same name in all caps at the top of a window. This book will use all capitals for filenames and extensions to make them easy to find and recognize. Publisher will automatically append the file extension .PUB to the filename.

3. Click the Backup button. Creating backups is also advisable. Unless you are constrained by disk space limitations, you should usually enable this option. Once it is set for a publication, Publisher automatically creates a backup copy each time you save.

Note

This procedure saves the file in the directory C:\MSPUB (or whatever directory you installed Publisher in). If you want to save the work from this chapter in another drive or directory, you must log onto that drive/directory first. To change drives, select a drive from the list in the Drives window. To select a directory from that drive, double-click on the directory in the directory tree.

4. Click OK. The dialog box closes, and the Publisher screen returns. The next time you want to save the publication, use the Save command. You should now see the name of the file in the Title bar.

Tip

Use CTRL-S *as a keyboard shortcut to save a file.*

Importing Text

Now that the Text frames for the main articles of the publication are in place, you can add text to them. This tutorial will use dummy text, supplied with Publisher, as the material for both articles in the newsletter. Such dummy text is usually written in an archaic language and may even be pure gibberish. It is generally known in the advertising and publishing trade as *greek*. Normally, of course, you would use your own material.

1. Click on the Text frame in the first (leftmost) column. The frame becomes active, and its handles and Connect button appear.

2. Click on File from the Menu bar and click on Import Text from the File menu. The Import Text dialog box will appear, normally displaying only Publisher files (files with a .PUB extension) in the File window, as shown in Figure 3-8. You can, however, change the specification for which files display to one or more other file types.

3. Click the arrow on the Type of Files list and click on Plain Text. The window closes and the File window changes to display files that have a .TXT extension. This is a common abbreviation for "text" used for unformatted files. Plain files can be read by most systems.

4. Double-click on CENTURY.TXT. The frame in column 1 fills with text, and the message shown in Figure 3-9 appears on the screen.

When the active frame is too small to accommodate all of the text from an imported file, Publisher lets you choose between automatically filling it into other frames, or placing it in the *overflow area*. The overflow area is invisible to you, but it will accommodate any amount of text as well as the overflow from multiple frames and their sources.

5. Click on No.

Chapter 3: *A Working Session* 59

Figure 3-8. Import Text dialog box

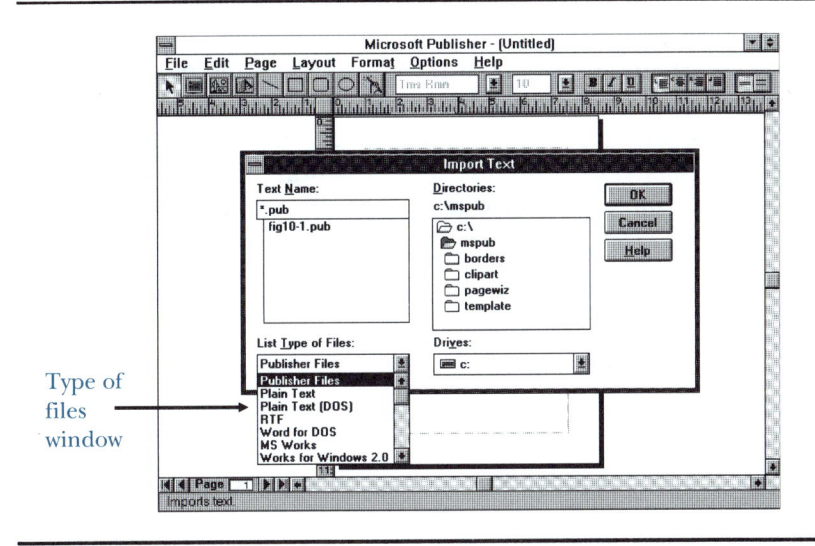

Figure 3-9. Autoflow dialog box

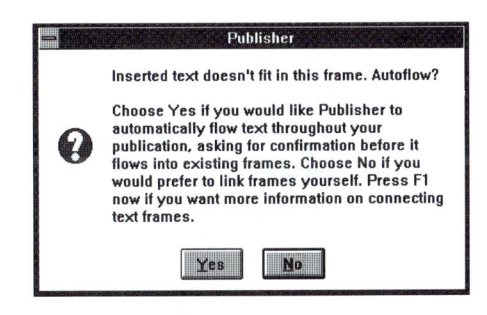

Flowing Text

Don't worry too much about the illegibility of the text at this point (it's greek anyway). You'll soon be able to read it more clearly. Take a look at the bottom of the frame. The small button on the bottom boundary at the right is called the *Connect button.* The Connect button lets you control the flow of text between frames. The three dots on the button are ellipsis marks. They indicate that there is an overflow of text for this frame, and that it is currently in the overflow area.

1. Point to the Connect button. When the cursor is over the Connect button, it changes from a pointer to a finger, as shown in Figure 3-10*a*.

2. Click on the Connect button. The finger changes to the icon of a pitcher, as in Figure 3-10*b*, indicating that you can now connect the text to another frame by "pouring" it in.

3. Click on the frame in column 2. The remaining text from CENTURY.TXT fills the second frame. Several other changes occur as well. The Connect button in the second frame now has a diamond in it, as in Figure 3-10*c*. The diamond is called the *endmark.* It

Figure 3-10.   *Changes in Connect button when text flows*

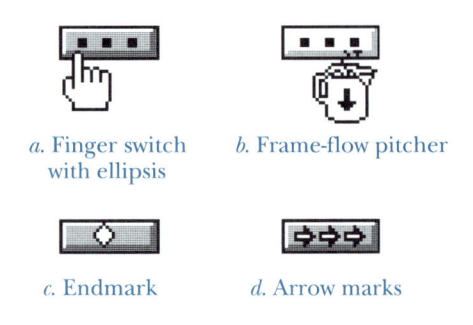

a. Finger switch with ellipsis

b. Frame-flow pitcher

c. Endmark

d. Arrow marks

Chapter 3: A Working Session 61

indicates that there is no longer any text in the overflow area for this file.

4. Click on the frame in column 1. The Connect button changes to a series of arrows, as in Figure 3-10d, to indicate that the text in this frame has been connected to another frame.

Connect buttons tell you a lot about how a frame is operating with other frames in the publication. Now you can import the text for the frames in columns 3 and 4 using the same process.

5. Click on column 3.
6. Select File from the Menu bar and select Import Text from the File menu.
7. Click the arrow on the window called "List Type of Files" and click on Plain Text.
8. Double-click on PROFILE.TXT.
9. Click on No (for Autoflow). Then click on the Connect button for the frame in column 3 and click on the frame in column 4.

Your publication should now look like the page in Figure 3-11.

Entering and Formatting Text

Importing text is only one of the ways to get text into a frame. You can also enter text directly. This is more common when the text itself is brief, as in a headline, subheading, or caption.

1. Click on the Text Frame tool.
2. Point to the fourth layout guide (beginning of column 4) at approximately 4 inches on the ruler line. Then drag the cursor across the width of column 4 and down to approximately 5 1/2 inches. Remember to move the rulers if you need help in measuring.
3. Click on Page on the Menu bar.

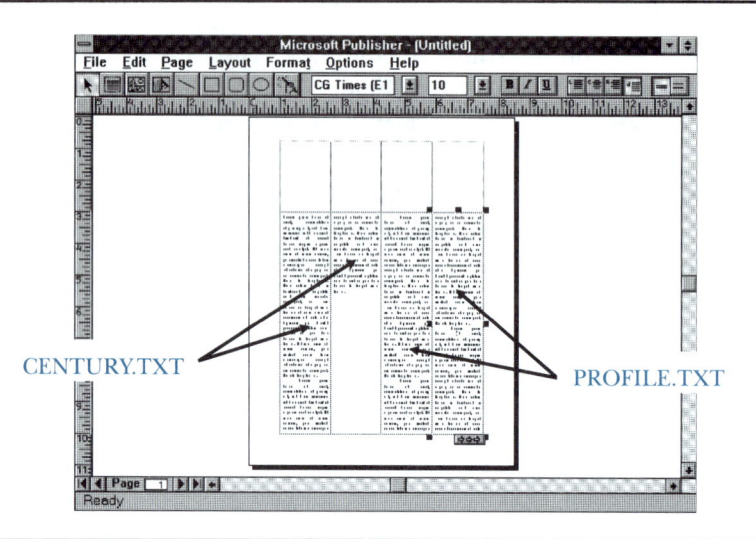

Figure 3-11. *Both text files have been added*

[Screenshot of Microsoft Publisher window showing a page with four columns of text; arrows point to CENTURY.TXT on the left and PROFILE.TXT on the right.]

Publisher will let you view the page area in different degrees of magnification, as shown on the Page menu in Figure 3-12. As you use Publisher more, you'll notice that each of these views is useful for different applications.

4. Click on Actual Size on the Page menu. The view changes so that the display of the area in focus is closer to its actual size, as shown in Figure 3-13. Publisher also zeroes in on the frame that you had already selected.

Within the frame is a vertical bar called the insertion point. Like the insertion point in a field, it acts as a text cursor within Text frames. Notice that Publisher has also accommodated the placement of this latest frame by flowing the text in column 4 around it. Publisher will continue to flow the text even if you move the frame.

Note

The insertion point was present when you created the four other frames on this page as well; however, the Full Page view made it too small to see.

Chapter 3: *A Working Session* 63

Figure 3-12. *Page menu*

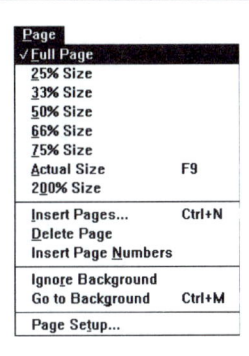

Figure 3-13. *Actual Size view*

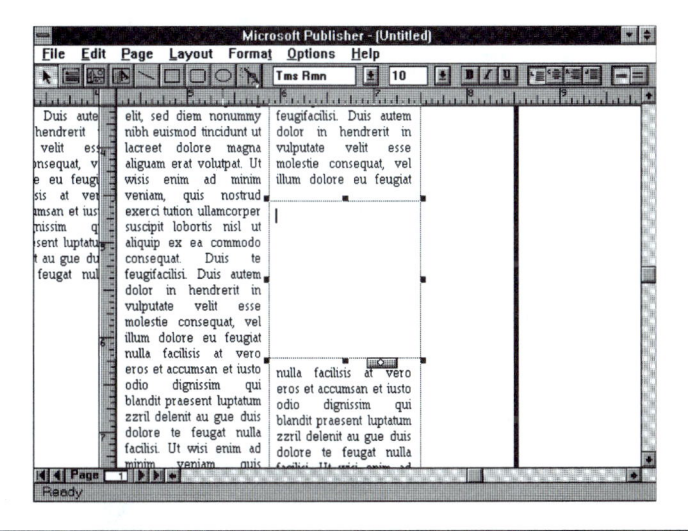

5. Point to the edge of the new frame near one of the handles, until the cursor changes to the icon of a moving van.

6. Press and hold the mouse button until the edges of the frame become a dotted line, and drag the frame down approximately 1 inch in the column. The text in column 4 adjusts to the new location of the overlaying frame.

Experiment with the effects of moving frames and text flow. You can even move the frame off of the page area completely and into the scratch area. If you do so, column 4 will assume its original appearance. Before continuing with this session, replace the frame in column 4 at or near its original location. Now you'll add text for the quotation.

7. Click in the Text frame and press (ENTER) twice.
8. Type **If you're serious about Spring....** This will form the text of the quotation that appears in the newsletter shown in Figure 3-1. At the moment, however, it is the same size and style as the rest of the text in the article. Changing it will require some of the buttons on the Toolbar, shown here:

9. Point to the letter *I* that begins the quotation and drag the cursor to the end of the next line in order to select all of the text, as shown here:

Chapter 3: A Working Session

10. Click on the Point Size list on the Toolbar and click on 14. The list of point sizes closes, and the selected text assumes the new size.
11. Click the Center button on the Toolbar. The text becomes centered within the frame. It should look like this:

> If you're serious
> about Spring...

These are examples of character and paragraph formatting. Many of these commands are also available from the Publisher menus. The most commonly used commands are on the Toolbar for your convenience.

12. Press F9.

Tip

F9 *is a keyboard shortcut for changing views. It switches between the Full Page view of the page and the Actual Size view. This is handy because you'll use Actual Size frequently in formatting and editing text (it's much more legible).*

13. Click on the Text Frame tool.
14. Point to the third layout guide at approximately 3 inches on the ruler line (the upper-left corner of column 3). Then drag the cursor all the way across column 4 and down to approximately 3 3/4 inches.
15. Press F9 to zoom in on the new frame and type **winter 1991**.
16. Drag the cursor across all of the text in the frame in order to select it. Then click on Format on the Menu bar and on Character on the Format menu. The Character dialog box, shown in Figure 3-14, appears. Now finish formatting the headline.
17. Click the Bold button, click the Italic button, and click the All Caps button.
18. Click the arrow on the Font list and click on Modern.
19. Click the arrow on the Point Size list, scroll down the list until 30 becomes visible, and click on 30.

Figure 3-14.   Character dialog box

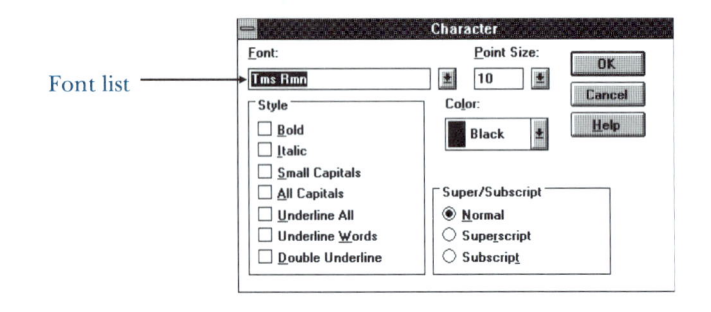

Getting Help

Publisher gives you access to its online help from all of the important dialog boxes in the system. As described in Chapter 2, when you select help from a dialog box it is context sensitive. In other words, Publisher displays help on the options available from the dialog box you are working with at the time. The help screen on formatting characters is shown in Figure 3-15. If you need help on other subjects, you can also display the help index by pressing the Help button.

1. Press (F1) and take a look at the information on the help screen.
2. Double-click the Control button to close the help screen.
3. Click OK. Then press (F9). Your publication should now look like the page in Figure 3-16.

Adding a Picture Frame

It's time to add some artwork to the publication. Blending text and pictures with ease is one of the features that clearly distinguishes a publishing

Chapter 3: A Working Session

Figure 3-15.   *A help screen*

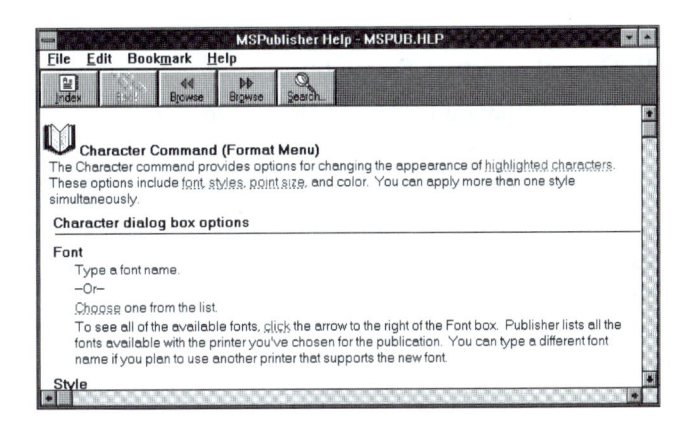

Figure 3-16.   *Completed headline for the second article*

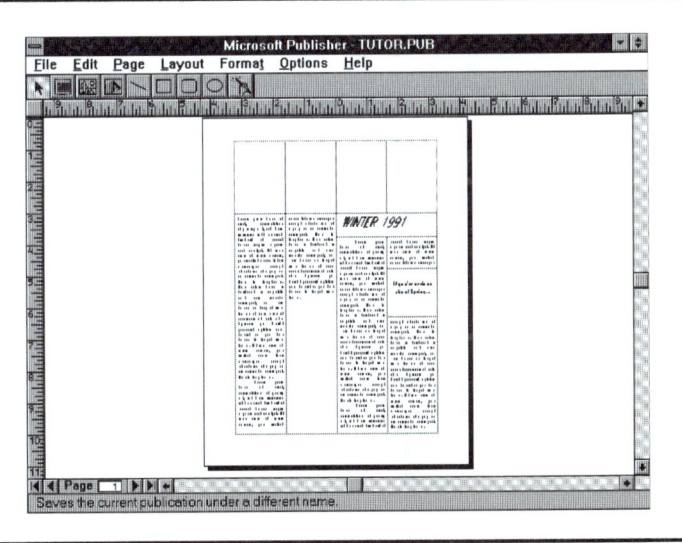

program from a word processor. With Publisher, working with pictures is even easier than importing text.

1. Click the Picture Frame button.
2. Point to the guide for the left margin at approximately 3 inches on the ruler line (the upper-left corner of column 1). Then drag the cursor all the way across column 2 and down to approximately 4 1/2 inches.

This is the Picture frame for the illustration of the globe in Figure 3-1. Your publication should now look like Figure 3-17. Like the addition of the two previous Text frames, Publisher moves the text in the underlying frame to accommodate the new Picture frame.

3. Click on File on the Menu bar and click on Import Picture from the File menu.
4. Double-click on the clip art directory in the directory tree. The File window displays a list of available clip art. The files are arranged in alphabetical order.

Figure 3-17.   Tutorial publication with Picture frame added

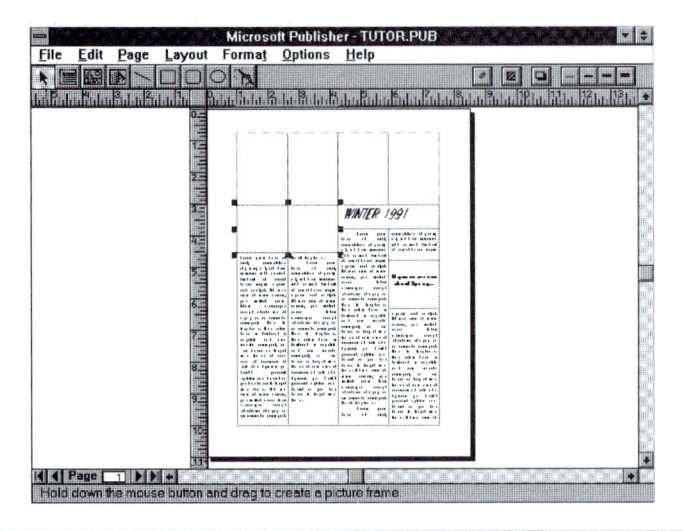

Chapter 3: *A Working Session* 69

There are over 200 illustrations available in the clip art directory, including some that come with Publisher, and over 100 that come with this book. These are taken from the Dover Publications Pictorial Archive Series. If you have not already installed the Dover drawings, see Appendix G for instructions on copying them into the clip art directory.

5. Scroll to the bottom of the list and click on WORLD2.CGM.
6. Click on Preview. The Preview window, shown in the Import Picture dialog box in Figure 3-18, lets you see a picture before actually importing it into the publication.
7. Click OK. The illustration of the globe appears in the new Picture frame.

Resizing a Frame

The art you bring into Publisher adapts itself to the size and shape of the frame into which it is imported. You can, however, easily change the Picture frame, and the illustration will adapt.

Figure 3-18.   *Import Picture dialog box*

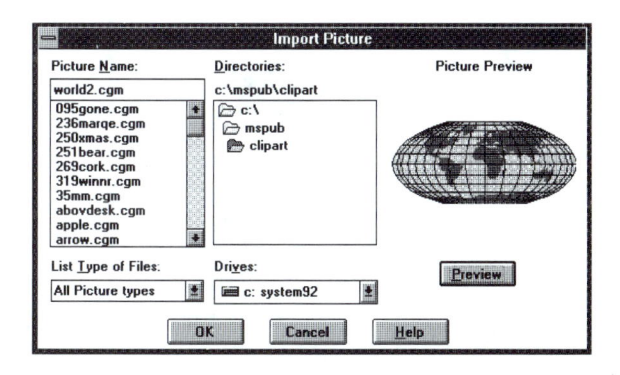

1. Point to the lower-middle handle of the Picture frame until the cursor changes into the resizing icon, as shown here:

2. Drag the handle down approximately 1 inch and release the mouse button. The globe becomes considerably more spherical in shape because the frame more closely approximates a square, as shown in Figure 3-19.

Resizing works for all of the frames in Publisher—Picture, Text, and WordArt—so changing the look of a publication is easy. Now you can restore the frame to its original shape.

3. Drag the handle back up approximately 1 inch and release the mouse button, or just Undo the command.

Figure 3-19.   *Resized Picture frame*

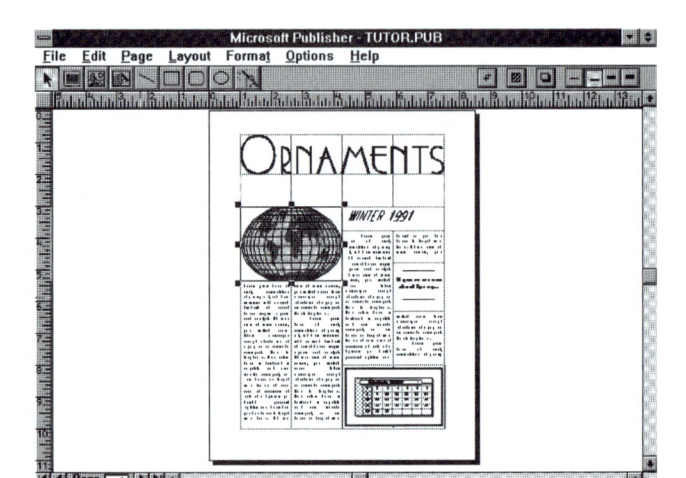

Chapter 3: *A Working Session* 71

Tip

To import an image in its original size, follow the same procedure described in this section without selecting a Picture frame. Publisher creates a frame using the proportions with which the picture file was initially created.

Creating Borders

Publisher lets you add graphics borders to any of the frames in a publication. Borders can consist of simple rules of varying thickness or of complex patterns provided by Publisher, called BorderArt. Since the design of this sample newsletter is fairly clean, a simple line border is appropriate.

1. Click on the Picture frame.
2. Click on the second of the four border tools, shown here:

Publisher surrounds the Picture frame with a border. Each of these tools creates a border with a different thickness. You can turn any of them on or off by clicking on them.

Using WordArt

WordArt lets you create graphics effects for text that are not available through the Text Frame tool. These effects include a variety of fancy typefaces and special embellishments for them. In this section you'll use WordArt to create the oversized letter for the article in column 1 and the headline for the newsletter. While creating the next few frames, remember to use different views of the screen ((F9)) to make frame creation easier.

1. Click on the WordArt button.
2. Point to the guide for the left margin at approximately 4 1/2 inches on the ruler line (the upper-left corner of column 1). Then drag the

cursor halfway across column 1 and down 3/4 inch. Publisher creates a WordArt frame and displays the WordArt dialog box, as shown in Figure 3-20.

The characters that you enter in the copy window are affected by the other options you set in the dialog box. Oversized first letters are one of the easiest effects to obtain. They are simply WordArt frames consisting of a single letter that is "spaced" across the entire frame. This is achieved using the Best Fit selection in the Size list.

3. Type **A** and click OK. The oversized letter should now appear in column 1. Next you'll create the headline.

4. Click the WordArt button again.

5. Point to the guide for the left margin at the top of the page (the upper-left corner of column 1). Then drag the cursor all the way across column 4 and down to approximately 1 1/4 inches.

6. After a moment the WordArt dialog box appears. Type **Ornaments**.

7. Click the arrow on the Font list and click on Langly.

Figure 3-20.   *WordArt dialog box*

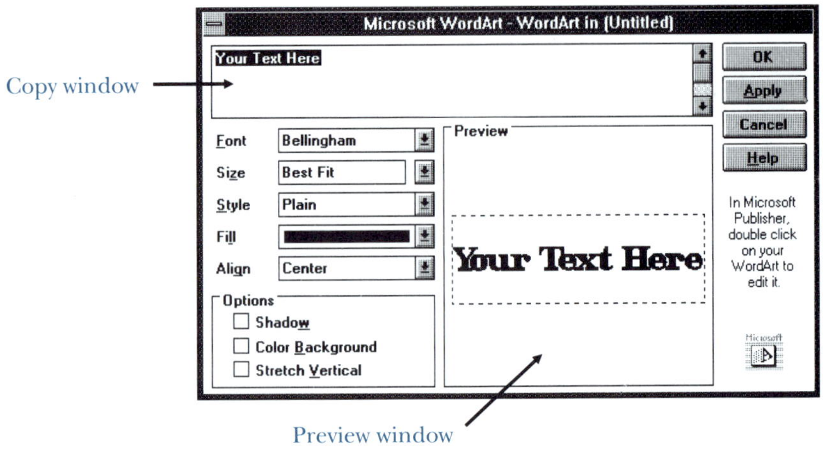

Chapter 3: *A Working Session* 73

8. Click the arrow on the Style list and click on Arch Up. The Preview window displays the newsletter title arched upward, as shown here:

While this is an interesting example of WordArt special effects, it's not quite what you want for the newsletter.

9. Click the arrow on the Style list and click Plain (you may have to scroll up in the window slightly to see it).
10. Click the arrow on the Align list, click Letter Justify, and click OK. Your publication should now look like the one in Figure 3-21.

Figure 3-21.   *WordArt added for headline and fancy first letter*

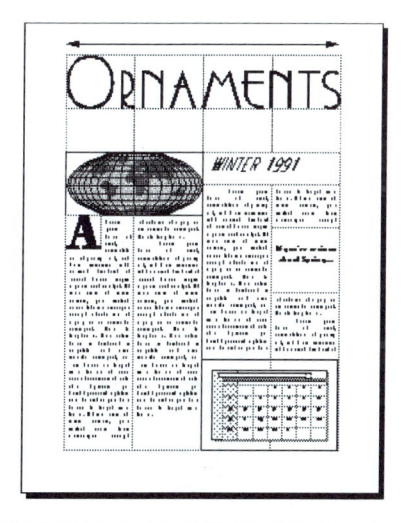

Using PageWizards

PageWizards are the quickest way to create publications and certain kinds of visual accents in Publisher. All you need to do is answer a few questions, and the PageWizard does everything else for you. When you use a PageWizard in an existing publication (as opposed to using it for creating a new one), you create a PageWizard frame first.

1. Click on the PageWizard button.
2. Point to the middle guide (the beginning of column 3) at approximately 8 inches on the vertical ruler and drag the cursor all the way across column 4 and down to the lower-right corner.

Publisher pauses and then displays the PageWizard selection window, shown in the following illustration. This is where you can indicate the type of PageWizard you want to use.

3. Double-click on Calendar. The first dialog box for this PageWizard appears.

Each PageWizard consists of a series of dialog boxes that give you choices about the frame. You must answer the questions in each by clicking on one of its option buttons and proceeding to the next dialog box. You can always return to previous boxes by pressing one of the "rewind" buttons. A typical PageWizard dialog box is shown in Figure 3-22. Many of the PageWizard dialog boxes have preview areas. As you indicate your preferences by selecting a button, the preview area changes to display a sample of what your choice will look like.

Chapter 3:   A Working Session   75

Figure 3-22.   PageWizard dialog box

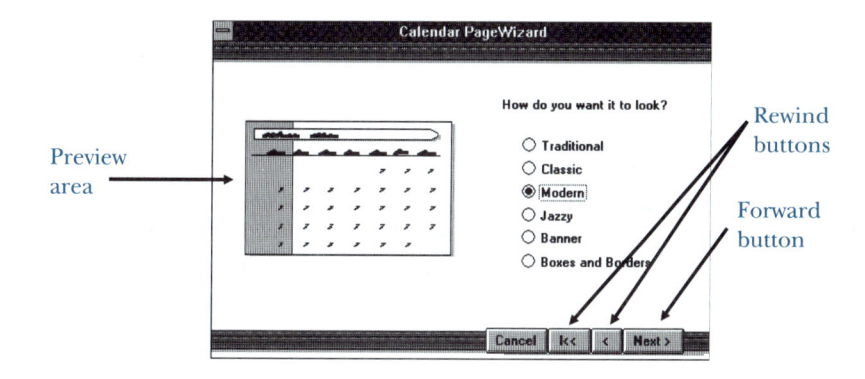

4. Click the Next button in the Calendar PageWizard dialog box. The dialog box that appears lets you decide on the scope of the calendar. You can create a calendar for a single month (of your choosing) or for all 12 months of the year. Then click the Year button. The preview area changes to show what a full year calendar would look like.

5. Click the Month button to reset the scope of this PageWizard to a month. The preview area reflects your change. Then click the Next button.

The dialog box that appears lets you select a style for the calendar. Publisher uses different typefaces and graphics to create the styles.

6. Click Modern. Then click the Next button twice.

The next dialog box gives you the option of including a picture with the PageWizard.

7. Accept the default (No)—since there really isn't enough room in the PageWizard frame for a calendar and a picture— by clicking the Next button.

This dialog box lets you include a border and pick a style for it.

8. Click the Classic button. Then click the Next button.

This screen and the one that follows let you establish the year and month for the calendar, respectively. The two screens following these let you choose abbreviations, initials, or full names for the days of the week, and the language for the names.

9. Accept the default values for all four screens by clicking on the Next button four times.
10. Click the Create It button.

The calendar is one of the most sophisticated PageWizards. It consists of many frames of different types, and although it takes a little while to create, Publisher does it a lot faster than you could. As Publisher is creating the PageWizard calendar, a dialog box like the one shown here appears in the lower-right corner of the screen explaining each step in progress:

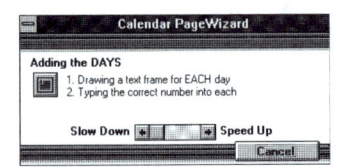

You can move the dialog box to a different part of the screen if it is blocking your view of the frame. You can also accelerate or decelerate the process by sliding the speed control to the left or right.

11. Click OK after the last PageWizard dialog box appears. Your publication should now look like the one shown in Figure 3-23.

Chapter 3: *A Working Session* 77

Figure 3-23.   *Finished PageWizard calendar*

Adding Graphics

Now you can use Publisher's drawing tools to add some final graphic flourishes to the publication. Start with a vertical rule down the center of the page.

1. Click the Line button. The buttons on the right side of the Toolbar change to accommodate the options available for the tool.

2. Click the second thickness button from the left. This creates a two-point line equal in thickness to the border you created around the Picture frame.

3. Point to the upper-right corner of the Picture frame (the center of the page) and drag the cursor to the bottom of the column creating a vertical rule down the center of the page like the one in Figure 3-24.

Now add some horizontal bars to highlight the quotation by setting it off from the rest of the text.

4. Click on the frame for the quotation and press (F9).

Tip

If you hold down (CTRL) while clicking any tool button, you can create multiple objects (frames, lines, and so on) without reclicking the button for each.

5. Hold down (CTRL) and click the Line button. Then click the first thickness line to create a one-point line.

6. Point to the area just above the letter *I* of the quotation and drag the cursor across the length of the text to create a horizontal rule.

Figure 3-24. *Vertical rule added*

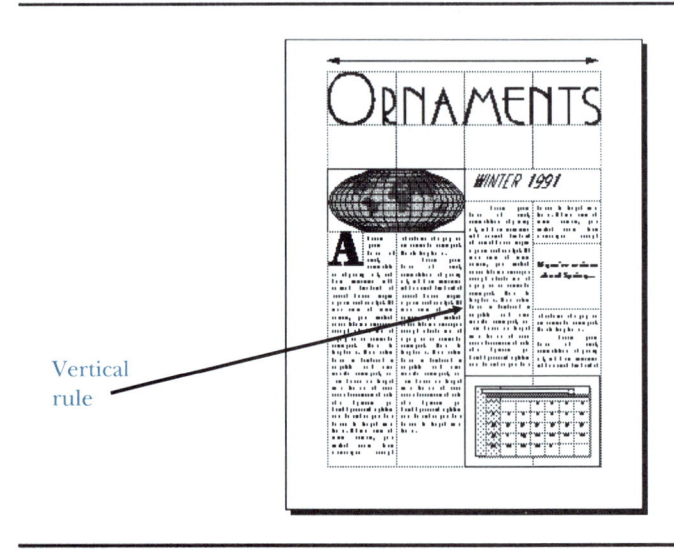

Chapter 3: A Working Session 79

7. Point to the area just below the letter *I* of the quotation and drag the cursor across the length of the text to create another horizontal rule. The frame with the quotation should now look like this:

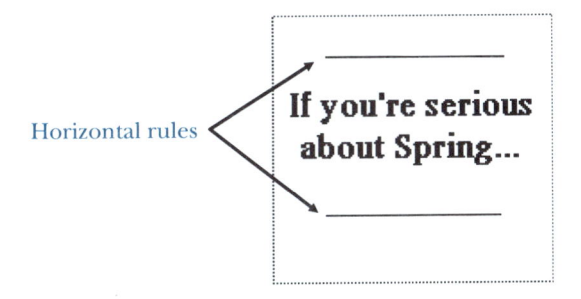

Horizontal rules

> If you're serious about Spring...

Finally, add the rule (double-headed arrow) shown in Figure 3-1 across the top of the newsletter title.

8. Press `F9`. The display returns to a full page.
9. Point to the area just above the *O* in the title, then drag the cursor across the length of the word "Ornaments" to create the rule.
10. Click on the double-headed arrow on the Toolbar, and then click anywhere in the scratch area to clear the Line tool. The publication should now look like the page in Figure 3-25.

Adding Pages

As a result of the Picture and WordArt frames you have added to the four original Text frames, the text from both articles no longer fits on this page. You can confirm this by clicking on the frames in column 2 or 4. The Connect button for each displays ellipsis marks (...) indicating that there is text in the overflow area. The newsletter now requires an additional page to accommodate the text overflow. When you begin a new publication, Publisher allocates only a single page to it. You must add more pages if you need them.

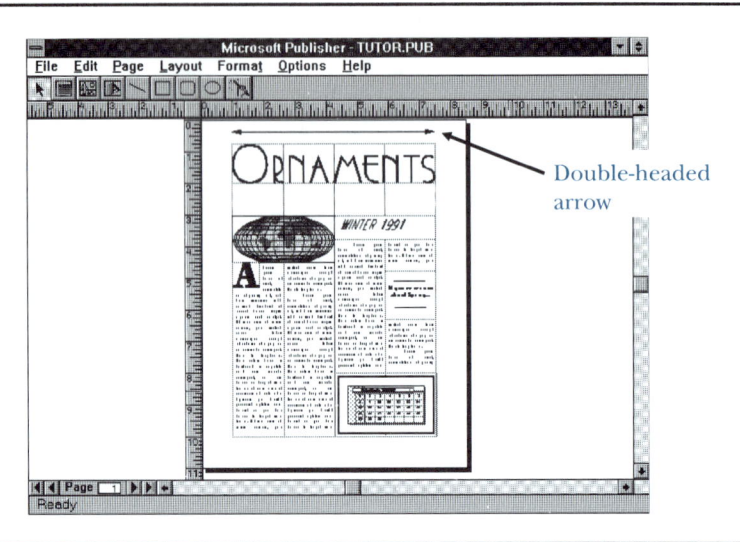

Figure 3-25.   *Additional line art*

1. Click on Page on the Menu bar and click on Insert Pages on the Page menu. The Insert Pages dialog box appears, as shown here:

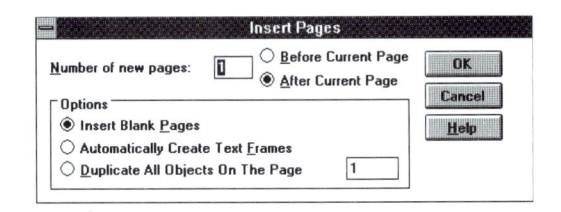

    The default setting for the number of new pages to insert is 1 (which is all you need to complete this publication). There is no need to change any of the other settings in this dialog box.

2. Click on OK. Publisher inserts a new blank page with the same layout guides as page 1. No frames, however, have been added. The page indicator in the lower-left corner of the screen displays the current page number (2).

Chapter 3: *A Working Session* 81

3. Hold down (CTRL) and click on the Text Frame tool.
4. Point to the top of the first layout guide (the upper-left corner of column 1). Then drag the cursor across all four columns and down 1/2 inch.
5. Point to the lower-left corner of the frame you just created. Then drag the cursor all the way across column 2 and down to the bottom margin.
6. Click anywhere in the scratch area to turn off the Text Frame tool. Page 2 of your publication should now look like Figure 3-26.
7. Click on the Previous Page button at the left of the page indicator to turn to page 1.
8. Click on the Text frame in column 2 and click on the Connect button for that frame.
9. Click on the Next Page button to turn to page 2 and click on the horizontal Text frame at the top of the page. The remaining text from the first article flows into this frame.

Figure 3-26.   Page 2 with Text frames added

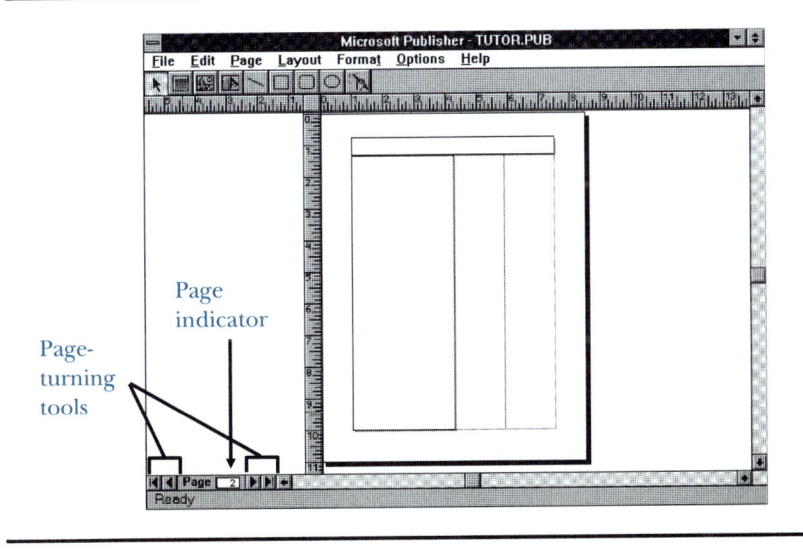

10. Click on the Previous Page button to turn to page 1.
11. Click on the Text frame in column 4 and click on the Connect button for that frame.
12. Click on the Next Page button to turn to page 2.
13. Click on the vertical Text frame on the left of the page. Both articles are now displayed in their entirety.

If you were completing the newsletter with additional articles, of course, you would probably now resize these frames to accommodate the actual amount of text that is in them, and make more room for other articles in the publication. For the purposes of this demonstration, however, you can leave them as they are.

The Background Page

Publisher's *background page* provides an easy means of causing certain items to repeat on every page of a publication. There's no need to re-create them each time. Anything that is placed on the background page automatically appears in the same location on all pages. The rule above the publication title (double-headed arrow), for example, can make an attractive header for each page.

1. Click on the Previous Page button.
2. Scroll up the page slightly to display a few inches of scratch area above the publication title.
3. Drag the rule into the scratch area above the page area, as shown here:

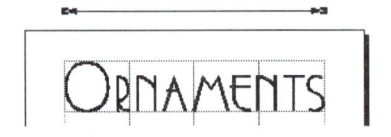

Chapter 3: *A Working Session*

4. Click on Page on the Menu bar and click on Go to Background on the Page menu. The background page looks just like a normal blank page, except that the page indicator displays a different icon, as shown here:

5. Click on the rule in the scratch area and drag it back into the page area in the top margin to the same location that it had originally on page 1.
6. Click on Page on the Menu bar and click on Go to Foreground on the Page menu. The rule appears on page 1 as it did originally.

Tip

`CTRL`-`M` *is the keyboard shortcut for switching between the foreground and background pages.*

7. Click on the Next Page button to display page 2. The rule appears in the same location at the top of page 2.

Note

You cannot select the rule as a graphics object unless you return to the background page.

Printing

Printing your publication is the easiest part. See "Printer Considerations" in Chapter 2 or Appendix H for details, if you are uncertain about printer configuration.

1. Click on File on the Menu bar.
2. Click on Print on the File menu and click on OK.

If you haven't done so recently, save the publication.

3. To quit Publisher after the print job is complete, double-click on the Control Menu box.

Printing concludes the working session covered in this chapter. You've now had a good first look at some of the major features in Publisher and have begun to learn how to use them. Each of the chapters that follows deals with specific parts of the Publisher program, and contains detailed instructions on how to use them. You may find it useful to return to this chapter for practice or for a quick reminder about how a certain function operates.

4

All About Frames

You manage information in a publication with frames. Each of the three frame types holds a different kind of material. Text frames contain only text. Picture frames contain only graphics. WordArt frames contain text embellished with special graphic effects. All Publisher frames behave in basically the same manner. Creating, moving, or setting margins for a Text frame, for example, is a virtually identical task for a Picture or WordArt frame.

You can place frames anywhere on the pages of a publication or in the scratch area. They can exist side by side, overlap, and link from one page to the next. Frames can also be resized, repositioned, or moved between pages or publications, and Publisher reformats their content instantly. This chapter discusses the properties common to all types of frames and how to use them. The differences between frame types are noted here, but explored more thoroughly in chapters 6 through 10.

The sections in this chapter are meant to give you a clear and thorough understanding of all major aspects of working with frames. Each section includes a working example and generic instructions for completing the task under discussion. Each example begins with the most elementary actions you need to learn a particular task. Everything you learn about Publisher, however, makes more sense in the context of a publishing project. To complete an example, you'll need to do some additional work, but it's usually worth spending the time. Getting all the way through an example is not essential to understanding a task, but it places the task in the context of a practical application. If you need a summary or a reminder about how to do something, you can find straightforward instructions for each task in a box at the end of the section.

Creating Frames

The three frame tools, shown in the following illustration, are the means of creating a frame in Publisher, and creating frames is the only thing that frame tools do.

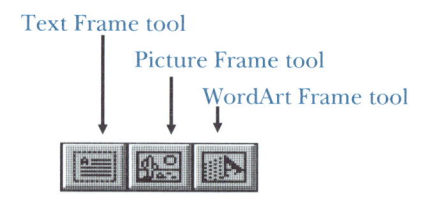

Text Frame tool
Picture Frame tool
WordArt Frame tool

Frame tools determine the type of frame you produce, the initial dimensions, and the position of the frame on the page. All frames are rectangular in shape. You can use the same technique to create Text, Picture, or WordArt frames. The only difference in the outcome lies in which tool you decide to use. In this section you'll see how to create the business card shown in Figure 4-1 using all three frame types. This example should also give you a good sense of how Publisher *blends* frames. It accommodates new frames by rearranging the material in existing ones in a manner that makes sense in the overall publication.

Start a new publication using a blank page. Then create a Text frame that matches the outline of a business card (3 1/2 inches wide and 2 inches long). First click on the Text Frame tool. Notice that the screen changes in several ways as a result. The Text frame button becomes colored, and the pointer changes to a crosshair (+) to indicate that the frame tool is now active. Frame

Chapter 4: *All About Frames* 87

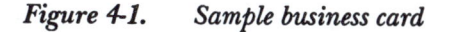

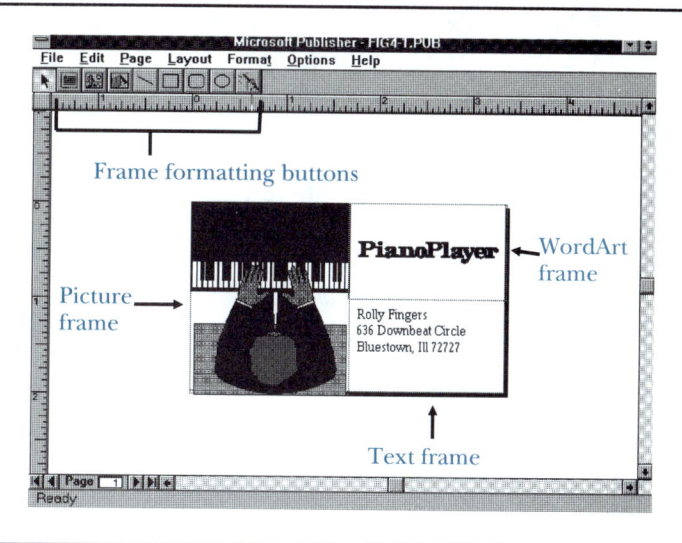

Figure 4-1. Sample business card

formatting buttons also appear on the right side of the Toolbar. Finally, hairlines appear on the rulers to mark the current location of the crosshair on the page. Before you begin drawing the frame, the hairlines move along the ruler and follow the crosshair around the page, as shown here:

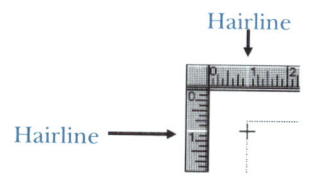

Tip

Use the Snap to Ruler Marks command on the Options menu to help create the frame with exact measurements. Move the rulers into the page area to make their tic marks easier to see.

The hairlines make it easy to pinpoint your starting location and measure the size of the frame as you create it. Point to a location for the upper-left corner of the frame, and then drag the crosshair left 3 1/2 inches and down 2 inches. It doesn't really matter where on the page you begin. As you drag the cursor, the size and shape of the frame changes. You can modify the appearance of the frame as much as you'd like before you release the mouse button to complete the frame. While you draw the frame, the hairlines shadow the frame along the ruler to indicate its actual dimensions, as shown here:

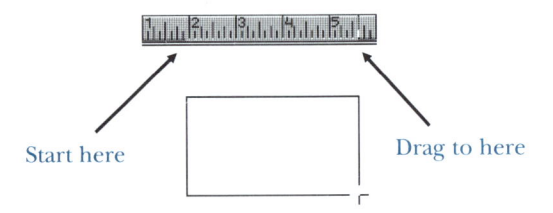

Start here   Drag to here

Tip

If you're a little jumpy, you may release the mouse button too early or end up with a shape that doesn't quite meet your expectations. If necessary, use Undo to delete the frame and start over again.

After you complete a Text frame the screen changes in several ways, as shown in Figure 4-2. The crosshair changes back to a pointer, and the Toolbar displays a number of different text formatting options. In addition, the finished frame appears with six handles and a Connect button. *Handles* let you resize a frame. You'll learn more about them later in this chapter. The Connect button lets you flow text from one frame to another. You can find information on flowing text in Chapter 6.

You'll need to add text to the frame before continuing. The Full Page view that Publisher uses when you start a new publication makes it difficult to see the text you type in its default size. Switch to Actual Size view by pressing (F9), or by selecting Actual Size from the Page menu. Now, type the following lines:

Rolly Fingers
636 Downbeat Circle
Bluestown, Ill. 72727

Next add the illustration of the pianist from the Publisher CLIPART directory. First you need to create a Picture frame on the left side of the card.

Chapter 4: *All About Frames* 89

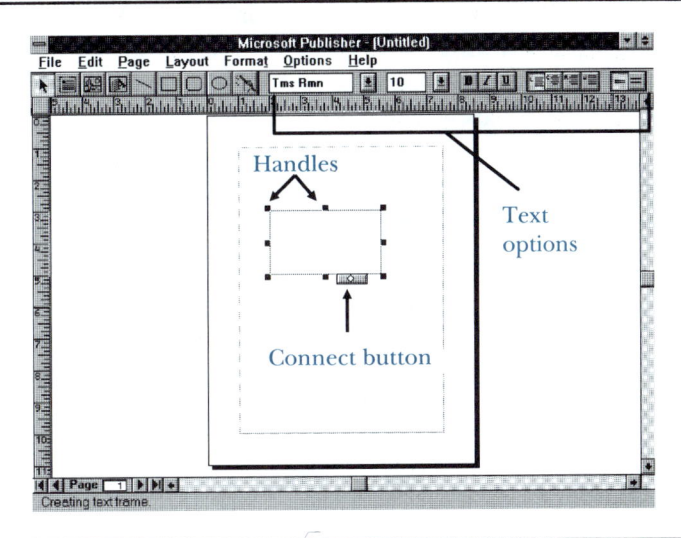

Figure 4-2. **Completed Text frame**

You can draw it right on top of the Text frame, and the text will *float* into the remaining space on the right side of its frame. Click on the Picture Frame tool. The screen and pointer change just as they did when you created the Text frame. Point to the upper-left corner of the Text frame and drag the crosshair halfway across and down to the bottom of the frame. The completed Picture frame should look like this:

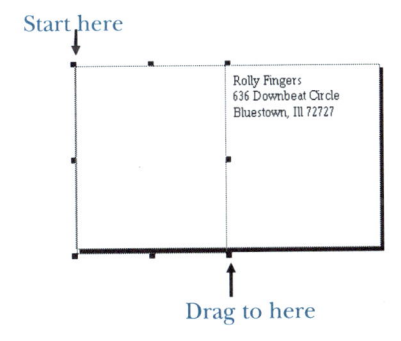

Now bring in the clip art. Select Import Picture from the File menu, and make sure that the current directory is set to \MSPUB\CLIPART. Scroll down the list of drawings until you see PINOPLR2.CGM, and double-click on it (the list is in alphabetical order). The pianist shown in the following illustration should appear in your publication.

To complete the card you need to add a final WordArt frame for Rolly's title on the upper half of the right side of the card. Click on the WordArt tool, and then draw the frame from the upper-right corner of the Picture frame halfway down and across the Text frame, as shown here:

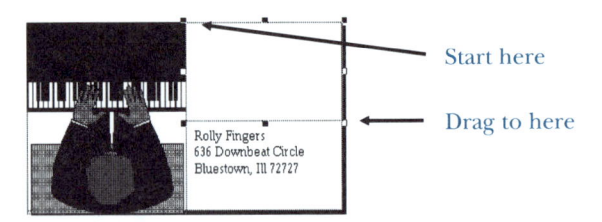

After you complete the frame, Publisher displays the WordArt dialog box. Type **PianoPlayer** and click on OK. The completed card should now look like the illustration in Figure 4-1. The original text for Rolly's name and address has been "shoved around" with the addition of new frames, but in the end it winds up in a very convenient location for this project. The way in which Publisher repositions material to accommodate new frames doesn't *always* come out quite so perfectly, but the results are usually close to what you're looking for. You can make adjustments afterwards using some of the techniques described in the remainder of this chapter.

How to Create a Frame

1. Click on one of the frame tools.
2. Position the crosshair at a location for one of the frame's corners.
3. Drag the cursor to the opposite corner of the frame.
4. Release the mouse button.

Chapter 4: *All About Frames* 91

Centering Frames

Publisher makes it easy to center any frame at a specific location. When you center a frame, it grows in opposite directions at the same time. In other words, as you drag the crosshair to the left, the horizontal sides of the frame extend equally to the left and right. Similarly, as you drag it downward, the vertical sides shrink or grow up and down concurrently. Centering a frame can be very handy as long as you're sure about the starting location. Use centering to create the Picture frame in the flyer shown in Figure 4-3.

Note

You may find it easier to position the crosshair for this publication if you use the 50% option from the Page menu. Since there is no layout guide marking the center of the page, the Snap to Ruler Marks setting is handy here too.

Start a new publication using Blank Page. Select the Picture Frame tool and position the crosshair at the center of the page (5 1/2 inches on the vertical ruler, 4 1/4 inches on the horizontal ruler). Press and hold CTRL while you drag the crosshair 2 inches up and 2 inches to the left, and then

Figure 4-3. *A flyer for Rolly's concert*

release the mouse button. As you move, a square frame forms around the starting location.

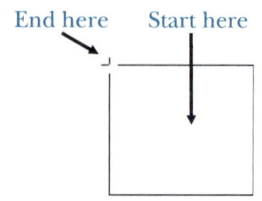

Always release the mouse button before the (CTRL) key when you center or square frames. Select Import Picture from the File menu to bring in the illustration called PINOPLR2.CGM from the CLIPART directory. More information on importing pictures can be found earlier in the section, "Creating Frames" or in Chapter 9. To complete the flyer, add two WordArt frames at the top and bottom of the page for the text shown in Figure 4-3. Because these frames are adjacent to both margins, you can create them more easily by dragging from left to right. If you begin at one of the margins and use centering, the frame will grow above (or below) the margin instead of remaining adjacent to it.

Tip

When you want to create several frames of the same type, hold down (CTRL) while you click on one of the frame tools. The Frame button and crosshair remain active after you complete the first frame, and stay that way until you cancel them by clicking somewhere in the page or scratch areas.

Hold down (CTRL) while you click on the WordArt tool. Then draw the first frame beginning at the top-left margin and moving across the page to the right margin and down 2 inches. When the WordArt dialog box appears, type **PianoPlayer** and then click on OK. Start the next frame on the left margin at 8 inches on the vertical ruler and drag the crosshair to the bottom-right margin. For the second WordArt frame, type the following lines, and then click on OK.

Rolly Fingers
Live at the South Street Cafe
September 11-16

Chapter 4: *All About Frames*

The completed flyer should look like the sample in Figure 4-3.

How to Center a Frame

1. Click on the frame tool that you want to use.
2. Point to what will be the center of the frame, then press and hold CTRL.
3. Drag the crosshair to create the frame. All vertical or horizontal measurements are made in both directions concurrently.
4. Release the mouse button first. Then release the CTRL key.

Squaring Frames

Publisher takes the guesswork out of making frames perfectly square. When you square a frame, the horizontal and vertical dimensions grow at the same rate in the same direction as shown here:

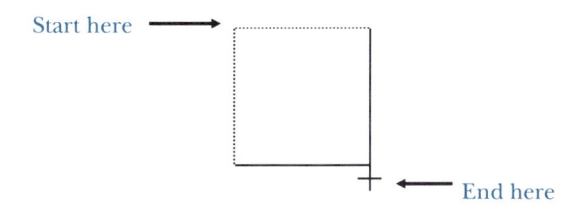

Start here →

← End here

Tip

Since the frames you create in this example are adjacent to the top and left margins, use Snap to Guides from the Options menu to make alignment easier. You may also find it simpler to see the characters you type by selecting Actual Size view from the Page menu (or press F9).

Start a new publication using a blank page. Now use squaring to create a WordArt frame for the following letterhead logo:

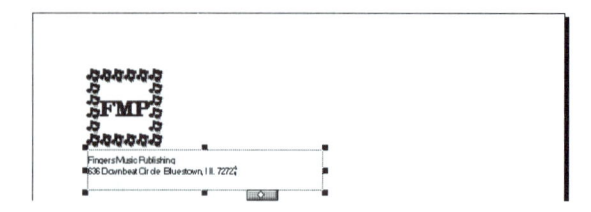

Click on the WordArt tool and point to the upper-left margin. Hold down (SHIFT) as you drag the crosshair down and to the right one inch to create the frame for the logo. Publisher makes it impossible to draw anything that isn't a square!

After you release the mouse button, type **FMP** in the WordArt dialog box, and click on OK. To complete the logo, you need to add some border art to the frame. Select BorderArt from the Layout menu. Scroll down the list of borders until you see Musical Notes. Then click on OK. The decorative border should appear around the frame.

To complete the letterhead, you should add a Text frame for the name and address of the company. First click on the Text frame tool, and then position the crosshair about 1/4 inch below the logo on the left margin. Drag the crosshair to the left 3 inches and down 1 inch to create the frame. Then type the following lines:

Fingers Music Publishing
636 Downbeat Circle - Bluestown, Ill. 72727

To use centering and squaring together, hold down (SHIFT) and (CTRL) while you draw a frame.

Tip

How to Square a Frame

1. Click on the frame tool that you want to use.
2. Point to what will be a corner of the frame, then press and hold (SHIFT).
3. Drag the crosshair to create the frame. All vertical and horizontal measurements are equidistant.
4. Release the mouse button first. Then release the (SHIFT) key.

Setting Frame Margins and Columns

Publisher uses the following default settings (in inches) for the margins and columns in each type of frame.

Frame Type	Left/Right	Top/Bottom	Columns	Gutter
Text	.08	.08	1	.33
Picture	.00	.00	None	None
WordArt	.00	.00	None	None

Text frames use a small default margin because text is easier to read when it is visually separated from adjacent material in a publication. You can adjust these settings for any individual frame, and you can change the default settings for each type of frame. When you adjust the default, all subsequent frames of that type use the new settings.

Use the newspaper review in Figure 4-4 as an example of how changing margins can affect your designs. Start a new publication with a blank page, then create a Text frame that covers the left side. Use Import Text from the File menu to read in a text file of at least one-half page in length. You can use

Figure 4-4. Rolly's Review

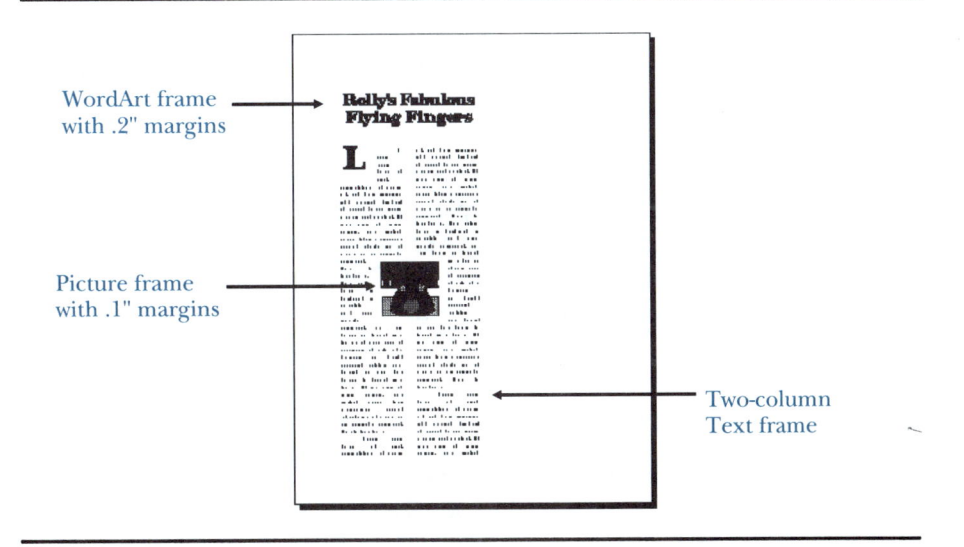

one of your own text files, or use the file PROFILE.TXT in the Publisher directory (this is the dummy file used in the tutorial in Chapter 3).

The file should display in a single column. Select Frame Columns and Margins from the Layout menu. The following dialog box appears:

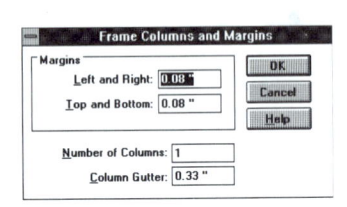

Type **2** in the Number of Columns text box to change the setting, then click on OK. The text in the frame reformats in two columns. By changing the setting *after* the frame was created, you have altered the column format for this individual frame. Subsequent Text frames that you create will still use a single column unless you format each one differently.

Note

The Column Gutter field determines the amount of space between columns when there are multiple columns in a frame. You can experiment with this too, if you like, but this application doesn't require any column gutter adjustment to make it attractive.

Next click on the WordArt tool to create a frame for the headline, but select Frame Margins from the Layout menu before you begin to draw the frame. Unlike Text frames, WordArt and Picture frames have no initial margin setting because graphic material often extends to the edge of a page or frame for aesthetic purposes. Type **.2** in the field for Left and Right, and then click on OK. By changing the setting *before* you draw the frame, you change the default for all subsequent frames of this type (WordArt). Create the headline frame by dragging the crosshair across the top of the initial Text frame and extending it down about 1 1/2 inches, as shown in Figure 4-4. Now type the following lines for the headline, and then click on OK.

Rolly's Fabulous
Flying Fingers

Notice that the frame uses the new margin settings of .2 inches. Create another WordArt frame for the oversized first letter in column 1 of the article.

This should be a square of about 1/2 inch (a great opportunity to try the frame squaring option described earlier in this section). When the WordArt dialog box appears, type **L**, and then click on OK. The oversized letter in this frame appears with a margin around the edges. If you check the Left and Right margin settings for this frame by selecting Frame Margins from the Layout menu, you'll see that it is .2 inches, the same as the default you set for the headline.

Finally, create the Picture frame for the center of the article. This is a 1-inch square centered between the two columns about halfway down the page (try the frame centering option here). After you draw the frame, use Import Picture from the File menu to select PINOPLR2.CGM from the CLIPART library. The completed article should look like Figure 4-4. You may want to add a small margin (about .1 inch) to the Picture frame. This will set it off slightly from the rest of the text.

How to Set Margins and Columns

1. To modify individual frames, click on the frame you want to change. To modify the default settings for a type of frame, click on one of the frame tools.
2. Select Frame Margins (Picture and WordArt frames) or Frame Columns and Margins (Text frames only) from the Layout menu.
3. Change any of the field values for margins, columns, or gutter width to meet the needs of your publication.

Selecting Frames

In order to work with a frame in any way—resize it, move it, format its text or graphic content, import material, and so on—you must first make the frame active by selecting it. Frame-oriented commands from the menus or Toolbar affect only the active frame. For most formatting purposes only one frame can be active at a time. You can, however, select multiple frames in order to move, copy, or delete them. You can always tell which frame is active by the appearance of its handles and, in the case of Text frames, a Connect button, as shown here:

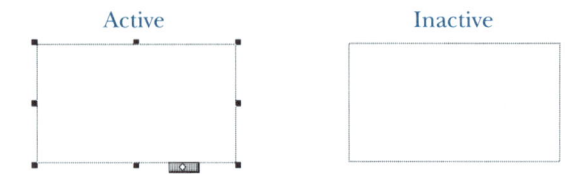

Active   Inactive

Publisher gives you several ways to select frames, depending on what you want to do with them. Use one of the existing Publisher templates for an example. Begin a new publication using the PRICELST.PUB template. This is a model for a company price list that contains numerous text and Picture frames carefully arranged in columns and rows, as shown in Figure 4-5. You can select any single frame by simply clicking on it. Try clicking on a few of

Figure 4-5.   PRICELST.PUB *template*

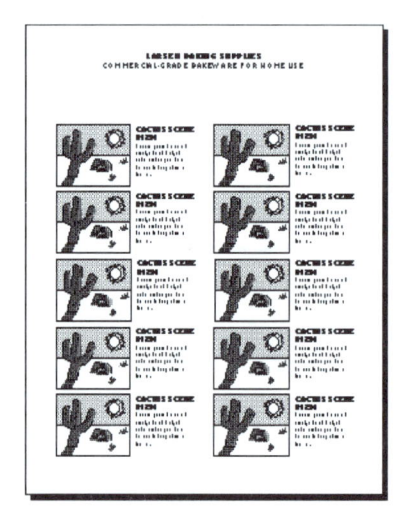

the frames to get a feel for it. Each time you select a frame its handles appear, and the handles on the previous frame you selected disappear. Selecting a frame cancels the selection of any other frame. You can also click in any empty spot on the Page or scratch areas to cancel the selection of a frame.

Tip: Make sure you can see all of the frames. Many of the templates are stored with the Hide Object Boundaries setting turned on. This is handy for seeing what a publication will look like when you print it, but it makes selecting frames a chancy business since you can't see their outlines. Use the setting on the Options menu for Show Object Boundaries to complete this exercise.

Selecting Multiple Frames

If you select multiple frames, you can move, copy, or delete them as a group. This is especially convenient in a number of situations. For example, you may have spent a considerable amount of time positioning several frames in relation to each other, and want to reproduce the group with the same spatial arrangement on another page in a publication. You may want to move the group into the scratch area to see what the publication looks like with a different frame configuration. Perhaps you just want to delete several frames and save some time by giving the command only once. In all of these cases, selecting multiple frames is extremely useful. When you select multiple frames, you can mix different types of frames—Text, Picture, and WordArt. Publisher will deal with them all as a group of objects regardless of their type.

One at a Time

Publisher gives you two ways to select multiple frames. One way lets you select any number of frames one at a time in succession, regardless of where they are positioned. You'll find this technique useful when frames are scattered around the page. To select frames like this, Hold down CTRL while you click on each frame. For example, the price list shown in Figure 4-5 might be a little too crowded for some applications. Click on the first Picture frame at the top of column 2. The first frame you select displays handles in the normal fashion. Hold down CTRL as you select the adjoining Text frame to the right. The handles of both frames appear shaded, as shown here:

Shaded handles

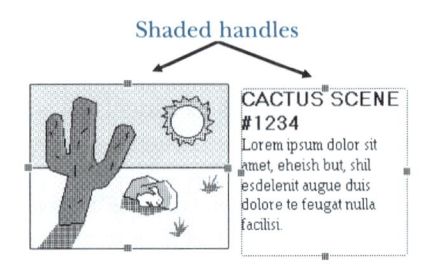

Tip: To remove individual frames from a group that you already selected, hold down CTRL while you click on the frame that you want to exclude.

Try removing alternating groups of Text/Picture frames to get the effect shown in Figure 4-6. Make sure that CTRL remains depressed each time you click on another frame for the group. After you select all of the frames, press CTRL-X to delete them. To cancel your selection, select a frame *without* pressing CTRL, or click on the Page or scratch areas.

Figure 4-6. The same price list with a sparser frame layout

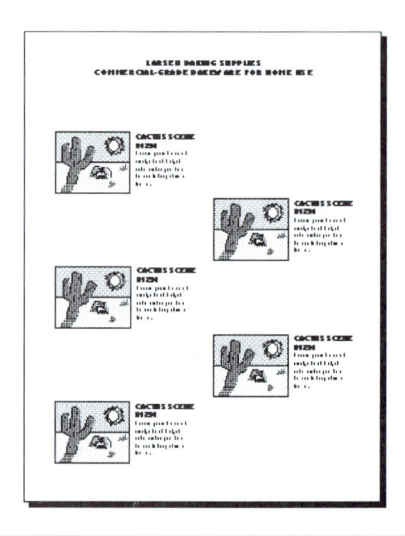

Chapter 4: *All About Frames* 101

> **Note**
>
> *You don't have to keep* CTRL *depressed constantly as you select multiple frames, only while you're clicking.*

Sometimes frames prove difficult to select because they overlay each other. If a frame plays hard to get, you can try one of the following steps:

- Click directly on each of its borders.
- Move the interfering frame temporarily to the scratch area.
- Select the overlaying frame and use the Send to Back command from the Layout menu in order to move it out of the way without actually repositioning it on the page. Then select the underlying frame and use the Move to Front command from the same menu to bring it into view.

Using the Marquee

When all of the frames you want to select fit within an area that can be framed itself (a rectangle) you can use the *marquee* to select them. The marquee is a temporary frame for selecting multiple objects all at once. For example, you might want to use only a single column of products per page in the price list, or copy an entire column of Text/Picture frames to another page. Since they can all fit together in a rectangle, the marquee is perfect for selecting them.

Point to the area just above and to the left of the first Picture frame in the second column of the price list. Drag the pointer down and to the right so that the border with the broken line (that's the marquee) surrounds all of the Text and Picture frames in column 2 of the price list, as shown in Figure 4-7. Then release the mouse button. All of the frames now appear with shaded handles. To see what the page looks like with a single column of product listings, click on any frame in the group and wait until the frame boundaries change to broken lines. Then drag the entire group of frames into the scratch area to the right.

> **Note**
>
> *The marquee selects graphic objects within its perimeter as well as frames, and the graphics become a part of the selected group. This makes it easier to move material that is physically related on the page.*

When you use the marquee, only frames that you surround *completely* are included in the selection. If any part of one or more of them is outside of the

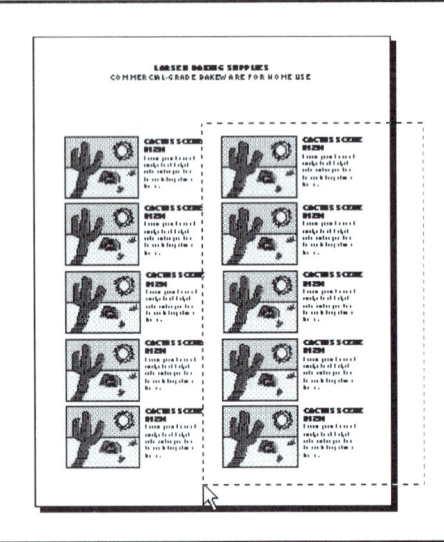

Figure 4-7. *Selecting a whole column with the marquee*

marquee it will be excluded from the group. If you leave out a frame accidentally, just try the selection over again, since selecting frames has no effect on the publication before you execute a command or press (CTRL) and click the frame you missed.

When you're having trouble getting a selection right with the marquee, try magnifying your view of the Page with one of the other selections from the Page menu.

Tip

How to Select Frames

1. To select an individual frame, click on it.
2. To select multiple frames, either hold down (CTRL) while you click on each frame in the group or surround them all with the marquee.
3. To cancel the selection of one or more frames, click on an empty spot in the page or scratch areas.
4. To cancel the selection of an individual frame from a pre-selected group, hold down (CTRL) while you click on it.

Chapter 4: *All About Frames* 103

Moving Frames

Publisher lets you move frames around on the page or scratch areas or move them between pages or publications without affecting the frames' contents. You may simply want to change the look of a publication by trying a new location for a Picture frame, or you may want to move an entire section of a newsletter or brochure to a new page. The easiest way to move frames, discussed here, is by dragging them with a mouse. You can also use the cut-and-paste techniques covered in the next section, but that method takes a little more time and is more useful for moving large groups of frames or moving frames between publications.

First create a new publication using the template called BIZCARD1.PUB, one of Publisher's templates for business cards. This is shown in Figure 4-8. Try moving the Picture frame to make a simple change in the card's design. Click on the picture of the cactus, and then point to the frame. The pointer changes into an icon for a moving van called the *mover* (). The mover indicates that Publisher is ready for you to make your move. Hold the mouse button down until the outline of the frame changes to a broken line and the

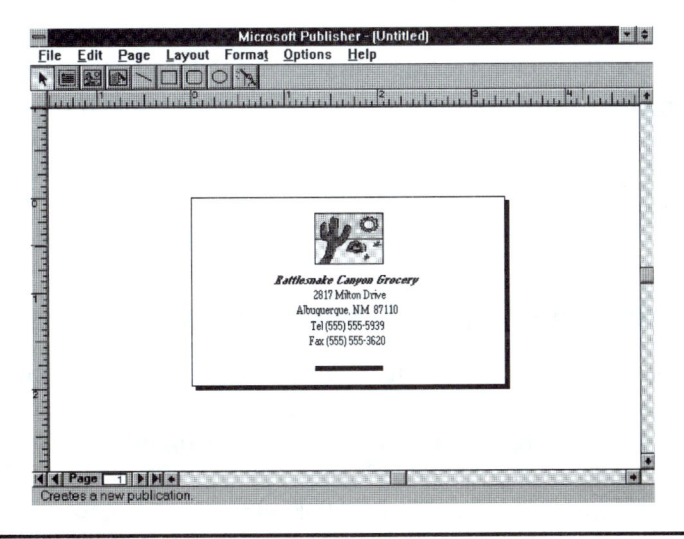

Figure 4-8. BIZCARD1.PUB

handles disappear. Drag the pointer to the upper-left corner of the business card. Moving frames around is just that simple. All types of frames—Text, Picture, and WordArt—move in the same way.

Tip

To keep a frame aligned with its original horizontal or vertical position, hold down (SHIFT) as you move the frame. Publisher will only allow the frame to move straight up and down or directly left and right. This is helpful if you've already taken the trouble to align a frame with another object on the page in one of these dimensions. Also, turn on either of the Snap to options (Ruler Marks or Guides) to make positioning a frame on the page easier. The frame will tend to stick at the tic marks or layout guides as you move it.

When you move frames on top of each other, different results occur depending on the frame types and other settings. Try moving the Picture frame in this business card into the middle of the text area:

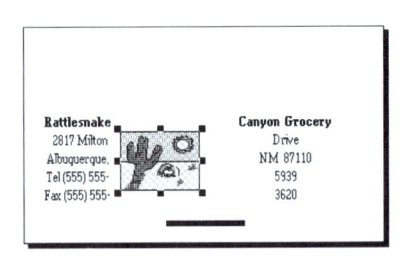

The text moves to any available space within the Text frame that it occupies. It may even seem to disappear if Publisher cannot find enough room in the frame to display it. If you reposition the Picture frame to its original location at the top of the card, the text floats back to its original position. Be aware that moving frames can affect the content of other frames in a publication.

Moving a Group of Frames Between Pages

Next you'll try moving a group of frames between the pages of a publication. This is a fairly complicated exercise, but is typical of the kind of redesign work that goes on when you're laying out a publication.

Start a new publication using BROCHURE.PUB. This is a two-page publication, as shown in Figure 4-9. First you're going to move all of the frames

Chapter 4: *All About Frames* 105

Figure 4-9. **BROCHURE.PUB**

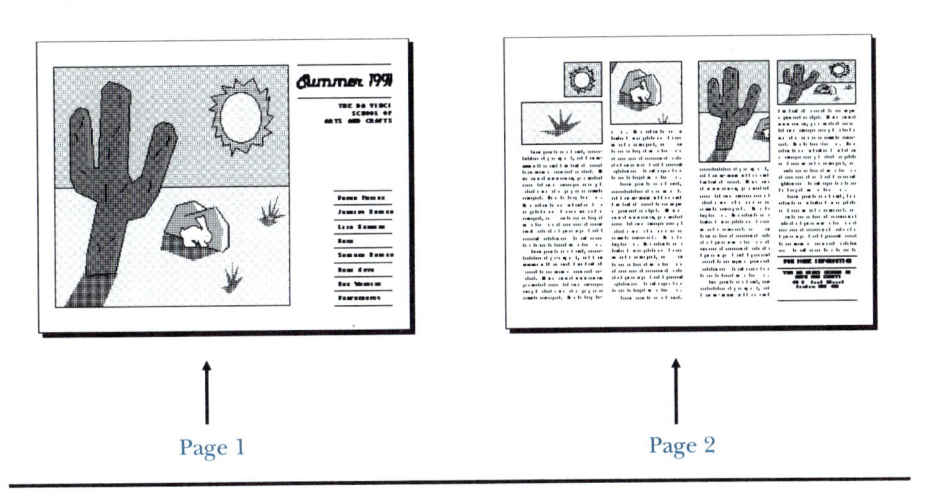

Page 1

Page 2

in the far right column of page 2 to a new page 3. Select all of those frames now using the marquee, and then drag them off the page and onto the scratch area to the right. After you select the frames, just move the cursor into the middle of the group. Be sure to wait until the mover appears before you press the mouse button. Then wait until the boundaries of the frames become broken lines before you start to drag the frames. This is an excellent time to use the (SHIFT) key with your move, since you are going to replace the frame group within the same top and bottom margins on the next page.

Note

When you want to move frames between pages using the scratch area, the frames must be completely off the page area. Otherwise they will remain on the original page. If there isn't enough room on the left or right of the page area for the objects you want to move, try scrolling above or below it. You can find additional scratch area that will accommodate different shapes in those locations. If there still isn't enough room to clear the edge of the page, you must use the cut-and-paste techniques described in the next section.

Next insert a single new page. Select Insert Pages from the Page menu, and click on OK to accept the default settings for a blank page. Publisher displays the newly added page 3, and the frames you moved off page 2 are still visible in the scratch area to the right. Drag them back onto the page and position them as the first column on the left of page 3, as shown in Figure 4-10 (beginning at the 10-inch mark on the horizontal ruler).

Tip

Undo works when you move frames. It can be particularly helpful if you make an error in a move because it restores the frame (or the group of frames) to a prior location with no effort on your part. Make sure you're happy with each segment of a move (to the scratch area, from the scratch area, and so on), because each is a separate command, and Undo only works on the most recent command.

Finally, you're going to move the Text frame on page 1 for "THE DA VINCI SCHOOL OF ARTS AND CRAFTS" to the background page. (It's just beneath the title "Summer 1991.") This will make it appear on every page of the publication. Turn to page 1 and click on its frame, as shown in Figure 4-9. Then drag it off the page in the scratch area to the right, and turn to the background page by either selecting Go to Background from the Page menu or pressing ALT-M.

Now drag the frame to the same location on the background page that it originally occupied on page 1. Return to the foreground by pressing ALT-M, and browse through all three pages. The frame appears as an attractive visual standard in the same location on each page of the publication.

Figure 4-10.   Reformatted pages

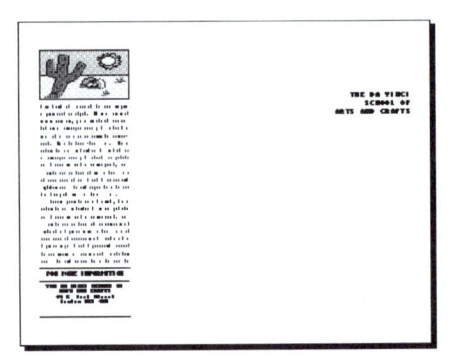

Chapter 4: *All About Frames*

Tip

When you're trying to move a Text frame, you must point between the handles on one of the boundaries of the frame in order to make the mover appear. When you want to move a Picture or WordArt frame, you can point practically anywhere in the frame in order to display the mover. Always wait for the mover to appear and the frame boundaries to change before you start to move a frame.

How to Move a Frame

1. Select the frame(s) that you want to move.
2. Point to the frame to display the mover (MOVE).
3. Press and hold the mouse button until the boundaries of the frame change to broken lines.
4. Drag the frame to a new location in the page or scratch areas.

Cut, Paste, and Copy

When you cut or copy a frame, Publisher sends the frame and its content to the Windows Clipboard. Cutting can be extremely handy when you want to move a large group of frames (too big to fit in the scratch area) between the pages of a publication or move frames between separate publications. Delete removes frames from a publication altogether (not to the Clipboard). Copy duplicates frames and their contents but leaves the original frame in position on the page. After you cut or copy a frame, use Paste to insert it on the same page, other pages, or in other publications. Cut, copy, and paste work with all three types of frames—Text, Picture, and WordArt. You can also use them with groups of frames, and mix different types of frames in a group.

Note

The Clipboard only holds one object at a time (the most recently cut or copied). If you're planning to paste something after you've cut or copied it, paste it right away! Otherwise, you may inadvertently overwrite the material with another command that affects the contents of the Clipboard.

Now try some examples. The Publisher template for a product catalog makes a good practice session because it has such an interesting array of Text and Picture frames. Start a new publication using the CATALOG.PUB template. This publication has three pages, as shown in Figure 4-11. Click on the Text frame on page 1. Then select the Delete Text Frame command from the Edit menu. Publisher removes the frame from the page.

Tip: The keyboard shortcut for deleting a Picture or WordArt frame is (DEL). For a Text frame use (CTRL)-(DEL).

Next you're going to move all of the frames on page 2 to page 1. Turn to page 2 and use the marquee to surround all of the frames on the page. After you release the mouse button, all of the frames should appear with shaded handles. This group of frames is too large to place in the scratch area, so using cut and paste is the only way to move them to another page. Use Cut Object from the Edit menu to cut the group, and then turn to page 1. To paste the group, select Paste Objects from the Edit menu (the literal menu selection changes to "Objects" because both Text and Picture frames are contained in the group). The entire group should now appear on page 1.

Tip: The Keyboard shortcut for cutting frames is (CTRL)-(X). For pasting use (CTRL)-(V).

Figure 4-11. CATALOG.PUB (three pages)

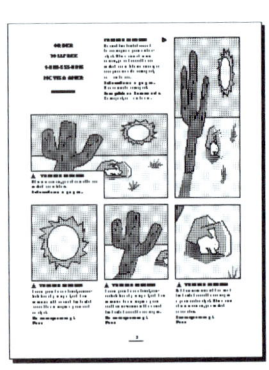

After you've cut or copied something to the Clipboard it remains there until you cut or copy something else. Since the frame group you just moved to page 1 is still on the Clipboard, you can use the same technique to paste the entire group of frames into another publication. Create a new publication beginning with a blank page. When Publisher asks if you want to save the changes that you made to CATALOG.PUB, click on No. After the blank first page of the new publication appears, use the Paste Objects command to copy them into the new publication.

Note: Undo works with Cut, Copy, and Paste. This fact should comfort you, since these commands can have some of the most powerful effects on the appearance of your publication. If you cut, paste, or copy frames and the results are not what you expected, remember to use Undo immediately! You can't reverse a cut if the last thing you did was paste.

Duplicating Frames

When you copy frames, the original frames remain in place in a publication, and a copy is placed on the Clipboard. Copying comes in handy when you want to be sure that two frames are identical or that the spatial relationship between several frames stays the same in a new location. This is a real time saver for detailed business publications such as forms. Consider the page of three-up labels in Figure 4-12. All 30 Text frames on the page have the identical dimensions and content. This is an ideal application for copying. You only need to create a single frame. Then you can copy progressively larger groups of frames to create the entire page in a hurry.

Start by creating a new publication from a blank page. You may find a 50 percent view helpful for this application. Create a single Text frame in the upper-left corner of the page approximately 2 1/2 inches wide and 1 inch deep as in Figure 4-13. Enter your own name and address for the label.

Copy the frame to the Clipboard, and paste it back into the publication. Select Copy Text Frame from the Edit menu, and then select Paste from the Edit menu. Publisher always pastes frames in the center of the screen, regardless of the location of either the pointer or the original frame. If this is not where you ultimately want the frame to appear—it usually isn't—you must move it to another part of the page after pasting. In this case, drag it up

Figure 4-12. *A page of three-up labels*

Figure 4-13. *Creating a page of labels*

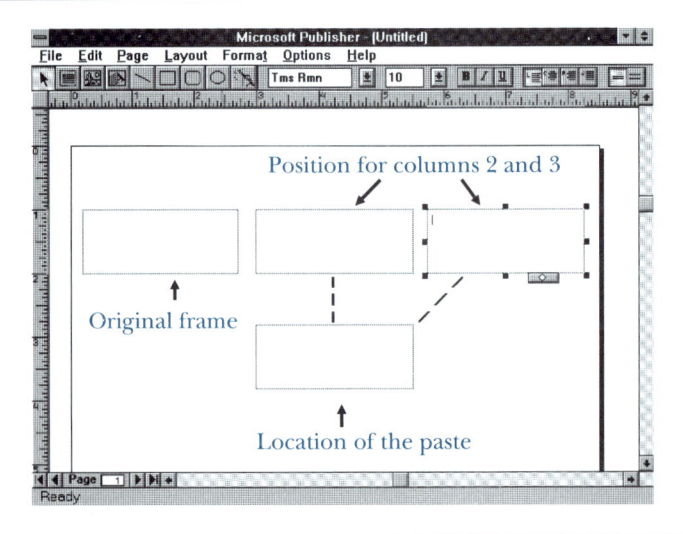

Chapter 4: *All About Frames*   111

next to the first frame to begin a second column of labels. Paste the frame again (remember it's still on the Clipboard) and move this copy to the top of column 3, as shown in Figure 4-13.

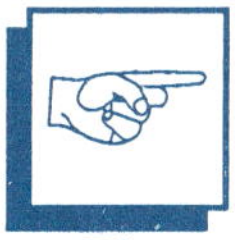

Tip

The keyboard shortcut for copying frames is CTRL-C.

Now select all three frames with the marquee. Use Copy and Paste to create a duplicate of the entire group, and move it up next to the first row of labels, as shown in the following illustration:

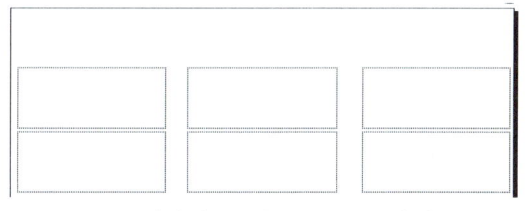

Escalate the copy process! Select the group of six and repeat the copy, paste, and move sequence to double the number of labels on the page from 6 to 12. Repeat the process until the page is filled. Toward the bottom of the page you may be left with a page area that will only accommodate one or two rows of labels. Just change the number of rows that you copy to suit the area that remains on the page.

Note

When you paste frames, they appear in the foreground and may block existing frames in the background.

How to Cut, Paste, and Copy Frames

1. Select the frame or frames that you want to cut or copy.
2. Select Cut or Copy from the Edit menu, or use one of the keyboard shortcuts for either of those commands. If you're not moving or copying the frames, this is the end of the procedure.
3. Turn to the page or load the publication you want to move or copy the frames to, if necessary.
4. Select Paste from the Edit menu, or use the keyboard shortcut.
5. Reposition the frames as needed.

Resizing Frames

With Publisher, you can change the size of a frame at any time. Its contents, if any, will adapt to the new dimensions. Resizing is one of the most powerful features in the program, because it lets you experiment with the composition of a page without worrying about the effects that design changes may have on its content. Once you're satisfied with the way frames fit together on the page, you can make adjustments to their content to suit the altered composition. Resizing frames is a very common and basic task for working effectively with any desktop publishing program.

You can use the same techniques to alter the size of any of the three types of frames: Text, Picture, and WordArt. If the frame is empty, its dimensions simply change, and there is no effect on the content. When you have already entered or imported material for a frame, however, the effects of the change will vary depending on its content. If you are resizing a Text frame, all of the text in the original frame may not fit in the new frame. In this case, Publisher stores it in the overflow area. For WordArt frames, the outcome varies based on how you format the WordArt. With Picture frames, the effects will differ depending on how you execute the change, and what kind of picture you have in the frame—pictures can become distorted either intentionally or unintentionally.

Note

When you select a Picture frame, the Cropping button (⌗) appears on the Toolbar. Cropping and resizing are not the same. For more information on cropping, see Chapter 9.

This section will deal only with the mouse-driven techniques you need to resize a frame. For more information on how to deal with the consequences of a change in size for each of the different frame types, refer to Chapter 6, to WordArt in Chapter 8, and to the sections on sizing, cropping, and scaling in Chapter 9.

You can use any one of the eight handles (■) that surround a frame to resize it. When you point directly to a handle, it changes into a *sizing icon,* as shown in the following illustration:

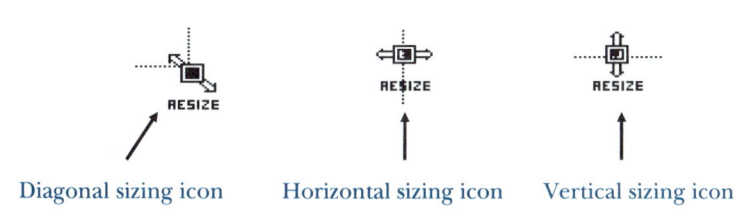

Chapter 4: *All About Frames* 113

Diagonal sizing icon   Horizontal sizing icon   Vertical sizing icon

The sizing icon indicates that Publisher is ready to resize a frame. Each handle has a slightly different icon designed to indicate which direction it will operate in. The horizontal sizing icon enlarges or reduces a frame's lateral size and shape from the side of the handle you select (the opposite boundary stays in place). The vertical sizing icon has a similar effect on the frame's height, from either the top or the bottom. The diagonal sizing icon affects both width and height, but only in one direction (NE, SE, SW, or NW).

Tip

Both Snap to Guides and Snap to Ruler Marks operate when you resize frames. They make it easy to align the new sides of a frame with specific locations on the page.

To experiment with resizing, start a new publication using REPORT.PUB, one of the Publisher templates for a report. In this exercise you'll redesign the report so it looks like the revised version on the right in Figure 4-14. Remember, if you make a mistake or get an unexpected result during this exercise, use Undo immediately to reverse the effects of resizing.

First click on the Picture frame in the middle of columns 2 and 3. Point to the handle in the lower-right corner of the frame and wait until the sizing icon appears. Then drag the handle down and to the right until the edge of the Picture frame meets the right margin. The Snap to Guides option is on for this template, so it should be easy to align the frame with the margin. You may notice a small Text frame for the picture caption lagging behind. After you resize the picture, move the Text frame for the caption beneath the Picture frame in its new location.

Tip

If you hold down (SHIFT) *while you drag the sizing icon, the frame retains the same proportion of length to width in the new size. If you hold down* (CTRL) *while you drag the sizing icon, opposite sides of the frame grow or shrink equally at the same time, and the frame remains centered at the original location.*

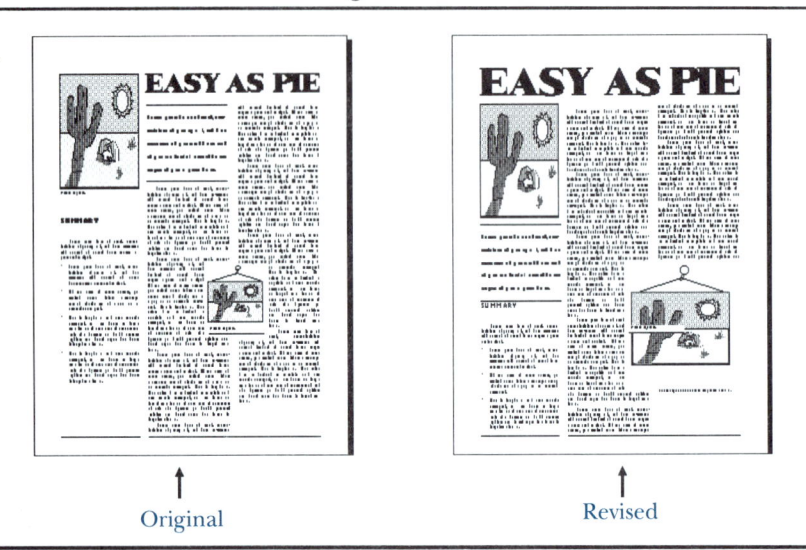

Figure 4-14.   REPORT.PUB: *original and revised versions*

Original   Revised

Next, move the Picture frame in the upper-left corner of the page down about 1 inch. You may want to switch to Actual Size view to facilitate this move. The top edge should be even with the adjacent Text frame, as shown here:

Now click on the WordArt frame containing the headline "EASY AS PIE" at the top of the page, and point to the handle in the middle of its left boundary. Drag the sizing icon to the left margin of the page as in Figure 4-14. Click on the Text frame in column 1, and point to the handle in the middle of the top edge of the frame. After you see the sizing icon appear, drag the top of the frame down about 3 inches.

Finally, click on the double-spaced Text frame at the top of column 2, and drag the frame to the middle of column 1 below the picture (this is strictly a

Chapter 4: *All About Frames* 115

move). If you followed all of this correctly, your publication should look like the left side of Figure 4-14. This exercise was a rapid-fire sequence of instructions, but it's a good drill for working with frames. If you need some more practice, reload the template and try it again.

Tip

Change your views of the page as often as necessary to see the portions of the page you're working with in sufficient detail. Don't try to move or resize objects within small increments of space while you're looking at a full page. The greater the magnification, the better the accuracy.

How to Resize a Frame

1. Select the frame that you want to resize.
2. Point to the handle on the side or corner that you want to move, and wait until the handle turns into a sizing icon.
3. Drag the sizing icon to the new location.

Frame Graphics

You can add graphic embellishments for borders, shading, and drop shadows to any of the three types of frames. Publisher provides buttons on the Toolbar, shown here, for adding these simple touches quickly and easily.

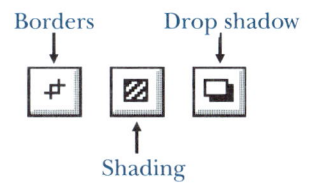

Borders Drop shadow

Shading

You can also find these options on the Layout menu, where more variations are available. This section discusses only the application of these commands from the Toolbar. See additional information for working with these options in Chapter 10. The effects you implement from either the Toolbar or the Layout menu have the identical effect on a frame.

Note

Whenever you select one of the frame tools, the right side of the Toolbar displays all of the graphic options just described. For Picture and WordArt frames, these options remain on the Toolbar after you complete the frame, and reappear whenever you select it. In the case of Text frames, the graphics options only appear before you create the frame. Afterward, and if you subsequently select a Text frame, Publisher displays text formatting tools instead. To change graphic characteristics for an existing Text frame you must use the Layout menu.

You can adjust these settings for any individual frame, or you can change the default settings for each type of frame. When you adjust the default, all subsequent frames of that type use the new settings. By changing the setting after a frame is created, you alter the format for the individual frame. By changing the setting before you draw a frame, you change the default for all subsequent frames of the type you selected.

Start a new publication using a blank page, and create a WordArt frame in the upper-left corner for the logo shown in Figure 4-15. Type **FMP Corp** in the WordArt dialog box and click on OK. Experiment with the border buttons by clicking on them. Each causes Publisher to display a border of different thickness around the frame. Once a button is activated, click on it again to turn it off or click on another border button. Now try clicking on the Drop Shadow button. This is simply a toggle that turns the drop shadow on or off. Before going on, give the WordArt frame a narrow border and leave the drop shadow turned on as in Figure 4-15.

Now draw another WordArt frame for the exclamation point you see to the left of the company initials. Type **!** in the WordArt dialog box. After Publisher redisplays the page, click on the Shading button. The Shading dialog box appears, as shown in Figure 4-16. All of these patterns and colors are available as backgrounds for any frame.

To get the background effect shown in Figure 4-15, click on the pattern in column 1 in the second row from the bottom and click on OK. Your publication should now look like Figure 4-15. Remember, all of these graphics options are explained in Chapter 10. However, you should feel comfortable

Chapter 4: *All About Frames* 117

Figure 4-15.   Using graphics options to create letterhead

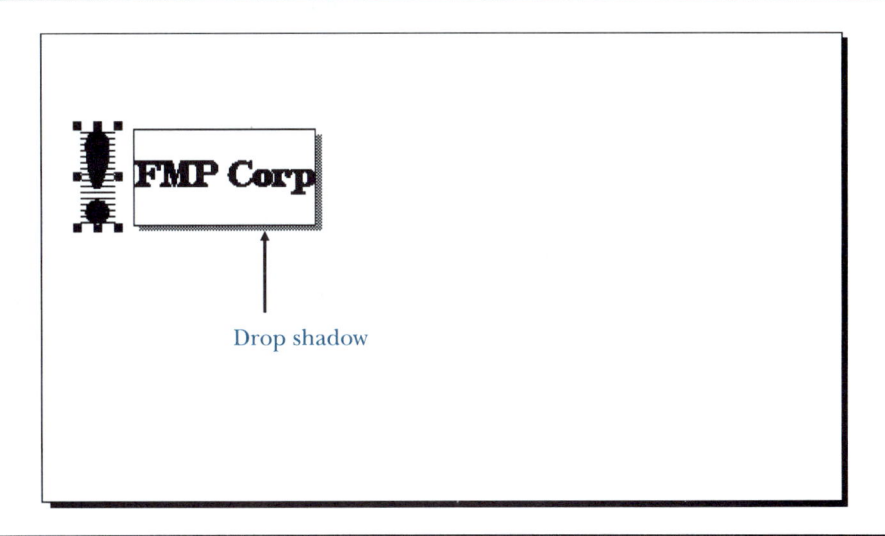

FMP Corp

Drop shadow

using them on the fly from the Toolbar because it makes Publisher more fun to work with.

Figure 4-16.   Shading dialog box

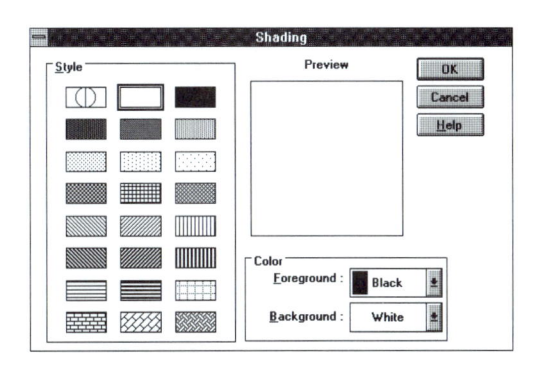

How to Add Graphics to a Frame Quickly

1. To modify individual frames, click on the frame you want to change. To modify the default settings for a type of frame, click on one of the graphics tools after you select the frame tool but before you create the frame.
2. Click on any of the borders or the Drop Shadow buttons to turn the options on or off.
3. Click on the Shading tool to add a background or color to a frame, and then select one of the background patterns or colors in the dialog box.

Review

Frames are showcases for text and graphics. They are the primary means you will use to get information across to the reader. You control their content by formatting the text and pictures inside them. Manipulating frames is essential to becoming an effective desktop publisher. Remember the tools at your disposal in working with frames.

- Each of the frame tools—Text, Picture, and WordArt—lets you display a different type of information.
- You can control all frames with the same basic set of commands. You can also change the default settings for each frame type.
- Frames can be resized and reshaped at any time, and Publisher automatically adapts their content to their new dimensions.
- It's easy to size and position frames exactly by using the rulers and the Snap options for rulers and guides.
- Options are available for drawing perfectly square or centered frames.
- Publisher lets you cut, copy, or paste frames anywhere within a publication or between publications, and with or without their content.
- You can select multiple frames concurrently, and cut, copy, paste, and drag the frame groups.
- The scratch area is extremely useful for moving frames between pages, or testing the effects of different frame configurations without having to delete material completely.
- Publisher has a handsome selection of graphics options for frames that let you add borders, shading, drop shadows, or patterns to enhance frame appearance.

5

All About Page Layout

Pages let you form the foundation of a publication and lay out its overall structure. All of the pages in a publication have the same structural characteristics, although some of these are more flexible than others. For example, page size remains constant throughout a publication whether you're designing a business card, a newsletter, or a book. It can't be changed without dramatically affecting all of the material in the publication. Since Publisher only displays a single page at a time, page size also has a significant impact on the appearance of the page area of the Publisher screen.

The layout guides you choose for a publication, on the other hand, only establish a general reference for the publication's appearance. Creating a publication is easier if you set guides that are applicable for placing major objects, but you can always override the guides when you apply frames and graphics. Positioning some frames askew from the main layout can add visual interest to a publication. Page size and the placement of guides are among the first jobs you should tackle in a new publication. While certain aspects of a layout do provide you with flexibility, you should always plan a publication carefully. If there are too many changes to the design that you start with, the project may become difficult to manage as your work progresses.

This chapter is meant to give you a clear and thorough understanding of how to design and view page layouts. Each section includes examples that let you practice and experiment with a specific task. Examples begin with the most elementary actions you need to learn a task and then go on to explore more elaborate usages. Examples are based both on Publisher templates and on material that you create from scratch. The templates contain so many good layouts that becoming familiar with them can only save you unnecessary work in the long run. Consider the samples in Figure 5-1. Using or modifying the layout from an existing template for one of these applications—when appropriate—is always faster than designing a publication from scratch. If you need a summary or a reminder about how to execute one of the tasks discussed in this chapter, you can find generic instructions in a box at the end of its section.

Page Formatting

Page formatting affects the way you see a publication on screen and how it looks after you print it. The choices available for some of the Publisher

Figure 5-1. *Layouts from some of the different templates*

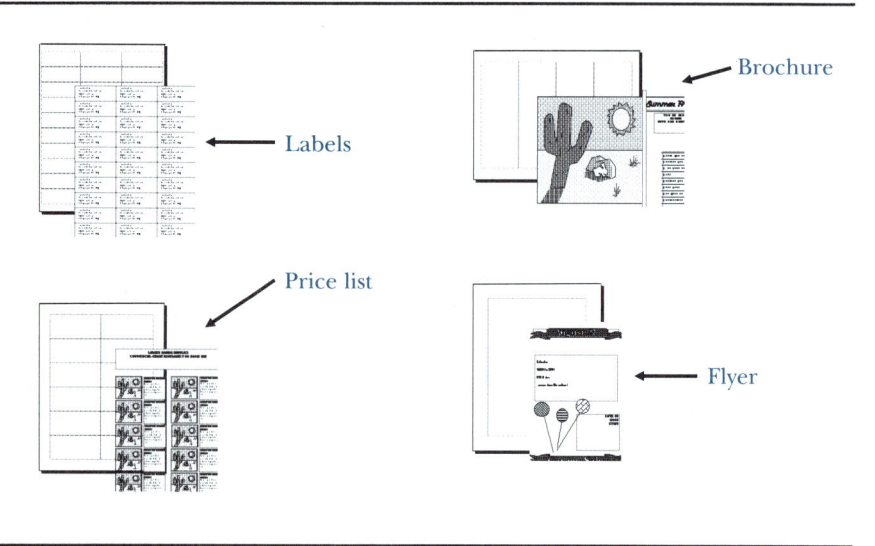

features discussed in this section are directly related to the type of printer that you have installed. For example, you cannot select a page length or width of 14 inches if you don't have a printer that accommodates legal-sized paper. You should always select the printer you intend to use *before* starting a publication, and especially before working with page formatting features. Publisher stores your printer selection along with all of the other information about your publication. If you try to open or print a publication using a different printer, you may get unexpected (usually unwanted and always unpredictable) results. For example, text may not flow in the same way, and pagination may change. You may need to redesign the layout completely in order to make it work with a different printer. Alternatively, you can reselect the original printer from within Publisher, and the publication will adopt its prior appearance.

Page Orientation and Paper Size

Page orientation lets you control the direction your material is printed in so that you can use the larger of a page's dimensions as the width if necessary. Figure 5-2 shows the same document printed on a letter-sized page (8 1/2 by 11 inches) in both portrait and landscape orientations. In *portrait orientation*—the more standard of the two—printing occurs from left to right, top to bottom. It's always available and usually the default setting for most printers. *Landscape orientation*, which gives you a much wider page, actually prints from bottom to top. If you were using a typewriter, you could simply rotate the page 90 degrees. Since many modern printers do not allow you to reorient the page, the direction of the printing itself is reoriented.

Orientation is *not* the same as paper size, although the two are closely related. For example, you can have either portrait or landscape orientation for both letter- and legal-sized paper. Paper size determines the maximum possible measurements for both the length and width of a publication. The measurement your printer uses for each dimension is a matter of orientation. Which orientation you decide on for a particular publication is largely a matter of taste. There are conventional settings for many applications, but being innovative in selecting a page orientation can have positive design results. Business cards, as seen in Figure 5-3, are normally designed in landscape orientation, but can be striking in portrait.

Figure 5-2.   *Portrait and landscape orientations*

Portrait

Landscape

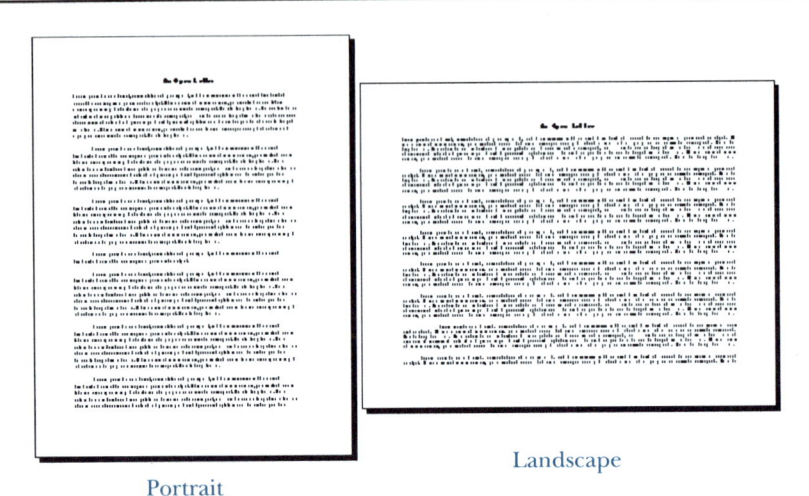

Figure 5-3.   *Business cards shown in portrait and landscape orientations*

Publisher uses letter-sized paper and portrait orientation as its default settings. To experiment with paper size and orientation, start a new publication with a blank page. Select Print Setup from the File menu. The Print Setup window appears, as shown in Figure 5-4. To change the orientation to landscape, just click on the Landscape button and click OK.

Publisher takes care of changing the page size and screen display for you when you change orientation for letter-sized pages, as shown in Figure 5-5. However, this is not the case for other paper sizes. Try changing the setup to legal-sized paper in landscape orientation:

- Select Print Setup from the File menu again.
- This time click on the Paper Size list and select Legal.
- Click on OK. When the Publisher screen appears, the page area is still letter sized.
- Now select Page Setup from the Page menu and look at the measurements for the Page size in the lower-left corner of the dialog box. They are still set for a letter-sized page.
- Change the width to **14** and the length to **8** for a legal-sized page in landscape orientation and click on OK. Publisher now displays the page area with the proper dimensions.

    The same problem occurs if you select either of the other European page size options (A4 or B5) in either orientation.

Figure 5-4.   Print Setup dialog box

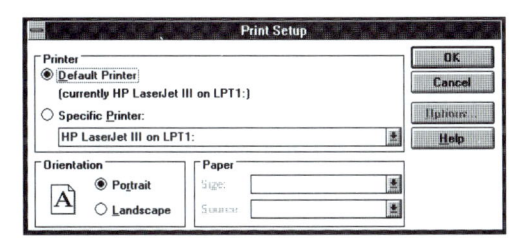

Figure 5-5. *Screen display for letter-sized paper in landscape orientation*

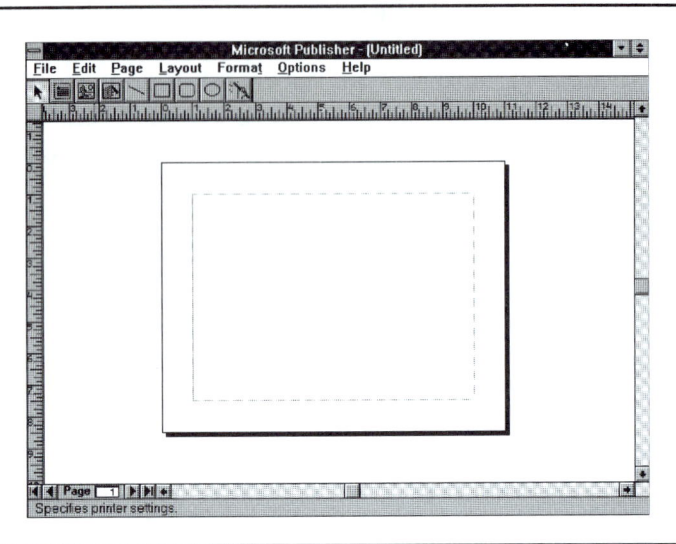

Note

If the appearance of the page area does not change to reflect a new orientation or paper size, you may need to adjust the page size manually. Make sure that all three settings—paper size, orientation, and page size—are correct before you start any detailed work on the publication. In the current release of Publisher (1.0) these settings do not update automatically for any paper size other than letter.

How to Change Page Orientation and Paper Size

1. Select File from the Menu bar and select Print Setup from the File menu.
2. Click on the orientation button that you want to use.
3. Click on the Paper Size window to open it, and select a new size.
4. Click on OK.

Publication Type

The ability to set a publication's type is one of Publisher's most unique features. It affects a publication's default page size, the appearance of the page area on the screen, and, in some cases, the order in which Publisher prints pages. There are seven types of publications.

Full Page
Book
Tent Card
Side Fold Greeting Card
Top Fold Greeting Card
Index Card
Business Card

Page size determines what part of the paper Publisher will use as a page. Whenever you select a type of publication, Publisher calculates a recommended page size and displays its actual measurements in the length and width fields of the Page Setup dialog box. You can reduce page size, but you can never enlarge it beyond the actual size of the paper you're using. For most applications, Publisher's recommendations are just fine.

For publication types other than Full Page, Publisher uses space on the paper in different ways. How much and what part of the paper varies depending on which publication type you choose. Publisher also fixes the dimensions for a Full Page view of the screen based on the page size. Except in the case of full pages, the entire physical page never appears until the print job is run. Figure 5-6 shows an example of how a page for an index card looks on screen, and how it appears on paper.

Full Page

Many publications may never require more than a full page. Full Page is the default publication type. To use it, just start a new publication using a blank page. Full pages are familiar and easy to understand. All of the space on the paper constitutes a page, and the pages that appear on screen are exactly like those that you print. The paper size and page size are equal. You can design hundreds of useful applications, from business forms and reports to newsletters and party invitations, all on full-page publications.

Figure 5-6.   *Screen page and printed page for a business card*

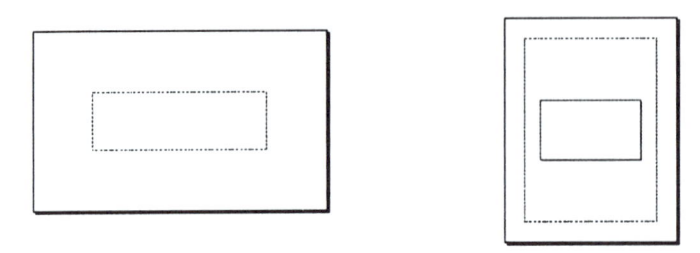

However, the other publication types can save you considerable time in formatting and printing for special applications. You can change the publication type by selecting **Page Setup** from the **Page** menu. The Page Setup dialog box appears, as shown in Figure 5-7. Click on the type of publication you want. As you click on the buttons for each of the publication types, the Preview window displays a thumbnail sketch of what the page will look like in relation

Figure 5-7.   *Page Setup dialog box*

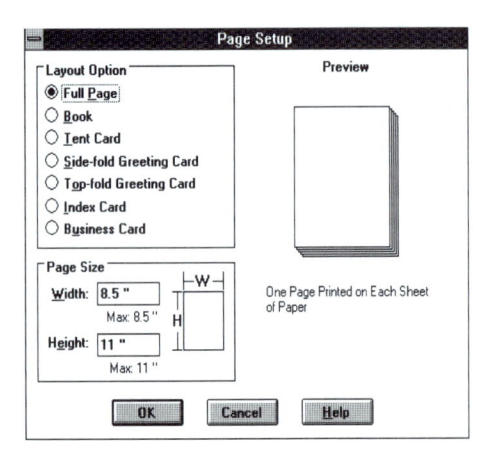

to the paper size. Try clicking on each of the options to get a picture of what each type does. The remainder of this section explains the major differences among the publication types.

Book

Book publications are printed as facing pages, or *spreads*. Publisher assumes that you want the pages to face each other as they do in a book. Publisher divides the paper size equally to form two pages, assuming that a collection of these sheets will be bound together at the center line to produce a multipage book. When Publisher prints the publication, it pairs the pages on each piece of paper to facilitate book binding: the first with the last, the second with the second to last, and so on. You can see this in Figure 5-8.

You can copy or paste successive pairs of these sheets back to back (1/12 and 2/11, 3/10 and 4/9, and so on) and fold them at the middle to create a book.

Tip

When you design a book, make sure that the total number of pages is divisible by 4, even if it means having some blank pages at the end of the publication. That way, you will always be able to pair the pages properly for binding. If necessary, insert the appropriate number of pages in order to bring the total page count to this level.

Figure 5-8.   *Order in which pages are printed in a book*

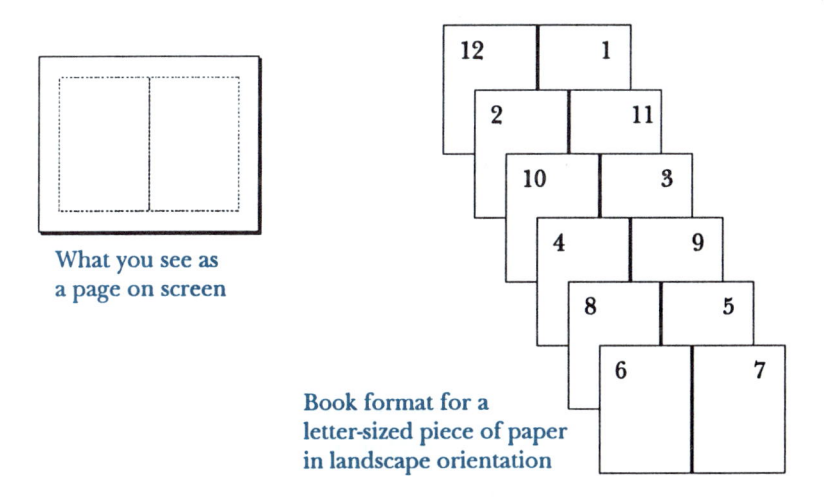

What you see as a page on screen

Book format for a letter-sized piece of paper in landscape orientation

For most applications, books are best designed with a landscape orientation. Otherwise the pages tend to be too narrow to display a significant line of text. For example, start a new publication using a blank page. Then select book format from the Page Setup dialog box, and click on OK. In portrait orientation a page is 4 1/2 inches wide. After you allocate room for margins, the area in which you can print will not be more than approximately 3 inches. Unless you're designing an unusual looking catalog or an ingenious multipage greeting card, this will probably be an inadequate area to print in. Now try setting the paper orientation to landscape. Select Print Setup from the File menu, click on the Landscape button, and then click on OK. The resulting page size is much more appropriate for a book than its portrait-oriented cousin.

Tip

A mirrored layout for the pages of a book helps to give the book symmetry. See the section later in this chapter on facing pages and mirrored layouts for more details on implementing this option.

Tent Card

Publisher prints *tent cards* with the assumption that you want to create a four-sided card using a single sheet of paper, with a single fold and printing on two sides. The paper size is divided equally to form a page, as shown in Figure 5-9. Since both pages will ultimately face outward, Publisher prints the text and graphics for the second page upside down. After you fold the paper, text will appear right side up on both pages. Tent cards can be attractive in both portrait and landscape orientation, and lend themselves easily to custom sizes. You can, for example, create a place card for a formal meal using a tent card with business-card proportions for the page size. Depending on the dimensions of the card, you may also want to experiment with different weights of paper: larger cards will need a heavier paper stock in order to stand up properly.

The best way to appreciate the special publication types is to work with them. To create the card shown in Figure 5-9:

- Start a new publication using a blank page and click on Tent Card from the Page Setup menu.
- Create a WordArt frame that matches the layout guides for the page margins and type **Sold!** for the text in the WordArt dialog box.
- Now click on Copy in the Edit menu to make a copy of the frame.

Figure 5-9. *How a tent card works*

How the card is folded

Tent Card format

- Select Insert Pages from the Page menu and click on OK to accept the default settings. Publisher displays page 2 of the piece.
- Click on Paste on the Edit menu to insert the frame on page 2. Move it into position on top of the layout guides. Finally, print the card.

Note: Always be sure to add a second page to your publication if you decide to create a tent card. Selecting a tent card only causes Publisher to divide the paper size in half, and print the second page upside down. It doesn't add the actual second page. You must select Insert Pages from the Page menu and explicitly add a second page for this publication type to print properly.

Side- and Top-Fold Cards

Side- and top-fold cards are printed with the assumption that a four-sided card with two folds will be produced from a single sheet of paper, with printing on all four sides. The paper size is divided equally from left to right and top to bottom in order to form four pages, as shown in Figure 5-10. Publisher assumes that this sheet will be folded twice, once at each center line. After it is completely folded, text will appear right side up on all four sides. The difference between side- and top-fold cards is the order of the folds. This affects the sequence of the pages and the edge from which the card opens.

Figure 5-10.   *A side-fold card*

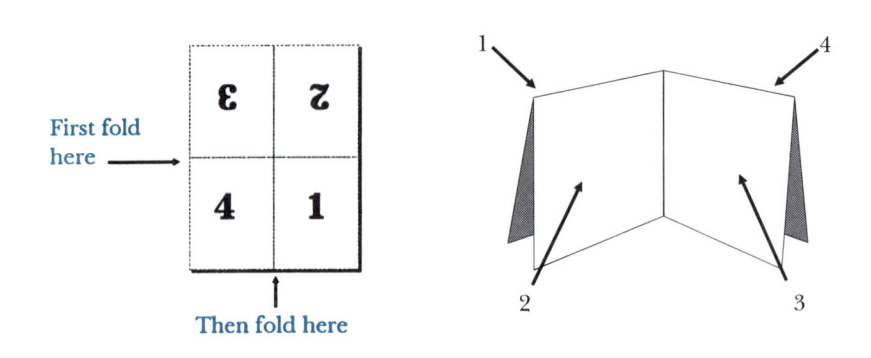

There is no standard preference for paper size or orientation for side-fold cards. You may find it easier to locate an envelope for one produced in letter size. If you haven't worked on these cards before, you ought to try creating one. These may seem a little complicated at first, but the design is quite ingenious. The PageWizard for greeting cards uses this format and does practically all of the work for you. After it's done, you can print the card and browse through the publication on screen to see how it works.

Start a new publication using PageWizards and select Greeting Cards from the PageWizard menu. If you're feeling lazy you can just click on Next to accept all of the defaults for the card. Otherwise alter any of the settings as you like (you can't really make a mistake with a PageWizard). When the last dialog box appears, click on Create It and watch Publisher do the work. Afterwards print the publication.

Note: *After you select this type of publication on your own, be sure to add three pages (in the previous example the PageWizard did it for you). Selecting the publication type causes Publisher to divide the paper size in quarters and print pages 2 and 3 upside down, but it doesn't add the actual pages. You must select Insert Pages from the Page menu and explicitly add three more pages for this publication type to print properly.*

Index and Business Cards

Index and business cards print on a single page, as shown in Figure 5-11. Index cards are approximately 3 by 5 inches, and business cards are approx-

Chapter 5: *All About Page Layout* 133

Figure 5-11. Index and business cards

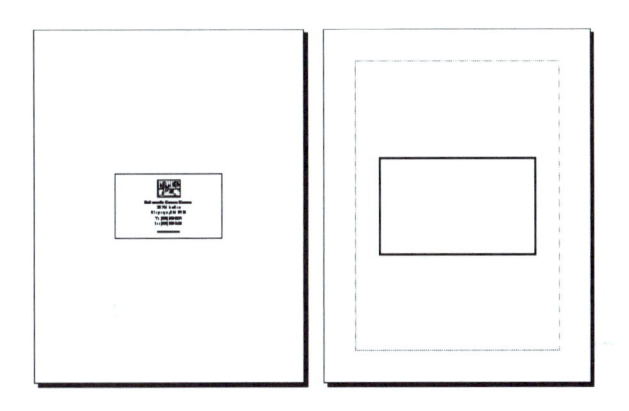

imately 3.3 by 2 inches. They do not use any special printing or folding techniques. You can use these publication types as mechanicals for submission to a commercial printer. A *mechanical* is a completed page design that is ready to be used for photo reproduction. Since both of these publication types use less than a full page, you should turn on the Crop Marks option when printing them. *Crop marks* indicate where the paper should be trimmed after printing in order to create the finished card.

If you want to print index or business cards using an in-house copier, you can create a sheet of them after you design a single card. This technique can save a lot of paper.

- Start a new publication using the Business Card publication type or one of the business card templates to design the card, and then change the publication type to Full Page.
- Use the marquee to select all of the frames that compose the card and move them to the upper-left of the page as shown in Figure 5-12.
- Use Copy and Paste to duplicate groups of cards until multiple sets are positioned on the page.
  See the section on Cut, Paste, and Copy in Chapter 4 for more information on how to propagate groups of frames on a page like this quickly.

Figure 5-12.   Creating a sheet of business cards

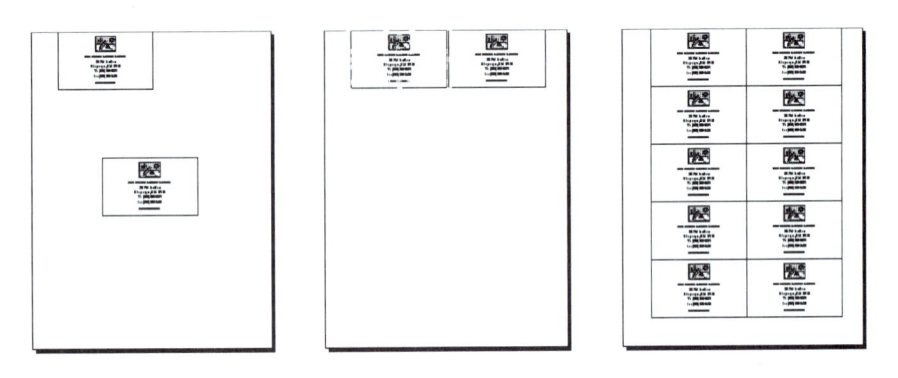

> **Note:** Publisher uses default 1-inch margins for all publication types. Naturally this is a little extreme for a business card with overall dimensions of 3.3 by 2 inches. When you select Business Card from the Page Setup dialog box, the following message appears:

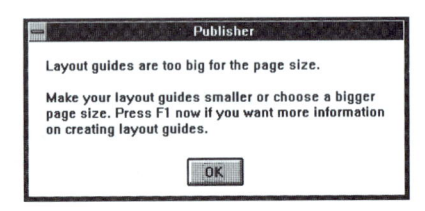

```
Publisher
Layout guides are too big for the page size.

Make your layout guides smaller or choose a bigger
page size. Press F1 now if you want more information
on creating layout guides.

                    [ OK ]
```

Just click on OK and adjust the guides for your design.

How to Select a Publication Type

1. Select Page from the Menu bar and select Page Setup from the Page menu.
2. Click on the publication type that you want to produce.
3. Click on OK.

Chapter 5: *All About Page Layout* 135

Page Size

Setting the page size determines which part of the current paper size Publisher uses as an individual page, and what the size of the page area will be on screen. When you start Publisher with a Blank Page, it uses the following default settings:

Publication type:	Full Page
Page size:	8.5 by 11 (letter sized)

If you select a different publication type, Publisher alters the page size and displays its new recommended dimensions at the bottom of the Page Setup dialog box as shown here:

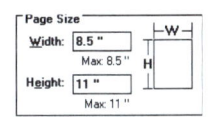

```
┌Page Size──────────────┐
  Width:  8.5 "          ┌─W─┐
          Max: 8.5 "   H │   │
  Height: 11 "            │   │
          Max: 11 "       └───┘
```

You can alter the page size by clicking on the Width and Height fields and entering new values. You must change the page size this way if you are using a size that Publisher does not list as a standard paper size or layout option, such as an envelope or custom-sized business card. To create an envelope, for example, change the width to 9.5 inches and the height to 4.1 inches. As you enter the new measurements, the preview area displays a thumbnail sketch of what the page size will look like in relation to the paper size (the preview area will only update after you select a button or field other than the one you change). After you click on OK, you will see the dialog box shown in Figure 5-13.

The maximum dimensions that you can use for page size will always be governed by the orientation and paper size you have selected under Print Setup. In this case, assuming that you are using letter-sized paper, you need to change the orientation to landscape before you print.

Note

Publisher takes care of updating the page size when you change between orientations for letter-sized pages. However, this is not the case for other paper sizes including legal, A4, and B5. If the appearance of the page area does not change to reflect a new orientation or paper size setting, you may need to adjust the page size manually. Make sure that all three settings—paper size, orientation, and page dimensions—are correct before you start any detailed work on the publication.

Figure 5-13.   *Dialog box that appears if your page is too large*

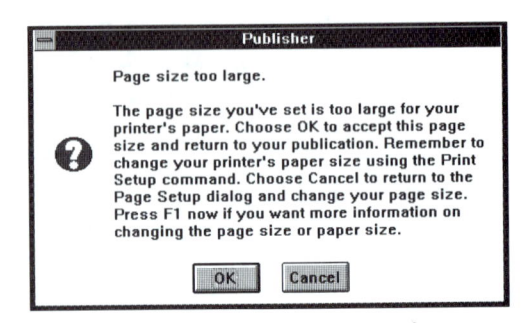

How to Change the Page Size

1. Select Page from the Menu bar and select **Page Setup** from the Page menu.
2. Click on the field (width or height) that you want to change from the group of fields under Page Size. Enter the measurements as needed. Partial values can be entered as decimals.
3. Click on OK.

Page Margins and Layout Guides

Layout guides let you establish an informal map for a publication's appearance. They provide an easy-to-use visual reference for positioning frames and graphics. Guides appear in the page area based on the margin, column, and row settings that you choose for a page's overall design. All margin settings—left, right, top, and bottom—are based on the page size (not the paper size). Margins are measured inward from their respective edge of the page; for example, the top margin is measured from the top edge. Margin guides appear on the screen in red on a color monitor. Columns divide the

Chapter 5: *All About Page Layout* 137

area inside of the margins vertically into equal sections. Rows divide the area inside of the margins horizontally into equal sections. Column and row guides both appear on the screen in blue. Publisher uses a default margin setting of 1 inch on all sides and a single column and row for all publication types. Figure 5-14 displays some other settings for layout guides.

The settings you choose for layout guides appear on every page of a publication. However, they only serve as a general reference. Unlike frames, which literally constrain the text and graphics contained in them, layout guides are simply signposts. The margins and number of columns or rows that you establish can be overridden in the way that you apply objects. While this flexibility exists, it is still a good idea to plan the layout carefully.

Tip

Page margins and frame margins operate independently of each other. For example, as a result of the default left margin setting for Text frames (.08 inch), the text in a frame that you position on the left margin of the page may not appear to be perfectly aligned with the margin itself or with other objects that you have positioned there. To correct this, eliminate the frame margin.

Figure 5-14.   Some sample layouts

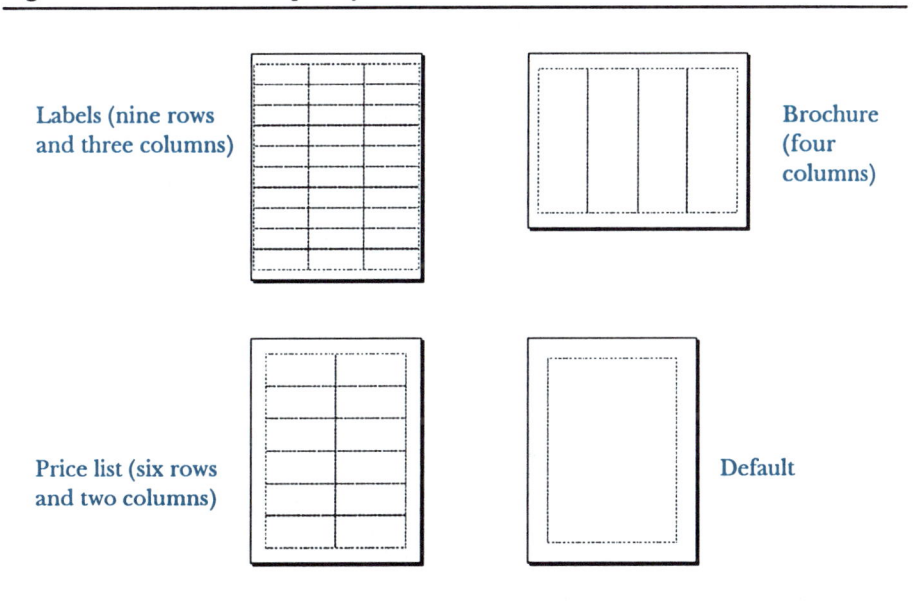

Labels (nine rows and three columns)

Brochure (four columns)

Price list (six rows and two columns)

Default

Try creating the layout for the brochure in Figure 5-1. It's a good example of how layouts are flexible guidelines: each of the objects on the page *works with* the guides, but does not conform to them completely. For example, the large picture sits squarely based in the lower-left margin, but extends only halfway across the third column. The three Text frames on the right are right *flush*—they all align with the right margin—but they extend at different lengths to the left, and none of them ends at a column guide. These are ways in which the designer has used discretion in both conforming to and overriding the layout. The easiest way to create this layout, of course, is to use the template BROCHURE.PUB and simply delete all of the frames.

If you want some practice at building layouts from scratch, however:

- Start a new publication with a blank page and use the Print Setup menu to change the page orientation to landscape.
- Select Layout Guides from the Layout menu. The Layout Guides dialog box appears, as shown in Figure 5-15.
- Type .5 for the left and right margins and .75 for the top and bottom. As you enter the new values, the image in the Preview window changes to reflect them.
- Finally, change the Number of Columns to 4 and click on OK. The revised layout should resemble the illustration for the brochure layout in Figure 5-14.

Figure 5-15.   Layout Guides dialog box

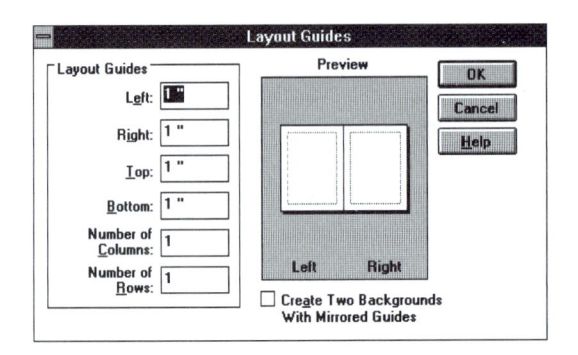

Chapter 5: *All About Page Layout*

How to Change the Margin and Layout Guides

1. Select Layout from the Menu bar and select Layout Guides from the Layout menu.

2. Click on any of the fields that you want to change, and enter new values as needed. Partial values can be entered as decimals.

3. Click on OK.

Display Options for Layout Guides

Publisher provides you with two important tools, Hide/Show and Snap, to make working with layout guides easier. These commands operate as toggles. Each time you select a *toggle* you either turn it on or off, depending on its previous state. If a toggle is in effect, it appears on the Options menu with a check mark to its left, or its opposite name appears, as shown here:

```
Options
 Check Spelling...

 Snap to Ruler Marks
√Snap to Guides         Ctrl+W
 Hide Pictures
 Hide Rulers            Ctrl+K
 Hide Status Line
 Hide Layout Guides     Ctrl+G
 Hide Object Boundaries Ctrl+Y
 Settings...
```

In this example, Snap to Guides is enabled and Hide Layout Guides appears (is on) instead of Show Layout Guides. If no check mark appears, the option is currently disabled. Toggles can be turned on or off at any time during a Publisher session.

Hide/Show Layout Guides simply turns the display of the guides on or off. Since layout guides do not print, this can help you get a more accurate sense of how your publication will appear after it is printed. Hiding the guides has no effect on your layout or the position of objects on the page. As your publication develops, frame boundaries and other objects begin to cover up the layout guides anyway. Part or all of the guides may become hidden in the course of your work. This toggle simply ensures that none of them appears.

Tip

The keyboard shortcut for toggling Hide/Show Guides is CTRL-G.

Snap to Guides causes the layout guides to become "sticky." If you're drawing a frame or a graphic object, the crosshair will tend to adhere slightly to any guide when passing over it slowly and "jump" to the next one as you move along. This makes it easy to align the starting and ending locations exactly with a set of guides. If you're moving or resizing a frame, the same effect occurs when the boundaries of the frame encounter a guide: they pause. If you've done a good job in designing a layout, Snap to Guides will be very useful in positioning most of the major objects in your publication.

Tip

The keyboard shortcut for toggling Snap to Guides is CTRL-W.

For material that you place askew from the layout, however, Snap can be an interference, especially in Full Page view. More magnified views display more distance between guides, so there are fewer sticky areas on the screen at one time. Try enlarging your view or turning Snap off if you're having trouble positioning material between guides. Snap doesn't make it impossible for you to place objects between guides, just easier for you to place objects on them. Hide/Show and Snap operate independently of each other (Snap will work even if the guides are hidden).

Note

Snap can also be toggled on or off for Ruler Marks as explained later in this chapter under "Working with Rulers." You cannot use Snap for both guides and rulers at the same time. When one of the two is enabled, turning on the other disables the first.

To Set Hide/Show or Snap for the Layout Guides

1. Select Options from the Menu bar.
2. Select Snap to Guides or Hide/Show Layout Guides from the Options menu. The menu closes, and the toggle switches the option to its new condition.

Mirrored Guides and Facing Pages

Books, and other publications where pages face each other, often use *mirrored layouts* for the right and left pages, as shown in Figure 5-16. This gives facing pages a symmetrical appearance, and also allows room for binding in the middle of the inside margin (called the *gutter*). If you request it, Publisher will automatically create a mirrored layout like this based on a design you create for a single page. Publisher recognizes the original page you designed as the right page and the mirrored page it creates as the left page. In mirrored layouts, vertical margins for both the left and right pages are measured from the point at which the two pages are bound. The left margin of the right page and the right margin of the left page become the inside margins. The other sides of each page become the outside margins.

None of the templates or PageWizards uses mirrored guides, so if you want to experiment with them you'll have to start a publication from scratch using a blank page. Then select Layout Guides from the Layout menu and change the right margin to 2 inches. After you close the field, the Preview window shows the new margin on the same side for both the left and right pages. Now click on the Mirrored Guide button, shown here:

☒ Create Two Backgrounds
   With Mirrored Guides

Figure 5-16.   *Mirrored layouts*

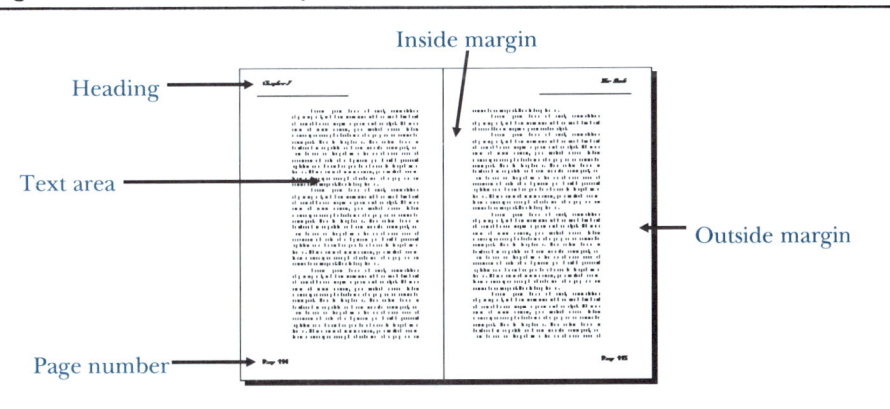

The names of the margin fields in the dialog box change to Inside and Outside, and the Preview window displays the new layout for the left page. The increased margin on the outside of the right page was *mirrored* to the outside of the left page.

You can confirm this in the publication as well. Click on OK, and then select Insert Pages from the Page menu. Creating a mirrored layout does not automatically add any pages to a publication. Click on OK to insert a second page with Publisher's default settings. Publisher displays the second page with the margin guides in their new mirrored location.

Tip

Any objects that you place on the background page before implementing mirrored guides are automatically copied and mirrored to the background for the new left page layout. You can use this for placing page numbers and other objects that repeat in book publications. See the sections later in this chapter on the background page and page numbers for more information on using these techniques.

When frames follow the layout of mirrored guides, they have symmetrical positions on left and right (even and odd) pages. In other words, their *absolute location* on each page—the distance from any two contiguous edges of the paper—will differ, depending on whether they are on an odd- or even-numbered page.

If you delete a single page, Publisher renumbers the pages that follow it in the publication. Odd-numbered pages become even, and even-numbered become odd. As a result, frames (and other objects) may no longer appear in the proper location to maintain symmetry between facing pages. When you add or delete pages in a publication that uses mirrored guides, use multiples of 2 in order to keep objects where you placed them on odd or even pages. Otherwise objects designed for the right page will move to the left, and will no longer conform to the layout.

Note

If you cancel mirrored layout guides, the original design (the right page) becomes the design for all pages. You may need to adjust the location of objects that were located on left pages. This is a good example of why major design decisions should be adhered to. Rearranging all of the left page objects in a multipage document can be extremely time-consuming and no fun at all.

> ### How to Implement Mirrored Guides
>
> 1. Place any objects that you plan to use on the background page.
> 2. Select Layout from the Menu bar and select Layout Guides from the Layout menu.
> 3. Change any of the margin, column, or row values.
> 4. Click on the Mirrored Guide button beneath the Preview window.
> 5. Click on OK.

Using Multiple Pages

When you begin a new publication, it contains only a single page. If your project requires additional pages, you must add them explicitly. This is the case for all publication types, including cards and books, for which the layout naturally anticipates more than one page. You can add or delete pages at any time and at any location in a publication. Publisher moves the objects that already exist to accommodate the change. This usually works out for the best; however, if you are working with a mirrored layout, you should follow a few precautions. Refer to the previous section in this chapter for tips on adding or deleting pages with a mirrored layout.

Inserting Pages

You can insert one or more pages at a time by using the Insert Pages dialog box, shown here:

New pages all take on the existing layout for the publication. You can insert new pages in front of or in back of the current page. Normally Publisher will insert blank pages. However, you can request it to create Text frames for you or duplicate all of the objects from a specific page in the publication.

Tip: The keyboard shortcut for inserting a single blank page is CTRL-N.

Now try adding some pages to one of the Publisher templates.

- Start a new publication using BROCHURE.PUB. Make sure that you can see both the layout guides and the object boundaries. Take a look at the Options menu if you're not sure and, if necessary, turn on either or both of them.
- Turn to page 2 of the publication and select Insert Pages from the Page menu.
- Click on the Before Current Page button and then click on OK. Publisher displays a new blank page and all of the objects that were on page 2 are moved to page 3.
- Now turn to page 3. Select Insert Pages again from the Page menu, but this time click on the button labeled Duplicate All Objects on the Page.
- Click on OK and turn back to page 4. Publisher copies all of the objects on page 3, frames and graphics, to page 4 in the same locations. The frames, however, are empty, as you can see in Figure 5-17.

This is the only way that you can "dump" frame content without deleting frames. There is no menu option for deleting a picture, for example, without deleting its frame as well.

Chapter 5: *All About Page Layout* 145

Figure 5-17.   *Moving objects*

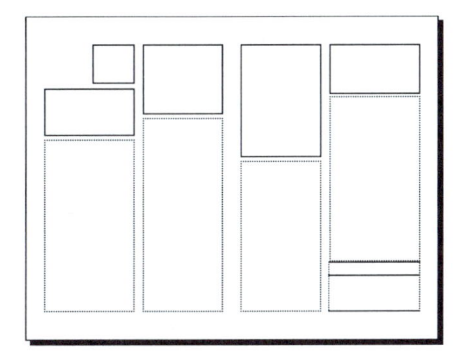

Tip

Be conservative when you're adding pages. Publisher lets you add as many pages as you like with a single command, but you can only delete one page at a time. They are considerably more tedious to get rid of than to create.

How to Insert Pages

1. Select Page from the Menu bar and select Insert Pages from the Page menu.
2. Enter the number, relative position, and frame composition for the new pages, if necessary, or accept the default values for inserting a single blank page after the current one.
3. Click on OK.

Deleting Pages

You can only delete one page at a time, the one you are currently working on. Deleting a page is simple, but there are a few things that you should be aware of. First and most important, *when you delete a page, all of the objects on the page are deleted as well.* Be careful—you can lose information! The scratch area is common to all pages. Objects in the scratch area remain unaffected by page deletions or insertions. If you want to retain some or all of the objects on a page you're going to delete, move them into the scratch area before the deletion. *They must be completely off the page area in order to avoid deletion.* If they don't fit in the scratch area, use Cut from the Edit menu to move them to the Clipboard and paste them on another page or in another publication.

If the page you delete contains Text frames that are linked to Text frames on previous or succeeding pages, the frames on the deleted page are removed but the flow of the text is maintained between the frames that still exist in the publication. If necessary, Publisher places excess text in the Overflow Area. Refer to Chapter 6 for more details on connected Text frames. Finally, Undo works with the Delete Page command. It will restore a deleted page if you execute it immediately after the deletion.

Caution

Publisher does not display a warning or confirmation message when you select the Delete Page command! Make sure you want to delete a page and that you are currently looking at the one you want to delete before executing the command. You may lose valuable information!

How to Delete a Page

1. Display the page that you want to delete.
2. Select Page from the Menu bar and select Delete Page from the Page menu.

Chapter 5: *All About Page Layout* 147

Paging

Publisher lets you move between pages by clicking on one of the page turning buttons or by clicking on the page indicator, located in the lower-left corner of the screen. Both of these tools are shown here:

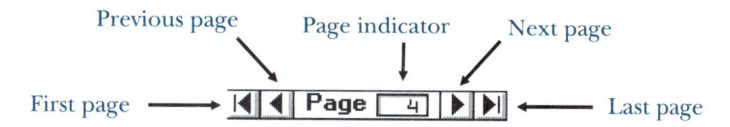

Previous page   *Page indicator*   *Next page*

First page → |◄ ◄ Page [4] ► ►| ← *Last page*

You can move to the page immediately before or after the page you are working on or directly to the first or last pages of the publication. You can also move to a specific page number. The number of the current page always appears in the Page Indicator box.

Tip

The keyboard shortcut for the next page is (F5). *For the previous page, it's* (CTRL)-(F5).

How to Change Pages

Click on one of the page-turning buttons or click on the Page Indicator box and enter a page number.

The Background Page

Multipage publications often contain information that appears in the same location on each page. The information may be simple, such as a page number or a border, or more elaborate, like a logo or detailed heading. Any object that you create on or move to Publisher's background page automatically appears on every normal (foreground) page. You only have to type it once. The background page is always present, even if you don't use it. If there's nothing on it, Publisher ignores it. The background page is also the only way to insert page numbers that paginate automatically in your publication.

Working on the background page is exactly like working on any other page in Publisher. Layout guides appear at the same location as they do on foreground pages. All of the menu commands operate normally, and frames behave in just the same way. The scratch area and Clipboard are common to both background and foreground pages, and can be used to move objects between both perspectives. To move objects to, from, or around the background page, use the same techniques that you would to move them on foreground pages. Cut, Paste, Copy, and the scratch area all work identically. Refer to Chapter 4 or Chapter 10 for more information on these procedures. You can switch back and forth between foreground and background pages at any time during a Publisher session. However, you can only select objects that exist in the current perspective: you cannot select background objects from a foreground page, or vice versa.

Now for some practice.

- Use Publisher's template for a product information sheet—PROD-INFO.PUB—as the basis for creating a catalog of product sheets, all with the same layout. Start a new publication using that template. Make sure that the Layout Guides are visible.

- Select Go to Background from the Page menu. The background page appears in the same view and at the same location as the page that you were working on. However, none of the objects from the foreground page are present (only the layout guides appear).

  The only way to tell for sure if you're looking at a background page is by the page indicator in the lower left of the screen. Instead of displaying the page buttons and the current page number that you normally see on foreground pages, Publisher displays an icon for the background page, as shown here.

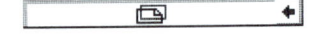

Tip

The keyboard shortcut for switching between the foreground and background pages is CTRL-M.

Chapter 5: *All About Page Layout* 149

- Now click on the Line tool and draw a horizontal rule across in the bottom margin, as shown in Figure 5-18. Switch back to the foreground page, and notice that the rule appears in the same location.
- Select Insert Pages from the Page menu, insert three pages, and browse through the newly added pages. Each is blank, except for the rule you placed on the background page.
- Return to page 1 and select the Picture and Text frames in the upper-right corner, as in Figure 5-18, and drag these into the scratch area to the right.
- Switch to the background page and drag them back onto the page in the same location that they had on page 1.
- Finally, return to the foreground and browse through all four pages. The heading appears on each at the same location.

Objects that you place on the background page always appear in the foreground unless they are blocked by foreground objects or you explicitly tell Publisher to ignore the background page in a specific instance. In that case, none of the objects on the background page appears on that foreground page. For example, return to page 1, and select Ignore Background from the Page menu. The rule and heading disappear, but are still visible on pages 2 through 4.

Figure 5-18. Objects created on background page appear on each page

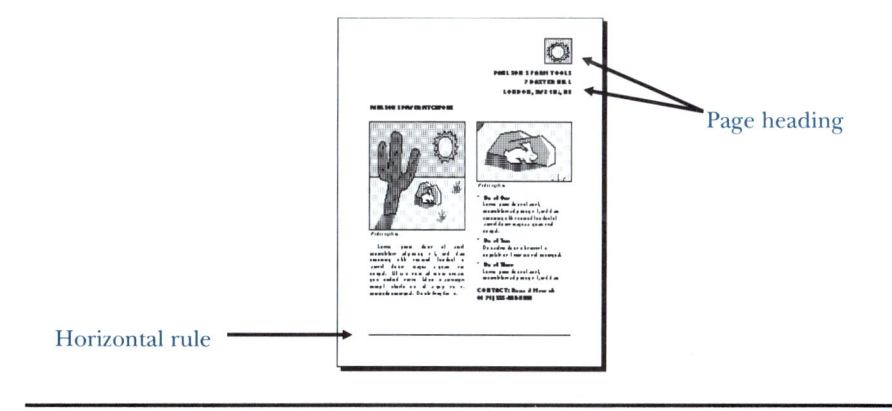

Page heading

Horizontal rule

To Repeat Objects on Every Page

1. Select Page from the Menu bar and select Go to Background from the Page menu.

2. Insert any of the objects that you want to repeat on all pages using any of the commands to create, copy, or move material in Publisher. You can also modify any of the objects that are already there.

3. To suppress the appearance of background material on any foreground page, turn to it and select Ignore Background from the Page menu.

Mirrored Guides and the Background Page

When you select a layout using mirrored guides, Publisher creates a separate background page for the left and right pages. If you switch your view to the background, the appropriate background page appears. Publisher displays two page indicators, as shown here:

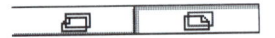

You can switch between left and right background pages by clicking on one of the indicators. Publisher highlights the one that you are currently looking at.

The layout guides for each background page are identical to their respective foreground pages. When you select mirrored guides, Publisher mirrors any objects you created on the normal (right side) background page at a symmetrical location on the left background page.

If you followed the exercise for working with the background page in the previous section, try this modification to the catalog you designed from PRODINFO.PUB. Enable the Mirrored Guides button in the Layout Guides dialog box. Then browse through all four pages of the publication. Right (odd-numbered) pages display the heading at the original location in the

Chapter 5: *All About Page Layout* 151

upper right of the page, as shown in Figure 5-19, whereas left (even-numbered) pages display it in the upper left.

> *Note — The text in the heading and the accompanying address appear flush right on left pages because the text is formatted that way in the frame. Publisher placed the frame itself in a mirrored location, but had no control over the formatting of the text inside of the frame. To correct this, select all of the text in the Text frame on the left background page, and then click on the Left Align button on the Toolbar.*

Any objects that you create on either of the background pages *after* selecting Mirrored Guides only appear on the page that you draw them on. Cut, Copy, Paste, and the scratch area also work normally for moving or duplicating objects between the background pages. See the section earlier in this chapter on using mirrored guides if you need more information.

Page Numbers

When you insert a page marker in a publication, Publisher automatically numbers pages and prints page numbers. This is the only way to print page numbers without creating them individually. You can only insert page markers in a Text frame on the background page. The frame can contain other

Figure 5-19.   *Headings in a mirrored layout*

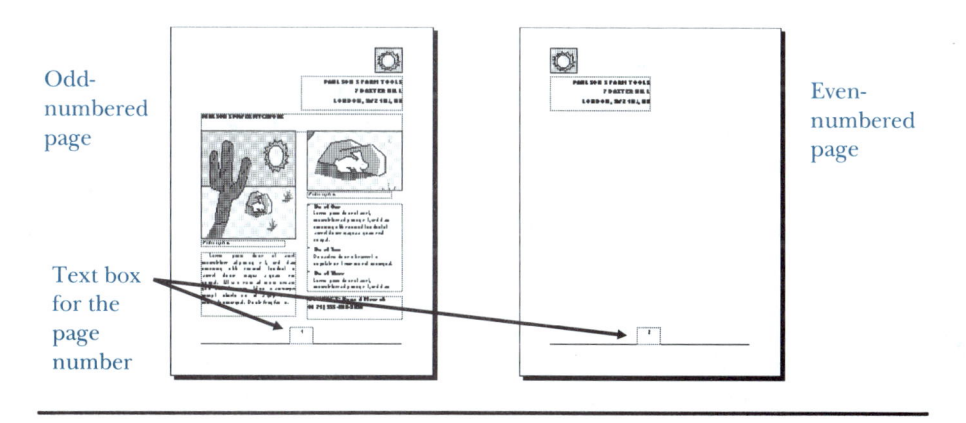

Odd-numbered page

Even-numbered page

Text box for the page number

text as well. If you create a page marker before activating the mirrored guides option, Publisher automatically copies it to the left page in a mirrored location.

Use the PRODINFO.PUB template to create page markers. If you haven't done so already, start a new publication using that template (if you've already been working with it while reading through earlier parts of this section, don't reload it, just continue adding to the publication with this exercise). Go to the background page and create a Text frame about 1/2 inch square just above the bottom margin, as shown in Figure 5-19. Then select Insert Page Numbers from the Page menu. Publisher inserts the page marker (#) in the frame, as shown here:

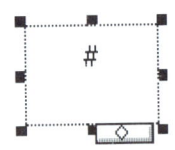

You may need to switch to Actual Size view in order to see it. Then switch back to the foreground. Publisher replaces the page marker with the correct page number on each foreground page.

Note

Since this page marker was created after you invoked mirrored guides, it will only appear on the corresponding foreground pages. You'd have to copy it to the other background page in order to see it in all pages of the publication.

Page markers only display or print Arabic numerals. If you want additional text, such as the word "Page" or dashes around the number, you must enter it yourself. Text frames that contain page markers are no different from other Text frames in a publication. You can treat the page marker itself just like any other text character. You can format and edit the frame and the characters in the frame using the same tools and commands that you normally would. Refer to Chapter 4 for more information about working with frames, and to Chapters 6 and 7 for more information on editing and formatting text.

Tip

Publisher normally begins numbering the pages in a publication on page 1 with the number 1. You can, however, cause it to begin with a different starting number. Select Settings from the Options menu. Enter a new starting page number, and click on OK.

The publication will now start with the new number, and each successive page will increment by 1.

> **How to Create Page Numbers**
>
> 1. Select Page from the Menu bar and select Go to Background from the Page menu.
> 2. Create a Text frame (or select an existing one) at the location where you want page numbers to print.
> 3. Select Page from the Menu bar and select Insert Page Numbers from the Page menu.
> 4. Add, edit, or format the page marker and any other text in the frame.

Working with the Publisher Screen

Publisher contains a number of visual aids to help you with your work. The remainder of this chapter discusses each of them. The visual aids of this kind available in Publisher are most powerful when used in concert. For example, repositioning the rulers is usually more effective with a magnified view. Experimentation is the best way to learn how to use these features effectively.

Switching Views

Normally Publisher displays the image of an entire page. If you're editing text or working on small-sized details, it's helpful to zoom in on a section of the current page in order to make it easier to see. On the other hand, getting a sense of how things fit together as a whole requires a view of the full page. Publisher lets you choose from eight different levels of magnification called *views*. For example, actual size, shown in Figure 5-20, is very useful for editing text. Changing your view of the page has no effect on the publication. If you select an object before you switch to one of the more magnified views, Publisher centers the new view around the section of the page that contains the object.

Positioning an object becomes easier when you're using the appropriate view. As you work more with Publisher, you'll find different applications for each of them. Never hesitate to try another view if you're having trouble seeing or positioning objects. It only takes a second. The following table describes which portion of the page Publisher displays for each view.

View	Displays
Full	Entire page
25%	3/4 page
33%	2/3 page
50%	1/2 page
66%	1/3 page
75%	1/4 page
Actual	Actual size
200%	Double the actual size

Figure 5-20.   A page in Actual Size view

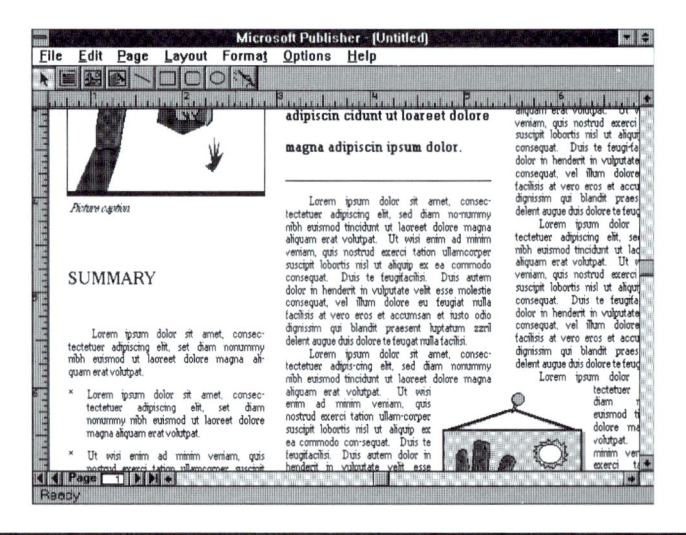

Chapter 5: *All About Page Layout* 155

Tip — **F9** *switches between Actual Size view and the last view you selected from the Page menu. If you haven't selected anything other than Full Page view during the current session, then that is the last view. Use* **PGUP** *and* **PGDN** *to scroll up and down the page in Actual Size view.*

> ### How to Switch Views
>
> 1. If you're going to switch to a more magnified view, select the object(s) you want to look at.
> 2. Select Page from the Menu bar and select one of the eight views.
> 3. Use the vertical and horizontal scroll bars or the scroll boxes to move around the page.

Working with Rulers

Publisher has vertical and horizontal rulers at the top and left side of the scratch area on the screen. The rulers are extremely helpful in positioning objects and measuring distances. You can move the rulers—separately or together—to any location on the screen in any of the views. You can also change the appearance of their tic marks in several ways. This makes dealing with even the smallest of measurements extremely easy.

Moving the Rulers

The more you use rulers the more you'll like them. This section gives you a little tour of the possibilities. Try this exercise:

- Start a new publication using the REPORT.PUB template.
- Move the vertical ruler next to the picture in the left column. Just point to the ruler until you see the double-headed arrow (⇔) appear, as shown in Figure 5-21, and drag the ruler over to the Picture frame. It's a lot easier to measure the size of a frame when the ruler is next to it.

- Now point to the intersection of the two rulers and wait until you see the diagonal double-headed arrow (⤢). The diagonal arrow indicates that both rulers are ready to move together.
- Drag both rulers so that they frame the upper-left corner of the other picture in the publication, as shown on the right in Figure 5-21. Then drag them back to the upper-left corner of the Publisher screen.

You can move the rulers together or separately at any time. If they get in your way, just move them back to the edge of the scratch area. Rulers have no effect on the content or appearance of a publication.

Figure 5-21.   *Moving the rulers*

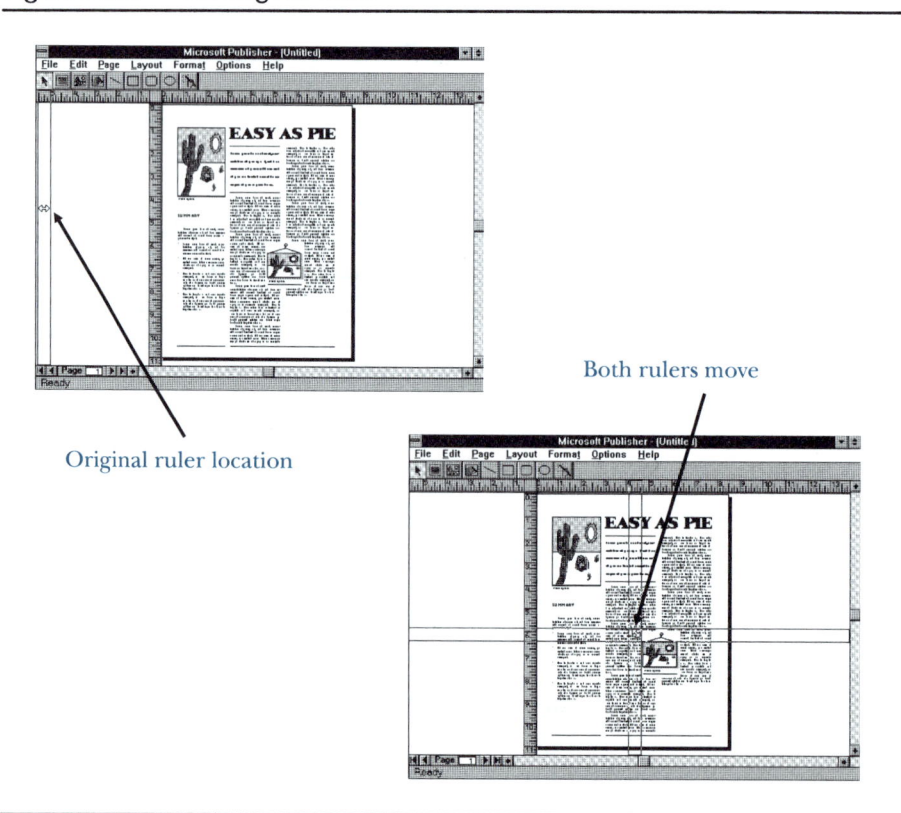

Original ruler location

Both rulers move

Chapter 5: *All About Page Layout* 157

> ### How to Move the Rulers
>
> 1. Point to the ruler you want to move, or to their intersection if you want to move both of them, and wait until the pointer changes to a double-headed arrow.
>
> 2. Drag the ruler(s) to the new location and release the mouse button.

Resetting the Ruler Tic Marks

Publisher normally aligns the zero marks of both rulers at the upper-left corner of the page area. Moving one or both of the zero marks makes it easier to measure object sizes and distances on the page.

- Click on the picture in column 1 and switch to Actual Size view.
- Drag the ruler down to the top edge of the picture. Currently it's not so easy to tell the width of the picture because the Picture frame begins and ends at awkward locations on the horizontal ruler.
- Now point to the left edge of the Picture frame so that the hairline on the ruler is aligned with it, and move the pointer onto the ruler.
- When the double-headed arrow appears, click the *right* mouse button. The location of the zero mark moves to the location of the pointer, and it's easy to see the width of the frame, as shown here:

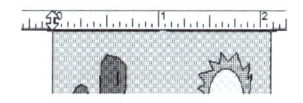

The tic marks can be moved on either of the rulers separately or both of the rulers at once. You control the new location for the zero mark by where you point on the ruler itself. You can also reset the tic marks to their original location. The location of the ruler on the screen and the zero marks on the ruler operate independently of each other.

Publisher also lets you change the unit of measure that appears on the rulers. When you change the unit of measure, it has no effect on the publication. Publisher automatically converts the size of existing objects to the new scale. You can switch between inches, centimeters, picas (6 per inch), and points (72 per inch). While inches or centimeters may seem more familiar when you begin using Publisher, points and picas are more common in the publishing world. Typefaces and line heights, for example, are always described in points. To change the unit of measure that appears on the rulers, select Settings from the Options menu. Then click on the Measurement window and select the new unit of measure from the list.

How to Set the Ruler Tic Marks

1. Point to the location on one of the rulers where you want the zero mark to appear, and wait until the pointer changes to the double-headed arrow. If you want to change the zero marks for both rulers, point to their intersection.
2. Click the *right* mouse button.
3. To reset both zero marks to their original location, point to the intersection of the rulers and double-click the *left* button.

Display Options for Rulers

Publisher provides Hide/Show and Snap options for rulers as well as layout guides. These commands operate as toggles. Each time you select a toggle you either turn it on or off, depending on its previous state. If a toggle is in effect, it appears on the Options menu with a check mark to its left, or its opposite name appears. For example, Hide Rulers may appear on the Options menu instead of Show Rulers. If no check mark appears, the toggle is currently disabled. Toggles can be turned on or off at any time during a Publisher session.

Hide/Show Rulers simply turns their display on or off. Turning them off makes more display room available on the Publisher screen. Snap to Rulers causes the tick marks on the ruler to become "sticky". If you're creating a frame, the crosshair will tend to pause slightly as it passes slowly over tic marks

Chapter 5: *All About Page Layout* 159

on the rulers. This makes it easy to align the starting and ending locations exactly with a ruler mark. If you're moving or resizing a frame, the same effect occurs with the boundaries of the frame—they pause when they pass by one of the tic marks. Snap doesn't make it impossible to place objects between marks, just easier to place objects in alignment with them. Hide/Show and Snap operate independently of each other (Snap will work even if the rulers are hidden).

Tip

You can also toggle Snap for layout guides, as explained earlier in this chapter under "Page Margins and Layout Guides." You cannot use Snap for both guides and rulers at the same time.

To Change the Display Options for Rulers

Select Options from the Menu bar and select Snap to Rulers or Hide/Show Rulers from the Options menu.

Other Screen Display Options

Publisher has three other Hide/Show toggles to help you in your work. Like their counterparts for layout guides and rulers described earlier in this chapter, they can be changed at any time, and have no effect on the content of a publication. Hide/Show Pictures suppresses or displays the content of any Picture frames. When pictures are hidden, Publisher redraws the screen much more quickly. On pages with complex or numerous graphics this can be a real time saver, especially if you change views frequently. Hide/Show Boundaries suppresses or displays the outline of any frames (Text, Picture, or WordArt). When frames have borders, these outlines are covered anyway, and this option does not affect their display. Since boundaries do not print, hiding frame boundaries helps to display your publication as it will appear on paper. Finally, Hide/Show Status line lets you control the appearance of the Status line at the bottom of the screen. When the Status line is hidden, there is more space available on the Publisher screen.

Review

Having a sound design for layout is the key to a successful publication, and creating one is a primary skill for page designers. Similarly, proceeding with an application before you establish a good layout will probably lead to frustration and lost time. Publisher provides a number of tools to help you develop a sound layout easily.

- Page size, paper size, and page orientation let you control a publication's dimensions. Your options in working with these factors may be limited by your printing equipment.
- Publisher has a unique feature called *publication type* that makes it easy to develop and print book- and card-style publications.
- Setting layout and margin guides can make it easy to create and position frames and graphics. Their appearance alone provides a strong visual reference during design. The Snap option takes the frustration out of precision placement and makes aligning multiple objects in a common format simple.
- Publisher accommodates multiple-page publications. Once a layout is established, it is echoed on every page and on new pages when they are added.
- Layouts can be mirrored for publications with facing pages.
- The background page lets you establish frames and/or graphics that repeat on every page of a publication. The background page can be suppressed for individual pages.
- The rulers can be moved and their starting points reset to any location on the screen in order to facilitate measuring distances. Snap can also be enabled for the ruler marks as an alternative guide for locating objects with precision.
- Views of the page with varying levels of magnification are available for dealing with different design issues. You can also get an on-screen preview of a publication's final printed appearance.

6

Creating Text

Publishers refer to the text for a publication as *copy*. Copy applies to everything in a publication from the name and address on a business card to the headlines and stories in a newspaper or the pitch in an advertisement. In Publisher, you use Text frames and WordArt frames to manage copy.

You can use Text frames for almost any kind of copy. They easily accommodate the lengthy amounts of text required in applications such as reports, newsletters, or catalogs. They can be used for everything from headlines to multipage articles. You can format the copy in a Text frame similarly to the way you might format text with a word processor. For example, Publisher supports common paragraph alignments like centering or justification, and the characters in Text frames can use all of the typefaces available on your printer.

WordArt frames, on the other hand, are more appropriate for small blocks of text when you want to dress up a publication with special visual effects. You can create oversized letters up to 14 inches in height or use offbeat styles, such as curved or angled headlines. WordArt is one of Publisher's unique features. Its special effects will operate with most modern printers. Text and WordArt frames can be blended together or used separately.

This chapter explains all of the ways you can affect copy inside of a Text frame. The topics covered include entering, editing, importing, and correcting text, and connecting Text frames. The chapter assumes that you are already comfortable with the fundamentals of working with frames—creating, moving, resizing, and so on. If you are not, refer to Chapter 4 for more details. Frame basics are predominantly the same for all types of frames. Chapter 7 discusses text formatting, and Chapter 8 deals with all aspects of WordArt.

Wherever feasible, sections in this chapter include examples that let you practice and experiment with a specific task. Some of the examples use files other than the Publisher templates. Occasionally you may not be able to find a file that's referenced in an example. Don't let it frustrate you—it's impossible to anticipate what every reader's computer has on it. In these cases do your best to find a substitute. If you feel comfortable with a topic but need a summary or a reminder about how to execute it, you can find generic instructions for tasks in a box at the end of many sections.

Where Copy Fits in Your Work Flow

In creating a publication, you should develop a general routine for working with copy. While the sequence of steps in the routine may be informal, it should give you a good sense of how to go about the job. Choices that you make about copy and pictures are more flexible than those that you make about a publication's page layout. Individual frames can be—and often are—modified during development without affecting the layout of an entire publication. Text-oriented frames may have more impact on the composition of a publication than Picture frames, simply because of the quantity of copy that must be accommodated. Pictures, on the other hand can be scaled and/or cropped to adjust for space without losing their content. The weight of each of these factors varies, of course, on the nature of the publication. As with most projects, try to tackle the aspects that influence the overall design first. Make sure that you have the page layout for a publication established before you begin to add copy. If you are unfamiliar with page layout, see Chapter 5 for more information. Then consider the following methodology for adding copy to a publication.

Chapter 6: *Creating Text*   163

1. *Create the major frames.* Think about why you're going to use each frame. Get a general idea how many frames you'll need and where you want them to appear on the pages. You should add Picture frames at this point too. Create as many of the important frames as possible to see how they will fit together. This can be especially important in a multipage publication where the number of pages may vary depending on the frame placement and design you use. In the sample newsletter in Figure 6-1, for example, the headline "Ornaments" (WordArt), the four columns of copy (text), the minor headline "WINTER 1991" (text), and the illustration of the globe (picture) are the building blocks of the page. The other frames are embellishments. Even in simpler projects, there are always essential and nonessential components.

2. *Get the copy.* Whether you type copy into Publisher yourself or bring it in from another program, you've got to place it in the publication before you can deal with its appearance. You must type in the copy for any WordArt frames (they can only accommodate about 250 characters anyway). While you can enter lengthy copy in

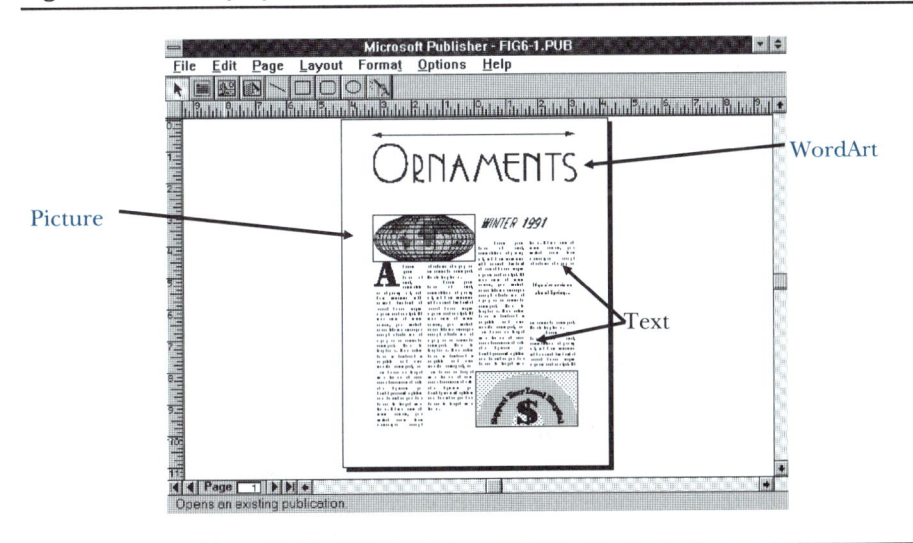

Figure 6-1. Major frames on a page

a Text frame, it is much easier to do so with a word processor and import its text files directly into Publisher. If you're including long text files, you'll probably need to flow the text across multiple frames and pages, so some additional frame design may be needed after you've brought the copy into Publisher. Try to work with files that have already been edited and are in their final version.

3. *Format the copy.*   After page layout, formatting is the second major task in publication design. Besides being an essential ingredient in the look of a publication, it can change the size requirements for frames and, in turn, the number of pages. Getting the copy (step 2) is just a preliminary for the design challenge of formatting it.

4. *Tune the publication.*   Publisher provides you with some powerful tools for refining the copy in Text frames—spelling, hyphenation, and global search/replace—once the publication is close to complete. It's easy to lose a character or two from a simple keyboard error during formatting. The spelling program lets you perform a final check for these kinds of errors. Hyphenation can tighten up the amount of text that fits in a frame and eliminate unnecessary white space that may be unsightly. The Search and Replace utilities let you make last minute global changes quickly.

Getting the Word Around

You can get words into a Text frame in two ways: type them in or copy them. With short blocks of text such as headlines or picture captions, the simplest approach is to type the words directly into a Text frame. While you can enter lengthy blocks of text, it is much easier to do so with a program designed especially for editing, such as a word processor, because its editing capabilities are so much more powerful. You can then import its files directly into Publisher. Large files may require more than a single page in order to display completely. When you need more than one page for a single file, Publisher lets you connect two or more Text frames so the same file flows between them. Connecting frames is the only way to spread text from a single source across multiple pages. From time to time you may also want to use the

Chapter 6: *Creating Text*

material from a publication in another program, or convert it from one file format to another. Publisher has options for saving text in a variety of popular file formats. This section discusses all of these aspects of manipulating text.

Entering and Editing Text

As soon as you select an empty Text frame, the insertion point appears at the top, as shown in Figure 6-2. To begin entering copy in an empty Text frame, just start typing. The insertion point behaves exactly as it does in a Windows field. It shows where the next character you type will appear on the screen. Like most word processing programs, Publisher Text frames have *word wrap*—if a line that you type ends in the middle of a word, Publisher automatically moves the entire word to the beginning of the next line, where typing continues. Only press (ENTER) if you want to begin a new paragraph.

Typing always occurs in *insert mode*. If there are any characters to the right of the insertion point, Publisher pushes them along in the frame to make room for the new ones that you type. If you want to make corrections to individual characters, use (BACKSPACE) or (DELETE) to remove characters and

Figure 6-2.   An empty Text frame

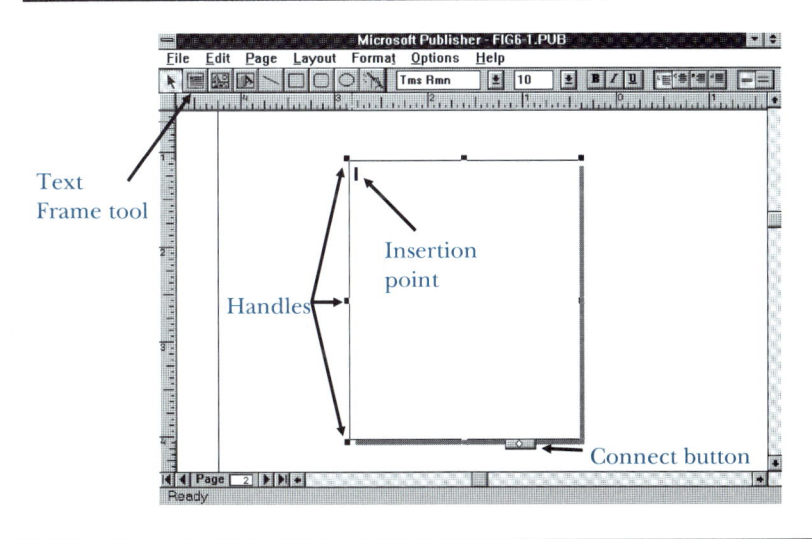

type new ones to replace them. If you need to reposition the insertion point for a correction, just point to the new location and click or use one of the cursor-movement keys.

Selecting Text

To edit a block of text that is longer than a single character—a word, phrase, sentence, paragraph, or even an entire file—you must first *select* it. If you're used to working with Windows or any of the other Microsoft products that incorporate text processing, Publisher's features will seem very familiar. If you're not, take a few minutes to familiarize yourself with the basics. Use the Publisher template BROCHURE.PUB for some practice. Start a new publication using it now and select the Text frame in the upper right of the cover page that reads "THE DA VINCI SCHOOL OF ARTS AND CRAFTS." Change your view to Actual Size before continuing (you'll almost always prefer to edit text in actual size because the characters are so much more legible). Select the word "SCHOOL" by double-clicking on it. Your screen should look like this:

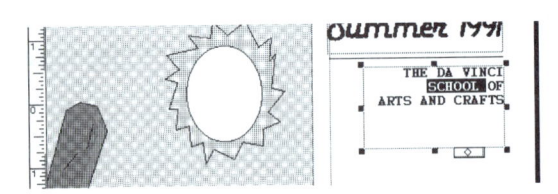

Now delete the word by selecting Delete Text from the Edit menu. Then type **INSTITUTE**, and remember to include a space at the end. Congratulations! You're on your way to becoming a great editor!

All text editing in Publisher follows the same sequence of actions: select the material that you want to change, and then execute a command to change it. Double-clicking selects a word and the single blank space following it. To select larger blocks of text, drag the pointer across the characters you want to affect. Select the words "AND CRAFTS" on the next line by pointing to space immediately to the left of the *A* and dragging the cursor over to the *S*. Your screen should now look like this:

Chapter 6: *Creating Text* 167

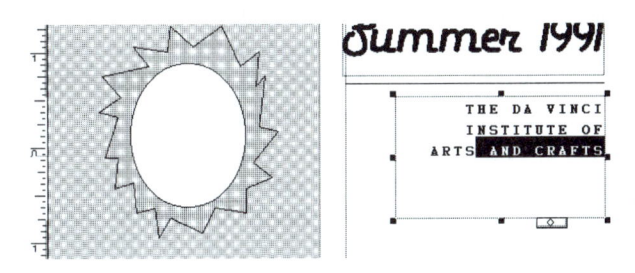

Press DEL (that's the keyboard shortcut for Delete Text) to delete the words you selected. Then click on the *A* at the beginning of the line and type **FINE** to change the name of the institution to FINE ARTS (remember to include a space at the end). The same technique works when you want to select (or delete) any amount of text in a single frame. Point to the first character of the block and then drag to the last. If you select the wrong text or change your mind about a selection, just click somewhere else in the frame. Publisher then clears the selection and displays the insertion point.

Publisher has a shortcut for selecting all of the text in a frame and any of the frames connected to it. You'll find this useful for getting rid of text in a hurry and for certain kinds of formatting. Click on the Text frame containing the topics for the brochure in the lower right of the page and select Highlight Story from the Edit menu. Publisher highlights all of the text in the frame, as shown here:

Highlighting an entire story and deleting it lets you retain the frame structure but remove the text. This is a convenient way to change the articles in a newsletter without altering the layout, for example. Highlight Story also selects the text in frames connected to the frame you first give the command in. The section later in this chapter on connecting frames discusses the effects of this in more detail.

Tip: *The keyboard shortcut for Highlight Story is* CTRL-A. *You can also select smaller blocks of text (by the word, by the paragraph, and so on) using keyboard shortcuts. If you are currently typing, the keyboard can be more efficient than picking up the mouse. When you hold down* SHIFT, *the insertion point becomes anchored in the same way as when you click and hold the mouse button. Once the insertion point is anchored, use* ↑, ↓, ←, *and* → *to extend the selection in any direction. There are some faster ways to position the insertion point using the keyboard detailed in Appendix D.*

Cut, Paste, and Copy

Cut and Paste let you move text. Copy and Paste let you duplicate it. Both Cut and Copy send words to the Windows Clipboard. From the Clipboard you can paste text to different parts of the current publication, to other publications, or to other Windows applications. Remember, however, that the Clipboard only holds one selection at a time, the one you most recently cut or copied there. If you intend to paste text, do it right after you cut or copy it. Otherwise you may inadvertently overwrite the selection on the Clipboard.

Before you can cut or copy text, you must first select it. Any amount of text—a character, word, sentence, paragraph, story, or anything in between—can be cut or copied. The selection techniques discussed in the previous section will work handsomely with either command. Once you've selected the text you want to work with, execute Cut or Copy from the Edit menu to send the selection to the Clipboard. To paste text from the Clipboard, click on a Text frame and position the insertion point where you want the material to begin in the frame. When you execute Paste from the Edit menu, Publisher places the contents of the Clipboard in its entirety in the frame beginning at that location.

Now try some of these editing techniques.

- Start a new publication using CATALOG.PUB and turn to page 2.
- Click on the Text frame in the lower-right corner of the frame and select the two-column list from the middle of the paragraph, as shown in Figure 6-3.
- To copy the list to the Clipboard, select Copy text from the Edit menu.

Chapter 6: *Creating Text* 169

Figure 6-3. *Copying a block of text*

- Click on the frame in the beginning of column 1. Click at the very beginning of the first line, and then insert the list at the top of the frame by selecting Paste from the Edit menu. The remainder of the text in the frame is pushed along to make room for the list. If you need more practice, try another edit. You can always reload the template if you want to start again with a clean slate.

If there isn't enough room left in the frame to accommodate all of the text after you Paste, Publisher displays the message shown in Figure 6-4. Click on No. In these cases Publisher pushes the remainder of the text into the overflow area. See the section later in this chapter on linking frames and the overflow area for more information on how Publisher deals with these situations.

If you make an error editing through Cut, Copy, Paste, or Delete, Undo will reverse the edit if you execute Undo immediately after the error.

Note

Figure 6-4.   *The Overflow message*

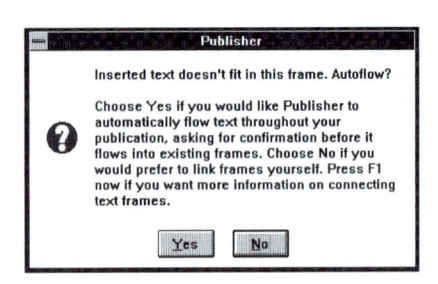

As you saw in the previous exercise, when you paste text into a frame that already contains some, Publisher normally preserves the original text in the frame. You can, however, elect to overwrite the old material with the text that you're pasting. For example, try this:

- Turn to page 3 of the catalog and cut all of the text for ORDER INFORMATION from the frame in the upper-left corner.
- Click on the adjacent Text frame to the right and select all of the text in that frame.
- Click on Settings from the Options menu and look at the Settings dialog box, shown here:

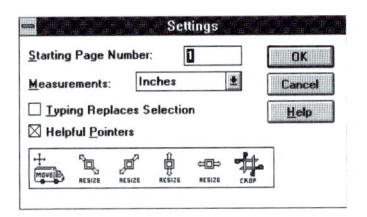

- Click on the button for Typing Replaces Selection to turn it on and click on OK.
- Finally, execute the paste. Publisher replaces the text that previously occupied the frame with the incoming material. This option can be

Chapter 6: Creating Text

useful for deleting text quickly, but you should use it sparingly. When you work with this option enabled, you can lose text very easily.

Tip

All of the editing commands have keyboard equivalents. DEL (Delete), CTRL-C (Copy), CTRL-X (Cut), and CTRL-V (Paste) can all save time, especially for work that occurs within a single frame because your hands may be on the keyboard already.

You can paste material into other publications using the same approach that you did here. For example, if you still have the ORDER INFORMATION block on the Clipboard, start a new publication using a blank page now. Then create a Text frame, and execute the paste. The block from the catalog should appear in the new publication. Always try to reuse material that is on hand if you're in a hurry.

How to Edit Text

1. Click on a Text frame.
2. Click next to a character to position the insertion point, or select the text that you want to change.
3. Select Edit from the Menu bar.
4. Select Delete, Cut, or Copy from the Edit menu.
5. To move or copy the text, click on another Text frame and/or location in a Text frame.
6. Select Edit from the Menu bar.
7. Select Paste from the Edit Menu.

Text and Other Applications

Publisher accepts text from a variety of sources besides the keyboard. You can transfer part or all of a file from Windows- or DOS-based applications into a publication. You must place the text that you add to a publication from an outside source in a Text frame, just like the text that you type. The frame can be empty, or it may already contain text from another source. Similarly, you can use the text from a publication in other applications.

Exchanging Text with Windows Applications

If you want to incorporate text from a Windows program in one of your publications, just copy it to the Windows Clipboard, and then paste it into a Text frame as you would normally. Most Windows applications contain an Edit menu with options for Cut, Copy, and Paste, just like Publisher. The Notepad and Write accessories that come with Windows, for example, both support these options. Computer environments tend to vary, especially outside of a single application such as Publisher, so it's difficult to provide you with a concrete example for this feature. Any suggestion for a program or file to practice on might not exist on your system.

In general, start the program and open the file that contains the text you want to paste into a publication. Then select the text that you want to include, and copy (or cut) it. While it's impossible to say for sure that the process will be the same in the other application, selecting, cutting, and copying text is very similar for all Windows applications. Switch back to Publisher using the Windows Task List or by clicking on the Publisher window. Select the Text frame that you want to paste the text into, and position the insertion point as you would normally to paste text using Publisher. Finally, paste it.

Note

When you copy text from any application to the Clipboard, it becomes compatible with Publisher immediately. You don't need to perform any further conversion in order to use it in Publisher.

If you want to export text to another Windows application, just use Copy (or Cut) to send it to the Clipboard, and then insert it in the other program. Virtually all Windows applications that contain text processing facilities have a Paste option on their Edit menu. If the other application does not contain a paste option, consult the manual for that software.

How to Exchange Text with Other Windows Programs

1. Use the Windows Program Manager to start Publisher and a second Windows application. The program that contains the text you copy is the *source*. The one that you insert the text into is the *destination*, or *target*.

2. Select text from the source using standard techniques. Selecting material by dragging the pointer across the text works in most Windows programs, including Publisher. In addition, different applications may have keyboard shortcuts for making a selection.

3. Copy (or cut) the selection to the Windows Clipboard. Use either command from the Edit menu of the source application, or use one of the keyboard shortcuts.

4. Switch to the target application either through the Windows Task List or by clicking on the appropriate window. If you intend to include the text in an existing file, open the file as well.

5. Position the insertion point (or a similar tool such as the cell cursor in a spreadsheet program) at the location where you want the incoming text to appear.

6. Select Paste from the Edit menu, or use the appropriate keyboard shortcut to insert the text in the destination program.

Exchanging Text with Non-Windows Programs

Publisher understands how to read files in a number of popular DOS formats that appear in the following list. If you want to use text from an application not included in this list, refer to the User Guide for that application for instructions on how to convert the text to ASCII file format and import the material as plain text. Almost all modern applications support some utility for converting text to ASCII.

Plain Text (ANSI format for Windows)
Plain Text (DOS) (ASCII format for DOS)
RTF (Rich Text Format)
MS Works
Word for DOS
WordPerfect 5.0 - 5.1
Wordstar 3.3 - 5.5

Once Publisher recognizes a format for the text that you want to import, incorporating it into a publication is easy. The source of the material doesn't really matter. You only need to know how to use Publisher. For example, begin a new publication using a blank page. Then create a Text frame that matches the guides for the default page margins. Next, select Import Text from the File Menu. Publisher displays the Import Text dialog box as shown in Figure 6-5.

Normally, Publisher displays its own files in the file window (those with a .PUB file extension). You can change the selection in the file window by clicking on the file types list and selecting an alternative. In this case, open the list and click on plain text. The list in the file window should change to display files with a .TXT file extension. If your screen looks different, you may have to change drives or directories. The Files window should now display the following choices.

Figure 6-5.   *Import Text dialog box*

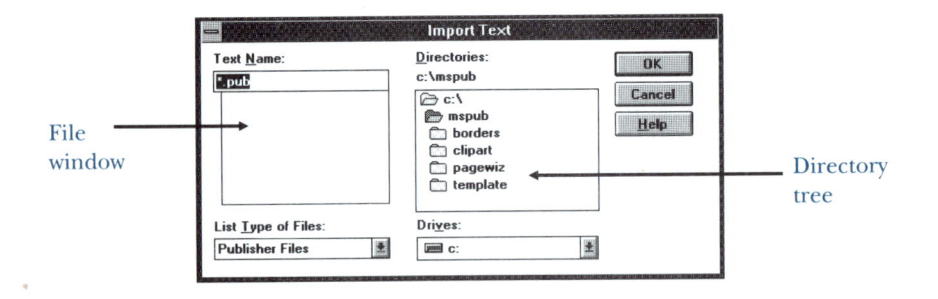

Chapter 6: *Creating Text* 175

```
PROFILE.TXT
CENTURY.TXT
README.TXT
```

Click on PROFILE.TXT, and a file of text should fill the frame that you created, as shown in Figure 6-6.

Note

This file is composed of dummy text. In this case it's written in an archaic language, but sometimes may even be pure gibberish. Dummy text is generally known in the advertising and publishing trade as greek. *Normally, of course, you would use your own material.*

You can combine imported text with other material in a Publisher Text frame in the same way. Just position the insertion point at the location that you want the imported text to begin. For example, move the cursor up two lines to the beginning of the last paragraph. Select Import Text from the File menu. Unfortunately, Publisher doesn't remember your last choice for file type. Click on the File Type list, and select Plain Text again. Then double-click

Figure 6-6. PROFILE.TXT *imported*

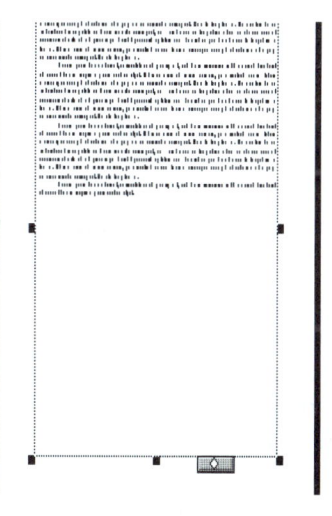

on CENTURY.TXT. Publisher appends the text from the new file to text in the frame.

> ### How to Import Text from a Non-Windows Program
>
> 1. Click on the Text frame into which you want to import text. If necessary, position the insertion point at the location in the frame where you want the incoming text to begin.
> 2. Select Import Text from the File menu. If necessary, switch to the drive or directory where the incoming file is stored.
> 3. Click on the list of files and select a file format or application program for the incoming text.
> 4. In the File window, double-click on the name of the file.

Publisher also lets you copy text out of a publication and use it in other application programs. If you have one of the versions of Word, WordPerfect, or WordStar that Publisher supports, try saving some material in the appropriate format during the following exercise. Use the plain text (ASCII) option as an alternative if there is a different word processor in your environment (just as most programs can export ASCII, they can also import it). Start a new publication using the RESUME.PUB template. You're going to export the text into the large Text frame in the center of the page, as shown in Figure 6-7.

- Click on the primary frame and select all of the text inside of it.
- Select Save As from the File menu. The Save As dialog box appears, as shown in Figure 6-8.
- Type **SAMPLETR** for the filename and click on the Save Selection As button. This indicates to Publisher that you want to save the content of a frame rather than the entire publication. Publisher appends the appropriate file extension based on the file type for the program you select.
- Click on the file type list and select the file format or program that you want to export the material to. Make a mental note of the drive

Chapter 6: *Creating Text* 177

Figure 6-7. RESUME.PUB

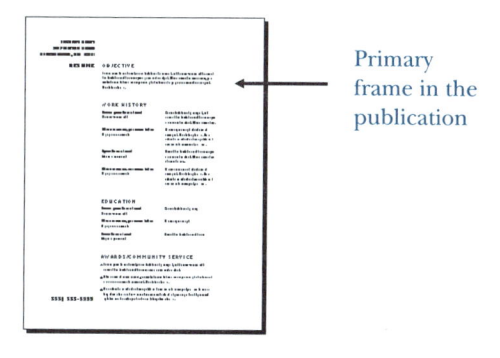

Primary frame in the publication

and directory that appear in the dialog box, because this is where Publisher will save the exported file. Change them now, if necessary.

- Click on OK. Publisher displays a moving bar chart showing its progress in converting the file and returns to the Publisher screen.
- Use the Windows Program Manager or Task List to switch to your word processing program, and load the file. Remember, you may have to change directories in order to find it.

Figure 6-8. Save As dialog box

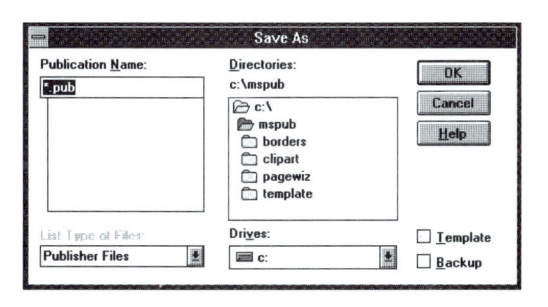

This feature can be useful for several purposes. You may simply want to include some material from a publication in another document that you created. On the other hand, some organizations require a higher quality of print reproduction than may be available in-house. In these instances, you may need to prepare a *copy sheet* for a commercial printer. A copy sheet simply contains all of the text for a publication with no special formatting or appearance. Exporting text to a word processor can help you to prepare a copy sheet quickly and save you the time it would take to input the text again. You may simply want to convert text from one file format to another. For example, someone may have written an article for your newsletter using Wordstar, but you want to edit it using WordPerfect. By importing the file—as described earlier—in one format and exporting it in another, Publisher makes it easy to convert the file from one format to another. The same file formats are available for import and export.

How to Export Text to a Non-Windows Program

1. Click on the Text frame from which you want to export text. Then select the specific text that you want to export.
2. Select Save As from the File menu. If necessary, switch to the drive or directory where you want to store the outgoing file.
3. Click on the Save Selection As button to enable it.
4. Click on the list of files and select a file format or application program for the outgoing text.
5. Click on the Publication Name field and enter a filename for the outgoing text and click on OK.

Connecting Text

Sometimes there isn't enough room in a single Text frame to accommodate all of the text that you want to include. This often happens when you import or paste material from another application, especially if it is a large file. It can also be a function of the way you want to lay out the frames on a page. By design, you may want text and pictures to appear interspersed, and for text to *flow* between frames. For some applications you may want to begin text on one page and continue it on another. In all of these instances you must connect two or more Text frames. With Publisher, you can connect any number of frames in a publication. Publisher links together the text in connected frames as a single body called a *story*. No matter which frame you use to edit a story, you're always working on the same body of text, wherever it appears in a publication. Some of the possible effects appear in Figure 6-9.

For example, reducing the size of the first frame (or any frame other than the last) causes more text to flow into later frames. A deletion or addition to the text in an early frame affects the content in the later frames in the chain. This section discusses all of the effects of connecting frames and the procedures necessary to do so.

The Connect Button

Whenever you select a Text frame, its Connect button appears as a small shaded box on the left of the bottom boundary of the frame. The Connect button tells you about the current connections for the text in the frame. It can display three different symbols, as shown in Figure 6-10. The *ellipses* indicate that there is more text in a story, but the frame is not currently connected to a later frame in the publication (there may or may not be earlier

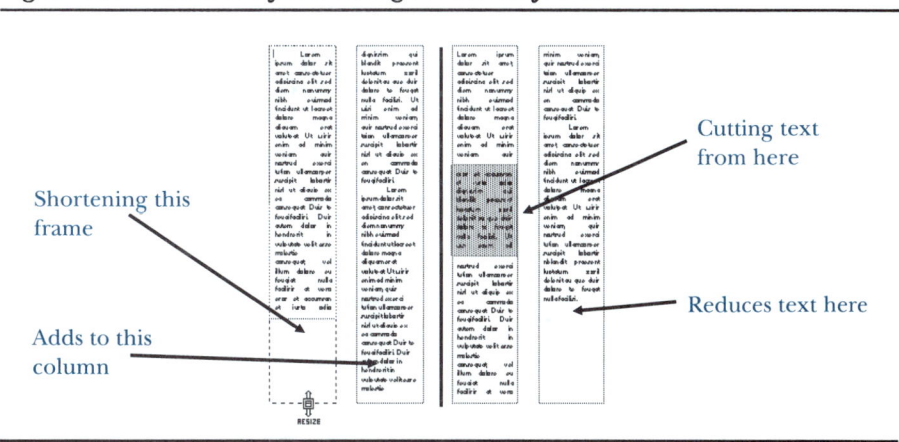

Figure 6-9.   How text flows through connected frames

frames in which the story started). When you see the ellipses, the remaining text for the story is currently in the overflow area, a temporary storage place for text from unconnected frames. The *connection arrows,* on the other hand, indicate that the story continues in at least one more frame.

The last of the three symbols is the endmark. Publisher displays the *endmark* on the last frame in a series of connected frames. When you see the endmark, there is no additional text for the story (it also appears on a single unconnected frame with no text in the overflow area). Connect button symbols may change as you work with Publisher to develop a publication. They always show the current state for any frame you select.

Autoflow

The easiest way to connect frames is to let Publisher do it for you. If you try to paste or import text into a frame that isn't large enough to display all of it, Publisher automatically shows the message displayed in Figure 6-11. When you click on No, Publisher places the remainder of the text for the story in the overflow area.

The overflow area can accommodate any amount of text from any number of stories (yes, it keeps all of the stories separate). It even holds text between editing sessions. There is no need to dispose of text in the overflow area or clean it up if you need to save your work or close Publisher. On the

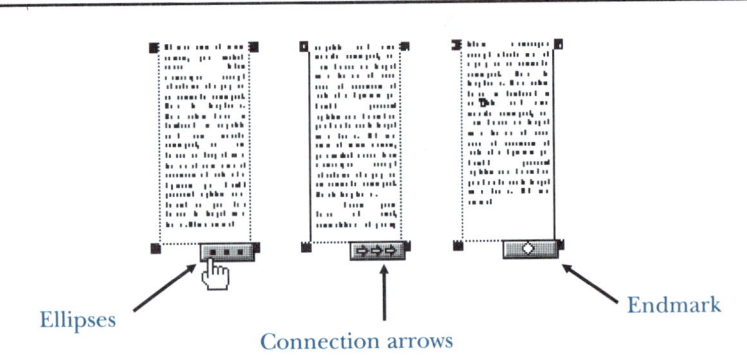

Figure 6-10.   Three ways that the Connect button can appear

Figure 6-11. *Autoflow message*

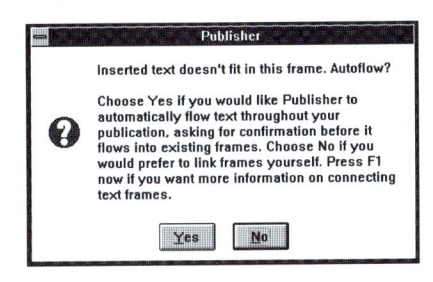

---

other hand, if you click on Yes when the Autoflow message appears, Publisher pauses at each empty Text frame in the publication, and displays this message:

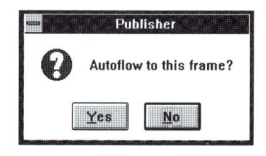

If you click on No, Publisher skips the frame and presents the same message at the next frame. If you click on Yes, the frame is filled, if possible.

This process continues until you have dealt with all empty frames in the publication. If more text remains in the story after Publisher has processed the last empty frame that you created, it creates as many frames as it needs to display the file in its entirety. The new frames appear one to a page and are a full page in size (they fit within the page margins for the publication you are working with). Publisher adds as many pages to the publication as it needs to accommodate all of the frames. Each of the frames that Publisher uses or creates with Autoflow is connected to the next. Autoflow processes a single story at a time.

If you haven't yet let Autoflow do the work for you, try this example.

- Start a new publication using a blank page and create a Text frame on the left side of the page as shown in Figure 6-12 on the left.

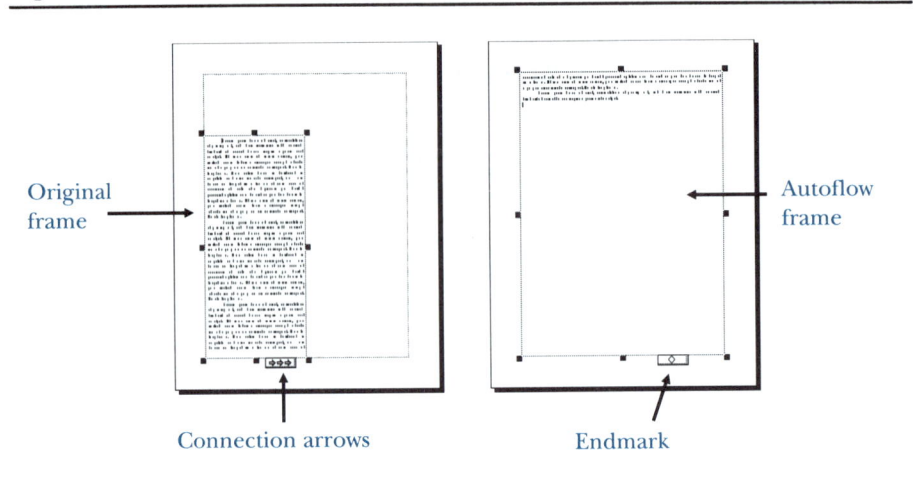

Figure 6-12.   *Working with Autoflow*

Original frame → [figure] ← Autoflow frame

Connection arrows — Endmark

- Select Import Text from the File menu, change the list of files to display Plain Text, and double-click on PROFILE.TXT (you must be in the MSPUB directory in order to locate the file).
- Publisher fills the frame you created and then presents the initial Autoflow message. Click on Yes. Publisher inserts a second page in the publication and creates a Text frame for it containing the balance of the story as shown in Figure 6-12. Notice that the frame on page 2 displays the endmark on the Connect button.
- Turn back to page 1 and click on the Text frame. Its Connect button displays the arrows, indicating that the story continues in at least one additional frame.

Connecting Frames Yourself

You can connect and disconnect the frames that hold a story at any time in a publication's development. In doing so, you control the flow of information in the piece. A story can flow in any direction around a single page or across multiple pages. Connect buttons and the overflow area make it easy to manage any number of stories. The best way to become familiar with connecting frames is by practicing.

Chapter 6: *Creating Text* 183

- Start a new publication with a blank page and create three Text frames, as shown here:

- Select the first frame on the left and import the dummy text called PROFILE.TXT (if necessary, see the previous section for instructions on importing a file).
- When the Autoflow message appears, click on No. Publisher fills the first frame on the page with the beginning of the story and places the remainder in the overflow area (notice that the Connect button in the first frame displays the ellipses).
- Point to the Connect button for the first frame. The pointer changes to the icon for an index finger, as shown in Figure 6-10.
- Click on the Connect button. The pointer changes to the icon for a pitcher. When you see the pitcher, Publisher expects you to *pour* text from the overflow area into a frame.
- Click on the middle frame, and the story flows into it, as shown here:

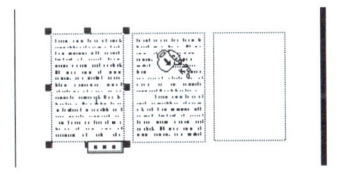

Repeat this process to connect the second frame on the page with the third. Click on the Connect button for frame 2, point the pitcher to frame 3, and then click on it. The remainder of the story appears there. Afterward, click on each of the frames and look at the Connect button. Frames 1 and 2 display the arrow marks to indicate that the text in each is connected. Frame 3 shows the endmark to indicate that it is the last frame in the series. Use the Save As command to store this publication under the name CONNECT. That way, if you make any unexpected errors while experimenting with frame connections in this section you can always return to this point by opening the publication again.

Tip: To track the sequence of frames that Publisher uses for a story, select one of the frames in the series and press CTRL-TAB. *Publisher selects the next frame that contains the story in the publication even if the frame is on a different page. Press* CTRL-TAB *again, and Publisher moves forward to the next frame in the series.* SHIFT-CTRL-TAB *makes Publisher track the frames in the opposite direction.*

When you disconnect a frame, the text that had appeared in it, and in any succeeding frames in the series, moves to the overflow area. The disconnected (empty) frames, however, remain in the publication. To disconnect a frame, click on the Connect button for the previous frame in the series. For example, click on the Connect button for frame 1. All succeeding frames clear. You disconnected frames 2 and 3 from the series, and sent the remainder of the story into the overflow area. You can now flow the text into another frame by clicking on it or click in some empty area of the page or scratch areas to cancel connecting. Of course, you can also create new frames and flow the text into them.

Note: When frames are connected, you can move them around the page area without affecting the flow of text between them. You can even move a connected frame to another page by dragging it to the scratch area. You cannot, however, use Cut and Paste without removing the frame from the series.

When you delete a frame from a series the story remains intact. If the frame is in the middle of the series the text that occupied it flows into the following frame. This effect *ripples* through all of the remaining frames in the series, and may move some of the text from the last frame into the overflow area. If you delete the last frame in a series, text goes into the overflow area immediately. Deleting the first frame in a series causes the story to begin in the next (second) frame, and a ripple effect also occurs: the text from the old frame 2 (new frame 1) flows into the old frame 3 (new frame 2), and so on throughout the series. Text from the last frame may be moved into the overflow area if there isn't sufficient room in the frame to accommodate it. When you delete pages that contain connected frames, the same effects occur based on where in the chain the frames were located.

Chapter 6: Creating Text

Tip

If you know that you're going to connect several frames with the same story, click on the right mouse button in the original frame. Then click normally on each of the frames that you want to connect. Publisher continues the flow through all of them until you cancel connecting by clicking in an empty part of the page or scratch areas.

If you need to work with newsletters, books, brochures, catalogs, or any elaborate multipage publication formats, spend some time experimenting with all of the ways in which frames interact. Feeling comfortable with these features is important when you work with complex design projects.

Tip

Highlight Story (from the Edit menu) can be a real time saver when you work with a series of connected frames. If you click on one of the frames in a series and then select Highlight Story, Publisher highlights all of the connected frames on the current page. When you Cut, Copy, or Delete a story using this option, the story is completely removed from the publication on all pages, but the Text frames remain in place.

How to Connect or Disconnect a Story Between Frames

1. Click on the Connect button for the previous frame in the series.
2. Click on the frame that you want to connect. To send text to the overflow area, click in an empty part of the scratch area.

Text Correction Tools

While Publisher is not meant to be a text processing program, it does provide several important text processing utilities found in modern word processors—spell checking, hyphenation, and global search/replace—to make working with text easier. For example, after adjusting paragraph alignment, text can often benefit from hyphenation. By tightening up the copy in a story, more characters appear on each line, and you can use the space in a publication more efficiently. You may also want to check the spelling of a word you've added or make sure that you haven't introduced any errors during your formatting work. It's easy to lose a character or two from a simple keyboarding mistake. Finally, the global search and replace functions let you locate text and make last minute changes easily. This can be especially useful in publications that contain several copy-heavy stories and multiple pages, such as brochures, catalogs, or newsletters.

Find and Replace

If you have done any word processing, you're probably familiar with both Find and Replace. These options are closely related to each other. Find (often called Search in other programs) lets you locate one or more characters anywhere in a Text frame and positions the insertion point at that location. Replace locates characters using Find and substitutes a different set of specified characters for them.

Using Find

Find is chiefly important for moving around a large publication quickly or for checking for the existence of a word or phrase in a story. For example, you might want to jump directly to the point in a story where you know that percentages are spelled out or that a parenthetical phrase was used. By searching for the % or (character, you can find what you're looking for easily. If there are no special characters to look for, you can enter a word, phrase, or sentence. You can also insist that the search be restricted to certain upper- and lowercase letters or other special characters.

Note

Find does not look through the overflow area! If you want to locate all occurrences of your entry, be sure that Publisher has displayed all of the text in the story.

The following paragraphs give you some practice with the Find options. To try them out, start a new publication using a blank page and create a single large Text frame that conforms to the standard margin guides. Then use Import Text to load the file README.TXT into the frame. When the Autoflow message appears, click on Yes. Publisher adds 11 pages to the publication in order to accommodate the file and positions you on the last page. Click on the Previous Page button to turn to page 11.

Chapter 6: *Creating Text* 187

Note

The README.TXT file should be in the main Publisher directory (MSPUB) on your system. You may have to change directories and/or drives in order to find it. If the file is missing or you can't find it, substitute another text file of your own for this exercise. If that is the case, you'll have to supply your own words for the searches as well.

Click on the Text frame on page 11 and make sure that the insertion point is at the very beginning of the frame. Find only operates in one direction at a time, starting at the location of the insertion point and searching forward or backward through the story. You should also switch to Actual View. Find works in any view you use, but it's difficult to see the text in broader views once Publisher locates it.

Select Find from the Edit menu. The Find dialog box appears, as shown here:

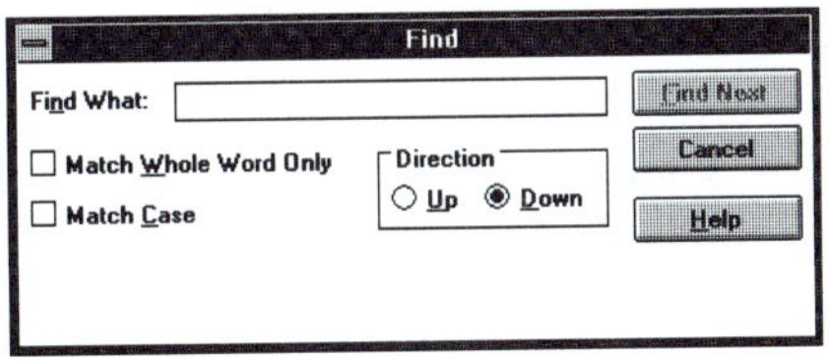

Type **WordArt** and click on Find Next. Publisher selects the first occurrence of "WordArt" on the page. In this instance, the word appears in all uppercase letters. Click on Find Next again. Publisher moves down the page and selects the next occurrence, this time spelled in both upper- and lowercase letters. Continue clicking on Find Next until you see this message:

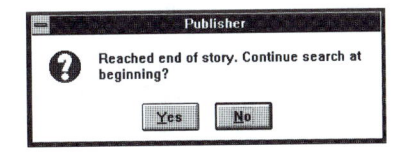

The first time that Publisher searches to the end of a story it asks if you want to start over at the beginning. If you began the search in the middle of the story, this is a handy way to cover all of the text without having to run the command again. In that case, the search would stop at the top of page 11. For now, click on No.

Now search back up the page. Click on the Up button in the Direction group, and then click on the Match Case button to enable it. These two settings cause Publisher to move back up the page, searching only for occurrences of "WordArt" with the same capitalization as the one you first entered. In this case, the versions with all uppercase or all lowercase letters get skipped over.

The other option button in the dialog box lets you restrict the scope of the search even further. For example, if you enter **Word** instead of **WordArt** and click on the button for Match Whole Words Only, Publisher skips instances of the letters *w-o-r-d* unless they have an empty space before the first letter and after the last. It will not, in this case, find "WordArt."

Publisher also has some special searching capabilities. You can look for carriage returns, wildcards, and other nonprinting characters. Whenever you press (ENTER), Publisher inserts a *carriage return* at the location of the insertion point. Carriage returns—while invisible—are what Publisher uses to separate one paragraph from another.

The *wildcard* character can stand for any character. It is handy for approximate searches if, for example, you're not sure how you spelled a word. The wildcard character is the question mark (?). Try searching through README.TXT for "?ord" and make sure that Match Case and Match Whole Word Only are turned *off*. Publisher finds words that begin with any letter followed by the letters *o-r-d*, such as "WordArt," "word," "border," "borders," and "order." The following list shows some of the other special characters that you can look for using Find.

^p	Carriage return
^t	Tab
^n	Forced line break
^w	White space (any combination of tabs, carriage returns, and spaces)
^?	Question mark

Note

If you select a block of text, Find only searches through the block. This can shorten the time required to complete a search. However, make sure that you do not have a block selected if you want to search throughout an entire story.

How to Find Text

1. Click on one of the frames that contains the story through which you want to search.
2. Select Edit from the Menu bar.
3. Select Find from the Edit menu.
4. Enter the text that you want to locate in the Find What field. Click on any of the option buttons to limit the scope or direction of the search.
5. Click on Find Next to search for successive occurrences of the text. You can alter any of the option settings each time that Publisher finds one of the matches.

Using Replace

Replace lets you substitute one group of characters for another. You can do so selectively throughout a story or have Publisher replace all instances of a group at once. This is particularly useful when the characters you want to replace occur frequently. For example, you might need to replace the reference to a day of the week because of a change in scheduling or the name of a character in a story. Replace can save you a lot of time in searching and typing. It has the added benefit of ensuring that all occurrences of the characters you're looking for get found. This isn't always the case when you try to make corrections by simply reading through a story.

Note

Undo works with Replace. When you select Undo immediately after a replacement session, Publisher reverses all of the replacements that it made since the command was last invoked.

Use the README.TXT file for some practice. If you haven't done so already, start a new publication using a blank page and create a single large Text frame that conforms to the standard margin guides. Then use Import Text to load the file README.TXT into the frame. When the Autoflow message appears, click on Yes. Publisher adds 11 pages to the publication in order to accommodate the file. Click on the First Page button.

Click on the Text frame on page 1 and make sure that the cursor is at the top of the frame. Then select Replace from the Edit menu. The Replace dialog box appears, as shown in Figure 6-13.

In order to replace characters you must first find them. The first half of Replace, consequently, operates just like Find. If you're not familiar with Find, refer to the previous section in this chapter for more information. You can use all of the Find options for matching characters when you execute the Replace command. Type **Publisher** in the Find What field, and then click on the Replace With field and type **Microsoft Publisher** in it. You're going to replace "Publisher" with "Microsoft Publisher."

> *Replace All is an extremely powerful command and can sometimes have unexpected and unwanted results. For example, if you type a word incorrectly in the Replace With field, the new error is introduced throughout the publication. Be careful. It's usually a better idea to review each replacement individually.*
>
> **Caution**

Click on Find Next. Publisher stops at the first occurrence of the word "Publisher." To make the change here, click on Replace. The next occurrence appears. To skip over this one and leave it as is, click on Find Next. Replace continues to move forward through the file, stopping at each occurrence of the word and giving you the option of replacing it or moving on to the next. Alternatively, you can click on Replace All. Publisher will stop asking you about individual occurrences and will make changes throughout the entire story.

Figure 6-13.   Replace dialog box

If you leave the Replace With field empty, Publisher simply removes the text specified in the Find What field. This is a handy way to make global deletions.

Tip

How to Find and Replace Text

1. Click on one of the frames that contains text you want to replace.
2. Select Edit from the Menu bar.
3. Select Replace from the Edit menu.
4. Enter the text that you want to replace in the Find What field. Click on any of the option buttons for matching to limit the scope of the search.
5. Click on the Replace With field and enter the text to substitute.
6. Click on Find Next to search for successive occurrences of the text you want to replace.
7. Click on Replace to make individual substitutions in each case or click on Replace All to have Publisher make substitutions throughout the file without confirmation.
8. Click on Cancel to terminate the session.

Hyphenation

The appearance of text can often be improved through hyphenation. Text that is fully justified can suffer in appearance from *rivers* of white space. Rivers occur because Publisher must spread words across a line in order to make them end exactly at the right margin, and this sometimes creates larger than desirable spaces between any two words as shown in Figure 6-14.

Text that is left aligned can also be smoothed along the right margin through hyphenation if it appears especially jagged. Publisher also lets you use hyphenation to check for the correct location at which to split an individual word.

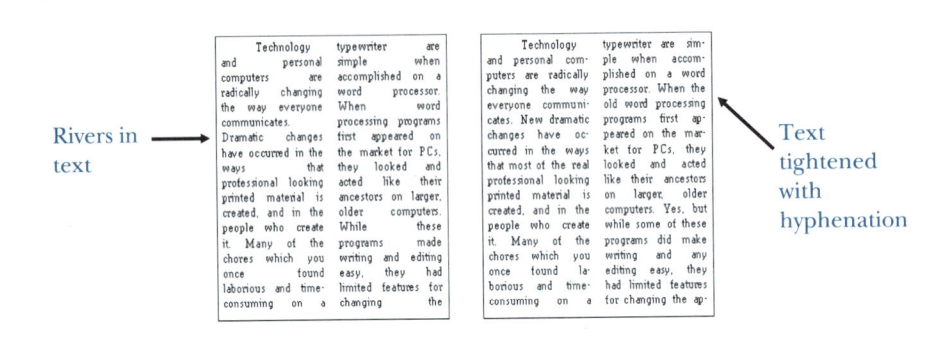

Figure 6-14. *How hyphenation can correct rivers of white space*

Rivers in text

Text tightened with hyphenation

When Publisher hyphenates a story for you, it inserts optional hyphens at the correct location in words that can be hyphenated, based on the amount of space left on a line and the margin settings for the frame. By using *optional hyphens*, Publisher can decide to suppress hyphenation for a word if you edit text or resize a frame so that hyphenation would no longer be useful. You can insert an optional hyphen in a word yourself by pressing CTRL-. Publisher also supports *nonbreaking* hyphens for words that always appear hyphenated but should never be broken onto two lines such as hyphenated last names. Press ALT-CTRL- to create a nonbreaking hyphen.

When you want to check the correct hyphenation for an individual word, click on the word and then select Hyphenate from the Options menu. The Hyphenate dialog box appears, as shown here:

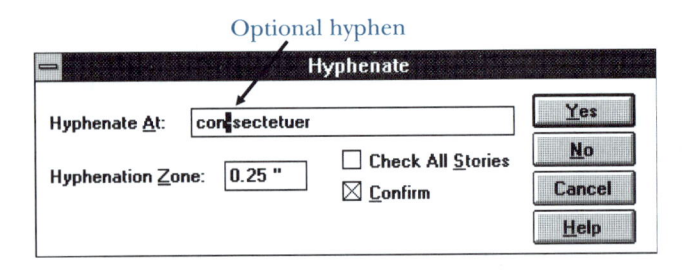

Optional hyphen

The word you selected appears in the Hyphenate At field. Publisher inserts optional hyphens wherever the word can be hyphenated. Publisher selects the location that seems best, but you can click on any of the alternatives if you want to hyphenate somewhere else in the word. When you're satisfied with the location of the hyphen, click on Yes to have Publisher insert it and return to the page area.

The *hyphenation zone* determines when Publisher will attempt to hyphenate a word at all. If the amount of space between the last character on a line and the right margin is less than the value set in the hyphenation zone, Publisher doesn't even attempt to hyphenate the next word, but rather places it on the next line. If the space remaining equals or exceeds the hyphenation zone, Publisher attempts to split the next word. You can adjust the hyphenation zone in order to tune the appearance of a frame. With a smaller zone, Publisher packs words more tightly on each line.

If you want Publisher to hyphenate all appropriate words in a story, just click anywhere in one of the frames that displays the story. Then select Hyphenate from the Options menu. The Confirm and Check All Stories buttons let you control the scope of the hyphenation session. Clicking on Confirm makes Publisher display each word it intends to hyphenate and lets you inspect and modify the hyphen location in the same way that you do for individual words. Once you're satisfied with how a word has been treated, click on OK. To skip hyphenation for the word and go on to the next, click on No. When Confirm is off, the entire story gets hyphenated automatically, with Publisher making the decision about locations for you.

When Publisher reaches the end of the story, the following message appears:

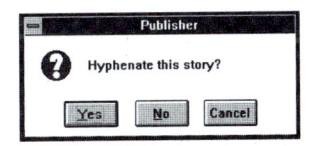

Click on Yes to have Publisher hyphenate the next story in the publication, or No to skip the story and proceed to the one after. Click on Cancel to stop the hyphenation session. If you're sure you want Publisher to hyphenate all of the stories in the publication, click on Check All Stories when the dialog box first appears.

> **How to Hyphenate**
>
> 1. Click on the Text frame that contains the story you want to hyphenate or select the word for which you want to check hyphenation.
> 2. Select Options from the Menu bar.
> 3. Select Hyphenation from the Options menu.
> 4. Adjust the hyphenation zone or click on any of the option buttons to refine the settings for the hyphenation session, if necessary.
> 5. Make any adjustments to Publisher's suggested hyphenation by clicking on one of the alternative optional hyphens, if necessary.
> 6. Click on OK to accept hyphenation for the current word or No to skip it.

Spelling

You can have Publisher check your spelling for individual words, for all words in a story, or for all stories in a publication. Even if you import most of the text for a story and it was checked by another system, it's always a good idea to check the spelling in a publication before going to press. When you're working on page design, it's easy to strike the wrong key inadvertently and introduce spelling errors. Few things in publishing are as frustrating as discovering a blatant spelling error in a piece you worked hard on to design well. Publisher has a substantial dictionary and can usually make good guesses for what you're trying to spell and how to spell it correctly. When you have spelled a word correctly but Publisher is not familiar with it, there is also an option for adding new words to the Publisher dictionary.

To check the spelling of an individual word, click on the word and select Check Spelling from the Options menu. The dialog box shown in Figure 6-15 appears. If you see the correct spelling among the list of suggestions, just click

Chapter 6: *Creating Text* 195

Figure 6-15. Check Spelling dialog box

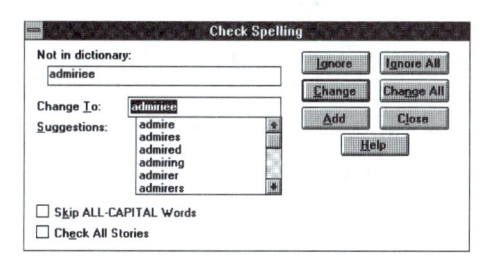

on it to have Publisher display it in the Change To field, and then click on Change to make the substitution in the publication.

When Publisher doesn't offer the correct spelling in its list of suggestions, you can correct the spelling yourself. Click on the word in the Change To field and edit it as you would any other field in a Windows program. Then click on Change. To retain the original spelling, click on Ignore. To retain the spelling and include the word in the Publisher dictionary, click on Add. Once you've added a word to the dictionary, Publisher recognizes it in future spelling sessions.

If you want to check the spelling for an entire story, click on any Text frame in the publication. Publisher always starts a spelling session at the beginning of the story, even if the insertion point is located elsewhere when you begin the session. Then select Check Spelling from the Edit menu.

In a long story when a word has either been incorrectly spelled throughout, or is used frequently but Publisher isn't familiar with it, two handy options are available. Change All will change the same mistake throughout a publication based on the first correction you make. That way you don't have to keep answering the same question over and over again. Similarly, clicking on Ignore All makes Publisher stop asking about a word it doesn't recognize once you have flagged the word as acceptable.

You can further adjust the scope of the spelling session by clicking on Skip ALL-CAPITAL Words. Since Publisher tends not to recognize proper nouns, this can also be a time saver. Finally, if you're sure you want Publisher to check the spelling in all of the stories in the publication, click on Check All Stories when the dialog box first appears.

How to Check Your Spelling

1. Click on the Text frame that contains the story you want to check or select the word for which you want to check spelling.
2. Select Options from the Menu bar.
3. Select Check Spelling from the Options menu.
4. Click on either of the option buttons to refine the settings for the spelling session, if necessary.
5. If the spelling of the word is incorrect, click on spelling alternatives in the Suggestions list or edit the spelling of the word yourself. Then click on Change to make an individual correction or Change All to revise all similar misspellings in the story automatically.
6. If the spelling of the word is correct but Publisher doesn't recognize it, click on Ignore to skip the current word or Ignore All to skip all similar words throughout the story automatically. Click on Add to retain the current spelling and update Publisher's dictionary. Spell checking then continues with the next word in the story.
7. Click on Close to terminate the spelling session.

Chapter 6: *Creating Text*

Review

The text editing and importing skills discussed in this chapter are simple, but critical to working effectively with Publisher. Page layout, frame positioning, and text formatting are really more at the heart of desktop publishing skills, but you must be able to manipulate text comfortably in order to get a publication to press. Remember the basic tools that Publisher provides you.

- You can create text directly in Publisher or bring it into a Text frame from almost any computer source.
- Basic editing tools are available for cutting, pasting, and copying text blocks of virtually any size. You can copy or move text within Text frames, between them, between publications, or between applications.
- Publisher lets you flow longer blocks of text through a publication by connecting frames. The sequence of frames in a series is completely under your control and can be changed at any time.
- Find lets you check for the existence of a word or phrase in a story, or position at a specific location in a story quickly.
- Replace lets you make last-minute changes to story content quickly and thoroughly.
- Hyphenation can tighten up the appearance of all of the text in a frame or provide you with the correct way to split an individual word.
- Spell checking helps to compensate for spelling errors that you may haphazardly introduce in the process of designing a publication.

7

Formatting Text

Publisher offers a rich selection of copy formatting options. Between text and WordArt, you can address most publishing needs. Certain formatting characteristics influence all copy, regardless of frame type. A frame itself—its shape, size, margins, shading, and so on—always affects the appearance of the copy inside it. As you can see in Figure 7-1, both Text and WordArt frames affect the amount of copy on the page and the way the copy fits into the publication layout. Paragraph styles, alignment, and spacing affect the copy within Text and WordArt frames differently, but all such modifications change the way the characters in a paragraph behave as a group.

Individual characters can always have different sizes and styles, but the selection of these differs between Text and WordArt frames. With Text frames, for example, you can italicize or boldface characters, as shown in the headline "WINTER 1991." With WordArt, you can stretch or enlarge the copy beyond the usual selection of sizes available for text, as in the oversized letter *A* or the curved headline and dollar sign in the solicitation for hospital donations.

This chapter assumes that you are already comfortable with the fundamentals of working with frames—creating, moving, resizing them, and so

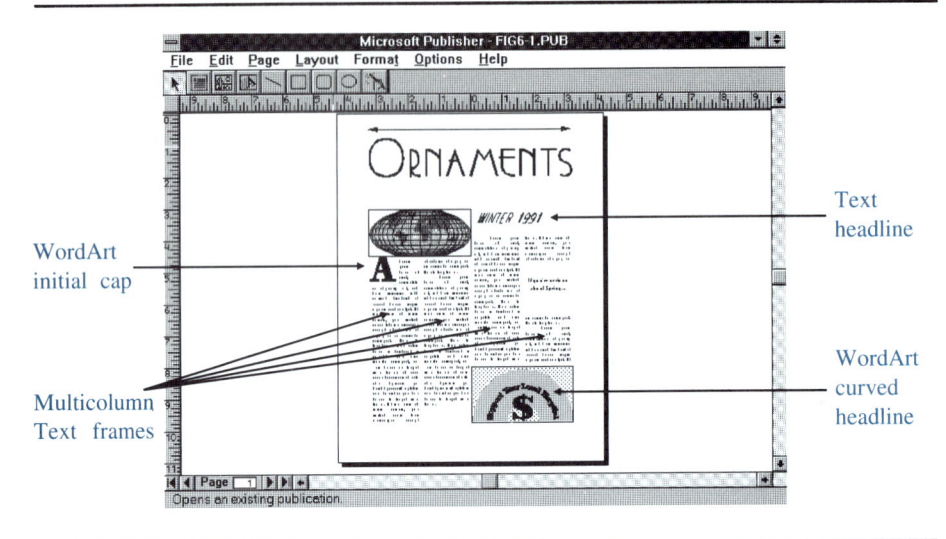

Figure 7-1.   *Some different applications of text and WordArt*

on—and entering, editing, and importing text. If you are not, refer to Chapter 4 or Chapter 6 for more details. Practical examples appear wherever appropriate. Generic instructions for tasks appear in a box at the end of most sections.

While text formatting accounts for much of a publication's style and appearance, most of the choices that you make about formatting text have little effect on its structure. As a result, you have considerable latitude to experiment with different formatting options without worrying about the larger design issues you encounter during page and frame layout. In short, text formatting is fun! As with most tasks, however, try to tackle the more influential aspects first.

Type size can be a notable exception to the freedom from structural issues you generally have in formatting. In copy-heavy publications, for example, increasing the size of the most frequently used characters by only a small amount can result in having to add several pages in order to accommodate the text overflow. As suggested in the previous chapter, it's a good idea to get the copy into most or all of the major frames before you begin formatting. The graphical impact of any formatting can only be evaluated or appreciated in the context of the entire page (and all of the other formats on it). Even in designing a simple greeting card with a single Picture frame and a Text frame, it's hard to make typographical decisions unless you can see how they blend with the image that they are meant to support.

One final word of advice—make liberal use of Actual View when formatting. Unless you're working on a large headline, it's difficult to see any of the formatting effects in one of the broader views.

In Publisher, you can apply text formatting in three ways: to characters, paragraphs, and frames. The *characters* that you can format include any of the standard symbols on your computer keyboard that you can display on a monitor or printer. Publisher recognizes all of the letters, numbers, punctuation marks, and other writing symbols, such as the asterisk (*) and ampersand (&), as characters that you can format. Tabs and carriage returns are also characters, and while Publisher lets you search for them—as you learned in Chapter 6—you cannot format them. You can apply formatting to characters, for example, by underlining, italicizing, or choosing different type styles and sizes for them. With character formatting, you can change the appearance of each character individually, or you can select a group of characters to format, such as a word, sentence, or paragraph.

Paragraphs refer to one or more characters that are separated in a frame from other characters by a carriage return or by the beginning or end of a story. (A carriage return, remember, is what Publisher automatically inserts in text whenever you press (ENTER).) Paragraph formatting affects all of the characters in a paragraph uniformly. Examples of paragraph formatting include double-spacing or centering.

Frame formatting lets you adjust the overall margins and the number of columns in the frame. Frame formatting affects all of the paragraphs in a frame uniformly. Figure 7-2 shows samples of character, paragraph, and frame formatting.

In Publisher, formatting commands, like editing commands, always affect the current selection. You must select a Text frame before you can execute a frame formatting command such as adjusting the margins. Similarly, you must select one or more characters or paragraphs in a frame before you can execute a formatting command such as centering or boldface. The commands that you decide on will only apply to the characters or paragraphs you have selected. All of the text selection techniques described in Chapter 6 operate perfectly for formatting. You can access the more commonly used character

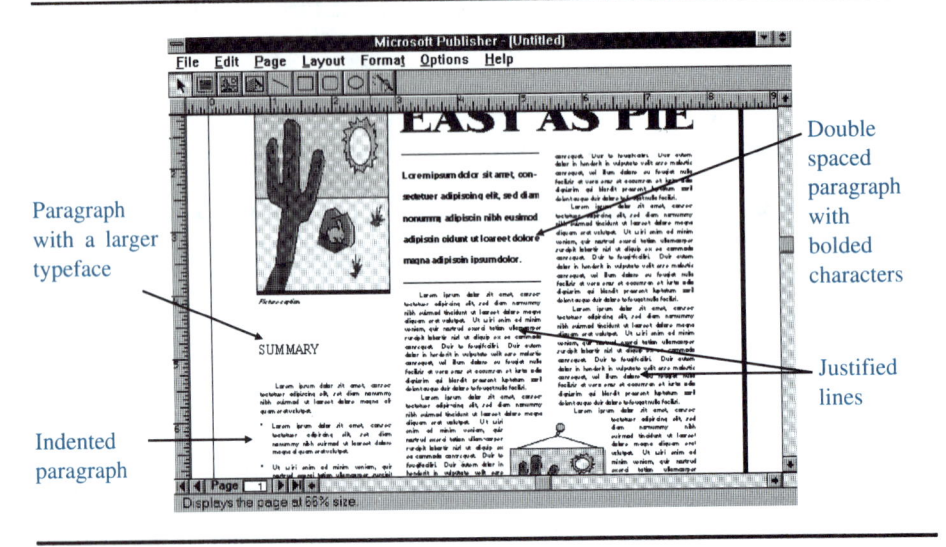

Figure 7-2. Some effects of text formatting

and paragraph formatting options either from the Toolbar or from the Format menu on the Menu bar. This section explores all of the ways that you can format text in Publisher.

Formatting Characters

Publisher offers five groups of formatting options for characters. The two most common of these, *style* and *position*, do not depend on any special hardware or software. Underlining is an example of a character style, and superscript is an example of position. The selection available for the other three groups—font, size, and color—is closely tied to the type of printer you have.

A font or *typeface* is a set of characters that all have the same design. Font sets have names like Courier, Helvetica, or Century Schoolbook. Figure 7-3 shows several complete font sets and a variety of font sizes. Font sets always include all of the upper- and lowercase letters, the numbers, and the standard

Chapter 7: *Formatting Text* 203

Figure 7-3. *Some popular fonts and sizes*

Times Roman
AaBbCcDdEeFfGgHhIiJjKkLlMmNnOoPpQqRrSsTtUuVvWwXxYyZz
1234567890 !@#$%^&*()-_=+

Courier
AaBbCcDdEeFfGgHhIiJjKkLlMmNnOoPpQqRrSsTtUuVvWwXxYyZz
1234567890 !@#$%^&*()-_=+

Helvetica
AaBbCcDdEeFfGgHhIiJjKkLlMmNnOoPpQqRrSsTtUuVvWwXxYyZz
1234567890 !@#$%^&*()-_=+

6 pt
8 pt
10 pt
12 pt
14 pt
18 pt
24 pt

36 pt
48 pt
72 pt

punctuation marks. Usually they also include the other keyboard characters, such as the dollar sign ($) and the pound sign (#).

In Publisher Text frames, the only fonts and font sizes that you can print are the ones that have been installed for your copy of Windows. Many modern printers—especially laser printers—can be modified to accommodate new fonts and font sizes, but these must be installed in your printer and under Windows before you can use them in Publisher. Similarly, Publisher supports color printing for text. However, while the selections you make for text color may appear on screen when you design a publication, they will not print unless you have a color printer. At the very best, they will print in shades of black, but they may not print at all.

> *Don't be alarmed if the specific selections for fonts and font sizes discussed in this section differ from the ones on your system. You can use the same principles for formatting text in any font. If one of the examples calls for a font that you don't have, simply substitute one that appears in your environment.*
>
> **Note**

Applying most character formats is easiest with the Toolbar. Just select the characters you want to change and click on any of the text formatting buttons. To experiment with some of the options, start a new publication using the PRODINFO.PUB template. This is the Publisher sample for a product specification sheet. Click on the Text frame in column 2 containing the three bullets. Then select the text in the first paragraph, as shown in Figure 7-4. Try clicking on the bold, italic, and underline buttons on the Toolbar. These are toggles, so each time you click on one you turn it either on or off depending on its previous state.

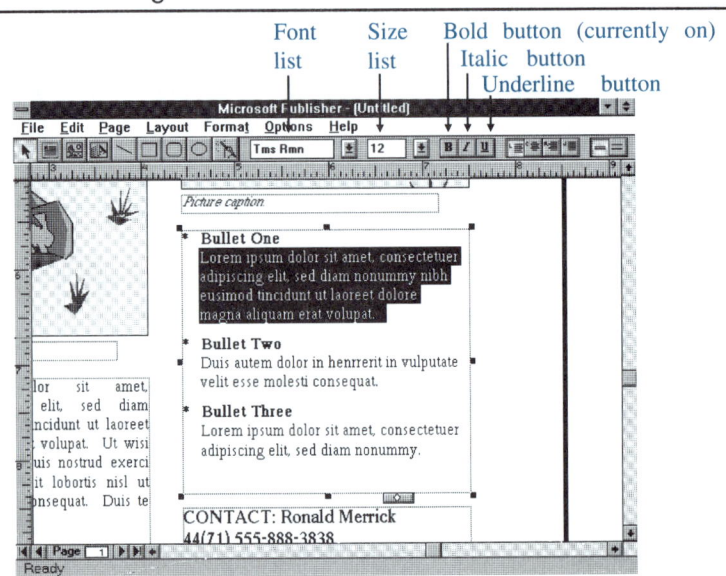

Figure 7-4.   Formatting text in PRODINFO.PUB

Chapter 7: Formatting Text

If the text you currently have highlighted has been formatted by one of the Toolbar buttons, the brightness of the button itself is slightly more intense on the Toolbar. You can use the buttons in conjunction with one another. For example, you can format the text as boldface and underlined.

Tip

To remove any style or position formats that you may have assigned, select the characters that you want to restore and press CTRL-SPACEBAR.

Next try clicking on the Font list. Publisher displays all of the fonts on your system. Clicking on any of these changes the font for all of the characters in your selection. Experiment with each of them to see how they affect the characters you selected in the spec sheet. Then try using different sizes for different fonts by clicking on the Size list and making a selection. The selection of sizes will probably differ for each font.

While font size affects both the height and width of a character, it is usually measured by height in *points*. A point is equal to 1/72 inch. There are 12 points (abbreviated pt) to a standard line and 6 lines to an inch. Most publications use a 10-point font for body copy. *Body copy* is a name for the most common text in a publication. In PRODINFO.PUB, for example, the paragraph below the picture on the left of the page, and the paragraphs beneath the headings for each of the three bullets are body copy. Using a 10-point character on a standard 12-point line allows just enough breathing room between lines to make single-spaced copy easy to read. Remember that all formatting options operate independently. For example, changes you make in the font do not necessarily affect the font size.

To see all of the options available for text formatting, select Character from the Format menu. The Character dialog box appears, as shown at the top of Figure 7-5. Choosing any of the options here affects the current text selection in the same way as using the buttons on the Toolbar. Similarly, options that you implemented from the Toolbar can be turned on or off here. The Character dialog box and the Toolbar are just different ways of doing the same thing. However, the dialog box offers several formatting choices that do not appear on the Toolbar. The text fragment at the bottom of Figure 7-5 shows samples of all of the different styles and positions for text in Publisher. To make selections in the Character dialog box, just click on any of the option buttons or select from any of the lists. You can change any or all of these text attributes before you close the dialog box.

Figure 7-5.   Character dialog box

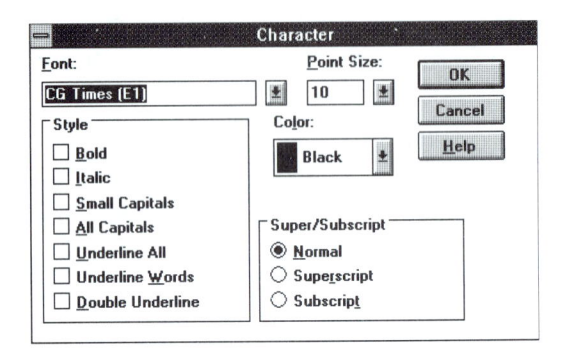

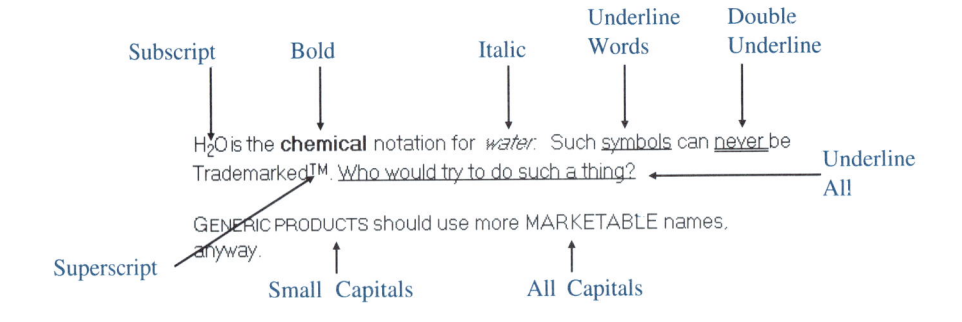

[Character dialog box showing Font: CG Times (E1), Point Size: 10, Style checkboxes (Bold, Italic, Small Capitals, All Capitals, Underline All, Underline Words, Double Underline), Color: Black, Super/Subscript options (Normal, Superscript, Subscript), and OK, Cancel, Help buttons.]

Sample text with labels pointing to: Subscript, Bold, Italic, Underline Words, Double Underline, Underline All, Superscript, Small Capitals, All Capitals:

H_2O is the **chemical** notation for *water*. Such symbols can never be Trademarked™. Who would try to do such a thing?

GENERIC PRODUCTS should use more MARKETABLE names, anyway.

To see the effects of some of the other formatting options, use the Publisher template for a resumé.

- Start a new publication using RESUME.PUB and click on the large Text frame on the right of the page.

- Switch to Actual View to get a more accurate look at the fonts and type styles on the page. All of the text in this frame uses a Times Roman font. Two different font sizes are used—8-point for the body text and 12-point for the section headings—and parts of the body copy are bold, as shown in Figure 7-6.

Chapter 7: *Formatting Text* 207

Figure 7-6.   *Different applications for type*

12-point Times Roman caps

SUM**E**   OBJECTIVE

Lorem ipsum dolor sit amet, consectectetuer adipiscing elit, sed diam no-nummy nibh euismod tincidunt ut laoreet dolore magna aliquam erat volutpat. Ut wisi enim ad minim veniam, quis nostrud exerci tation ullamcorper suscipit lobortis nisl ut aliquip ex ea commodo consequat. Duis te feugifacilisi.

8-point Times Roman

WORK HISTORY

Lorem ipsum dolor sit amet
Diam no-nummy nibh

Consectectetuer adipiscing elit, sed euismod tincidunt ut laoreet dolore magna aliquam erat volutpat. Ut wisi enim adum.

Minimim veniam, quis exerci tation
Aliquip ex ea commodo

Ullamcorper suscipit lobortis nisl ut consequat. Duis te feugifacilisi. Duis autem dolor in henderit in vulputate velit esse molestie consequat, vel illum.

8-point Times Roman bold

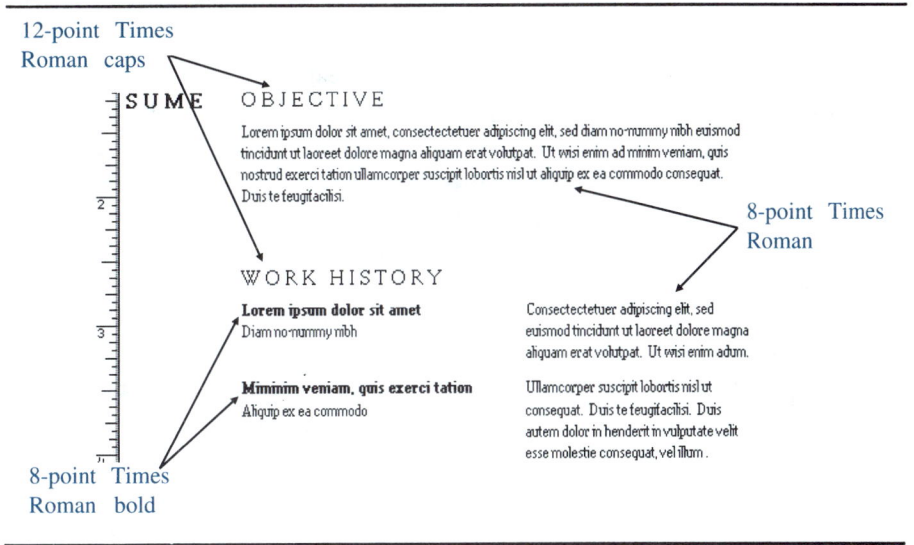

- Use Highlight Story to select all of the text in the frame quickly. Then click on the Font list and select **Helvetica**. The typeface changes for all of the characters in the frame, but the other character formats, their size for example, remain the same.

- Next, italicize each of the section headings for "OBJECTIVE," "WORK HISTORY," "EDUCATION," and "AWARDS/COMMU-NITY SERVICE." First click somewhere in the Page area to clear the current selection. Then select those titles separately and click on the Italic button on the Toolbar for each.

- Switch to 50% View to get an overview of how the publication has changed. Small changes to the fonts in a publication can have subtle but distinctive effects.

- The 8-point font used for the body copy in the resumé is neat looking, but it's hard to read (even in actual size view). See what the first paragraph under the OBJECTIVE heading looks like in a 10-point font. Select that paragraph now. Then click on the Size list and select 10. The result makes the publication considerably more legible and should probably be used as the standard size for the body copy throughout the resumé.

Unfortunately, you can't simply select all of the text in the frame at once and reset its size as you did with the font. The change to Helvetica was uniform for all of the characters, because all of the text in the frame was formatted in Times Roman. Not all of the text, however, has the same size, so resetting it all at once will eliminate some of the sizes you want to retain.

Is it easier to set the entire frame in 10-point and reset the section headings in 12-point, or individually set each paragraph in 10-point and leave the section headings undisturbed? This is exactly the sort of decision that you encounter quite frequently during formatting. In this case, the difference is negligible, since there are only four subheads, and the body text could be selected in three groups of paragraphs under each subhead. However, these questions are always worth considering. Finding the proper answer can often save you time.

For now, select all of the paragraphs between "WORK HISTORY" and "EDUCATION." Then open the Size window and click on 10 pt. The results appear disastrous. Unfortunately, as characters get taller, they also get wider to remain in proportion. The result, in this case, is that fewer of the larger characters will fit on a single line, and, because of word wrap, some of the text automatically extended to the following line. Don't panic—this is only practice! If you can't stand looking at the mess, select Undo to correct the error.

Effects such as these are not uncommon when you work in desktop publishing. A small change in point size (in this case 1/36th inch per character) can have dramatic effects on the entire publication. If you look at RESUME.PUB more closely following the change in point size, you will see also that there is no longer enough room on the page for all of the text. Of course, Publisher provides a variety of methods for you to correct that and still use a 10-point font for the body copy in the resumé. You could widen the frame, adjust the line spacing, remove unnecessary lines between sections, or some combination of all of these adjustments, as you will see in the next few sections in this chapter. You might even decide to print the resumé on two pages, although many people prefer one. These are all considerations you must address as the designer. The most important issue for you is to understand what your alternatives are.

Chapter 7: *Formatting Text*

Note

Publisher usually displays as much information as possible on the Toolbar about the current text selection in the publication. For example, the font name and size appear, and any of the selected formatting buttons are slightly brighter. When multiple and conflicting formats occur in your text selection, for example, both 8-point and 12-point type, the Toolbar displays no information for that characteristic. In this case, the Size list would be empty.

How to Format Characters

1. Select the characters that you want to change. Use any of the selection techniques described in Chapter 6. Any size block of text can be included from a single character to an entire story.
2. Click on any or all of the character formatting tools on the Toolbar.
3. If you want to apply formatting characteristics that aren't on the Toolbar, select Layout from the Menu bar and select Character from the Layout menu.
4. Click on any of the options in the dialog box.
5. Click on OK.

Kerning

Font designs can be classified in several ways. For example, *serif* fonts, such as the Times Roman shown in **Figure 7-3**, have short horizontal strokes at the top and bottom of the character's vertical strokes. *Sans serif* fonts, such as Helvetica, do not. Serif and sans serif are two ways of describing font design.

The use of proportional spacing is another characteristic of font design. *Monospaced* fonts, such as the Courier shown in **Figure 7-3**, allocate the same amount of horizontal space for each character in a word. *Proportionally spaced* fonts, such as Times Roman or Helvetica, vary the amount of space for each letter depending on the design of the character. The letter *i*, for example, gets less room than the letter *m*, because the character itself has less strokes and requires less space. With proportionally spaced fonts, characters *nuzzle* to-

Figure 7-7. *Proportional spacing after kerning*

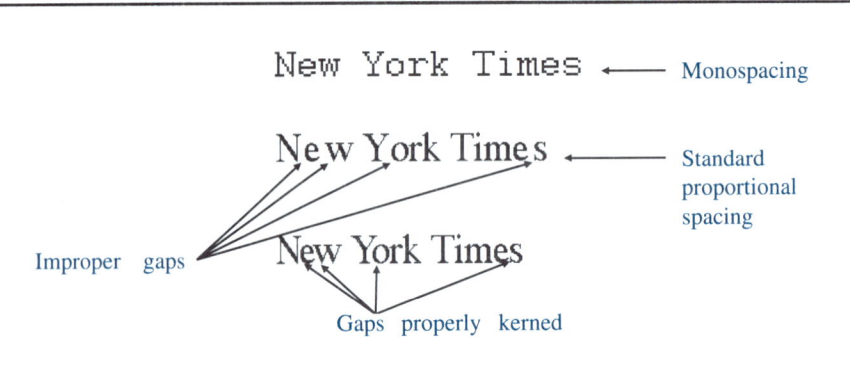

```
                New York Times  ←——— Monospacing

                New York Times  ←——— Standard
                                       proportional
                                       spacing
    Improper  gaps
                New York Times
                Gaps properly kerned
```

gether attractively because of these different space allocations, and the result is a more professional look to the copy in a publication.

Occasionally, depending on which characters are adjacent to each other, two characters will not fit together as well as they could. Consider the example in Figure 7-7. Without adjustment, the capital letters in each of the first two words in the proportional font are too far from the second letters that follow them, and in both the first and last word, the last letter is too far from its predecessor. *Kerning* lets you adjust the distance between individual characters. In Publisher, kerning adds or subtracts space to the right of the character you have selected. Space is usually measured in points (72 per inch), but can be entered in any of the other scales that Publisher uses (inches, centimeters, or picas).

- In the example in Figure 7-7, to move the *N* and *e* closer together, click on the *N* and select Spacing Between Characters from the Format menu. Publisher displays the corresponding dialog box as shown here:

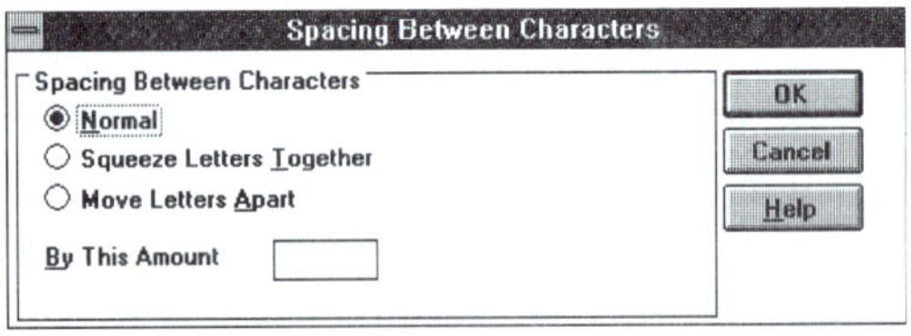

Chapter 7: Formatting Text

- Click on the button for Squeeze Letters Together and click on OK to accept the default value of 1.5 pt. The result should look like the first word in the third sample in Figure 7-7.
- Repeat the same process for the *e* in the first word, the *Y* in the second word and the *e* in the last word. You can, of course, override the default setting for distance, but Publisher's suggestion is usually a good starting point.

Kerning also allows you to spread letters out when they are too close together. This can occur from the same problems that give rise to excess spacing.

Note: *Kerning is especially important in headlines and other applications that require larger font sizes. While spacing problems may occur between the same characters of a font in any point size, they are most noticeable in larger type. Besides, you don't want to spend the rest of your life kerning every word in a publication. Only apply it when the spacing problems become noticeable.*

How to Kern Characters

1. Select the character immediately to the left of the space you want to adjust.
2. Select Format from the Menu bar and select Spacing Between Characters from the Format menu.
3. Click on the appropriate button to increase or decrease the amount of space to the right of the selected characters, type a specific value for the spacing, or click on normal to restore the original spacing.
4. Click on OK.

Paragraph Formatting

There are three groups of formatting options for paragraphs in Publisher—alignment, indentation, and spacing. Most of these should be familiar if you have experience using a word processor. They are all printer independent. Alignment defines the way that paragraphs position with respect to the boundaries and margins of a Text frame. For example, paragraphs can be centered (equidistant from the left and right margins) or flush left (aligned with the left margin but not the right), among other formats.

Selecting Paragraphs

A paragraph is a group of characters separated from the characters immediately before and after it by a carriage return. Publisher automatically inserts a carriage return whenever you press (ENTER). Pressing (ENTER) is the correct (and only) way to separate the text in one paragraph from another. Paragraphs are usually, but not always, collections of words and sentences (they can be an individual word or letter, too). Because paragraph formatting commands affect all of the lines in a paragraph, the choices you make about how to divide text into different paragraphs impact your ability to format.

Tip

To force a new line without starting a new paragraph, press (SHIFT)(ENTER).

When you want to use similar paragraph formatting styles on succeeding lines of text, keeping the text together in a single paragraph can make formatting easier. You don't actually have to highlight an entire paragraph before you format it. The insertion point, however, must be somewhere inside the paragraph. On the other hand, separating text that you want to format differently into different paragraphs is essential. In the following example, if you tried to achieve the effect on the top for a centered title line, but wound up with the effect on the bottom, you probably forgot to divide the text into two paragraphs.

Chapter 1
The Beginning of It All

Lorem ipsum dolor sit amet, consectetuer adipiscing elit, sed diem nonummy nibh euismod tincidunt ut lacreet dolore magna aliquam erat volutpat. Ut wisis enim ad minim veniam, quis nostrud exerci tution ullamcorper suscipit lobortis nisl ut aliquip ex ea commodo consequat. Duis te feugifacilisi. Duis autem dolor in hendrerit in vulputate velit esse molestie consequat, vel illum dolore eu feugiat nulla facilisis at vero eros et accumsan et iusto odio dignissim qui blandit praesent luptatum zzril delenit au gue duis

Too much centering →

Chapter 1
The Beginning of It All

Lorem ipsum dolor sit amet, consectetuer adipiscing elit, sed diem nonummy nibh euismod tincidunt ut lacreet dolore magna aliquam erat volutpat. Ut wisis enim ad minim veniam, quis nostrud exerci tution ullamcorper suscipit lobortis nisl ut aliquip ex ea commodo consequat. Duis te feugifacilisi. Duis autem dolor in hendrerit in vulputate velit esse molestie consequat, vel illum dolore eu feugiat nulla facilisis at vero eros et accumsan et iusto odio dignissim qui blandit praesent luptatum zzril delenit au gue duis

Tip: To find a carriage return in a text file, use Find from the Edit menu and type ^p in the Find What field. Publisher will position the insertion point at the location of the first carriage return in the frame (carriage returns are invisible). Click on Find Next to search for other carriage returns in the frame.

Indents, Alignment, and Spacing

Indentation is space that you can add to each paragraph on the left or right to effectively increase the individual margins. Bulleted lists, for example, are often indented in order to set them off from the rest of the text in a frame and call attention to them. *Spacing* affects the height of the lines in a paragraph and the number of lines between paragraphs. Examples of some of these effects can be seen in Figure 7-2.

Applying paragraph formats is easiest with the Toolbar. Just select the paragraph(s) you want to change and click on the appropriate button. To experiment with some of the options, start a new publication using RE-SUME.PUB. This is the Publisher template for a resumé.

- Click on the Text frame containing the name and address in the upper-left corner of the page and select all of the text in the frame.
- Click on the Left Align button on the Toolbar. All of the text becomes flush left. (With this alignment, the frame should be moved slightly to the right, just for aesthetic purposes.)
- Click on the main frame in the center of the page and separately select each of the section headings. For each, click on the Center Align button to center it. The publication should now look something like the sample in Figure 7-8.
- Finally, select the paragraph below the heading "OBJECTIVE" and try the Double Space and Single Space buttons.

The alignment buttons are mutually exclusive. For example, since a single paragraph cannot be both left aligned, right aligned, justified, and centered at the same time, whenever you select any one of these buttons the others become deactivated. The same applies for the spacing buttons, since a paragraph can't be single and double spaced at the same time. You can, however, combine choices for spacing and alignment. If a paragraph you

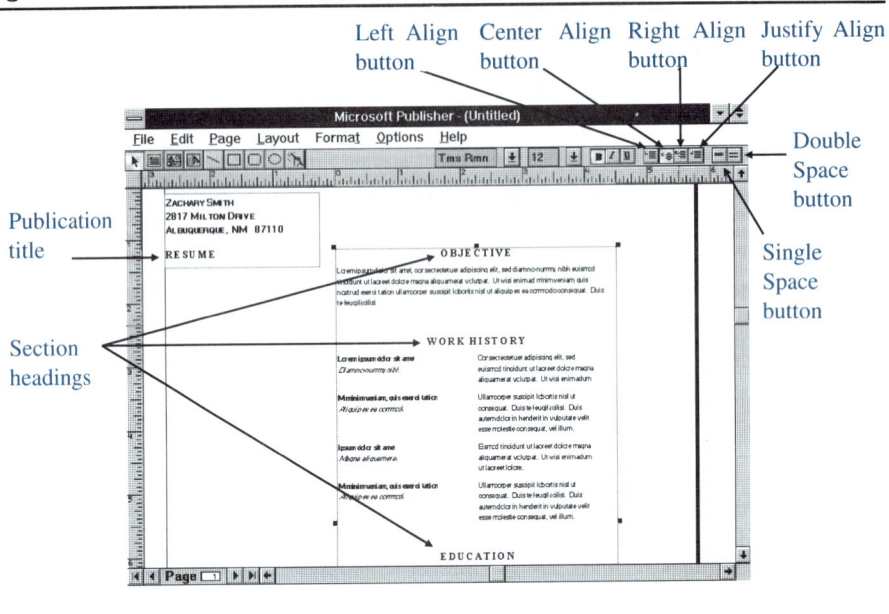

Figure 7-8. RESUME.PUB

select has been formatted, the brightness of the corresponding button appears slightly more intense on the Toolbar.

To remove any paragraph formats that you may have assigned, select the paragraphs that you want to restore and press CTRL-Q.

Tip

To see all of the options available for paragraph formatting, select Indents and Spacing from the Format menu. The associated dialog box appears as shown in Figure 7-9. Clicking on any of the options here affects the current text selection in the same way as the options you implement from the Toolbar, and the options that you implemented from the Toolbar can be turned on or off here. The Indents and Spacing dialog box and the Toolbar are just different ways of executing the same commands.

There is, however, one group of formatting options available here that does not appear on the Toolbar—indents. An indent is space that you add to the left or right margin for an individual paragraph. You can assign a special

Chapter 7: *Formatting Text* 215

indent for the first line of a paragraph that gets added to the overall left indent, as shown here:

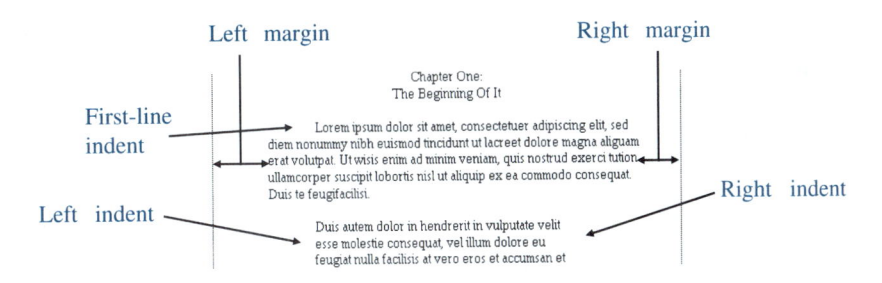

The bulleted points at the bottom of **RESUME.PUB** under the heading "AWARDS/COMMUNITY SERVICE" also have a left indent. To make selections in the Indents and Spacing dialog box, just click on any of the option buttons or type new values in any of the fields. You can change any or all of the attributes before you close the dialog box.

Note

You can type measurements in any of the fields in inches ("), centimeters (cm), points (pt), or picas (pi), regardless of which measurement Publisher uses to display information for a field. If you want to use a different unit than the one in which the field appears, be sure to follow the value with the proper symbol (", cm, pt, or pi).

Figure 7-9. Indents and Spacing dialog box

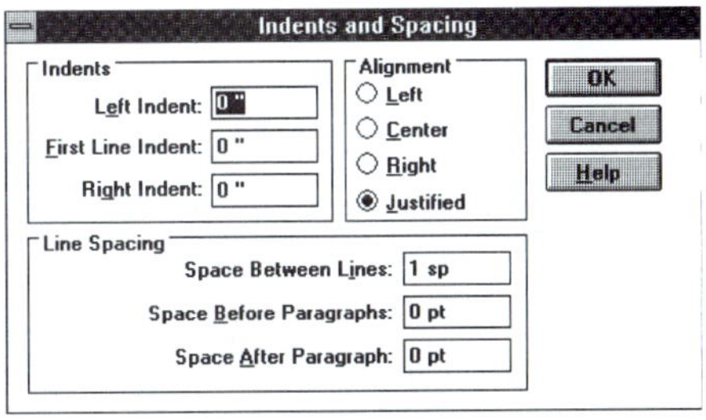

Leading

Publisher normally allocates 12 points (1/6 inch) to the height of a line. This is visually pleasing for 9-point to 11-point fonts. However, it is too small for larger fonts and too large for smaller fonts. When you select a different font size, Publisher usually takes care of adjusting the line height for you. Occasionally, you can do a better job. Consider the two samples from RESUME.PUB shown in Figure 7-10.

The sample on top shows the 8-point characters under the heading "OBJECTIVE" on a 12-point line. The template comes like this. The sample on the bottom shows the same characters on a 10-point line. The tighter spacing is more appropriate and visually pleasing. The vertical space between lines is called *leading*. You can adjust the leading for each paragraph by entering different values in the Space Between Lines field in the Indents and Spacing dialog box. You can also alter the leading between paragraphs by typing values in the Space Before Paragraph or Space After Paragraph field. The leading between paragraphs is a more stylistic decision than the leading inside of paragraphs. You may prefer an open look for some parts of a publication.

Figure 7-10.   *Adjusting the leading*

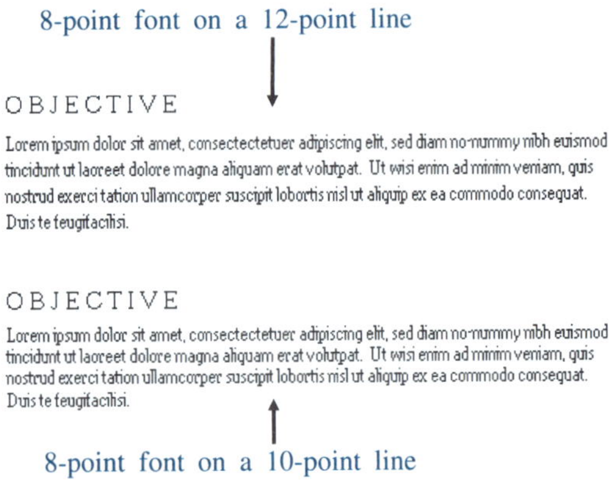

8-point font on a 12-point line

OBJECTIVE

Lorem ipsum dolor sit amet, consectectetuer adipiscing elit, sed diam no-nummy nibh euismod tincidunt ut laoreet dolore magna aliquam erat volutpat. Ut wisi enim ad minim veniam, quis nostrud exerci tation ullamcorper suscipit lobortis nisl ut aliquip ex ea commodo consequat. Duis te feugitacilisi.

OBJECTIVE

Lorem ipsum dolor sit amet, consectectetuer adipiscing elit, sed diam no-nummy nibh euismod tincidunt ut laoreet dolore magna aliquam erat volutpat. Ut wisi enim ad minim veniam, quis nostrud exerci tation ullamcorper suscipit lobortis nisl ut aliquip ex ea commodo consequat. Duis te feugitacilisi.

8-point font on a 10-point line

Chapter 7: *Formatting Text* 217

How to Format Paragraphs

1. Select the paragraphs that you want to change. Use any of the selection techniques described in Chapter 6. You can include any number of paragraphs from one to an entire story.
2. Click on any or all of the paragraph formatting tools on the Toolbar.
3. If you want to apply formatting characteristics that aren't on the Toolbar, select Layout from the Menu bar and select Indents and Spacing from the Layout menu.
4. Click on any of the buttons or change any of the field values in the dialog box.
5. Click on OK.

Tabs

Tabs let you align text at specific locations in a paragraph. The easiest way to think of applying tabs is in a table, as in **Figure 7-11**. For example, tabs

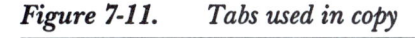

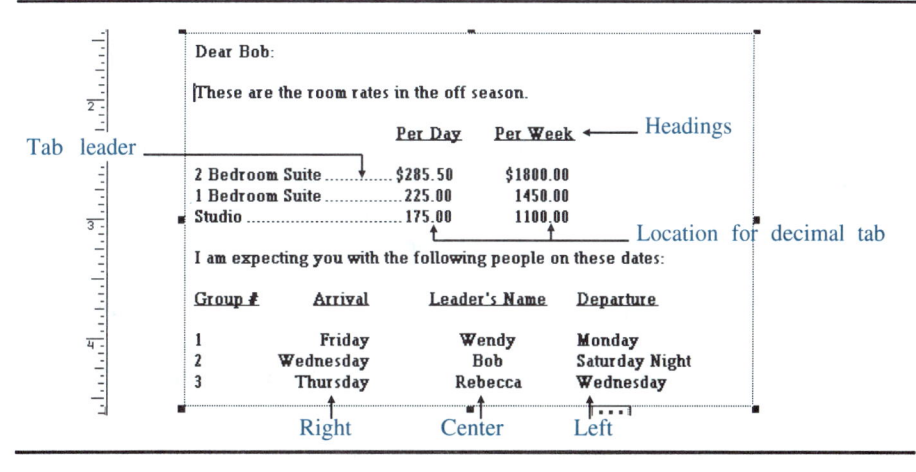

Figure 7-11. Tabs used in copy

```
Dear Bob:

These are the room rates in the off season.

                         Per Day    Per Week   ←——— Headings
Tab leader
            2 Bedroom Suite ......↓...... $285.50    $1800.00
            1 Bedroom Suite ............. 225.00     1450.00
            Studio ........................ 175.00     1100.00
                                    ↑          ↑
                                    └──────────┴─ Location for decimal tab
            I am expecting you with the following people on these dates:

            Group #    Arrival        Leader's Name    Departure
            1          Friday         Wendy            Monday
            2          Wednesday      Bob              Saturday Night
            3          Thursday       Rebecca          Wednesday
                           ↑              ↑              ↑
                         Right          Center          Left
```

cause the prices to align in the two columns of numbers. There are several good reasons to use tabs (instead of spaces) for any columnar work in Publisher. For one thing, tabs make it much easier to line up text quickly. Once you set a tab, it only takes a single keystroke to position the insertion point there. Using the (SPACEBAR) key could require many more. Tabs also take the guess work out of measurement. When you set a tab, it has a specific physical location in a frame. The text that you position at that location all starts at the same exact place. Finally, when you work with proportionally spaced fonts, tabs are the only means of making text align properly at any location other than the margins. Because different amounts of space are allocated between the characters in a proportionally spaced font set, using spaces to line up columns of text almost always results in a jagged edge for the column.

Tabs actually have two parts to them. A *tab stop* is a location, measured from the left margin of a frame, where the insertion point stops after you press the (TAB) key. A *tab character* is an invisible character that Publisher inserts in a paragraph when you press the (TAB) key. The tab causes the insertion point to move to the next tab stop to the right of its current location. The tab separates the last character to the left of the tab stop from the first character at the tab stop.

When you create a Text frame, Publisher assigns default tab stops every 1/2 inch to all paragraphs. If you're not familiar with how tabs work, start a new publication using a blank page and create a Text frame. Switch to Actual View so that you can see what's going on a little more clearly. Press the (TAB) key several times. The insertion point skips across the line at 1/2-inch intervals. Then press (BACKSPACE) several times. Tabs can be erased like other characters by using any of the text editing keys.

Note — *Remember that Text frames have a default left and right margin of .08 inch, so the first default tab stop actually occurs at .508 inches from the left boundary of any frame. For applications where you need to set complex tab stops, it's sometimes easier to eliminate the left margin and use paragraph indents to make up the difference.*

Tab stops come in four flavors with three different toppings. Figure 7-11 contains examples of most of these (use it as a reference while reading through this paragraph). Left-aligned tab stops are familiar to anyone who has worked with a typewriter. The column for Departure is a good example. The text at left-aligned tab stops aligns on the left side. All of Publisher's default tab stops are left-aligned. Right-aligned tab stops do just the opposite: they align on the right edge, and text extends back toward the left. The Arrival column shows you how right-aligned tabs work. Center-aligned tab stops cause text to center *around* the tab stop as in the Person's Name column. Finally, decimal tab stops are for aligning columns of numbers like the two price columns. At decimal tab stops the first characters you type (presumably numbers, commas, or dollar signs) align to the right until you type a period. Subsequent characters (presumably the fractional amount to the right of the decimal point) align to the left. Money looks best at a decimal tab stop, because all amounts line up around the decimal point.

Any of the four tab stop types can include a *leader*. A leader appears in Figure 7-11 between the name of each accommodation type and the daily price. Leaders fill the space occupied by a tab with an appropriate number of characters to fill the gap. You can choose between dots, dashes, and underscores for Publisher to use as the leader character. Dots are shown in the figure. Leaders are terrific for menus and tables of contents.

When setting tab stops, you may find it helpful to drag the horizontal ruler down to the top boundary of the frame to help visualize locations. It's also useful to reset the zero mark on that ruler to the left edge of the frame. If you need more information about these procedures, refer to the section, "Working with Rulers," in Chapter 5. Use the following exercise for some practice setting tab stops.

Try creating the two columns of numbers shown in Figure 7-11. These use decimal tab stops at 2 inches and 3 inches in the frame.

- Start a new publication using a blank page and create a Text frame about 3 inches high and 5 inches wide. Then switch to Actual View to get a better look at what you're doing.
- Type **2 Bedroom Suite** and select Tabs from the Format menu. The Tabs dialog box appears, as shown in Figure 7-12.
- Type **2** in the tab field. Click on the Decimal button in the alignment group and click on the Dot button in the leader group. Then click on Set. Publisher displays the location for the first tab stop in the tab list.

Figure 7-12. Tab dialog box

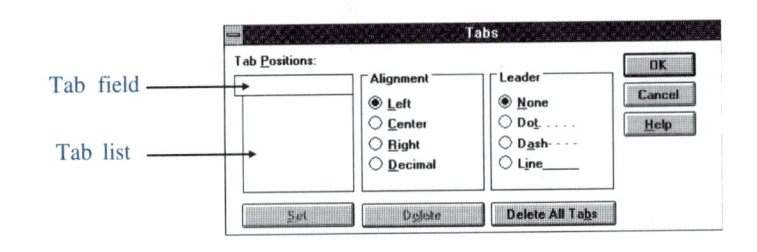

- Type **3** and then click on the None button in the Leader window. Click on Set again and click on OK to complete the settings for this paragraph. The Publisher screen returns.
- Press (TAB), and then type **$285**. The characters move out to the left.
- Type **.00** and then press (TAB) to move the insertion point to the next tab stop.
- Type **$1800.00** and then press (SHIFT)(ENTER) to force Publisher to begin a new line within the same paragraph.
- Complete the second and third lines of the table as shown in Figure 7-11. Be sure to separate each column by pressing (TAB) and to end the second line by pressing (SHIFT)(ENTER).

Tab stops are actually part of a paragraph's format. When you enter new tab stops, Publisher clears all of default settings to the left of your entry. This only applies, however, to the current paragraph. By ending each line with a forced line break instead of a carriage return, you keep all of the lines in the table in a single paragraph with the same tab stop settings. This makes editing much simpler if you decide to change a tab stop location, because you only need to make the change once (for a single paragraph). The headings for the decimal columns in the previous exercise, by the way, are part of a paragraph with different tab stop settings. They are center-aligned at 2 inches and 2.9 inches, respectively. Tables are often composed of two sets of tab stops: one for the headings and one for the data in the table. The importance of keeping

Chapter 7: *Formatting Text* 221

---

the number of paragraphs to a minimum (by using forced line breaks) becomes more obvious as the complexity of a table grows.

Tip

When you copy a Text frame, Publisher retains the tab stops for the first paragraph in it, even if you delete the text. When you copy a paragraph, Publisher retains the tab stops in it as well as the text. You can delete the text and retain the tab stops for the paragraph as long as you don't delete the carriage return at the end of the paragraph. You can also duplicate the tab stop settings in another paragraph by moving the insertion point to the left of the first character in the paragraph and pressing ENTER. *The one-line paragraph that Publisher creates immediately above the insertion point copies all of the tab stops and none of the text from the current paragraph. If you've taken the trouble to create a complex series of tab settings and want to use a similar format in another frame or publication, copy the initial frame or paragraph. If you do a lot of tabular work, you may even want to create a template that contains frames with different frequently used tables.*

How to Set and Format a Tab Stop

1. Select the Text frame in which you want to set tab stops.
2. Position the insertion point in the paragraph for which you want to set tab stops.
3. Select Tabs from the Format menu.
4. Enter the location for a tab stop and click on any of the tab formatting options for alignment or leader characters, if necessary.
5. Click on Set to complete the individual setting.
6. Repeat steps 4 and 5 as many times as necessary for additional tab stops.
7. Click on OK.

When you clear a tab stop the text that was positioned there moves to the prior tab stop location to its left. This location can either be one of Publisher's defaults or one that you set yourself. For example, make sure that the insertion point is still in the paragraph that you set tab stops for in the previous exercise.

Select Tabs from the Format menu, and click on 3 in the tab list. Then click on Delete to remove the setting. Finally, click on OK. The text in column 3 moves to the left and repositions at Publisher's default tab stop at 2.5 inches.

Note

To move or change a tab stop, you must first delete it and then enter a new setting in its place. The tab, however, remains in the paragraph. When you set a new location for the tab stop, the old tab moves the text that was positioned at it to the new location.

How to Clear a Tab Stop

1. Select the Text frame in which you want to clear tab stops.
2. Position the insertion point in the paragraph for which you want to clear tab stops.
3. Select Tabs from the Format menu.
4. In the tab list, click on the location that you want to clear, or click on Delete All Tabs to clear them all.
5. Click on Delete to clear the individual setting.
6. Repeat steps 4 and 5 to clear additional tabs.
7. Click on OK.

Frame Formatting

Frame formatting lets you adjust the margins and the number of columns in a Text frame. These settings affect *all* of the paragraphs in the frame. Publisher uses a default setting of .08 inch for the top, bottom, left, and right margins of a Text frame. Text frames use a small default margin so that there is some space between the end of a line in one frame and the beginning of another in the next on a page which contains several adjacent Text frames. Text frames also use a single column of text by default. When you increase the number of columns in a frame, Publisher automatically computes a size

Chapter 7: Formatting Text

for the gap between the columns (called the *column gutter*), and shortens the line length for each column in order to make room in the frame. You can adjust all of these settings in the Margins and Columns dialog box.

- Use the price list template that comes with Publisher (PRICELST.PUB) to start a new publication, and select the Text frame that contains the title at the top of the page. You're going to reposition the title so that it is left aligned on the page instead of centered.
- Select all of the text in the frame, and then click on the Left Align button on the Toolbar. The title moves left, but if you take a closer look at the frame, shown in Figure 7-13, it doesn't quite line up with the column of illustrations. These are positioned on the left margin of the page. The left margin in the frame keeps the title from aligning properly.
- Now select Frame Columns and Margins from the Layout menu and type **0** for the Left and Right Margins. Then click on OK. The title moves to the proper location on the page margin.

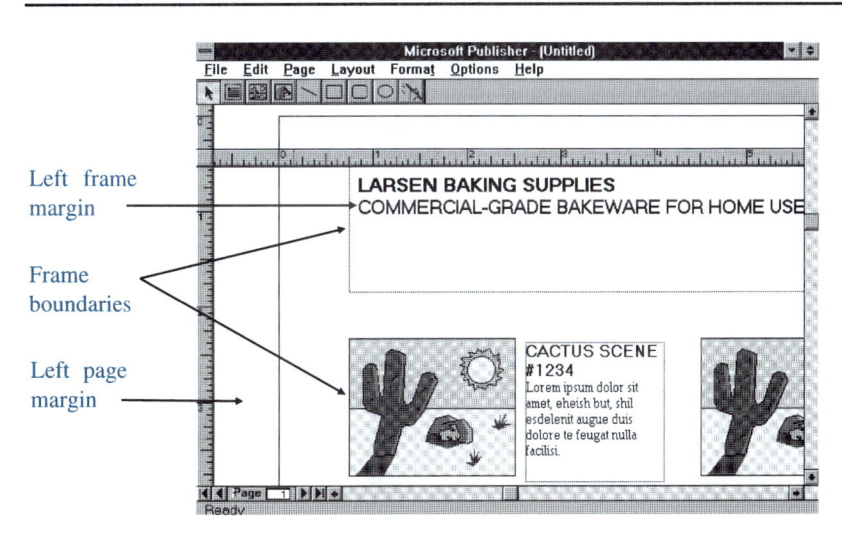

Figure 7-13.   *Adjusting the frame margin to align with the page margin*

> *To alter the default margin or column settings for Text frames in a publication, make changes to the values in the Margins and Columns dialog box before you draw the frame.*
>
> *Tip*

The next exercise involves a design problem that you might encounter producing a report or newsletter. To complete this you'll need to understand how to import text and copy frames.

- Start a new publication using a blank page and create a Text frame for the left side of the page.
- Fill the frame with some dummy text. Try using Import Text from the File menu and bring in the file called PROFILE.TXT from the MSPUB directory.
- Select Frame Columns and Margins from the Layout menu and change the number of columns in the dialog box to 2, as shown here:

> *With multicolumn Text frames, text can appear choppy or with rivers of white space running through the column, as shown in Figure 7-14. Having Publisher automatically hyphenate files can correct these visual problems by allowing more characters to fit on a line. For more information, see the section on hyphenation in Chapter 6.*
>
> *Tip*

- Now copy the frame, and paste the copy. Position it on the right side of the page as shown in Figure 7-14.
- Notice that the gutter between the two middle columns on the page is smaller than the gutter between either pair of outer columns. Publisher uses a default column gutter of .33 inch between columns in a frame. However, the left and right margins of each frame are .08 inch, which only adds up to .16 inch of space between the middle columns.

Chapter 7: *Formatting Text* 225

Figure 7-14. Creating a uniform column gutter

- Adjusted column gutter
- Default column gutter
- Rivers of space

- To even the gutter between all columns on the page, change the column gutter setting in the Frame Columns and Margins dialog box for each frame to .16 inch.

Within a multicolumn frame you can force a new column to begin to the right of the insertion point by pressing CTRL-ENTER.

Tip

How to Change Frame Margins and Columns

1. To change the settings for an individual frame, select the frame. To change the default settings, click on the Text Frame tool.
2. Select Layout from the Main menu and select Frame Columns and Margins from the Layout menu.
3. Change any of the values for margins, columns, or the column gutter.
4. Click OK.

Review

Text formatting is one of the most powerful tools in desktop publishing. It opens up a world of options to the designer, especially in light of the flexibility of modern printers and the availability of an enormous range of type fonts. *Typography*—the art of formatting text—can dramatically impact everything about a publication from its size, legibility, and frame layout to the indirect visual influences it has on pictures and line art. Remember the tools that are at your disposal as a typographer.

- Characters can be individually formatted. All of the standard character styles and positions can be assigned to any font.
- Numerous fonts may already be available on your system. More can be added for special applications, and Publisher can make use of them.
- Publisher can adjust kerning and leading so solutions to difficult typographical problems are within your reach.
- Standard paragraph alignment and a broad selection of tab settings make formatting text for different applications fast.
- Tabs make it easy to align proportionally spaced fonts in multiple columns.
- Text frames can be adjusted to display multiple columns automatically.

8

Working with WordArt

WordArt is the alternative to text for displaying copy. It is one of Publisher's most unique and innovative features. With WordArt, as with text, you can affect the format of frames and the characters and paragraphs inside them. Your options for character and paragraph formatting, however, are different in WordArt. For example, the lines in a WordArt paragraph can be arched or inverted. An entirely different selection of fonts and font sizes is available for WordArt characters.

Some of the most common applications for WordArt are in creating accents, highlights, special effects, and in publications where you need a very large type size, but nothing adequate for text is available on your printer. The headlines in a newsletter or the banner in an advertisement, for example, are ideal applications in a copy-heavy publication. You might even consider using WordArt for the body copy of an invitation or greeting card for which a fanciful font is appropriate. You can only enter a limited number (250) of characters in a WordArt frame, so it's not practical for body copy in long projects. Examples of WordArt using some of the Publisher templates appear in Figure 8-1.

Figure 8-1. Some uses of WordArt

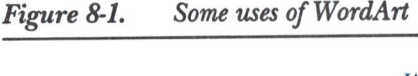

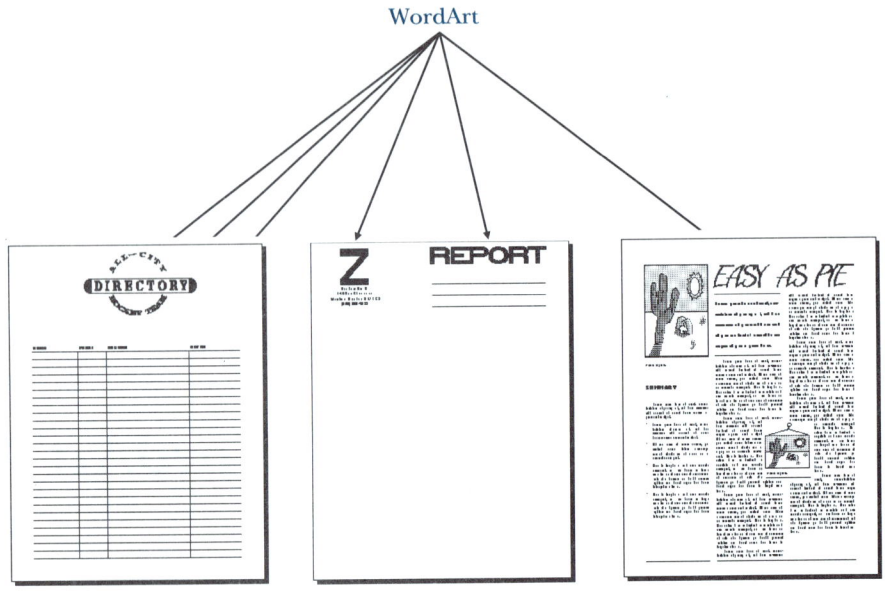

Many of the same guidelines for developing a publication apply to both WordArt and text. Like text, most of the choices you make in formatting WordArt—except for character size—have little effect on the structure of a publication. Some of the more unusual paragraph orientations, such as slanted or curved, can also affect the placement of adjacent frames. Even if you're uncertain about the art direction for the font or style in a particular frame, get the text into all of the WordArt frames early in the project, preferably when you enter text. It's impossible to experiment with the effects of formatting unless you have some material to work with.

In general, formatting WordArt is one of the most entertaining aspects of working with Publisher. The WordArt font sets do *not* depend on those installed on your printer or under Windows. Likewise, the special paragraph formats are all printer independent. Given the selection of WordArt fonts (a total of 19), you are likely to try a number of different options before settling on the one you want. The unique possibilities that Publisher has for styling

Chapter 8: *Working with WordArt*

WordArt fonts make the variety of choices extremely robust. When you work with special effects, it's natural to try lots of different combinations before you find what you're looking for. When you're working with WordArt, the results can be unexpected, but the process is usually fun!

This chapter assumes that you are already comfortable with the fundamentals of working with frames and with entering, editing, and formatting text. Practical examples appear throughout the chapter that use both Publisher templates and material that you create from scratch. Some of the Publisher templates also appear with modifications. Don't become frustrated if you can't locate a file that appears exactly like one used here. It's always easy to change a template using the Publisher tools and techniques you already know about. Since special effects are so relevant to WordArt, many of the examples are geared to creating only a small part of a publication.

At this point in the discussion, it is assumed that you know when to start a new publication in order to complete an example. Summaries appear for editing and formatting text. Since they are all implemented as lists or buttons from a single dialog box, you should feel comfortable with using them. Finally, the PageWizards make liberal use of WordArt and are an excellent source of reference for applying it. When you're feeling stuck for a new idea, it's always fun to let Publisher come up with something by running a PageWizard.

Entering and Editing WordArt

WordArt operates a little differently from text. To begin with, Publisher assumes that you will type in the characters for a WordArt frame at the keyboard. It has no explicit commands for importing text from other Windows applications or from non-Windows applications. Since WordArt is generally used for shorter blocks of copy, this isn't very much of an inconvenience. In addition, you cannot enter or edit WordArt in a frame directly. You must use the WordArt dialog box to change the content of a WordArt frame.

Tip

If you copy text from a Publisher Text frame or another Windows application to the Clipboard, press (SHIFT)-(INS) *to paste it into the Copy field of the WordArt dialog box. Be careful, however, that the text that you copy to the Clipboard (or the combined amount of text that ends up in the dialog box) does not exceed 250 characters, or some of them may get lost.*

Try creating a WordArt frame now to see how the basics work:

- Create a WordArt frame that conforms to the margin guides on a blank page. After you complete the frame, Publisher takes a moment to display the WordArt dialog box, shown in Figure 8-2. When the dialog box appears for a new WordArt frame, Publisher always displays the words "Your Text Here" in the Copy field. Since that text is already selected, you can just start typing.

- Type **Fire Sale!** Publisher deletes the words, "Your Text Here," and replaces them with the ones you enter.

- Click on the Style list. As soon as you close the Copy field, your entry appears in the Preview window. Notice that the copy fills the window from left to right just as "Your Text Here" did, even though your entry contains four fewer characters. This is due to the current selection for Best Fit in the Size list.

- Scroll down the Style list until you see Slant Up (More), and then click on it. In the Preview window, Publisher will slant the text from the lower-left to upper-right corners. This is one of the special

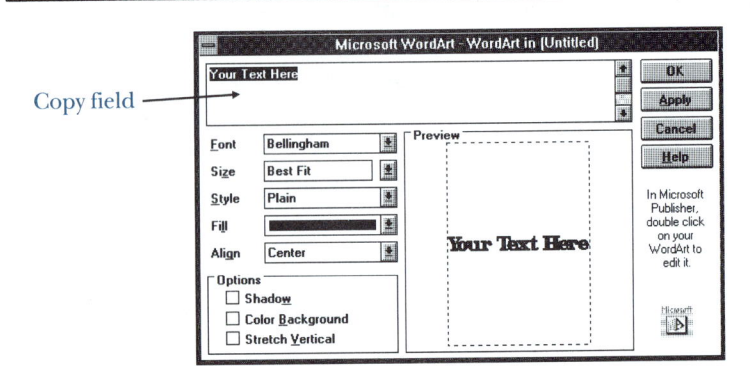

Figure 8-2.   *WordArt dialog box*

Chapter 8: *Working with WordArt* 231

WordArt paragraph styles. The new style appears in the Preview window as soon as you close the list.

When you click on the Apply button, Publisher lets you see how your formatting looks in the actual publication. Usually—and this case is no exception—the WordArt dialog box blocks your view of the frame, and you must drag the box out of the way. Try clicking on Apply now. Then click on the Title bar of the dialog box, and drag it down the screen far enough to reveal the WordArt frame that you're working with, as shown in Figure 8-3. WordArt can often have unexpected effects, especially as you begin to experiment with formatting. The Apply button is a real time saver because you don't have to keep opening and closing the dialog box in order to see how special effects blend in the context of the page you want them to appear on.

Note

Whenever you click on Apply, the text in the Copy field actually becomes the current text of the frame in the publication. You cannot click on Cancel to reverse the effect of Apply.

Figure 8-3.   Dragging the WordArt dialog box aside to see your text

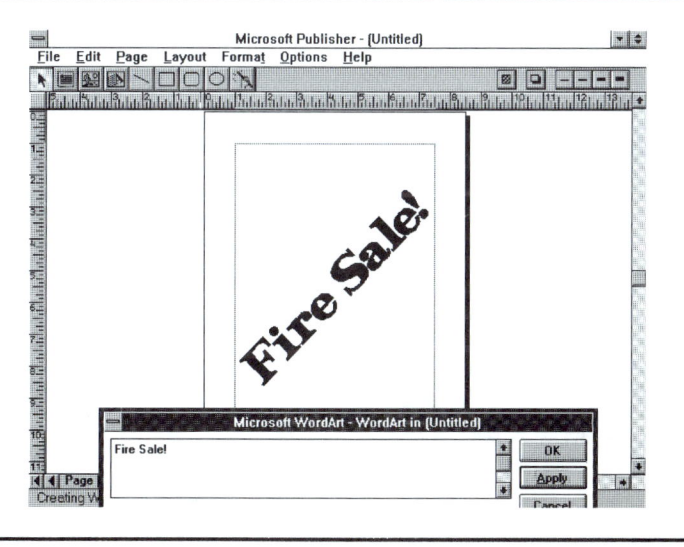

Now change the copy for the frame to "Tag Sale."

- First select "Fire." The Copy field operates like any other Windows field. You can place the insertion point at any location by clicking, and select characters by dragging or by double-clicking. All of the standard field-editing techniques you've learned about will work in the Copy field. It just happens to be a very large field!
- Delete "Fire" and type **Tag**. Click on Apply to see how the change looks in the publication.
- Click on OK to close the dialog box and return to the Publisher screen.

Note

Pressing ENTER *does not close the WordArt dialog box as it does most other dialog boxes in Windows applications. If you happen to press* ENTER *while the Copy field is open, you will insert a new line in the field. This can affect the appearance of the frame dramatically. For example, if you add a line to the Copy field in the previous exercise, the size of the text in the frame is reduced substantially. In this case the size reduction occurs because the frame uses the Best Fit setting for size, and adding another line changes the number of characters and lines that Publisher must fit in the frame. Because there are so many WordArt settings in which Publisher adjusts some formatting characteristic for you, surprising results can occur if you inadvertently add extra lines or spaces.*

When you want to edit the copy in an existing WordArt frame, click on the frame. Then select Edit WordArt Object from the Edit menu. If you want to change only some of the characters in the Copy field, you must first clear the text selection before you begin typing. Then use the same field editing techniques described earlier to change the copy or any of the formatting options. There are no tab stops available in WordArt, and Publisher treats all paragraphs for a single WordArt frame in the same way. Consequently, pressing ENTER is the only way to terminate a line in the Copy field. You can only determine the effects of word wrap—if any—by looking in the Preview window or applying the change. The margins that affect word wrap exist in the frame, not in the Copy field.

Tip

To display the WordArt dialog box, double-click on the WordArt frame that you want to edit.

Chapter 8: *Working with WordArt* 233

If you draw a WordArt frame and then click on Cancel in the dialog box, Publisher is no longer sure about what type of frame you want. The frame remains on the screen, but if you try to edit it the only active option is Insert Object. The Insert Object dialog box opens, as shown here:

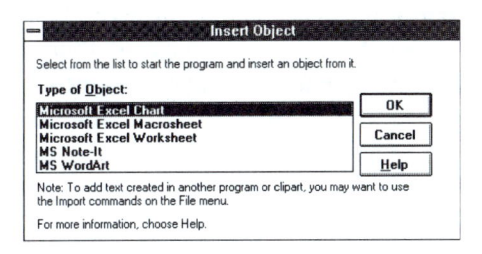

```
┌─────────────────────── Insert Object ───────────────────────┐
│ Select from the list to start the program and insert an object from it. │
│ Type of Object:                                             │
│ ┌─────────────────────────────┐  ┌────────┐                 │
│ │ Microsoft Excel Chart       │  │   OK   │                 │
│ │ Microsoft Excel Macrosheet  │  └────────┘                 │
│ │ Microsoft Excel Worksheet   │  ┌────────┐                 │
│ │ MS Note-It                  │  │ Cancel │                 │
│ │ MS WordArt                  │  └────────┘                 │
│ └─────────────────────────────┘  ┌────────┐                 │
│                                  │  Help  │                 │
│ Note: To add text created in another program or clipart, you may want to use │
│ the Import commands on the File menu.                       │
│ For more information, choose Help.                          │
└─────────────────────────────────────────────────────────────┘
```

If you select MS WordArt from the window in this dialog box, the WordArt dialog box appears and you can treat the frame as WordArt. The remainder of the selections in this window, however, let you link pictures from other applications. When you select one of them, Publisher treats this frame as a special type of picture frame. See Chapter 9 or Appendix A for more information on these options.

How to Enter or Edit Copy in WordArt

1. Click on the WordArt tool and draw a frame, or double-click on an existing WordArt frame.
2. Use standard Windows field editing techniques to edit the characters in the Copy field.
3. Click on Apply to see the effects of your entry in the frame without closing the dialog box.
4. Click on OK.

Formatting WordArt

The formatting commands for WordArt can be broken into the same categories as those used for text. Publisher provides options for formatting characters, paragraphs, and frames; however, there are distinct differences from text. For each formatting command there are different choices for WordArt. It also has some formatting commands that are completely unique. For example, paragraph alignment is available for both text and WordArt, but the selection of alignments is broader and more unusual for WordArt. Paragraph styles such as upside down or bottom to top are simply not available for Text frames.

Like the process of entering or editing copy for a WordArt frame, you can only format WordArt through the dialog box. You can format it when you first create a WordArt frame or later on. Whether you are entering copy for the first time or editing existing copy, the formatting choices you make using any of the lists or buttons affect *all* characters in the Copy field uniformly. Selecting individual characters has no effect. You cannot, for example, choose two separate fonts for different characters in the same frame.

Likewise, paragraph formatting affects all paragraphs equally. When you want to combine different WordArt effects that Publisher would otherwise reject in a single frame, you must use multiple frames. Each formatting option can be enabled, disabled, or changed at any time. Vertical stretching, for example, can be turned on or off for any style of type and at any time before or after you change a character's font.

How to Format WordArt

1. Click on the WordArt tool and draw a frame or double-click on an existing WordArt frame.
2. Make choices from any of the lists or click on buttons in the WordArt dialog box.
3. Click on Apply to see the effects of your formatting in the frame without closing the dialog box.
4. Click on OK.

Formatting Characters

Part of what makes WordArt fonts so unusual is that they are *scalable*: they can be sized to any proportion in relation to a WordArt frame, from extremely small to almost 14 inches in height. Likewise, they can be stretched and distorted in a variety of ways to create unusual visual effects. You can also print WordArt fonts in color, if you have an appropriate printer. Most of the special effects have different results when used in different combinations. Experimentation is the best way to become familiar with WordArt. This section discusses each of the different formatting options for WordArt characters. These are all available as buttons or lists on the WordArt dialog box.

Font

Most of the WordArt font sets are geared to attracting attention. These should be used sparingly or a publication will appear busy and difficult to read. The fancier fonts are ideal for creating *logotypes*—logos composed of letters only—and other applications that require a strong typographical identity. You could easily apply the WordArt in the letterhead shown in Figure 8-4, for example, to a complete range of stationery products including envelopes, business cards, labels, and so on. The newsletter title, on the other hand, uses a modern font with a digital look to reinforce the identity of a publication from a machine-oriented industry.

Figure 8-4.   Using WordArt fonts for identity

To create the logo for Formal Evening Entertainment:

- Draw a WordArt frame about 5/8 inch high and 2 inches long. When the WordArt dialog box appears, type **EFE** in the Copy field.
- Click on the font list to display the selection of WordArt fonts, as shown here:

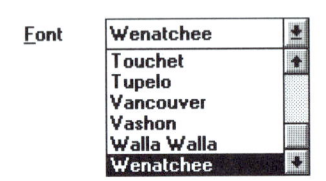

Font	Wenatchee
	Touchet
	Tupelo
	Vancouver
	Vashon
	Walla Walla
	Wenatchee

- Scroll down the list until you see Wenatchee and click on it. Then click on OK to complete the frame.
- Create a second WordArt frame that is 2 inches high and 5/8 inch wide.
- When the dialog box appears, type the same letters, but follow each by pressing (ENTER) so they all occur on separate lines.
- Use the same procedure described for the previous frame to select Wenatchee as the font. Then click on OK to complete the frame.
- Move one frame over the other until the central letter (*F*) in both frames exactly overlaps (yes, this will take a little doing, but that's part of the job).

The border around the logotype was created using the rectangular drawing tool with an 8-point line thickness. If you're feeling adventurous, you can try adding it now. Otherwise you'll have to wait until Chapter 10.

The title for the magazine is even simpler to create.

- Use a WordArt frame about 3/4 inch tall and 8 inches wide. Type the title in the Copy field.

- Select Touchet as the font and Letter Justified as the alignment. The positioning statement beneath the title is similarly letter justified, but uses Longview as the font. Notice that none of these examples requires you to specify a type size. They all let Publisher take care of determining the type size by using the Best Fit option described in the next section.

The design for a few of the WordArt fonts is on the conventional side. There are serif and sans serif sets that more closely resemble the style of type you could use for headlines or body copy in an application with a conservative tone. It's easy to use them in conjunction with text fonts when the size or spacing available from the latter is too limited. Ellensburg and Inglewood, for example, are very similar in appearance to Times Roman, and Longview closely resembles Helvetica. Times Roman and Helvetica are two of the most popular text fonts found on many laser printers. Use the following table as a guideline for applying WordArt type styles.

Conventional	Borderline	Offbeat
Bellingham	Anacortes	Duvall
Inglewood	Ellensburg	Enumclaw
Longview		Langley
Vancouver		Marysville
Vashon		Mineral
		Omak
		Sequim
		Snohomish
		Touchet
		Tupelo
		WallaWalla
		Wenatchee

Given this spectrum, you're almost certain to find a typeface that meets your requirements. A complete reproduction of each of the font sets can be found in Appendix C.

Size

Most font sets for text are available in only fixed sizes. Courier, for example, is almost always a 12-point font. The more common proportional fonts are typically found in 10, 12, 14, 18, and 24 points. Depending on your printer and the way that Windows has been configured, you may have access to other sizes as well. It's even possible that you have scalable text fonts if you have a printer that can accommodate them. Whether you do or not, all WordArt fonts are scalable. In addition to the popular sizes that come with the program, shown in Figure 8-5, you can have Publisher create a size for you based on the size of a frame. This method of scaling type is called *Best Fit* in Publisher.

Standard sizes are useful when you have fixed typographic specifications. You may want to use WordArt in a headline, for example, and the publication requires a 36-point type for the lead article. If you create a WordArt frame and select a type size that's too big for the frame, Publisher displays this message:

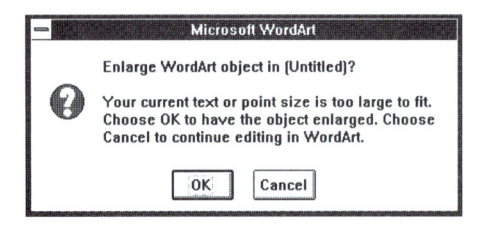

If you click on OK, Publisher will actually enlarge the frame to accommodate the type size you requested, although the new dimensions may not fit attractively in the publication.

Best Fit, on the other hand, lets Publisher take care of sizing the type for you. It scales the type size to the height and width of the frame, based on using a centered alignment. For the most part, Best Fit is a terrific time saver. It keeps you from laboring over exact type specs and lets you create the correct size by eyeballing the application. It can save you time for the same reason if you change a frame's size. Occasionally, however, the Best Fit setting will behave unexpectedly. For example, when characters formatted with Best Fit use a plain (horizontal) paragraph style, Publisher assigns a larger point size

Chapter 8: *Working with WordArt*

Figure 8-5.   *Fixed sizes available for WordArt*

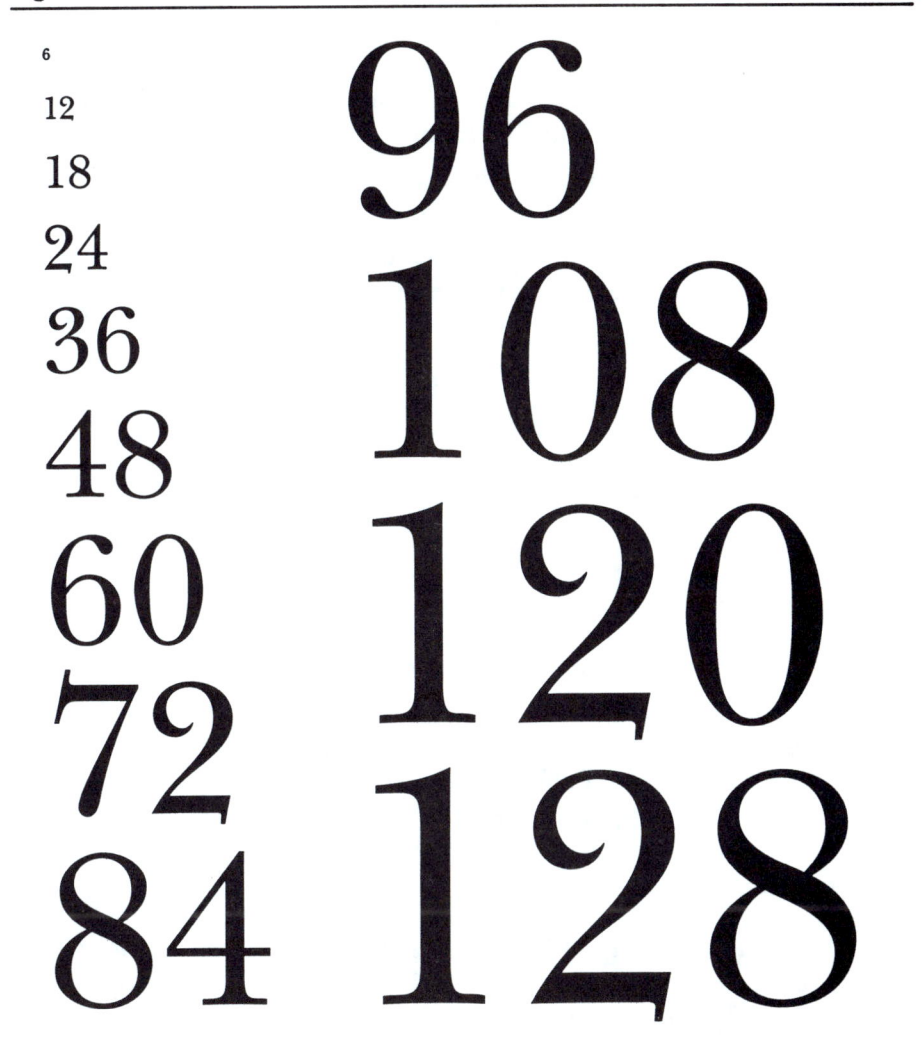

6
12
18
24
36
48
60
72
84

96
108
120
128

to them than when the paragraph uses a slanted style, even though there appears to be more room in the latter case.

- Try creating a square WordArt frame with approximately 2-inch sides and click on **OK** to accept the dummy text that comes with the frame.
- Copy the frame and paste it back into the publication. Drag it alongside of the first frame.
- Double-click on the duplicate frame to edit the WordArt and change the style to Slant Up (Less).
- Finally, click on **OK**. Both frames have the same dimensions and use Best Fit to determine the type size.

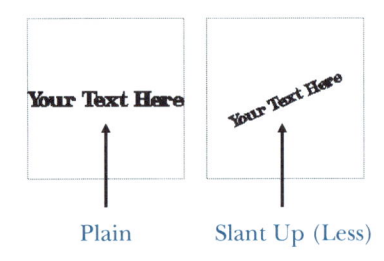

Plain   Slant Up (Less)

The results, however, are surprising, considering what appears to be more room in the frame on the right.

This sort of automatic adjustment can be easily overcome by resizing the frame, and doesn't really represent a problem. You should, however, be aware of this type of effect. Publisher often tries to do so many things with WordArt that the results are unexpected. In this example, if you had used a fixed point size, the type size would have remained the same, regardless of the change in paragraph style.

Note

If you reduce the size of a WordArt frame that contains characters with a specific point size, Publisher may not be able to display all of them. In these cases, the characters that won't fit are chopped off of both ends. This is known as cropping.

WordArt frames are transparent by default. No matter what size you make a frame, you can usually place the copy as near to other objects as necessary by overlapping the frames. In the following example, the WordArt frame with

Chapter 8: Working with WordArt 241

the diagonal banner ("Held Over 2 Days!") overlaps the frame with the main headline of the ad:

Overlapping frames

Fancy first letter

Best Fit is also the easiest way to create a fancy first letter. Just create a WordArt frame over a Text frame, and type the individual letter in the Copy field. Publisher takes care of all the rest. You can, of course, create fancier first letters using border art and shading. These topics are discussed in Chapter 10. The method described here, however, is extremely simple and very effective.

Stretch Vertical

When you stretch a font vertically, you intentionally distort it. You can use vertical stretching to your advantage to fill subtle gaps or to create striking visual effects. The catalog cover applications in Figure 8-6 show you some of the possible effects. All three examples use Langley as the font, but only the two on the left use Stretch Vertical. Fonts all have the same height when Stretch is turned on, regardless of their actual point size. In the sample on the left, however, the thinness of the 18-point characters betrays their actual point size. The sample in the middle uses Best Fit based on a 72-point font. The final sample on the right is unstretched (108-point). It's simply there to give you a reference for the size of the other two samples.

You needn't use Stretch Vertical for such extreme measures. For example, while it's easy to line frames up with each other, getting the text inside of them to line up with other objects on the page isn't always so simple. In the following sample from REPORT.PUB, the headline gets aligned with the top

Figure 8-6.   *Vertical stretching with different size settings*

of the neighboring picture by using Stretch Vertical (the frame boundary was in the right position to begin with). There is minimal distortion to the font, as shown here:

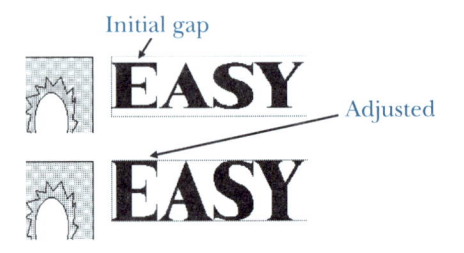

You can try this yourself with the REPORT.PUB template. Just edit the WordArt frame for the main headline ("EASY AS PIE") and click on Vertical Stretch.

Fill

The Fill option lets you add color to the characters in a WordArt frame. For the most part, color is printer-dependent. While it may show up on your monitor, it won't print unless you have a color device. You can, however,

Chapter 8: *Working with WordArt* 243

create dropout lettering using a standard black and white printer. *Dropout letters* appear in white on a black or patterned background. For example:

- Create a WordArt frame about 3 inches high and 5 inches wide, and type **Blackout!** in the Copy field.
- In the dialog box, click on the Fill list to open it.
- Scroll up the list and click on White (it's the first in the list, and may be invisible if your Windows color configuration uses a white background). The copy in the Preview window becomes hollow, as shown here:

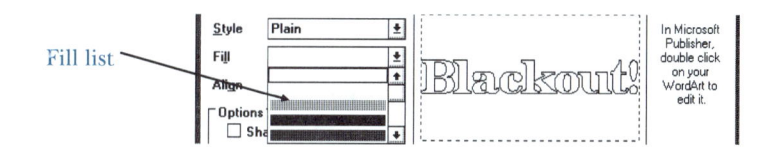

- Now click on the Color Background button. Publisher fills the frame in with a black background creating the dropout text shown here:

Note

While the stenciled look you created before coloring the background was only an intermediate step, it might be interesting for other applications.

Shadow

Shadow creates an outline behind each character. For thinner, stringier fonts such as Marysville or Langley, the shadow comes across without affecting the weight of the font. With the heavier fonts, on the other hand, the shadow almost gives a three-dimensional effect to the characters, as you can see here:

Shadows SHADOWS

Shadows are appropriate for applications in which you want to create a lighter, more relaxed feeling.

Formatting Paragraphs

Paragraph styles and alignments give you access to some of Publisher's most interesting visual effects. Styles let you change the orientation of lines in a WordArt frame. Unlike some of the options available in formatting WordArt characters, such as Font or Size, there are no equivalents for style in Text frames (they are all Plain). Most of the alignment options for WordArt, on the other hand, resemble those that you have already become familiar with in working with Text frames. Combining styles and alignments can yield unusual results. With the exception of the Button style, Publisher treats all of the paragraphs (lines) in a WordArt frame in the same way.

Tip

If you browse through the templates that come with Publisher, you'll see that Best Fit is often used with the more offbeat applications. While it's not a cure-all, Best Fit is usually a good setting to use when you try out a new effect (that's probably why it's the default setting for size). If you've drawn a frame accurately, the size that Publisher establishes will probably fit your needs. You can always fine-tune the size of the characters later. Choosing a fixed point size, on the other hand, can limit the impact of some of the formatting options. Best Fit also spares you the trouble of calibrating the type if you decide to change the size of a frame.

Style

WordArt styles are either plain, rotated, or rounded. An easy way to remember all of the options is by relating them to a clock. Each of the styles comes from running a line of copy around the clock, so to speak, as shown in Figure 8-7.

Plain style is what you normally think of for text. Copy appears on a flat line reading from left to right. The *Slant Up* options move up from 3 o'clock toward 12, where they become Bottom to Top. The *Slant Down* options tilt downward from the same point toward 6, where they become Top to Bottom.

Chapter 8: *Working with WordArt* 245

Figure 8-7. WordArt styles

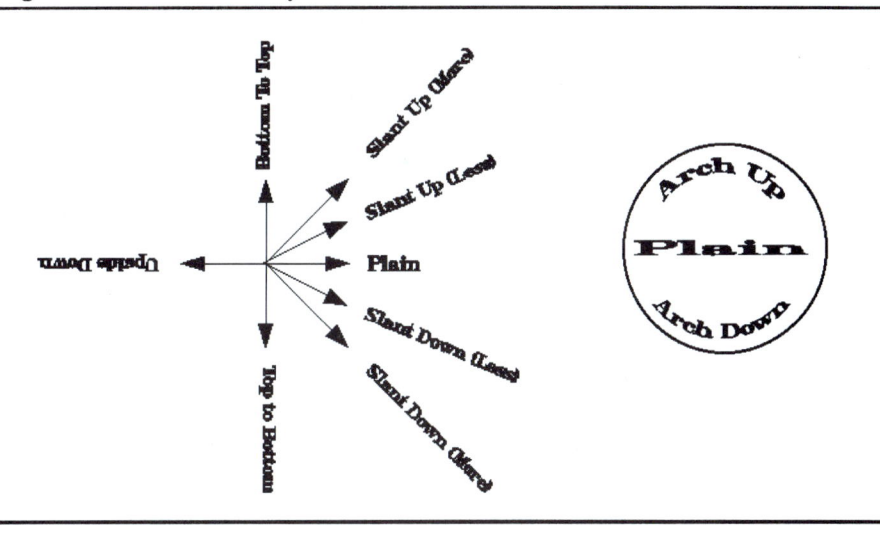

Upside Down is a full flip to 9 o'clock. The *Arch* options (Up and Down) each move from 9 to 3 through either 12 or 6. The *Button* uses all three lines, including both Arches and Plain on the middle line. Just think *clock*!

Some of the styles have more obvious applications than others. Bottom to Top, for example, is a natural for stationery. It presents an elegant but unusual appearance. The slanted styles, while very simple, are actually more attention getting than you would expect. Warnings and other exclamatory statements usually appear on an angle like this because they are in stark opposition to plain text. The arches and the button all present a softer contrast to plain text, and are appropriate for casual or humorous applications. These suggestions are, of course, general guidelines.

Buttons use the first three lines that you enter in the Copy field to form the top, middle, and bottom lines of the button respectively. Publisher ignores any other lines that you enter after the third. You can enter different text for each of the lines to vary the message in the button. If you leave the middle line blank, Publisher will produce opposing up and down arches. This is handy if you want to place an illustration or photo in the middle.

Consider the evolution of the buttons in **Figure 8-8**. You can start by creating a WordArt frame about 2 inches square.

- Type **HENRY FOR PRESIDENT** and separate each word by pressing (ENTER), so each is on a different line. Then click on Apply, and drag the dialog box out of the way so that you can see the result. It should look like the first example on the left.
- Change the size of the characters to 12-point and apply the change. It should look like the middle version.
- Finally, try setting the alignment to Fit Horizontally. You should get the example on the right.

This exercise is fairly representative of how you might go about modeling a button. (And you can certainly continue—there's no reason to stop now!) You really can't tell the full effect of many of these formatting options until you see them implemented with the exact characters that you're going to use them with.

Alignment

Alignment defines the way paragraphs are positioned with respect to the boundaries and margins of a frame. You already know about four of the six alignment options for WordArt from your work in formatting text. Left-aligned copy is flush with the left margin of the page and ragged on the right. Right-aligned copy is the reverse. It's aligned on the right side of the page and ragged on the left. Centered copy is equidistant from both margins. *Word Justified* is the WordArt equivalent to Justified copy for text. Publisher spreads

Figure 8-8.   Using WordArt to create a button

the words across each line so that both the left and right sides are aligned with their respective margins.

With *Letter Justified*, Publisher spaces the letters of an individual word across each line in order to make it flush with both the left and right margins, as shown here:

H E R E   N   O
N O W   WHERE

If multiple words occur on the same line, the line is effectively word justified by Publisher instead of letter justified. Little if any justification occurs between the letters of each word. Fit Horizontally is a more extreme way to justify text. It distorts the characters on each line laterally in order to make them justify.

HERE   NO
NOW   WHERE

You might say that Fit Horizontally is the cousin of Stretch Vertical. They both maximize character size in different dimensions.

Formatting Frames

Like Text frames, you can change the margins of WordArt frames and reshape them after you have added material to them. In these cases, Publisher adapts the contents of a frame as best it can, and it usually does a pretty good job. However, changing the dimensions of a frame can affect the formatting inside dramatically, especially if you have used any of the self-adjusting formats such as Best Fit, Stretch Vertically, or Fit Horizontally. These effects can be positive or negative. Experimenting with WordArt is the best way to learn its use most effectively.

The Color Background option is limited. If you select white fill for the copy and a color background, Publisher supplies a black background. If you select another color for Fill, Publisher provides a gray background. To get a more significant selection of background colors, you must supply a color or pattern for the frame itself, as explained in Chapter 10. In any case, none of these colors will appear in your finished publication unless you have a color printer, although they may appear on screen.

Review

WordArt can add substantial interest to any publication. Whether you're looking for a subtle embellishment to a headline or some substantial comic relief, WordArt is the best tool that Publisher has for the job. Many of Publisher's most unique and intuitive features are brought into your hands. Remember these characteristics when you work with WordArt.

- You must use the WordArt dialog box to enter, edit, or format WordArt copy.
- Any formatting that you use affects all characters and lines in a WordArt frame in the same way.
- The Apply button lets you experiment with different effects and view them in the context without closing the WordArt dialog box.
- WordArt has a unique and completely printer-independent set of fonts.
- The WordArt fonts are totally scalable. You can adjust their point size and distort them horizontally or vertically.
- Special effects such as coloring and drop shadows are available for all of the characters in a WordArt frame.
- WordArt copy can use different orientations to slant, invert, or curve lines of text.
- WordArt's Best Fit setting automatically scales type, based on frame size.

9

Working with Images

A publishing program is distinguished by its ability to blend text and graphics smoothly. If there are no graphic elements to a publication, it may be easier to use a word processor to create it than to bother with the page layout issues inherent in publishing. Graphics are a form of information in their own right. While the value of a picture may not always equate to a thousand words, illustrations and photographs convey details as accurately and effectively as copy and, in many instances, with more impact. Whether you're designing an amusing card or an executive report, images are a big part of the message.

Publisher is capable of creating original images through the drawing tools covered in Chapter 10, but anything more than the very simplest graphics are best brought into a publication from a program designed specifically to work with pictures and drawings. Publisher can include images from a variety of popular graphics programs designed for drawing, painting, and creating charts and spreadsheets. Once this material is in a publication, it can be cropped and scaled to suit the needs of the piece. Publisher even comes with a number of ready-to-use clip art illustrations that are copyright-free. You can include them in any publication.

Note: The supplementary disk included with this book contains over 100 illustrations from the Dover Publications Pictorial Archive Series. The Dover material contains attention-getting icons (called dingbats) that Microsoft didn't have room to include in the initial release of Publisher, as well as numerous other general-purpose figures. Be sure to take a look at the Dover images. They're handy and easy to use for a broad variety of applications. If you haven't installed the Dover clip art yet, see Appendix G for more information.

This chapter assumes that you are already comfortable with the fundamentals of working with frames. While it doesn't require that you understand text editing, text formatting, or WordArt, the more you know at this point, the better. Practical examples that use Publisher templates and clip art appear throughout the chapter. Many of the examples are geared to creating only a small part of a publication. At this point in the discussion, you should know when to start a new publication in order to complete an example. As usual, you can find generic instructions for most tasks in a box at the end of a section.

Where Graphics Fit in Your Work Flow

Like the sequence for text discussed in Chapter 6, you should develop a routine for working with graphics. The process may be informal, but it will help the publication to develop smoothly. The biggest payoff for following a general procedural guide is that you avoid redesign, which usually requires twice the time it takes to implement an original design correctly. Working with graphics can be very absorbing and pleasurable, but also time-consuming. Discarding work that you put your heart into is frustrating.

As with Text and WordArt frames, the choices you make about Picture frames are more flexible than those you make about page layout. Individual frames can be, and often are, modified during development without affecting an entire publication. Cropping and scaling an image in many cases lets you retain its full composition and has a minimal impact on page layout. While there are, of course, practical limits to how small you can make a picture, these tend not to be as restrictive as those imposed by text—you simply can't fit a ten-page story in a two-page newsletter without making it illegible. The choices that you make about line art and borders are even more flexible because they have little or no impact on a publication's structure. Consider the following steps as a suggested methodology for working with graphics when you're publishing a piece. These occur concurrently with their text counterparts.

1. *Create the major Picture frames early in a publication's development.* Decide where you need pictures and where you don't. Think about why you're using them. Create as many of the important frames as possible to see how they affect other copy, Picture frames, and the composition of individual pages. Too many pictures can clutter a page. By creating the frames in their initial sizes, you can get a good sense of whether the overall design you have in mind can work once it's on the page.

2. *Load the images.* Remember, pictures are information too! You can't make an informed judgment about the size of a Picture frame until you see if the information inside of it is clear. In addition, not all graphic file formats are compatible with Publisher, as detailed later in this chapter. You may need to check file compatibility and possibly make conversions. If you're not planning to use a lot of imported artwork, this may never be a problem. However, you're better off knowing about these issues before you're sitting on top of a *drop-dead date* (publishing slang for the latest possible deadline at which you can go to press).

3. *Scale and crop the images.* At this point you can adjust Picture frame size and have some fun developing the pages. Since all of the publication's major components are in place, you can tune the frames until you achieve the overall balance and composition you're looking for. When this stage—and its complementary steps for copy—are complete, you should have established the overall look for the publication, and not need to return to layout or frame issues except to make minor modifications.

4. *Add line art, borders, and shading.* Since these added touches affect structure the least, they are best left until last.

Creating Pictures

Images that you bring into a publication all reside in Picture frames. Creating Picture frames is no different than creating any of the other frame types in Publisher. Just click on the Picture Frame tool and use the mouse to draw the frame. Once you complete the frame, Publisher gives you four ways to get images into it—import, paste, insert, and embed. The method you decide to use depends on the source of the picture and how you plan to use it in your publication.

Importing Images

Importing images is easy and fun when everything goes right, and with Publisher it usually will. There are, however, some rules of the road that you should know about graphics files. You may not have gambled on learning quite this much about computer images right now, but strange things can happen when you try to import or resize pictures. It's useful to have some background when problems occur so you can understand what may be going on, and how to correct them.

Images, like all other computer data, are stored in files. Just as different text processing programs use their own file formats for storing words, graphics programs use different formats for storing images. Publisher supports the following graphics file formats.

Format/Source	Extension
Windows Bitmap	.BMP
PC Paintbrush	.PCX
Scanned	.TIF
Encapsulated PostScript	.EPS
Windows Metafile	.WMF
Micrografx Designer	.DRW
Computer Graphics Metafile	.CGM

If the file you want to use in a publication is in one of these formats, you can probably use it with no problems. There are, however, slight deviations from even these standards. If the file you want to use is in another format—

Chapter 9: *Working with Images*

such as .IMG or .GIF—or Publisher has trouble recognizing the file format, you may need to use a conversion program such as HiJaak or Import for Windows. These programs can transform image data from one format to another.

Note

Both the clip art that comes with Publisher and the Dover clip art that comes with this book are Computer Graphics Metafiles (.CGM) and are completely compatible with the program. You won't have any problem using them.

Importing is the easiest way of dealing with outside images. All you need is a picture on a disk in one of the file formats that Publisher accepts. You don't even have to create a Picture frame. Just select Import Picture from the File menu, and the dialog box appears, as shown in Figure 9-1. Publisher normally displays all of the files for the formats it accepts in the File window. If you need to look at the selection from a different drive or directory, use the directory tree or the drive list to switch to a different disk area. These techniques are the same as those described for importing text files in Chapter 6.

Scroll down the list of graphics files until you find the one you're looking for. Filenames can be cryptic. To make sure that a file contains the image you want, click on the Preview button. Preview is a time saver if you're not sure about the content of the file. To import a file, click on OK or double-click on the filename. Publisher creates a Picture frame for the file using the exact proportions that the image was created with. Importing a picture in this

Figure 9-1. Import Picture dialog box

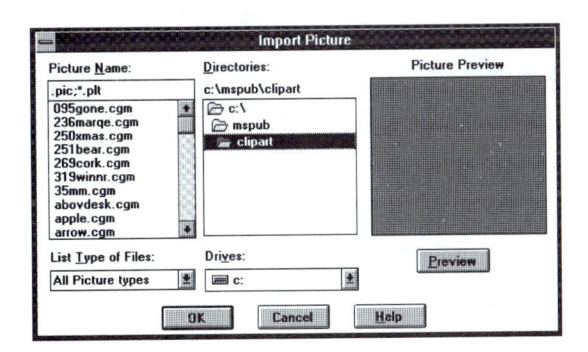

manner is the only way to ensure that its original proportions are preserved in the publication.

> *Normally, all of the Microsoft and Dover clip art resides in a directory called \MSPUB\CLIPART on the drive on which you installed Publisher. You may have to switch to that drive or directory in order to find this material for the exercises in the remainder of this chapter.*
>
> Note

Try this exercise:

- Start a new publication and select Import Picture from the File menu.
- When the dialog box appears, double-click on 35MM.CGM. The clip art image of a camera appears in the publication, as shown in Figure 9-2 on the left. It's a bit too large for most practical applications (Publisher always creates very large frames on its own), but its proportions are accurate. You can maintain these proportions and

Figure 9-2. Two different importing results

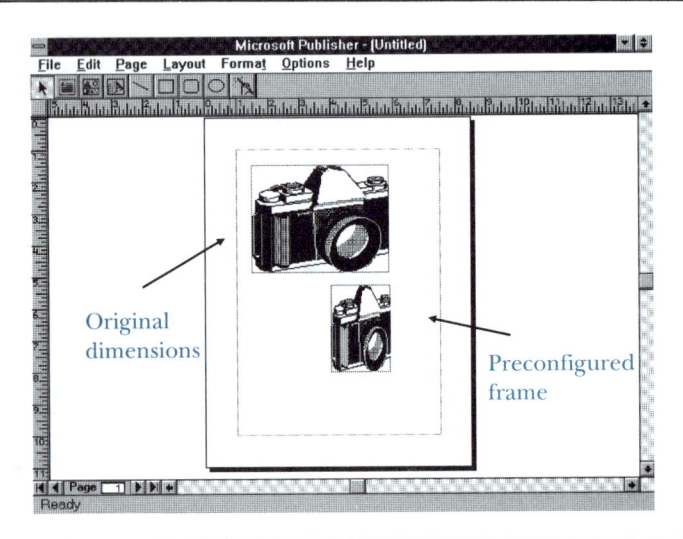

Chapter 9: *Working with Images*

scale the image to fit properly in the publication. (More information about scaling is available later in this chapter.)

- For now, delete the Picture frame by selecting it and pressing (DEL).
- Create a Picture frame about 4 inches square in an empty part of the same page.
- Select the frame and repeat the process described before. Select Import Picture from the File menu, and double-click on 35MM.CGM. In this frame, the image is somewhat distorted: it's tall and thin. Publisher fit it into the frame you created, but in so doing had to alter the original proportions of the image.

The lesson here is simple. Don't go jamming pictures into frames where they may get bashed. Whether you use the Preview Window to get a glimpse of the actual dimensions or just import the picture letting Publisher create a frame, be sure you know what it's supposed to look like before you make plans for the size of the frame that will ultimately house it. This underscores the importance of using a consistent overall methodology for creating a publication.

How to Import Pictures

1. Create or select a Picture frame, unless you want Publisher to create a frame for you.
2. Select File from the Menu bar and select Import Picture from the File menu.
3. Click on the directory tree or drive list, if necessary, to change the current directory.
4. Click on the file you want to import in the file list.
5. Click on Preview if you want to get a look at the image before using it in a publication.
6. Click on OK.

Pasting Images Between Windows Applications

If the image you want to use is in another Windows application, just copy it to the Windows Clipboard. Then switch to Publisher, select a Picture frame, and paste it. This method is ideal if you have no plans to change or update the image once it's in a publication. Most Windows applications contain an Edit menu with options for Cut, Copy, and Paste, just like Publisher. The Paintbrush accessory that comes with Windows, for example, supports these options. If you're familiar with Paintbrush, try this exercise:

- Start a new publication using CATALOG.PUB and turn to page 2.
- Switch to Paintbrush using the Windows Task Manager.
- Use Paintbrush to draw a simple image, as shown in Figure 9-3 on the left.
- Select the object and copy it to the Windows Clipboard.

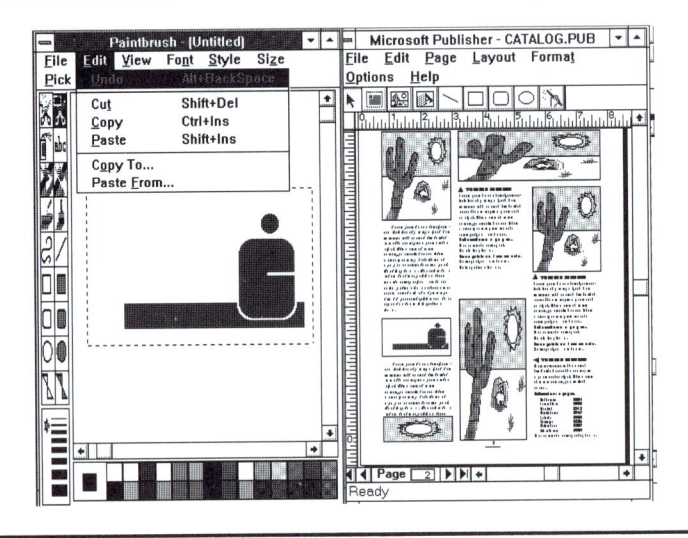

Figure 9-3.   *Pasting an image from Paintbrush*

Chapter 9: *Working with Images* 257

- Switch to Publisher and click on the middle frame in the first column of the page.
- Click on Paste from the Edit menu. The warning message shown in Figure 9-4 appears.
- Click on OK to paste it into the frame. Publisher only displays this message when a frame already contains an image.

It's impossible to say for sure that this process will be the same for all Windows applications, but selecting, cutting, copying, and pasting images is usually very similar. If you want to send a picture to another Windows application, just cut or copy it from Publisher and use Paste in the other application. The process is virtually indentical.

Tip

If the image you want to use is from another publication, just use the Clipboard to copy or cut the entire frame. Then paste the frame into the new Publisher application. Remember, the Clipboard only holds one selection at a time, the one you most recently cut or copied there. If you intend to paste an image, do it right after you cut or copy it. Otherwise you may inadvertently overwrite the previous selection on the Clipboard.

Figure 9-4. Import warning message

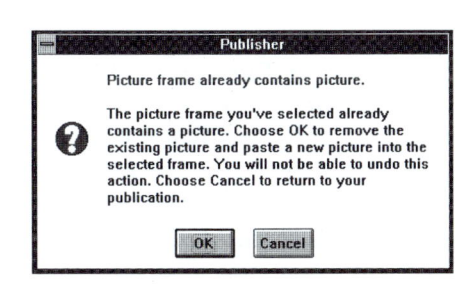

> ### How to Paste Images Between Windows Programs
>
> 1. Use the Windows Program Manager to start Publisher and a second Windows application. The program that contains the picture you want to copy is the *source*. The one that you insert the picture into is the *destination*.
> 2. Select an image from the source using standard techniques. Selecting images by clicking or using a marquee works in most Windows programs, including Publisher. In addition, different applications may have keyboard shortcuts for making a selection.
> 3. Cut or copy the selection to the Windows Clipboard. Use either command from the Edit menu of the source application or use one of the keyboard shortcuts.
> 4. Switch to the target application either through the Windows Task List or by clicking on the appropriate window. If you intend to include the image in an existing file, open that file as well.
> 5. Select the frame or location where you want the image to appear.
> 6. Select Paste from the Edit menu, or use the appropriate keyboard shortcut, to insert the image in the destination program.

Inserting and Embedding Objects

Publisher gives you two sophisticated ways to deal with information and images from other Microsoft applications. In some cases the information is actually an image. In others, the Picture frame is used for special situations. These alternatives are convenient for several purposes. The first of the two—*inserting*—starts another application program altogether, right from within Publisher. Use this method of creating or editing when it's easier to handle the material in its *native environment*, the one that was used to create it. For example, it's more convenient to edit a chart from Excel or a drawing from Paintbrush in one of those applications than in Publisher.

Chapter 9: *Working with Images* 259

The second method—*embedding*—automatically updates a publication with the latest version of a file from another application. There's no need even to open the application. For example, if you published a monthly newsletter containing certain financial data that you tracked in Excel, it would be ideal to embed some or all of the Excel spreadsheet. Whenever you opened or printed the publication, it would automatically contain the latest figures from the Excel file.

Note

Both inserting and embedding depend on a Microsoft technology known as object linking. *Not all Microsoft products support this process and of those that do, some support it differently than others. Word for Windows, for example, lets you embed a file in a publication, but only displays an icon in the embedded frame, whereas Excel displays your exact selection, and the Windows Notepad in Windows 3.0 doesn't recognize embedding at all. While there is some method to this madness, it can be frustrating if you're not prepared for differing results. Use these features when they are convenient and it makes sense to do so. Don't go to extremes to make them perform. If the only way that you can get a picture into a frame is to paste or import it, just do so and get the publication to press.*

Inserting Objects

Having read sufficient words of warning, take a look at what *will* run on your system using these special options.

- Create a Picture frame and select Insert Object from the Edit menu. The Insert Object dialog box should appear, as shown in Figure 9-5.

Figure 9-5.   *Insert Object dialog box*

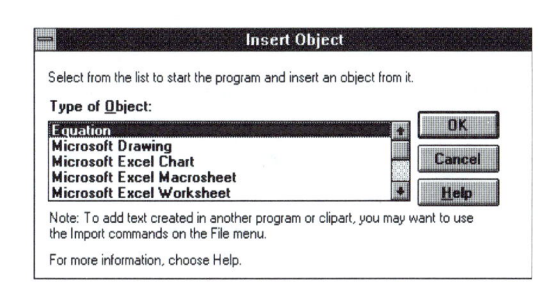

The actual programs that appear on the list in this box will vary depending on what's in your computer environment. Publisher checks various settings in Windows in order to produce this list. The options shown here, for example, are from Microsoft Word 2.0 (Drawing) and Excel (Chart, Macrosheet, and Worksheet). Note-It (discussed later in this chapter) and WordArt support object-linking, so they're always in the list.

- If you've come this far and there is an option other than Note-It or WordArt in your list, double-click on it. Publisher activity halts, and the other application takes over. In the example shown here, Excel has taken charge.

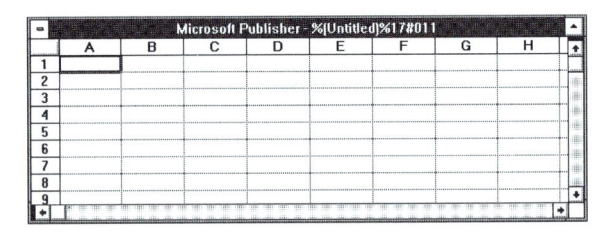

At this point, a normal Excel session is in process, just as it would be if the program had been started directly from the Windows Program Manager. Notice that Publisher has also put some special notation in the Title bar to indicate that this file is linked to another program and should be treated differently from a standard worksheet.

- After you finish creating the material in this (other) application, click on the File menu.

- When you access other applications through Insert Object, this menu displays options for either Exit and Return or Update instead of the standard Exit option. Select the one that appears on your menu, and Publisher returns with the new material in the Picture frame you started in. If you decide to edit the material in the future, Publisher will load the application automatically.

> **How to Insert an Object from a Microsoft Application**
>
> 1. Create or select a Picture frame.
> 2. Select Edit from the Menu bar and select Insert Object from the Edit menu.
> 3. Select an application from the list in the dialog box. This application is the source.
> 4. Create the image or other type of material in the source application.
> 5. Select File from the Menu bar in the source application and select Exit and Return or Update from the File menu.
> 6. To edit an inserted object, click on the frame and select Edit Object from the Edit menu.

Using Note-Its

A *Note-It* is a special Microsoft object that lets you leave messages in a publication. They operate like the paper Post-It notes that you may have used to remind yourself of a change, thought, or idea. Publisher lets you stick a Note-It on a publication in much the same way that you would place one on a paper document. A Note-It, however, has a variety of different covers, and all of the advantages of electronic editing come along with it. An open Note-It appears in Figure 9-6. The size of the Note-It depends on the size of the Picture frame that you create for it. You can move, resize, cut, copy, paste, and perform any of the other editing tasks on a Note-It that you normally would on a Picture frame. The only difference is in how a Note-It behaves when you double-click on it: it displays a message. After you've read it, click anywhere in the scratch or page areas to suppress the text of the message. The text of a Note-It can be fairly lengthy. Popping it up and down like this is convenient and doesn't clutter the work areas.

When you create a Note-It, its dialog box appears, as shown in Figure 9-7. The Window on the left has a choice of pictures that will appear in the frame

262   *Microsoft Publisher Made Easy*

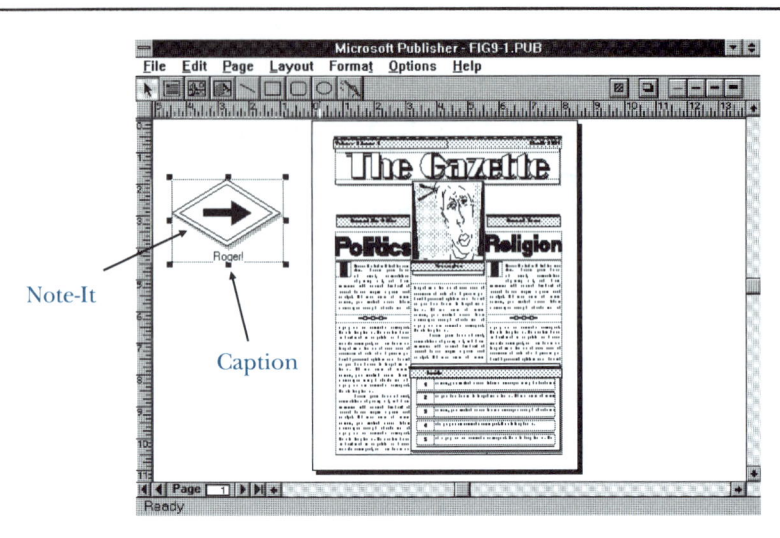

Figure 9-6.   Note-It in action

over the note. The selection is broad and rather humorous. Take a moment to scroll through the list. The caption appears in the frame below the picture. Typically for a caption, you might enter a tickler for the subject matter of the note. If you're working in a network environment, you could enter the name of another person who's working on a publication with you. The large field

Figure 9-7.   Note-It dialog box

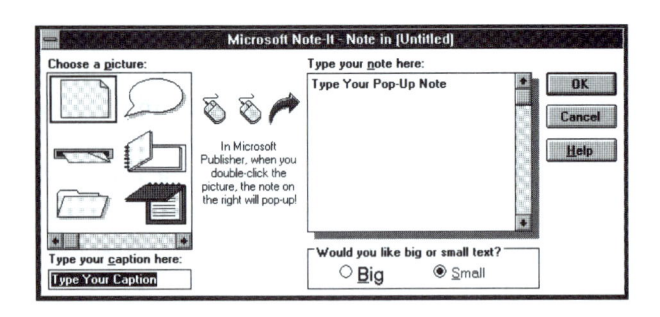

Chapter 9: *Working with Images* 263

on the right is for the text of the note. It can hold up to 25 lines of 40 characters each. This field operates just like the Copy field in the WordArt dialog box. All of the standard text editing keys and commands are available when you work on the text of a Note-It.

How to Create a Note-It

1. Create or select a Picture frame.
2. Select Edit from the Menu bar and select Insert Object from the Edit menu.
3. Select Note-It from the list in the dialog box.
4. Select a picture from the picture window. Use the scroll bar to display all of the alternatives.
5. Type a caption for the cover of the note.
6. Click on the text window on the right and type the text of the note.
7. Click on OK.

Embedding Files

When you *embed* a Picture frame with a file or file fragment from another application, Publisher automatically updates the publication with the latest version of the file. To embed an object you must first open the application from which you want to embed information. Like inserting an object, embedding only works with applications that support object linking. If you don't have an application that supports this process, don't even try the following exercise, just read along. If you do have one other than Excel, which appears in the example, you can try to substitute commands in the appropriate places. In any case you'll get a sense of how this function operates.

- First, use Program Manager to start the compatible application (the source). If you have a file that you want to embed from, open it as well. Otherwise, create a sample file.

- Once the information you want to reference is on the screen, select it. In the example shown here, a portion of an Excel worksheet has been selected:

21				
22	Revenues			
23	Shipments	500,000		750,000
24	Returns	125,000		187,500
25	Freight & Handling	20,000		30,000
26	Net Sales	355,000	100%	532,500
27				

- Copy the selection to the Clipboard as you normally would. Then use the Task Manager to switch to Publisher, or click on the Publisher window.

- Now, create a Picture frame for the embedded information. Then select Paste Special from the Edit menu. The following dialog box appears, presenting several options for embedding the material:

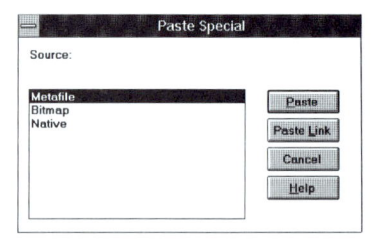

```
                    Paste Special
Source:

Metafile                              Paste
Bitmap
Native                              Paste Link

                                     Cancel

                                      Help
```

The only way to actually embed the information from Excel so that it will update each time you start Publisher is to select Native from the list in this dialog box. Embedding material as Native means that *information* from the source application is placed in Publisher. The other two options—Metafile and Bitmap—only embed a *picture* of the information. Such pictures are *static* and will not update each time you open the publication. Of the two, Metafile is the preferred choice. It is Windows' own format for transferring graphic information. Choose Bitmap as a last alternative for pictures when Publisher won't accept the source information as a Metafile.

If you've followed the example this far and can do so, select Native, and then click on Paste Link. If you can't select Native format, Paste Special will be inactive, and you must use Paste. The material from the source application should appear in the Picture frame. If you want to test the link between the programs—and that's always a good idea when you're working with computers—go back and make a change in the source application. When you return to Publisher you should find current information in the frame.

> ### How to Embed Material from a Microsoft Application
>
> 1. Use the Windows Program Manager to start Publisher and a second Windows application that supports object linking. The program that contains the material you embed is the source.
> 2. Create or select material from the source using standard techniques. Selecting material by dragging the pointer, clicking, or using a marquee works in most Microsoft programs.
> 3. Cut or copy the selection to the Windows Clipboard. Use either command from the Edit menu of the source application, or use one of the keyboard shortcuts.
> 4. Switch to Publisher either through the Windows Task List or by clicking on the appropriate window.
> 5. Create or select the frame into which you want to embed the material.
> 6. Select Paste Special from the Edit menu.
> 7. Select a format for the embedded file.
> 8. Click on Paste Link to embed "live" information. Click on Paste to embed a picture of the information.

Editing and Formatting Pictures

All of the basic frame manipulation techniques you learned about in Chapter 4 operate on Picture frames, whether they're filled with simple pictures or linked objects. Except for cropping and scaling, you've already been introduced to all of these topics. The first part of this section, then, constitutes a review, with an emphasis on the special effects that these commands may have on pictures. Cropping and scaling are treated as new topics.

Cut, Copy, Paste, and Move

Cut and Paste let you move pictures. Copy and Paste let you duplicate them. Both Cut and Copy send Picture frames to the Windows Clipboard. From the Clipboard you can paste them to different parts of the current publication or to other publications. You can also drag Picture frames to the scrap area to move them between pages, or for temporary storage if you're experimenting with different layouts.

Tip

All of the keyboard equivalents work for Picture frames. (DEL) (delete), (CTRL)-(C) (copy), (CTRL)-(X) (cut), and (CTRL)-(V) (paste) can all save time if your hands are already on the keyboard.

Before you can cut or copy a Picture frame, you must select it. Like WordArt frames, you can only select a Picture frame as an entire object. Publisher has no provisions for selecting a section of a picture (or for editing a section either) as you would a section of a text file. This is the sort of shortcoming that limits Publisher's graphics capabilities. The standard selection techniques all operate with Picture frames. You can click on a frame or use the marquee to surround several frames. When you select multiple frames, you can include Text and WordArt frames, and even drawn objects, in the selection. This flexibility makes it easy to retain a frame layout if you want to move it between pages. If you've spent some time positioning objects, you'll appreciate this convenience.

Try using the PRODINFO.PUB template to move a group of frames, as shown in Figure 9-8. Select all of the frames in the body of the right column, and drag them into the Scratch area on the right. As you can see, the frames move as a group, and remain in the same position relative to each other.

Note

If you make an error using Cut, Copy, Paste, Delete, or by dragging, Undo will reverse the error if you're careful to execute the command immediately.

Margins

You can modify the margins on a Picture frame by clicking on the frame and selecting Frame Margins on the Layout menu. Normally, Picture frames have a margin of 0 on all sides. Margins can be useful when you place pictures

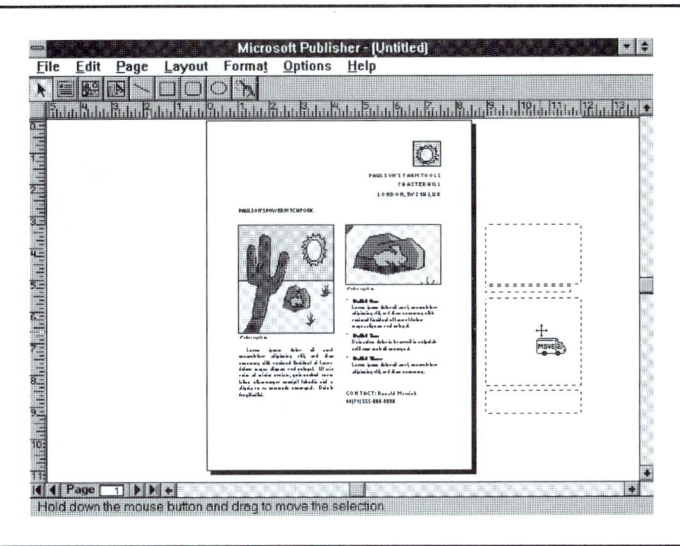

Figure 9-8.   *Selecting a group of frames and moving them all together*

in the middle of text, because they give the image a little breathing room. However, they also reduce a picture's size. Figure 9-9 shows three examples of *run-arounds*, places in a publication where text flows around a picture. Each of the three was developed using a different technique. The first example on the left uses no margins in the frame. Even with a margin of 0, Publisher leaves some room around the Picture frame. The second example, in the middle column, contains the same picture in a frame with the identical dimensions, but a .1-inch left and right margin. Notice that Publisher actually scales the image by squeezing the sides together to accommodate the margin setting. While the distortion is minimal because of the smallness of the margin setting, it is noticeable, nonetheless. As you will learn later in this chapter, you could crop the picture instead, and accommodate the margin without distorting the image.

The third example, in the right column of Figure 9-9, uses multiple Picture frames underneath the one that actually has the image. This causes a rounder and somewhat smoother run-around, which is particularly useful for curved or irregularly shaped images. Because you can layer and size any number of

Figure 9-9. Different ways to implement margins in run-arounds

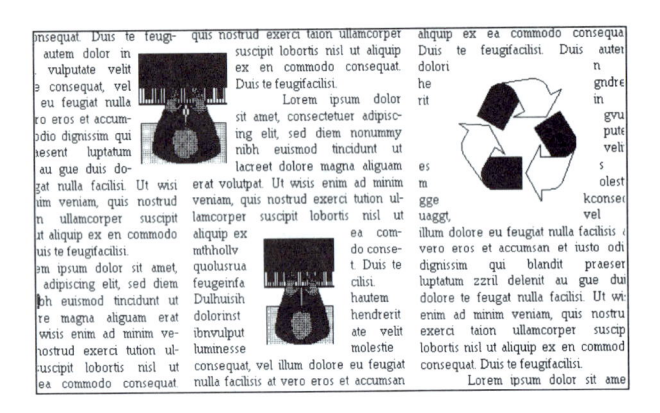

frames to shape the run-around, very subtle effects are possible. The following illustration shows the technique used in the underlying frames in Figure 9-9.

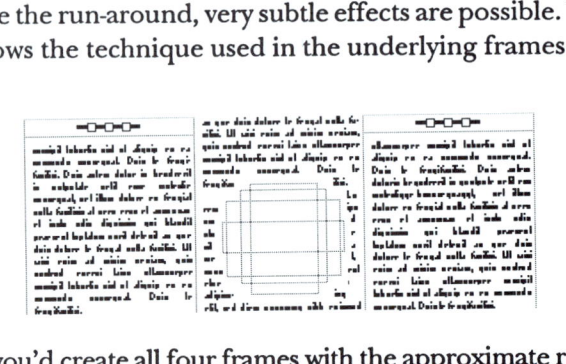

Typically, you'd create all four frames with the approximate relationships to each other as you see here. Their actual size and shape will depend on the shape of the image that you want the text to run around. You can move the frame containing the actual image to the scratch area while you work with the underlying frames, for convenience, and drag it back when the work is complete. The more frames you add, the smoother the curves of the run-around.

Repeating and Replacing Pictures

You can place pictures on the background page just as you would with text or WordArt. You can copy them, move them, or create them from scratch. Any Picture frame that you place on the background appears at the same location on every page in a publication. Placing a small logo on the background in the heading area of the page, for example, can be very attractive in a newsletter, brochure, or catalog. It helps to reinforce a visual identity throughout the publication. With a larger image on the background in a greeting card, on the other hand, you can play some interesting visual tricks by uncovering a different part of the image on each page:

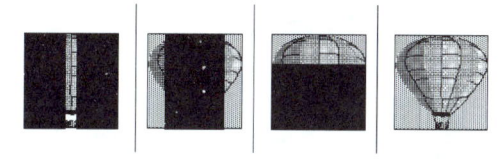

You could achieve this effect by placing the balloon image on the background page and drawing colored shapes over different parts of it on each of the foreground pages. The shapes can be drawn from Picture frames or with the Box tool using a solid background.

You can change the picture in a frame by selecting the frame and importing or pasting in new material. Earlier in this chapter, in fact, you replaced a picture by importing another. The incoming image completely replaces the original image in the frame. Publisher always displays a warning message before completing the replacement, to give you a chance to change your mind. There are no facilities for deleting the contents of a frame without deleting the frame itself.

To replace a picture by importing a new one, double-click on the Picture frame. Publisher displays the Import Picture dialog box immediately.

Tip

Display Options for Pictures

Publisher's two display options for working with pictures can come in handy. First of all, each time you change views or turn pages, Publisher has to redraw pictures on your monitor. If there are a lot of pictures on a page or any are very detailed, this can take some time and become annoying, especially if you're not working on pictures at that moment. Select Hide Pictures from the Options menu to suppress the appearance of all pictures in the publication. They're still there, but they don't show up until you select Show Pictures from the same menu. The screen redraws much more quickly.

When Hide Pictures is in effect, Publisher also hides the contents of WordArt frames.

Hide Boundaries can help you get a realistic idea of what a page will look like in print. Unlike Text frames, which have a white background by default, Picture frames are transparent, as you can see here:

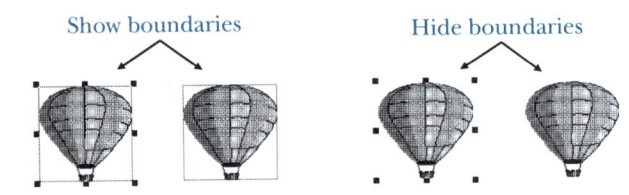

Show boundaries   Hide boundaries

If the image in a frame doesn't cover its entire area, the outline of the frame is visible. This effect becomes more distracting as the number of frames on the page increases. The page appears busier than it actually is. Select Hide Object Boundaries from the Layout menu to suppress the appearance of frame outlines. You'll get a better sense of what the final piece will look like, since frame outlines don't print. On the other hand, it's difficult to manipulate frames unless you can see them (although it is possible). Select Show Object Boundaries to make them visible again.

Scaling Pictures

Before explaining the details of scaling, there are a few more things you should know about images. All computerized images are collections of dots that appear on a screen or printer. Depending on how densely the dots are packed and the pattern in which they are arrayed, a computer can display any conceivable shape or shading. Programs that create these dot patterns do so using one of two methods. *Bitmapped images* are simply a matrix of dots that exist as a *single* object. A program that displays a bitmapped image only has instructions to display (or not display) each dot in the image at a specific location on a page.

Object-oriented images—also known as *vector graphics*—are more like programs themselves. They are *collections* of very simple geometric objects used in combination to form the primary image. Along with object descriptions, vector images contain instructions for how each object relates to the others in the image. The locations and density of dot patterns that result from an object-oriented image vary depending on the size to which the image is scaled. The following tables describe which of the Publisher-compatible graphic file formats fall into each category.

Bitmapped Format/Source	Extension
Windows Bitmap	.BMP
PC Paintbrush	.PCX
Scanned	.TIF

Object-Oriented Format/Source	Extension
Computer Graphics Metafile	.CGM
Micrografx Designer	.DRW
Windows Metafile	.WMF
Encapsulated Postscript	.EPS

The bottom line, from a publishing point of view, is that you can resize object-oriented graphics easily without distorting them. You can even distort them slightly without ruining their composition or the extent to which they can be recognized. Finally, they maintain the highest quality of resolution possible on your screen or printer. Bitmapped images, on the other hand, can become faded or jagged when you enlarge them, and are easily distorted beyond recognition if you try to change their proportions. They are also *device dependent*. In other words, their clarity and resolution is tied to the capabilities of the equipment that was used to create them, and you may not be able to take advantage of a high-resolution device—such as a laser printer—when you reproduce them. There are positive aspects to bitmapped images as well, but a more thorough discussion of computer imaging is beyond the scope of this book.

You can resize Picture frames in the same way that you would Text or WordArt frames. When you resize a Picture frame, however, Publisher automatically scales the image to the new dimensions of the frame. This is something like what happens to WordArt when you use any of the self-adjusting font features, like Best Fit, Stretch Vertical, or Fit Horizontal. The effects on an image, however, can be a bit more surprising. Consider the samples in Figure 9-10. The images on the left were produced from an object-oriented file. The images on the right are bitmaps. In both cases, the image on top contains the original proportions. The one on the bottom has been resized by flattening the height and stretching the width. While the distortion is much more pronounced in the bitmapped version, resizing clearly affects both. This is also a worst-case scenario for the bitmapped image. Bitmaps tend to improve in quality when you reduce them, and degrade when you enlarge them. Vector images, on the other hand, retain the same resolution at any size. Notice that even though the enlargement of the vector image is distorted, it still has the full detail of the original. The resolution of the bitmap, on the other hand, is beginning to break up badly, especially in the upper-right of the image, where the dot density was light to begin with.

Remember, to insert a picture in a publication with its original dimensions—the ones that were used to produce it—select Import Picture from the File menu without selecting a Picture frame first. Publisher creates a very large frame for the image when you bring it in this manner, but you can scale it down

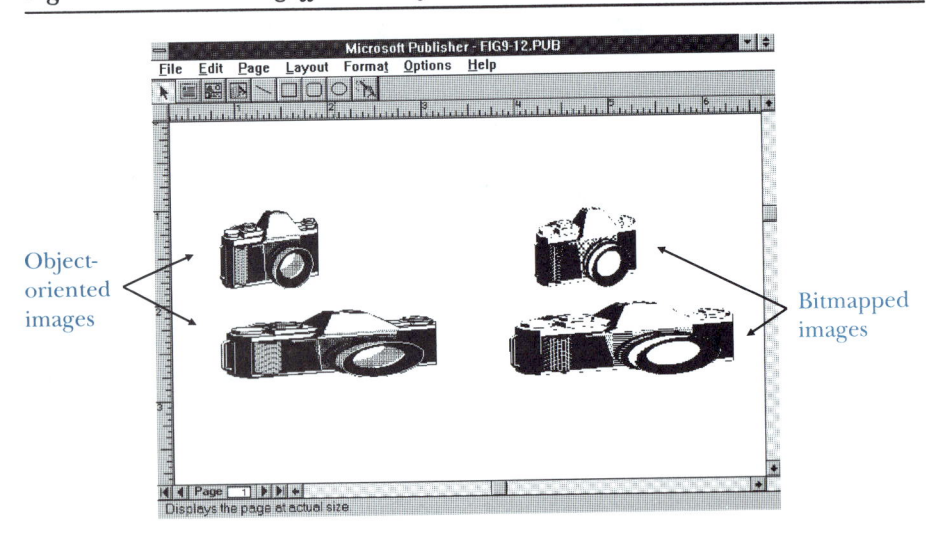

Figure 9-10.   Scaling effects on object-oriented and bitmapped images

Chapter 9: *Working with Images* 273

to an appropriate size for your publication by reducing the size of the frame. If you hold down (SHIFT) and resize using one of the corner handles, the picture retains its original proportions while you reduce or enlarge it, as shown here:

Tip

To restore a picture to its original size, click on the frame and select Scale Picture from the Layout menu. Click on the Original Size button, and then on OK. The picture returns to its originally imported size (very large), and you can scale it again, if necessary.

For most applications, you'll want pictures to appear in their original dimensions. It's fun to experiment with distorted images, and they have some novel uses, but these are occasional. If an image doesn't fit correctly in a publication in its original proportions, you can use frame margins to scale it *slightly*, include a border to fill space, or crop it. More information on cropping appears later in this chapter.

Tip

Undo reverses the effects of scaling if you execute it immediately after you complete the work. Be sure to work at a decent magnification level when you're scaling a picture. Otherwise—and especially if you lack a steady hand—it's easy to perform the operation twice, inadvertently. In this case, Undo only affects the second attempt at resizing, and you can't restore the picture to the exact original dimensions.

How to Scale a Picture

1. Select the frame that contains the picture.
2. Point to one of the handles until the pointer turns into the resizing icon ( ).
3. Drag the handle to a new location. To retain the current proportions of the frame, hold down the (SHIFT) key as you drag and use a handle from one of the frame's corners.

9

Cropping

Cropping is the only way Publisher lets you alter the composition of an image. When you crop an image, you can cut sections from any of its edges without affecting its scale, as shown in Figure 9-11. Cropping is useful when you want to focus on only one section of an image or fit an image into a limited space on a page. Sometimes only a small change in the size of a Picture frame can let you fit it smoothly on a page without reorganizing other frames. That, in turn, can mean the difference between getting all of the text for a story on one page or being forced to deal with overflow and additional pages. Often an image can be trimmed on several sides without lessening its impact or removing essential pieces of the composition. Clearly, this is a preferable alternative to reduction through nonproportional scaling. You can also enlarge a Picture frame through cropping. This simply adds empty space to the image on the side(s) you enlarge. It has the effect, however, of increasing the margin in the frame, without the distortion that goes along with adding to the margin through the Layout menu.

Cropping and scaling often go together. When you first import an image using its original proportions, it is far too large for most publications.

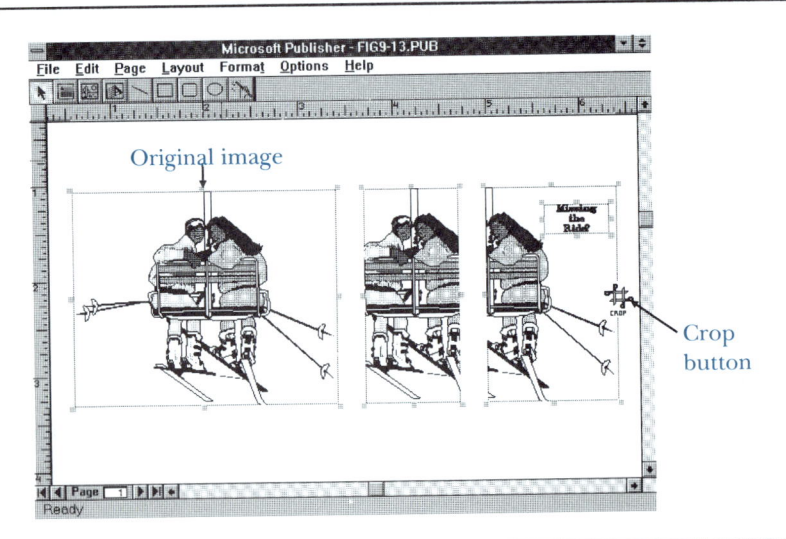

Figure 9-11.   *Two different crops of the same image*

Chapter 9: *Working with Images* 275

Proportional scaling, described earlier in this chapter, lets you reduce its dimensions to an approximate size for placement on a page. Then you can crop for an exact fit. On the other hand, you may recognize immediately that only a part of an image is relevant for an application. In this case you would crop first, then scale down, and then perhaps crop again.

To crop an image, click on the Crop button on the Toolbar. The button brightens slightly. Then select a Picture frame and point to one of the handles until you see the cropping icon appear ( ). Drag the handle inward toward the center of the picture to trim the side, or outward to add blank space. When you're satisfied with the crop, release the mouse button. Each of the side handles controls its corresponding side of the picture. Each of the corner handles controls its two adjacent sides concurrently.

Tip

Holding down the CTRL *button while you crop affects opposite sides of the frame equally at the same time. For example, if you crop inward with the bottom handle, the picture is reduced on both the top and bottom. If you use any of the corner handles, all four sides are reduced concurrently and in proportion.*

The following exercise is representative of the work you might do in putting together a catalog. You'll need many of the technical skills you've developed using Publisher to complete it. You're going to use the layout in PRICELIST.PUB as the basis for a page and substitute some of Publisher's clip art for the existing pictures.

- Start a new publication using the PRICELIST.PUB template and measure the size of one of the Picture frames. They all use the same dimensions, so once you've learned them, you can use that size as the basis for cropping and scaling all of the pictures you want to include. The easiest way to measure is to click on the intersection of the rulers and drag both of them to a corner of one of the frames.

- Double-click to reset the zero marks to the corner. Just in case you're feeling lazy about this part of the exercise, the pictures are 1 3/4 inches wide and 1 7/16 inches high.

- Now import the clip art drawing for a camera (35MM.CGM) from Publisher's clip art library. Make sure that none of the frames on the page has been selected, so the picture comes in with its native proportions. When it first arrives, it will cover most of the screen.

- Move it next to the vertical ruler so that its top edge aligns with one of the major tic marks, and use proportional scaling (hold down SHIFT and scale from a corner handle) to reduce its height to approximately 1 1/2 inches.
- Go to Actual View, drag the rulers to the corner of the frame and continue to scale proportionally until the height of the frame is 1 7/16 inches, as shown in Figure 9-12. If you enable Snap to Ruler marks, this should be easier.
- Notice that when you scale the height to the correct size, the width of the frame is slightly too large (1 7/8 inches) for the frame in the page layout (1 3/4 inches). This minor difference (1/8 inch) can be accommodated by cropping the left or right side of the camera. Because of the nature of this picture, trimming it slightly on one of these sides will not seriously affect the information in the picture.
- Drag it over to the page area so that it exactly overlays one of the cactus pictures on three sides.

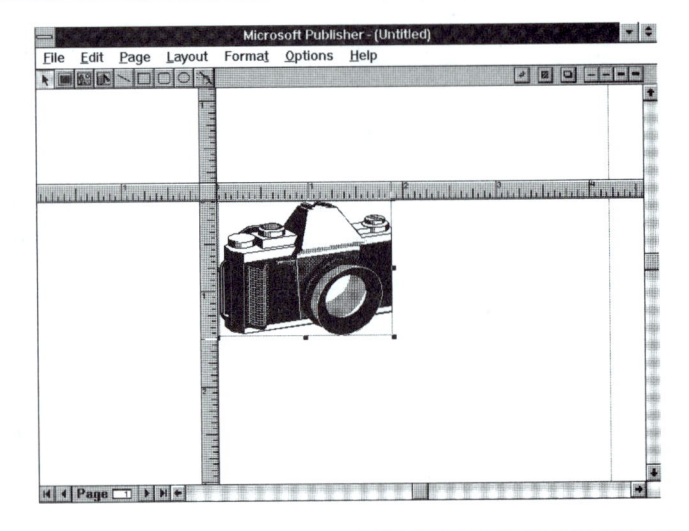

Figure 9-12.   Using the rulers to scale and crop

Chapter 9: *Working with Images* 277

- Click on the Crop button and drag the handle for the side that overlaps until the two frames are flush on the fourth side. It may be easier to turn Snap to Ruler Marks off before doing this, depending on where you left the rulers.

Now try the same procedure using the clip art bicycle (BICYCLE.CGM). When you scale this image down to the proper height (1 7/16 inches), it is still much too wide (3 1/16 inches). In addition, if you crop the bicycle, you will seriously impair the reader's impression of the merchandise either by cutting off half of each wheel or the front or rear of the bike!

- To solve this design problem, continue scaling the picture down proportionally until the width is correct (1 3/4 inches). Now, of course, the height is too small (1 1/16 inches), but you can use cropping to add to the top and bottom margins without distorting the image.
- Drag it on top of the frame below the camera so that it overlays the left and right boundaries and is equidistant from the top and bottom, as shown here:

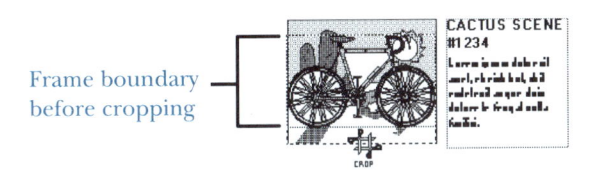

Frame boundary before cropping

- Use cropping to add space to the top and bottom of the image. If you hold down (CTRL) while you crop outward, both edges will grow at once.

To complete the publication, of course, you would have to delete the underlying cactus pictures, scale and crop images for all of the other Picture frames, and change the text descriptions in each of the adjacent Text frames. This exercise takes a lot of work, but is typical of the kind of detail necessary in implementing a page design. If you made it through both sections of the exercise, you're turning into a real pro!

Note

The cropping icon remains activated until you click on the button again. It then returns to the resizing icon.

How to Crop an Image

1. Select a Picture frame.
2. Click on the Crop button (⌗).
3. Point to the frame handle for the side that you want to crop.
4. When you see the cropping icon appear, drag the handle in toward the center of the frame to trim the image, or outward to add empty space (margin) to the frame.

Chapter 9: *Working with Images*

Review

In this chapter, you learned about how to deal with images in Publisher. These skills help you to balance text and pictures in a publication in order to maximize clarity and impact. Fluency with manipulating images in page layout is another arrow in your design quiver.

- Images can be brought into Publisher from a variety of outside sources including Windows applications and other popular graphic file formats.
- Bitmapped and vector images behave differently when scaled.
- The Clipboard deals with text and images similarly for cutting, copying, and pasting pictures.
- Scaling lets you reduce or enlarge an image by changing its dimensions but retaining the proportions that were used to create it.
- Cropping lets you reduce or enlarge an image by trimming the image on its edges or adding empty space to it.
- Images can be placed on the background page when you want them to repeat in the same place on each page in a publication.
- Publisher works with object-linking technology to let you insert and embed special files from other Microsoft applications.

10

Line Art, BorderArt, and Shading

Graphic accents are another form of visual information. They make a strong statement about a publication's style. Even subtle graphics, such as a rule between columns or one that separates headings from the body of the page, can make a difference in the publication's look. Graphics can direct the reader's attention to certain parts of a page or publication. They can even make a piece easier to read, and in this sense, provide information about *how to look* at a publication. Because the reader's eye is drawn to them, visual embellishments say something very overt about the thought that went into designing a publication. Figure 10-1 has some examples of how graphics can help to distinguish an application. It was, incidentally, developed with the PageWizard for newsletters.

You can apply three kinds of graphic accents in Publisher. To begin with, there are four drawing tools for creating *line art*—combinations of simple geometric shapes. You can combine simple shapes to create more elaborate figures. Secondly, you can fill any of the frame types or line art with colors and patterns. A drop shadow effect is also available to give these objects the

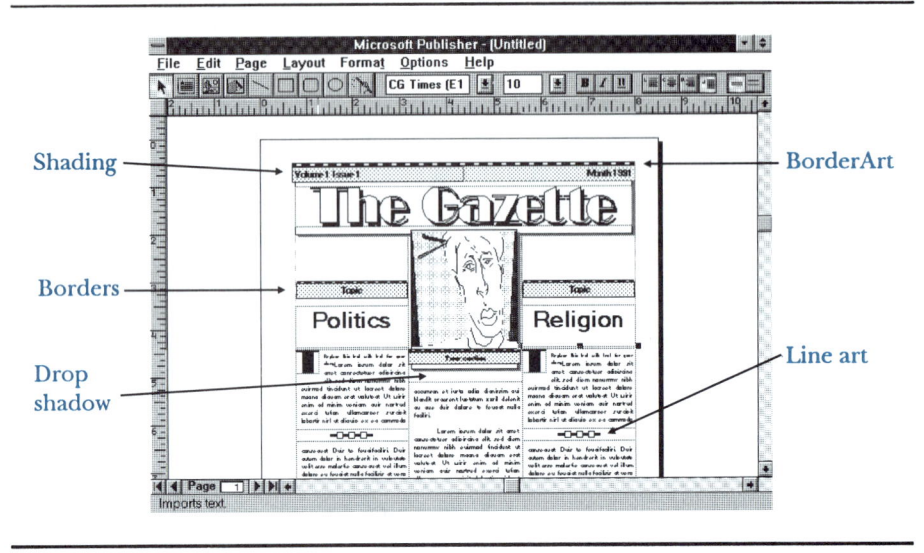

Figure 10-1.   Using graphic accents

appearance of depth. Finally, Publisher has an extraordinary collection of decorative borders, from simple lines to extremely elaborate and fanciful designs. There are over 100 BorderArt patterns in all. You can apply borders and BorderArt to frames or line art.

Well-executed graphic embellishments are usually spare in design. They rarely succeed from excess. As simple as these three tools may sound, they put a lot of graphics control in your hands. Adding graphic accents is usually one of the last stages in a publication's development. The choices you make are strongly influenced by all of the more rudimentary design issues that came before, from page layout to font selection. These decisions are even more flexible than those that you make about pictures. They have little or no impact on a publication's structure. However, if you introduce graphic accents before the frame and page structure is *frozen*—fixed in its development—you may be wasting your time. Working with graphics can be very absorbing and fun, but also time-consuming and full of detail. A slight change in page layout can have you repositioning objects for hours.

Chapter 10: *Line Art, BorderArt, and Shading*

If you're working with a multipage project and plan to use any repeating graphics, place the objects on the background page before you begin adding other graphics to foreground pages. Otherwise background material may become overlaid with foreground objects, and you may have to reposition or discard them. For most applications, start out simple. Too many accents can clutter a publication and make it unattractive and difficult to read.

This chapter assumes that you are comfortable with all other major features of Publisher, including layout, frames, and creating and formatting text and pictures. Practical examples appear throughout the chapter that use both Publisher templates and material that you create from scratch. As usual, you can find generic instructions for most tasks in a box at the end of a section.

Line Art

Publisher's drawing tools let you create four simple geometric shapes. You can fill the solid shapes with colors or patterns and add shadows to them just as you can with frames. The drawing tools in Publisher are terrific for adding highlights to a publication, such as rules, arrows, bullets, and so on. When used with shading, they can provide subtle tones that add to developing the style of a publication. You can also combine Publisher's four shapes to create simple illustrations. Figure 10-2 shows some examples of both types of application.

Figure 10-2. Some applications of line art

Remember, drawing is not one of Publisher's strong points. If you want to include sophisticated line art in a publication, you're better off creating it in a program designed for drawing and then importing the material to Publisher as a picture. For example, in Publisher you can only assign a color or pattern to one of the three solid shapes. While you can draw a triangle using three lines, each is a separate object, so the final result can have no shading. You can't rotate objects either, so changing a square into a diamond becomes a major undertaking. The ability to create new shapes or rotate them is elementary in a program designed for drawing. Given the selection of clip art and BorderArt that comes with Publisher, there's no reason to struggle with the drawing tools when there are better ways to solve a design problem.

The four tools are the line, box, rounded box, and oval. Like frames, each of these appears as a button on the Toolbar:

Creating an object with the drawing tools is like creating a frame. Just click on one of the tools to activate it. The pointer changes to a crosshair. Click and hold the mouse button at the starting location for the object. Then drag the crosshair to the ending location, and release the button. The Toolbar is the only way to create one of these objects. There are no menu or keyboard equivalents. If you haven't used them yet, try clicking on the drawing tools and experimenting with a few basic shapes.

Many aspects of line art operate similarly to the way that frames do. You can select one or several line art objects by clicking on them or surrounding them with the marquee. You can include line art in a selection with frames of any type. The Clipboard's cut, copy, and paste features are all available for line art. You can move them around the page or to the scratch area by dragging them. Line art objects have handles. You can enlarge or reduce objects by clicking on a handle with the resizing icon and dragging it to a new location. Like frames, you can change the defaults for each object type by selecting one of the options, such as shading or thickness, before you create the object. The only real difference between line art objects and frames is that line art doesn't hold anything (like text, WordArt, or pictures).

Chapter 10: *Line Art, BorderArt, and Shading*

How to Create Line Art

1. Click on the tool for the shape you want to create.
2. Point to the starting location for the object.
3. Click and hold the mouse button, then drag the crosshair to the ending location for the object.

Solid Shapes

Three of the line art objects are solid shapes. These are the box, rounded box, and oval:

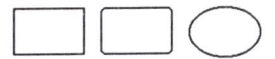

You can produce shapes that are not available from the Toolbar by combining and overlaying the ones that are. Examples of this type of overlaying are shown in Figure 10-3. To create the chair-like image on the left, draw a box with solid black shading and then draw two boxes with solid white shading on top of it. Details on how to create shading and color effects appear

Figure 10-3.   *Combining line art to make new shapes*

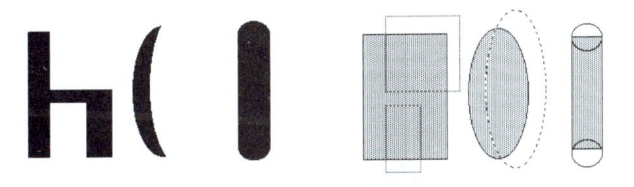

later in this chapter. Similarly, you can create the crescent by drawing over a solid black oval with a solid white one. The bar with rounded ends uses a box with circles positioned halfway off of each end. All three objects use the same black shading to make them appear as one.

Centering and squaring also work in creating or resizing line art objects as they do for frames. When you hold down (CTRL) while dragging, the object expands or contracts in opposite directions concurrently and at the same rate. Using (SHIFT) with the box or rounded box creates a perfect square. With the oval, it creates a perfect circle. Using (SHIFT) and (CTRL) together makes your starting location the center of the circle or square.

Creating Bullets

Circles and squares are the most effective way to create text bullets in Publisher. Since these are usually on the small side, they can be troublesome to line up. There are few sights quite as unattractive as misaligned bullets in an otherwise stunning presentation. Create a bullet and then use Copy and Paste to duplicate a dozen of them. Use the rulers and/or Snap options to align a full column. Then save the bullets as a template. When you want to use them in a publication, select them all and copy them in. Move them as a group to the proper horizontal location for the text you want to bullet, as shown in Figure 10-4. Then use (SHIFT) when you drag them to their correct vertical locations. In this way they always remain aligned. Select and delete the bullets that you don't need.

Figure 10-4.   How to handle bullets easily

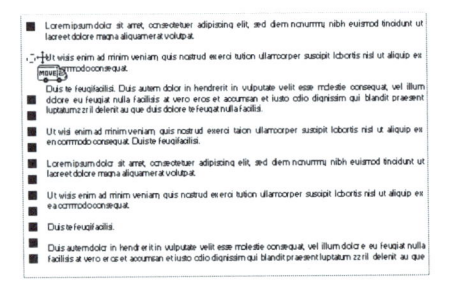

Lines

Publisher lets you format lines by adjusting their thickness or by adding arrowheads at either or both of their ends. When you click on the Line button, the Toolbar changes to display these options:

You can change some line attributes on the Toolbar, or you can add color or increase the thickness of a line to 10 points through the Line dialog box, as shown in Figure 10-5. To display the box, click on a line and then select Line from the Layout menu. You can select colors or a heavier thickness by clicking on the appropriate button. All of the line art options from the Toolbar can also can be turned on or off here as well.

Lines have only two handles. They appear at either end of the line. Since lines are two-dimensional, you can only resize them by dragging a handle to change their length. If you resize a line using the CTRL key, it grows or shrinks in both directions at once. Resizing is also the only way to rotate a line. Click on one of the handles and wait until you see the resizing icon. Then drag the handle to a new location at a different angle. The other end of the line remains in place. To pivot the line around its center, resize it using the CTRL key, as shown here:

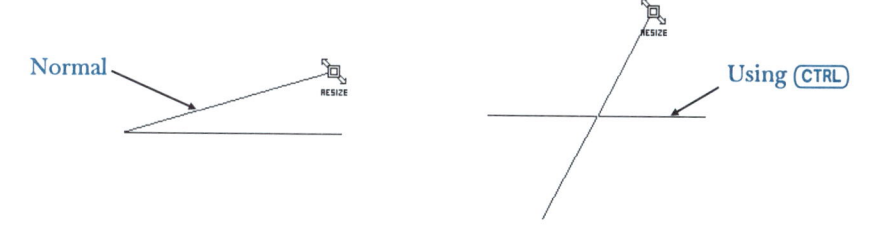

Normal   Using CTRL

Since lines only have two dimensions (length and width), there are no options for shading or shadows.

Switching the Visual Plane

Normally, objects that are created on top of or moved into an area already occupied by another object overlay the latter object. This applies to all frame

Figure 10-5. **Line dialog box**

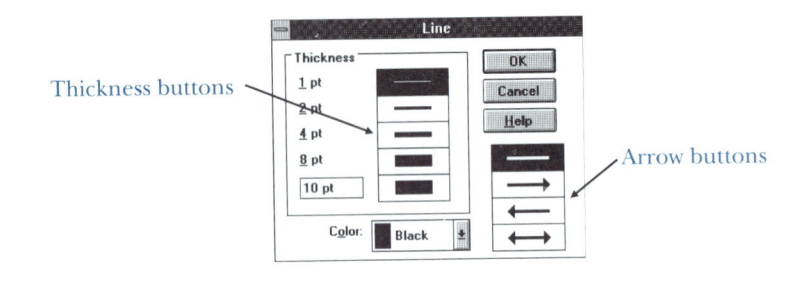

types and line art. However, objects can be shuffled in the visual plane much like playing cards. Objects in the foreground can be moved to the background, and vice versa. Interesting visual effects can be achieved with combinations of Picture frames and art objects in different visual planes. Foreground objects cover background objects unless the foreground objects are transparent. For the most part, this works to your advantage. Consider, for example, the illustration in Figure 10-6. If you draw the oval over the

Figure 10-6. **Using the visual plane**

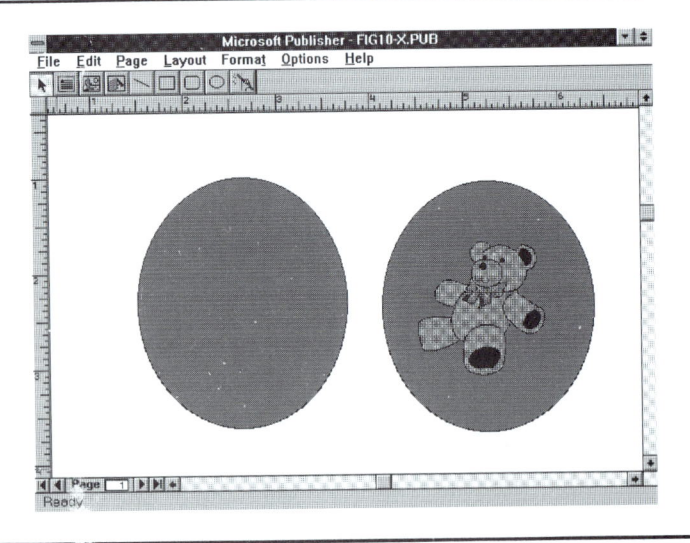

picture, it covers it. By placing the oval in the background, it gives the appearance of a rounded frame.

How to Switch the Visual Plane of an Object

1. Select the object to reposition.
2. Select Layout from the Menu bar.
3. Select Send to Back or Bring to Front from the Layout menu.

Shading, Shadows, and Colors

Publisher lets you accent frames by giving them a color, a pattern with or without color, or a drop shadow. These options are simple in nature, but can produce interesting effects that enhance a publication, whether it's a letterhead, logo, or brochure. The options apply to all frame types and line art, although they have some different default settings for each object. You can change the default settings of these options for each type of object by selecting an object and clicking on the Shading or Shadow button before you create it. All subsequent objects will use the same settings. You can change an individual object by clicking on it and then altering the settings. Remember, colors will not print unless you use a color printer. Although they may look fine on screen, they will print in black, or not print at all on a black-and-white printer.

Shading and Color

Each object has two visual planes, as shown in Figure 10-7, although it's not necessary to use both of them. In addition, frames have a third plane. The lowest plane is the background. By default, the background of Picture frames, WordArt frames, and line art is transparent, whereas Text frames have a solid white background. The only way that Publisher lets you alter the background is by adding a color to it. The middle plane is the foreground (even though it's not the topmost layer for frames). For the foreground you can assign a pattern and a color. The foreground color is assigned to the lines or dots that compose the actual pattern. The background color, if any, appears through the open space between the lines and dots that form the pattern. If you do have a color printer, you can achieve very subtle effects by using different colors for the pattern and background. The final plane contains the image, WordArt, or text that the frame was designed to display. This is truly transparent, and displays the foreground and background colors and patterns in any area that is not covered by the copy or image it contains.

Create a Text frame and import one of Publisher's dummy text files (PROFILE.TXT or CENTURY.TXT), or use one of your own. Notice that the Shading button appears on the Toolbar after you select the Text Frame tool and while you draw the frame. After completing the frame, however, the Toolbar changes to display text formatting options. The same change occurs if you select a Text frame at a later time. If you want to change the colors or patterns for a Text frame, you must select Shading from the Layout menu. When you create a picture or WordArt frame, the Shading button remains on the Toolbar after you complete the frame and reappears each time you select the frame. However you access it, the Shading dialog box appears, as shown in Figure 10-8.

Publisher offers a selection of 24 patterns and eight colors. You can select any of the patterns by clicking on them, and any of the colors by opening the list and clicking on the color. The Preview window functions like a painter's palette in this case, and lets you mix colors and patterns until you find the

Figure 10-7.   Three levels of a frame

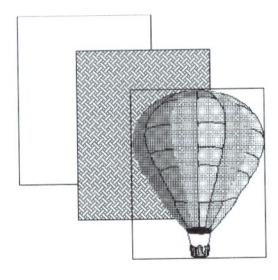

Figure 10-8. *Shading dialog box*

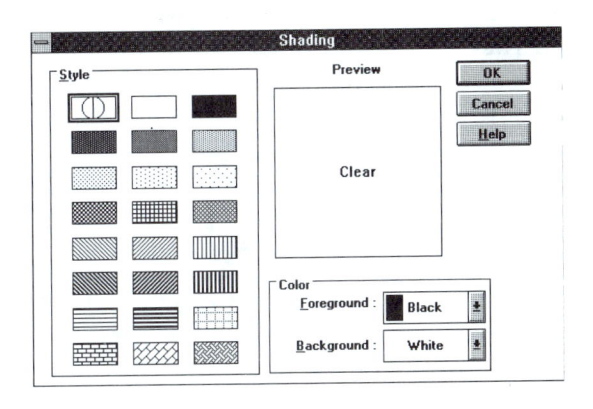

combination you're looking for. Since changes can be very subtle when you're working with color and patterns, the Preview window is a real time-saver.

Note: The choices that you make about shading, colors, and shadows have the same effect from wherever you implement them. When you make a change through the Toolbar, for example, the corresponding selection appears in the Shading dialog box or on the Layout menu.

How to Add Shading and Color to a Frame

1. Click on the frame for which you want to add shading or color.
2. Click on the Shading button or select Shading from the Layout menu.
3. Click on the background and/or foreground color lists, if necessary, and select a color.
4. Click on a pattern, if you like.
5. Click OK.

Shadows

Drop shadows give a frame or line art objects a feeling of depth and perspective. They are a terrific quick fix when you're in a hurry to lend some jazz to a publication and you've got to spend the time you have on more difficult layout issues. Here is a frame with a shadow:

Shadows, however, are limited in scope. You have no control over the color or placement of the shadow. The shadow is always grey (some people prefer black) and you can never adjust its position. If you want shadows that use a different color or are positioned to show more depth, you can make your own by creating a frame or drawing an object that exactly matches the dimensions of the frame you want to shadow. You can use the Mover to position the frame on your own in order to change the level of apparent depth, and then select any of the colors or patterns to use as the shadow.

Like Shading, the Shadow button is only available on the Toolbar for Text frames prior to frame creation. Afterward, you must access it through the Shadow option on the Layout menu. Wherever you implement the option from, it is a toggle and can only be turned on or off. With Text frames, the menu option appears with a check mark next to it when it is active. With Picture or WordArt frames, the Shadow button becomes slightly brighter when you select a frame for which Shadow is enabled. Figure 10-9 has an example of how you could use Shading and Shadows to lend interest to a calendar. This sample was created using the PageWizard for calendars.

Figure 10-9.   Using shading and shadows for style

Borders and BorderArt

Borders are one of Publisher's strongest design features. You can surround any frame or line art from the box tool on any number of sides with a solid border. There are buttons on the Toolbar for creating 1-point, 2-point, 4-point, or 8-point thicknesses. A 10-point option is available from the Borders option on the Layout menu. You can also assign any one of eight colors to a border. Like shading and shadows, you can change the border default for each of the three frame types. In addition, Publisher has over 100 decorative borders with a rich variety of themes ranging in tone from conservative to downright wild! Borders and BorderArt automatically adjust when you change the size of a frame.

Simple Borders

You can create simple borders from either the Toolbar or the Border dialog box on the Layout menu. As with shading and shadows, either method affects objects in the same way. Similarly, you can only use the buttons for Text frames before you create the frame. Afterward you must use the Layout menu. Create a Picture frame and then click on one of the thickness buttons on the right side of the Toolbar. A border surrounds the entire frame and overlays the frame boundary. The button you selected brightens to let you know that it is currently on. Try clicking on the other thickness buttons to change the width of the border. Selecting one deactivates any other. To suppress the border completely, click on a button that is currently active. If you want to experiment with the other border options, click on the frame and select Borders from the Layout menu. The dialog box appears, as in Figure 10-10. Any selection for thickness that you made from the Toolbar is highlighted in the thickness group on the right of the box. You can also select colors by clicking on the color list.

The Border group on the left of the box lets you choose which sides of the frame will use a border. You can also specify a different thickness for each side. Mixing thicknesses can lend some stylish elements to even a simple application. Consider the FAX cover sheet in Figure 10-11. Each of the frames has a thick left border, a thin bottom border, and no border at all on the top and right sides. Normally all four sides are included when you click on one

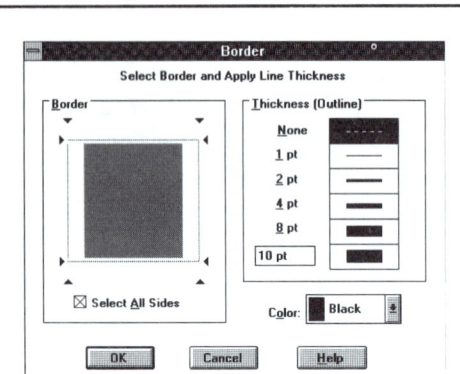

Figure 10-10.   *Border dialog box*

of the Toolbar buttons. If you want to specify individual settings, click on the side you want to change in the border group on the left. Then click on one of the thicknesses in the group on the right. To remove a border from a side, select the side and click on None for thickness.

How to Add a Border

1. Click on the frame for which you want to add a border.
2. Click on one of the thickness buttons or select Border from the Layout menu. From the Layout menu you can select individual sides and thicknesses for the border.

How to Delete a Border

1. Click on the frame from which you want to delete a border.
2. Click on the active thickness button or select Border from the Layout menu. From the Layout menu you can set individual sides or all sides to None.

Chapter 10:   *Line Art, BorderArt, and Shading*   295

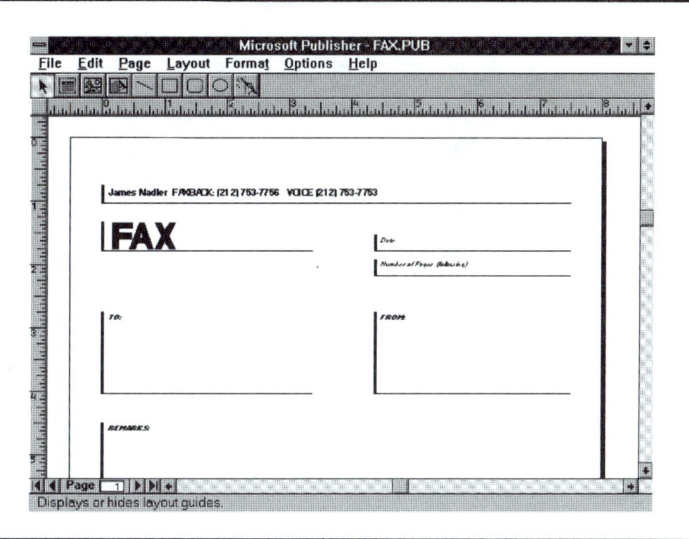

Figure 10-11.   *Using partial borders for effect*

BorderArt

BorderArt is one of the simplest features in Publisher to use, and yet one of its most powerful. The most difficult aspect of working with it is trying to decide which pattern to use and where to use it! The balloons, palm trees, and arched scallops will usually find a better home on a party invitation than a business form. However, don't underestimate the usefulness of levity in an otherwise straight-laced publication. Sections of a company report or a sidebar in a newsletter can often benefit from some comic relief as long as it is applied judiciously and in good taste. Figure 10-12 contains a small sampling of Publisher's BorderArt.

You can apply BorderArt to any frame or line art created with the box tool. Create a box and select BorderArt from the Layout menu. Then click on Balloons...Hot Air. The dialog box should look like Figure 10-13. The Preview window can give you a thumbnail of the border as it would appear in a square frame. Scrolling through the list and previewing the selections is the best way to become familiar with all of the BorderArt options.

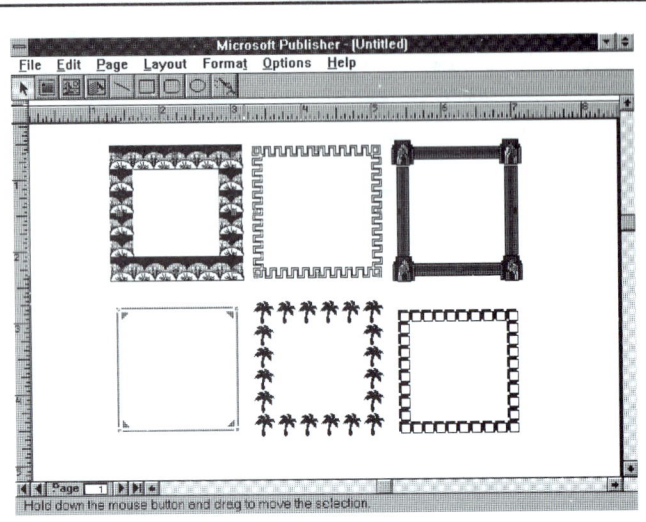

Figure 10-12.   Samples of BorderArt

Like simple borders, BorderArt automatically resizes when you adjust the dimensions of the frame to which it applies. Click on OK to complete the selection. Remember, this is powerful stuff! While it's not exactly a weapon, too much of it can be lethal for a publication's **appearance.**

Figure 10-13.   BorderArt dialog box

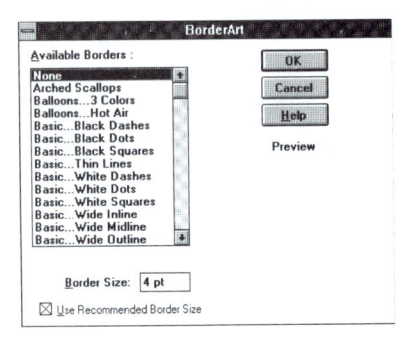

Chapter 10: *Line Art, BorderArt, and Shading* 297

You can also use BorderArt to create some novel thumbnail illustrations or for horizontal and vertical lines composed of some of the more character-like BorderArt figures. Consider these examples:

To create either of the lines, draw a square frame using the rectangular drawing tool. Then click and drag on one of the handles to reduce the frame height to 0 for a horizontal line, or its width to 0 for a vertical line. Use one of the corner handles to reduce both the height and width to 0 in order to create an individual character. Publisher also lets you alter the size of the characters used in the pattern. If you disable the Use Standard Point Size button, you can enter your own height for the characters. You might consider using small thumbnails as text bullets in a presentation.

How to Add BorderArt

1. Click on the frame for which you want to add BorderArt.
2. Select Layout from the Menu bar and select BorderArt from the Layout menu.
3. Scroll through the list of patterns and use the Preview window to find the pattern you want to use.
4. Click on OK.

How to Remove BorderArt

1. Click on the frame for which you want to delete BorderArt.
2. Select Layout from the Menu bar and select BorderArt from the Layout menu.
3. Scroll to None at the top of the list of patterns.
4. Click on OK.

Review

In this chapter, you learned about how Publisher deals with line art and other graphic accents. These graphics are a complement to typography in a publication. Learn to balance text, pictures, and graphics to polish a publication and give it a style all your own. Even the most subtle embellishment can add to a publication's character.

- Publisher can create simple line art for adding graphic accents and rudimentary illustrations to a publication.
- Line art objects can be combined to create illustrations.
- Frames and line art can use shading patterns, colors, borders, and drop shadows to enhance their appearance.
- Borders range in style from simple lines to extremely fanciful BorderArt.
- All objects can exist in the background or foreground, and you can adjust their position in the visual plane for different graphic effects.

A

Menu Reference

This section explains each of the commands and associated dialog boxes that appear on all of the Publisher menus. It's a cross-reference for the chapters in the book. The organization of chapters is functional—each of the Publisher commands is explained in the context of a publishing task; for example, paper size is a part of the discussion about page layout. This appendix is organized according to the menu structure of the program. It is meant to make finding out about specific Publisher commands easier once you've become familiar with the program.

Each listing for a command or dialog box always includes these categories of information:

Title	Purpose
Name	The name of the command
Usage	How Publisher implements it (menu selection or dialog box)
Description	What the command does
Procedure	Necessary and sufficient steps to execute the command

Where relevant, listings may also have some or all of the following information.

Title	Purpose
Buttons, lists, and fields	Descriptions of how each of the options in a dialog box affects a command.
Special cases	Situations where the command operates differently.
Defaults	Default values for any of the fields or lists.
Related topics	Other subjects that bear directly on the current one; for example, Page Numbers relate to the background, since they can only be created there.
Keyboard shortcuts	Keystroke equivalents for executing a command.

File Menu

The File menu controls Publisher's basic input and output systems. You can load publications, save them to disk, import external text and graphics files, and control all printing options from this menu.

Special Cases   *Recently accessed files*   In addition to the standard menu options described here, the names of the last five publications you worked with appear at the bottom of this menu. For convenience, you can open any of these files with a single click, and avoid looking through different drives and directories to find the material you worked with most recently.

Create New Publication

Usage   Dialog box

Description   The Create New Publication dialog box lets you open a new publication using a blank page, one of the Publisher templates, or through a PageWizard, as shown in Figure A-1.

Appendix A: *Menu Reference* 301

Figure A-1.   Create New Publication dialog box

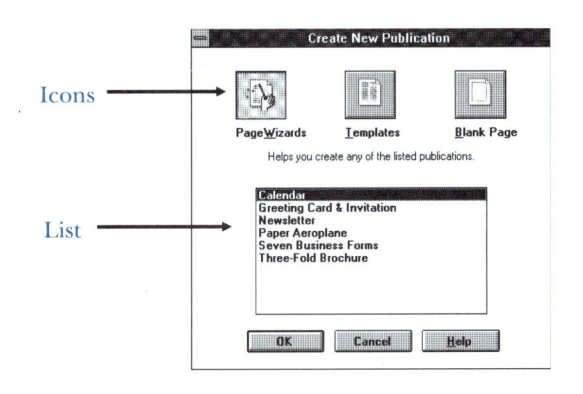

Icons

List

Procedure   Click on one of the icons at the top of the screen. Both PageWizards and Templates let you select a process or file from the list in the window below. Use the scroll bars, if necessary, to view additional choices, and indicate your selection by clicking on it. Double-click the selection or click on OK to start the new publication.

Defaults   The default is the PageWizard icon.

Keyboard Shortcuts   ALT-F C

Open Existing Publication

Usage   Dialog box

Description   The Open Existing Publication dialog box lets you select a publication to work with, as shown in Figure A-2.

Procedure   Scroll through the file list to find the publication you want to work with. Select it and click on OK, or double-click on the file to open it. You can also enter a filename directly into the field.

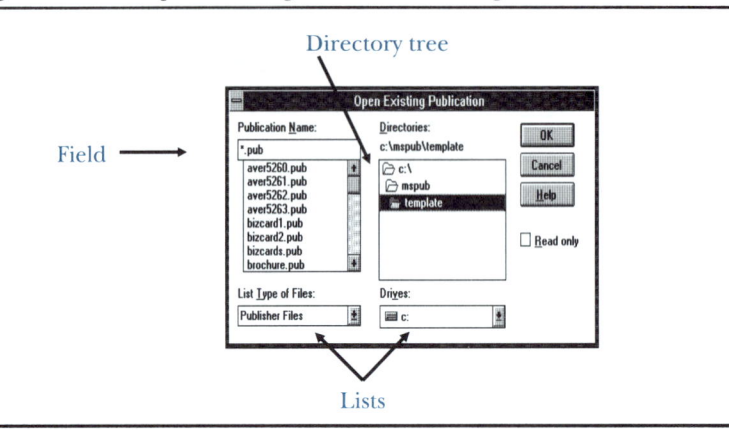

Figure A-2.   Open Existing Publication dialog box

[Open Existing Publication dialog box illustration with labels: "Directory tree" pointing to the directories panel, "Field" pointing to the Publication Name field, and "Lists" pointing to the list areas below.]

Buttons, Lists, and Fields   In the Open Existing Publication dialog box:

Read only   Enable this button if you want to ensure that a publication remains unchanged while you look at it. You'll be able to save the publication under a different name using Save As or copy material from it, but you cannot Save the file under its current name if you make changes to the original.

Drives   This list contains all of the logical disk drive designations for your system. If the publication you want to open is stored on a different drive than the current one, click on the drive list and select an alternative. The Directory tree displays the current directory for the drive you select.

Directory tree   This window displays the current directory, parent directories, and one level of subdirectories for the current drive. If the publication you want to open is stored in a directory other than the current one, double-click on one of the directories in the tree. This procedure operates similarly to the directory tree in the Windows File Manager.

Type of Files   Normally Publisher displays only publications (files with a .PUB extension) in the File window. To change the selection of files displayed in the window, click on the Type of Files list and click on an alternative file type.

Appendix A: *Menu Reference*

Related Topics   Save, Save As

Keyboard Shortcuts   [ALT]-[F] [O]

Close Publication

Usage   Command

Description   Close Publication terminates the Publisher session for the current publication.

Procedure   Click on Close Publication.

Special Cases   Safety   If you haven't saved your work first, Publisher displays the dialog box shown in Figure A-3. Click on Yes to close the file and save the publication with any changes you made during the current editing session. Click on No to abandon the changes from the current session. The previously saved version remains intact. Click on Cancel to return to the current editing session (the current version remains unchanged).

Keyboard Shortcuts   [ALT]-[F] [C]

Figure A-3.   Warning message when you try to close a file you haven't saved

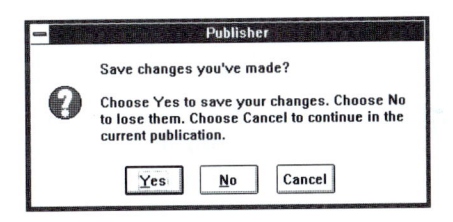

Save

Usage   Command

Description   The Save command stores the current publication on disk with any changes you have made during the current editing session.

Procedure   Click on Save.

Special Cases   *Untitled work*   If the current publication is untitled, Publisher displays the Save As dialog box so you can provide a filename.

Related Topics   Save As

Keyboard Shortcuts   CTRL-S

Save As

Usage   Dialog box

Description   The Save As dialog box lets you name a publication for the first time, or make a copy of an entire publication by saving it under a different name. Save As uses the dialog box shown in Figure A-4.

Procedure   Enter a filename for the publication, using up to eight characters. You can use all standard DOS file naming conventions including letters, numbers, dashes, and underscores. You cannot, however, leave any blank spaces in the name. Publisher will automatically append a .PUB file extension to the name.

Buttons, Lists, and Fields   In the Save As dialog box:

> *Template* Enable this button if you want to save the publication as a template. Publisher automatically stores the file in the \MSPUB\TEMPLATE directory on the drive where you installed the program. In addition, the file will appear in the future on the list of templates in the Create New Publication dialog box. When you create a new publication

Appendix A: *Menu Reference* 305

Figure A-4. *Save As dialog box*

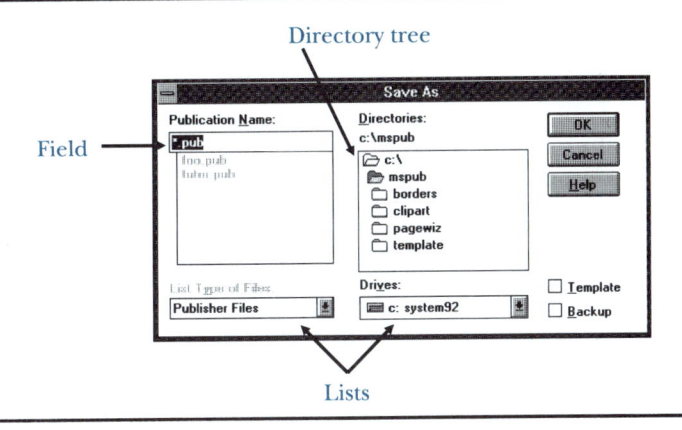

[Figure A-4: Save As dialog box, with labels pointing to "Directory tree", "Field", and "Lists". The dialog shows Publication Name field with "*.pub", foo.pub, fubu.pub entries; Directories list showing c:\mspub with c:\, mspub, borders, clipart, pagewiz, template; List Types of Files: Publisher Files; Drives: c: system92; checkboxes for Template and Backup; buttons for OK, Cancel, Help.]

using a template, an untitled copy of the publication is loaded into the program. The template itself remains on disk unchanged.

Backup Enable this button if you want to maintain a backup version of the publication. When you use this feature, each time you save a publication the previously saved version will also be saved using the same filename and a .BAK file extension. This is a recommended option for all files unless you are short on disk space.

Drives This list contains all of the logical disk drive designations for your system. If you want to store the publication on a different drive than the current one, click on the drive list and select an alternative. The Directory tree displays the current directory for the drive you select.

Directory tree This window displays the current directory, parent directories and one level of subdirectories for the current drive. If you want to store the publication in a directory other than the current one, double-click on one of the directories in the tree. This procedure operates similarly to the directory tree in the Windows File Manager.

Special Cases *Save Selection As* If you want to export text from a publication for use in another program, select a Text frame and the text inside of it that you want to export. Then select Save As from the File menu. When the

Save As dialog box appears, you will see this additional button above the Type of Files list.

☐ **S**ave Selection As:

1. Click on the button.
2. Select a format from the Type of Files list. This determines how Publisher will save the file.
3. Provide a filename for the text. Publisher will automatically provide file extensions based on the type of file you select. If necessary, you can supply your own file extension by typing it directly in the filename field.

Defaults   Publisher files (.PUB file extension)

Related Topics   Highlight Story, Create New Publication (template)

Keyboard Shortcuts   [ALT]-[F] [A]

Import Text

Usage   Dialog box

Description   The Import Text dialog box lets you include text from a DOS application in a Text frame in the current publication. It uses the dialog box shown in Figure A-5.

Procedure   Click on the Text frame into which you want to import text. If necessary, position the insertion point at the location in the frame where you want the incoming text to begin. Select Import Text from the File menu. In the File window, double-click on the name of the file you want to import.

Buttons, Lists, and Fields   In the Import Text dialog box:

Drives   This list contains all of the logical disk drive designations for your system. If the file you want to import is stored on a different drive than

Appendix A: *Menu Reference*

Figure A-5.   *Import Text dialog box*

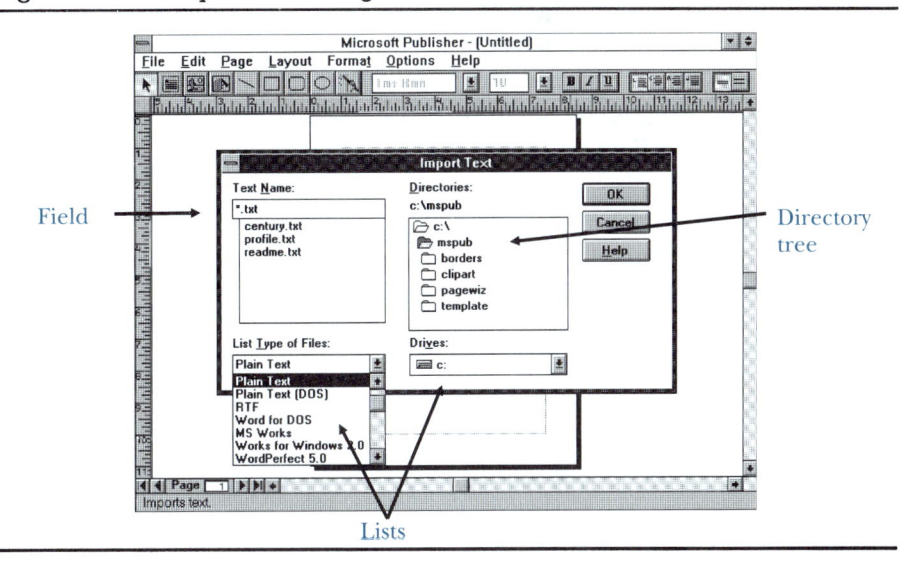

the current one, click on the drive list and select an alternative. The Directory tree displays the current directory for the drive you select.

Directory tree   This window displays the current directory, parent directories, and one level of subdirectories for the current drive. If the file you want to import is stored in a directory other than the current one, double-click on one of the directories in the tree. This procedure operates similarly to the directory tree in the Windows File Manager.

Type of Files   Normally Publisher displays only publications (files with a .PUB extension) in the file window. To change the selection of files displayed in the window, click on the Type of Files list and then click on an alternative file type. You will almost certainly have to change the file type during this process; however, the default type reverts to PUB after each import.

Special Cases   *File Formats*   Publisher understands how to read files in a number of popular DOS formats. These appear in the following list. If you want to use text from an application not included in this list, refer to the *User's Guide* for that application for instructions on how to convert the text to ASCII file format, and then import the material as plain text. Almost all modern applications support some utility for converting text to ASCII.

>Plain Text (ANSI format for Windows)
>Plain Text (DOS) (ASCII format for DOS)
>RTF (Rich Text Format)
>MS Works
>Word for DOS
>WordPerfect 5.0-5.1
>WordStar 3.3-5.5

Defaults   Publisher files (.PUB file extension)

Related Topics   Paste Text, Paste Special, Insert Object

Keyboard Shortcuts   ALT-F M

Import Picture

Usage   Dialog box

Description   The Import Picture dialog box lets you include in a publication graphics files created with other software programs. It uses the dialog box shown in Figure A-6.

Figure A-6.   *Import Picture dialog box*

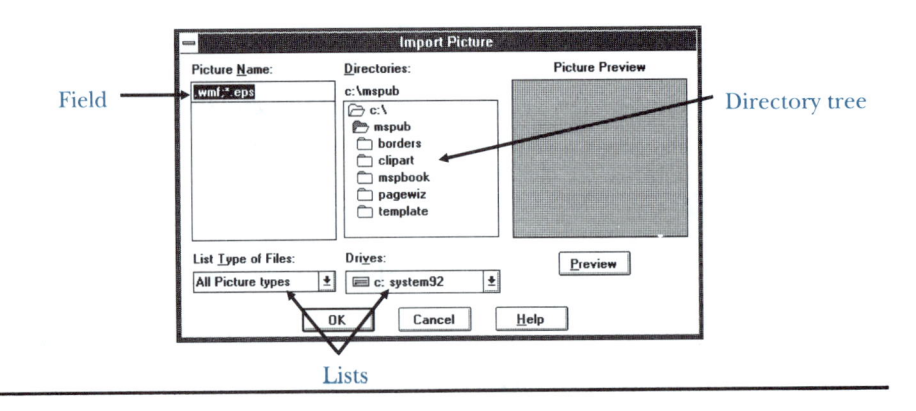

Appendix A: *Menu Reference*

Procedure   To import a picture using its original size, select Import Picture from the File menu and select a picture from the files in the list. Double-click on the file or click on OK to have Publisher create a frame and import the picture. Alternatively, you can create or select a Picture frame and follow the same procedure. Publisher then scales the picture to the size of the frame you selected.

Buttons, Lists, and Fields   In the Import Picture dialog box:

> *Preview*   Use Preview if you want to make sure that a file contains the image you want, before using it in a publication.
>
> *Drives*   This list contains all of the logical disk drive designations for your system. If the image you want to import is stored on a different drive than the current one, click on the drive list and select an alternative. The Directory tree displays the current directory for the drive you select.
>
> *Directory tree*   This window displays the current directory, parent directories, and one level of subdirectories for the current drive. If the image you want to import is stored in a directory other than the current one, double-click on one of the directories in the tree. This procedure operates similarly to the directory tree in the Windows File Manager.
>
> *Type of Files*   Normally Publisher displays files for all formats that it supports. You can restrict the scope of files that appear in the file list by changing the selection in the Type of File list.

Special Cases   *File Formats*   Publisher supports the following graphic file formats. There is considerable variation among graphic formats, and it is possible to find a file with one of these extensions that is incompatible with Publisher. For example, .PCX is used as an extension by a number of programs, but not all .PCX files are the same. If you run into compatibility problems, you may need to use a file conversion program such as HiJaak or Import for Windows.

Format/Source	Extension
Windows Bitmap	.BMP
PC Paintbrush	.PCX
Scanned	.TIF

Format/Source	Extension
Encapsulated PostScript	.EPS
Windows Metafile	.WMF
Computer Graphics Metafile	.CGM

Defaults   All acceptable graphics file formats

Related Topics   Paste Picture, Paste Special

Keyboard Shortcuts   ALT-F I

Print

Usage   Dialog box

Description   The Print dialog box lets you send a publication to the printer and control certain factors about how it will be printed. The Print dialog box is shown in Figure A-7.

Procedure   Select Print from the File menu. Make any necessary modifications to the options and click on OK.

Buttons, Lists, and Fields   In the Print dialog box:

Figure A-7.   *Print dialog box*

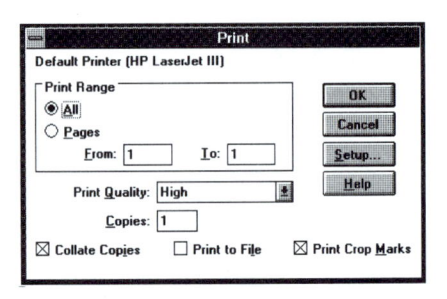

Appendix A: *Menu Reference* 311

Print Range This group of options lets you indicate which part of a publication to print. Within the Print Range group, the All and Pages choices are mutually exclusive. By selecting All, you decide to print an entire publication and cannot enter a specific sequence of pages. If you select Pages, All is automatically deselected, and you can enter beginning and ending page numbers for the print job in the From and To fields.

Print Quality The choices on this list affect the speed and resolution at which a publication prints. In general, higher quality means slower speeds, and lower quality means faster ones. However, this will also depend on your printer. Some lasers, for example, print at their highest speed regardless of the resolution you select in Publisher. The Draft option prints a publication without printing its pictures. Since graphics require more computation, this almost always speeds up the print job, no matter which printer you're using.

Copies This field determines the number of copies of the publication that print.

Collate Copies When you print multiple copies of multipage publications, Publisher normally prints all copies of each page before going on to the next. Enable this option to have Publisher print the pages of each copy in sequence.

Print to File This option lets you create a disk file of the print job. A disk file is useful if you plan to print the final copy of a publication on an output device other than your normal one. Most PC-based laser printers, for example, have a maximum resolution of 300 DPI. This is somewhat less than the resolution used by professional publications (1200 DPI or better). By sending the publication to a file, it becomes portable. For example, you can copy the file to a disk, and take the entire print job to another location where a higher-quality printing device is available. If you select this option, Publisher prompts you for a filename before completing the job.

Print Crop Marks Crop marks are used when the size of the pages in a publication will ultimately be smaller than the physical page on which they are printed. These are commonly found, for example, on a mechanical for business cards. Crop marks indicate where a page should be cut to make a final publication. They appear as small corner-shaped lines that frame the final page area.

Setup This option brings up a separate dialog box, detailed later in this section, which lets you adjust the paper size and other printer selections.

Defaults   The default settings on the Print dialog box are

Range	All
Print Quality	High
Copies	1
Collate	Yes
Print to File	No
Crop Marks	Yes

Related Topics   Print Setup

Keyboard Shortcuts   CTRL-P

Print Setup

Usage   Dialog box

Description   The Print Setup dialog box lets you change printers and settings for page size and orientation, as shown in Figure A-8.

Procedure   Select Print Setup from the File menu or the Setup button in the Print dialog box. You must return to the Print dialog box in order to run a print job.

Buttons, Lists, and Fields   In the Print Setup dialog box:

Printer The options in this group control which printer Publisher uses to output publications. Default Printer is the current default printer installed for Windows. The selections in the Specific Printer list are the other printers you have installed under Windows. If you select one of these, Publisher will use the alternative printer, regardless of what is

Appendix A: *Menu Reference* 313

Figure A-8.   *Print Setup dialog box*

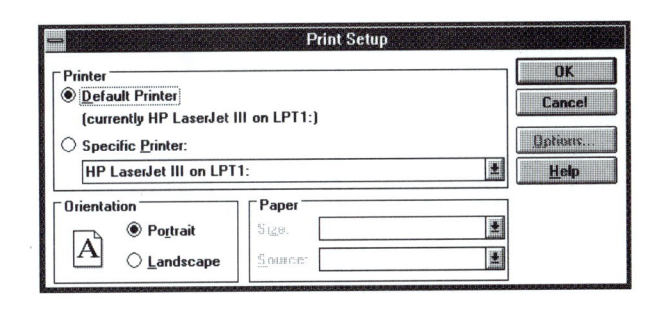

currently selected under Windows. This is simply a method of overriding the printer selection in the Windows Control Panel.

Remember *Using a different printer than the one you designed a publication with can affect the appearance of the publication dramatically. For example, between laser printers, the font selection may vary. With other devices, the selection of different page sizes may be limited. If the design of the publication calls for an element that is not found in the new printer, you may not like the substitutions that Publisher makes.*

Orientation   Page orientation lets you control the direction that Publisher prints in—left to right or bottom to top. In Figure A-9 you can see the same document printed on a letter-sized page (8 1/2 by 11 inches) in both portrait and landscape orientations. In portrait orientation, printing occurs from left to right. Portrait is the more standard of the two orientations. It's always available and usually the default setting for most printers. In landscape orientation, printing occurs from bottom to top in order to use the larger of a page's two dimensions as the width. If you were using a typewriter, you could simply rotate the page 90 degrees. Since many modern printers do not allow you to reorient the page in its carriage, the direction of the printing itself is reoriented.

Paper   This list lets you select one of the standard American (letter/legal) or European (A4/B5) paper sizes.

Figure A-9.   *Portrait and landscape orientations*

Portrait orientation   Landscape orientation

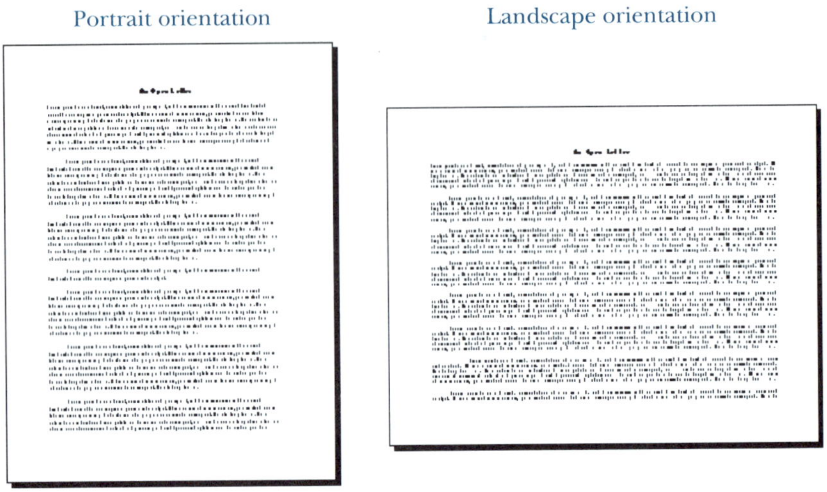

Source   This list lets you select from different paper feeds. For example, some printers have 2 paper trays, each for a different size of paper. In such a case, you can select one of the two trays to draw paper from for a particular print job. If the printer you're using has only a single source, the list is inactive.

Options   The selections available from this dialog box vary depending on the printer you are using.

Defaults   The default settings on the Print Setup dialog box are

Paper Size	Letter
Orientation	Portrait
Printer	Default

Related Topics   Page Setup, Format Characters, Print

Keyboard Shortcuts   (ALT)-(F) (R)

Exit Publisher

Usage   Command

Description   Exit Publisher closes the current publication and terminates the current Publisher session.

Procedure   Click on Exit.

Special Cases   *Saving*   If you haven't saved the publication first, Publisher displays the dialog box shown in Figure A-10. Click on Yes to close the file and save the publication with any changes you made during the current editing session. Click on No to abandon the changes from the current session. The previously saved version remains intact. Click on Cancel to return to the current editing session, and the file is neither saved nor abandoned.

Keyboard Shortcuts   ALT-F X

Edit Menu

The Edit menu lets you manipulate objects and the material inside of them. It contains selections for Text frames, WordArt frames, Picture frames, and line art. Objects can be cut, copied, and pasted within or between publications using the Windows Clipboard. You can edit text and invoke

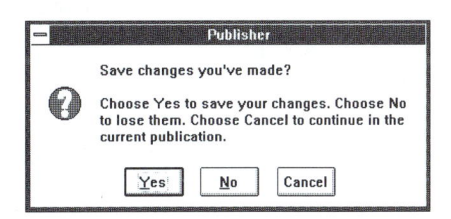

Figure A-10.   Warning message when you exit Publisher before saving

search and replace options within Text frames. The Edit menu also gives you access to functions that make use of Microsoft's object-linking technology.

Special Cases   *Menu changes*   The literal text for the options on this menu changes more frequently than any other in Publisher, depending on what type of object you currently have selected, and the nature of the last command you executed. For example, if you delete a picture, the Undo option reads "Undo Delete Object" whereas if you type some characters in a Text frame, the option appears as "Undo Typing".

Undo

Usage   Command

Description   Undo reverses the effects of the most recent command you issued. This applies to most of the commands on the Edit menu, and many other commands in Publisher, including moving or scaling objects by dragging them with the mouse. If you've made an error in resizing a Text frame, for example, or accidentally deleted a piece of line art, Undo will correct the error and return the publication to its condition immediately before the last command. However, it will only affect the very last command you executed. If you make an error and want to correct it using Undo, use it immediately!

Note   *Undo does not function with all commands. For example, if you open a new publication without saving the one you were working in, Undo cannot correct the error.*

Procedure   Click on Undo from the Edit menu.

Special Cases   *Redo*   When you use Undo to correct a mistake, the Undo command becomes the last command you issued, so the Undo line on the Edit menu reads "Redo", and pertains to whatever you had undone in the command before. For example, "Undo Delete Text" becomes "Redo Delete Text". Redo remains on the menu until you issue another command besides Redo or Undo.

Mouse moves   Using Undo when you're experimenting with frame layout is very helpful. For example, after you've spent time positioning an object (or group of objects), you may want to move them out of the way to see how

Appendix A: *Menu Reference* 317

a page looks without them. You can move them back to their prior location by selecting Undo Move Objects, as long as you select Undo immediately after the move. Using Undo to reverse a move ensures that the objects return to their *exact* original location.

Keyboard Shortcuts   ALT-BACKSPACE

Cut

Usage   Command

Description   Cut removes the currently selected object(s) from a publication and sends it to the Windows Clipboard. It operates with all frames, the text inside of a Text frame, and all line art. Used together, Cut and Paste let you move objects or text within a publication, between publications, or between Windows applications.

Procedure   Select the object(s) or text that you want to Cut. Any amount of text or any number of frames and line art objects can be cut together. Then select Cut from the Edit menu to send a copy of the selection(s) to the Clipboard.

Related Topics   Copy, Paste, selecting objects, selecting text

Keyboard Shortcuts   CTRL-X

Note

The Clipboard only holds one selection at a time, the one you most recently cut or copied there. If you intend to paste an object, do it right after you cut. Otherwise you may inadvertently overwrite the selection on the Clipboard.

Copy

Usage   Command

Description   Copy leaves object(s) in place in a publication and sends a duplicate to the Windows Clipboard. It operates with all frames, the text inside of a Text frame, and all line art. Used together, Copy and Paste let you duplicate objects or text within a publication, between publications, or between Windows applications.

Procedure   Select the object(s) or text that you want to Copy. Any amount of text or any number of frames and line art objects can be copied. Then select Copy from the Edit menu to send a copy of the selection(s) to the Clipboard.

Related Topics   Cut, Paste, selecting objects, selecting text

Keyboard Shortcuts   CTRL-C

Note

The Clipboard only holds one selection at a time, the one you most recently cut or copied there. If you intend to paste an object, do it right after you copy. Otherwise you may inadvertently overwrite the selection on the Clipboard.

Paste

Usage   Command

Description   Paste places a copy of the current contents of the Clipboard in a publication. It operates with all frames, the text inside of a Text frame, and all line art objects. Paste inserts objects roughly in the middle of the screen, regardless of the current selection, or the original location of the source. Paste inserts text in a Text frame starting at the current location of the insertion point. Used together, Cut and Paste let you move objects or text within a publication, between publications, or between Windows applications. Copy and Paste let you duplicate objects between the same resources.

Procedure   Cut or Copy an object or some text to the Clipboard. Select the desired location (a Text frame or another page of the publication) and select Paste from the Edit menu.

Special Cases   *Cloning objects*   The contents of the Clipboard remain intact until another object is Cut or Copied there. If you want to make multiple copies of an object, copy it to the Clipboard and then keep executing Paste.

Appendix A: *Menu Reference* 319

If you paste an object multiple times, Publisher places each copy on top of the previous one so that the copy overlays it perfectly. You can't even tell that there are multiple copies until you click on the stack and drag one away.

Related Topics   Cut, Copy, Typing Replaces Selection

Keyboard Shortcuts   CTRL-V

Note   The Clipboard only holds one selection at a time, the one you most recently cut or copied there. If you intend to paste an object, do it right after you cut or copy it. Otherwise you may inadvertently overwrite the selection on the Clipboard.

Paste Special

Usage   Command

Description   Paste Special lets you embed a Picture frame with a file or file fragment from another application. Publisher automatically updates the publication with the latest version of the file. There is no need to open the source application to obtain any subsequent update.

Procedure   Follow these steps to use Paste Special:

1. Use the Windows Program Manager to start Publisher and a second Windows application that supports object linking. The program that contains the material you embed is the source.
2. Create or select material from the source using standard techniques. Selecting material by dragging the pointer, clicking, or using a marquee works in most Microsoft programs.
3. Cut or copy the selection to the Windows Clipboard. Use either command from the Edit menu of the source application, or use one of the keyboard shortcuts.
4. Switch to Publisher either through the Windows Task List or by clicking on the appropriate window.
5. Create or select the frame into which you want to embed the material.

6. Select Paste Special from the Edit menu. The Paste Special dialog box appears, as shown in **Figure A-11**.
7. Select a format for the embedded file.
8. Click on Paste Link to embed live information. Click on Paste to embed a picture of the information.

Special Cases   *File formats*   The only way to actually embed the information from an application so that it will update each time you start Publisher is to select Native from the list in the Paste Special dialog box. Embedding material as Native means live information from the source application is placed in Publisher. The other two options—Metafile and Bitmap—only embed a picture of the information. Such pictures are static and will not update each time you open the publication. Of the two, Metafile is the preferred choice. It is Windows' own format for transferring graphic information. Bitmap is a last-case alternative for pictures when Publisher won't accept the source information as a Metafile.

Object linking   Embedding depends on a Microsoft technology known as object linking. Not all Microsoft products support this process, and of those that do, some support it differently than others. Word for Windows, for example, lets you embed a file in a publication, but only displays an icon in the embedded frame, whereas Excel displays your exact selection. The Windows Notepad, on the other hand, doesn't recognize embedding at all. Don't be surprised if you only have limited opportunities to use embedding.

Figure A-11.   *Paste Special dialog box*

Appendix A: *Menu Reference* 321

Related Topics   Cut, Copy, Paste, Insert Object

Keyboard Shortcuts   `ALT`-`E` `A`

Delete

Usage   Command

Description   Delete removes objects from a publication without using the Clipboard. Material on the Clipboard remains unaffected. Delete operates with all frames, the text inside of a Text frame, and all line art objects.

Procedure   Select the object(s) or text that you want to delete. Any amount of text can be deleted and any number of frames or line art objects. Then select Delete from the Edit menu.

Related Topics   Undo

Keyboard Shortcuts   `DEL`

Delete Text Frame

Usage   Command

Description   Delete Text Frame removes a Text frame from a publication. If the frame is not connected to any others in the publication, Publisher also deletes the text inside the frame. If the frame is connected, the text flows as described under Special Cases.

Procedure   Select the Text frames that you want to delete. Then select Delete Text Frame from the Edit menu.

Special Cases   *Connected frames*   When you delete a frame from a connected series of frames, the story remains intact. If the frame is in the middle of the series, the text that occupied it flows into the following frame. This effect ripples through all of the remaining frames in the series, and may move some of the text from the last frame into the overflow area. If you delete the last frame in a series, text goes into the overflow area immediately. Deleting the first frame in a series causes the story to begin in the next (second) frame, and a ripple effect also occurs: the text from the old frame 2 (new frame 1) flows into the old frame 3 (new frame 2), and so on throughout the series. Text from the last frame may be moved into the Overflow area if there isn't sufficient room in the frame to accommodate it. When you delete pages that contain connected frames, the same effects occur based on where in the chain the frames were located.

Related Topics   Undo

Keyboard Shortcuts   CTRL-DEL

Highlight Story

Usage   Command

Description   Highlight Story highlights all interconnected frames on the current page. When you cut, copy, or delete a story using this option, the story is completely removed from the publication on all pages, but the Text frames remain in place. If you want to export an entire story to another application through the Save As option, use Highlight Story to select it first.

Procedure   Click on a Text frame that you know is part of a series and select Highlight Story from the Edit menu.

Related Topics   Save Selection As

Keyboard Shortcuts   CTRL-A

Edit WordArt Object

Usage   Dialog box

Appendix A: *Menu Reference*

Description   The WordArt dialog box lets you modify text in a WordArt frame. You can change the content of the copy window or modify any of the formatting options shown in **Figure A-12**.

Procedure   **Select a WordArt frame and select Edit WordArt Object from the Edit menu.** Use standard Windows field editing techniques to edit the characters in the Copy field or modify any of the option buttons or lists.

Buttons and Lists   In the WordArt dialog box:

Apply   Click on Apply to see the effects of your entry in the frame without closing the dialog box. You may need to drag the WordArt dialog box out of the way to see the frame you are working on.

Preview   Click on Preview to see the effects of your changes in the Preview window.

Font   WordArt fonts are completely independent of the font selection available through Windows. The design for a few of the WordArt fonts is on the conventional side, although most of them are geared toward attracting attention. Use the following table as a guideline for applying WordArt type styles.

Figure A-12.   *WordArt dialog box*

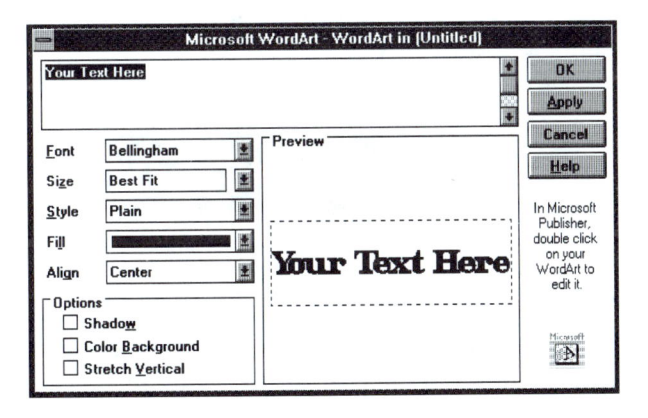

Conventional	Borderline	Offbeat
Bellingham	Anacortes	Duvall
Inglewood	Ellensburg	Enumclaw
Longview	Langley	Omak
Vancouver	Marysville	Sequim
Vashon	Mineral	Snohomish
		Touchet
		Tupelo
		WallaWalla
		Wenatchee

Size All WordArt fonts are scalable. In addition to the popular sizes that come with the program (6, 12, 18, 24, 36, 48, 60, 72, 84, 96, 108, 120, and 128 points) you can have Publisher create a size for you based on the size of a frame. This method of scaling type is called Best Fit in Publisher. These characters always adjust to the size of a WordArt frame, even if you resize it. Best Fit can create characters up to 14 inches in height.

Style WordArt styles are either plain, rotated, or rounded. An easy way to remember all of the options is by relating them to a clock. Each of the styles come from running a line of copy around the clock, so to speak, as shown in Figure A-13.

Fill The Fill option lets you add color to the characters in a WordArt frame. Color is printer dependent. It may show up on your monitor, but it won't print unless you have a color output device. You can, however, create dropout lettering using white fill for the letters on a color background, as shown here:

Blackout!

The dropout effect will occur with all printers.

Align Alignment defines the way that paragraphs are positioned with respect to the boundaries and margins of a frame. WordArt has the following options for alignment.

Appendix A: *Menu Reference* 325

Figure A-13.   WordArt paragraph styles

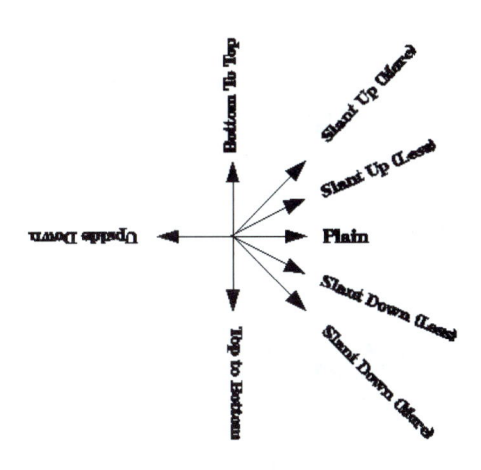

Left	Copy is flush with the left margin of the page, and ragged on the right.
Right	Copy is flush on the right side of the page and ragged on the left.
Centered	Copy is equidistant from both margins.
Word Justified	The words in the copy are spread across each line so that both the left and right sides are aligned with their respective margins.
Letter Justified	Publisher spaces the letters of an individual word across each line in order to make it flush with both the left and right margins, as shown here:

HERE   NO
NOW   WHERE

Fit Horizontally Individual characters are laterally distorted on each line in order to make them justify:

HERE NO
NOW WHERE

Shadow Shadow creates an outline behind each character:

Shadows SHADOWS

Color Background If you select white fill for the copy, Publisher supplies a black background. If you select another color for Fill, Publisher provides a grey background. To get a more significant selection of background colors, you must supply a color or pattern for the frame itself.

Stretch Vertical This option scales the type in the copy window to the full height of the frame. Unlike Best Fit, which makes the characters as large as possible but preserves the proportions of the font, stretching the font vertically always distorts it, as shown here:

TALL

Special Cases *Buttons* Button styles use the first three lines that you enter in the copy field to form the top, middle, and bottom lines of the button

Appendix A: *Menu Reference* 327

respectively. Publisher ignores any other lines that you enter after the third. You can enter different text for each of the lines to vary the message in the button. If you leave the middle line blank, Publisher will produce opposing up and down arches.

Defaults   The default settings on the WordArt dialog box are

Font	Bellingham
Size	Best Fit
Style	Plain
Fill	Black
Align	Center

Related Topics   Frame Colors, Patterns, and Borders

Keyboard Shortcuts   `ALT`-`E` `O` or double-click on the WordArt frame you want to edit.

Insert Object

Usage   Dialog box

Description   The Insert Object dialog box lets you select an application from within a Picture frame, as shown in Figure A-14. Publisher then starts the application program, directly from the Picture frame. When the application terminates, Publisher returns with the material from the application in the frame. Use this method of creating or editing when it's easier to handle the material in its native environment, the one that was used to create it. For example, it's more convenient to edit a chart from Excel or a drawing from Paintbrush in one of those applications than in Publisher.

Procedure   Follow these steps to use the Insert Object feature:

1. Create or select a Picture frame.
2. Select Edit from the Menu bar and select Insert Object from the Edit menu.

Figure A-14.   *Insert Object dialog box*

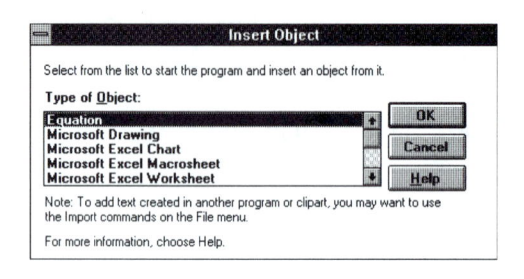

---

3. Select an application from the list in the dialog box. This application is the source.
4. Create an image, chart, spreadsheet, or other material in the source application.
5. Select File from the Menu bar in the source application and select Exit and Return or Update from the File menu.

Related Topics   Paste Special

Keyboard Shortcuts   ALT-E B

Note   *Insert Object only functions with applications that support a Microsoft technology known as object linking. Two of Publisher's features, WordArt and Note-Its, do. Object linking is meant to be used with Picture frames. If you don't have any other applications that support this process, don't try to use this function.*

Find

Usage   Dialog box

Description   The Find dialog box lets you search through a story for a series of characters such as a word, phrase, or sentence. You can restrict the search to match certain upper- and lowercase letters, complete words or other special characters, by enabling the option buttons shown in **Figure A-15**.

Figure A-15. Find dialog box

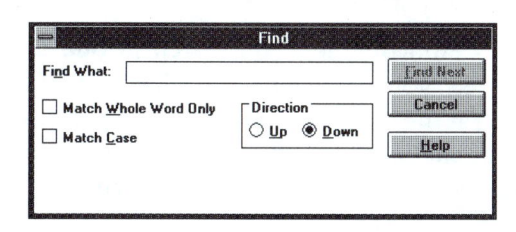

Procedure   Follow these steps to use the Find feature:

1. Click on one of the frames that contains the story through which you want to search.
2. Select Edit from the Menu bar and select Find from the Edit menu.
3. Enter the text that you want to locate in the Find What field. Click on any of the option buttons to limit the scope or direction of the search.
4. Click on Find Next to search for successive occurrences of the text. You can alter any of the option button settings each time that Publisher finds one of the matches.

Buttons and Lists   In the Find dialog box:

Match Whole Word Only   When this option is enabled, Publisher skips instances of the letters in the Find What field unless they have an empty space before the first letter and after the last. For example, if you search for the letters *t-h-e* with this button disabled, Publisher finds them in words such as "these", "bother", "them", "there", and "the". If you enable this option, Publisher only stops at "the".

Match Case   When this option is enabled, Publisher skips instances of the designated letters unless they exactly match the upper- and lowercase letters you entered in the Find What field. For example, if you search for the letters *T-h-e* with this button disabled, Publisher finds them in different combinations such as "THE", "the", and "The". If you enable this option, Publisher only stops at "The".

Direction   Find only lets you search in one direction at a time. These buttons lets you determine the direction of the search. Find begins searching at the location of the insertion point, and moves either forward (down) or backward (up) through the story. The first time that Publisher searches to the end or beginning of a story, it asks if you want to start over at the other end.

Special Cases   *The overflow area*   Find does not look through the overflow area. If you want to locate all occurrences of your entry, be sure that Publisher has displayed all of the text in the story.

Text selections   If you select a block of text, Find only searches through the block. This can shorten the time required to complete a search. However, make sure that you do not have a block selected if you want to search throughout an entire story.

Special characters   You can look for the following nonprinting characters with Find:

?	Wildcard
^p	Carriage return
^t	Tab
^n	Forced line break
^w	White space (any combination of tabs or spaces)
^?	Question mark

The wildcard character can stand for any character, and can be included in any position of the Find What field. For example, if you search for "?ord", Publisher finds words that begin with any letter followed by the letters *o-r-d*, such as "WordArt", "word", "border", "borders", and "order".

Views   Switch to Actual View when you use Find. It works, no matter which view you use, but it's difficult to see the text in broader views, once Publisher has located it.

Defaults   The default settings on the Find dialog box are

Direction	Down
Whole Words	No
Case	None

Appendix A: *Menu Reference* 331

Related Topics   Replace

Keyboard Shortcuts   (ALT)-(E) (F)

Replace

Usage   Dialog box

Description   The Replace dialog box lets you substitute one group of characters with another. You can do so selectively throughout a story or have Publisher replace all instances of a group at once. You can select any of these options from the dialog box shown in Figure A-16. Replace always operates forward in a file from the location of the insertion point.

Procedure   Follow these steps to use the Replace feature:

1. Click on one of the frames that contains the text that you want to replace.
2. Select Edit from the Menu bar and select Replace from the Edit menu.
3. Enter the text that you want to replace in the Find What field. Click on any of the option buttons to limit the scope of the search.
4. Click on the Replace With field and enter the text to substitute.

Figure A-16.   *Replace dialog box*

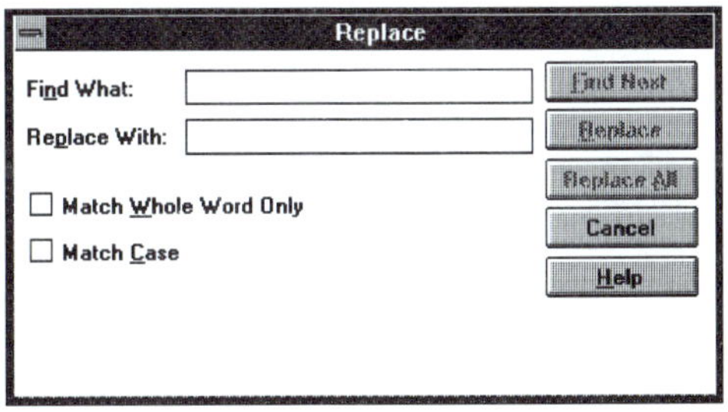

5. Click on Find Next to search for successive occurrences of the text you want to replace.
6. Click on Replace to make individual substitutions in each case, or click on Replace All to have Publisher make substitutions throughout the file without confirmation.

Buttons and Lists   In the Replace dialog box:

Match Whole Word Only   When you enable this option, Publisher skips instances of the letters in the Find What field unless they have an empty space before the first letter and after the last. For example, if you search for the letters *t-h-e* with this button disabled, Publisher finds them in words such as "these", "bother", "them", "there", and "the". If you enable this option, Publisher only stops at "the".

Match Case   When you enable this option, Publisher skips instances of the letters in the Find What field unless they exactly match the upper- and lowercase letters you entered. For example, if you search for the letters *T-h-e* with this button disabled, Publisher finds them in different combinations words such as "THE", "the", and "The". If you enable this option, Publisher only stops at "The".

Special Cases   *Undo*   Undo works with Replace. When you select Undo immediately after a replacement session, Publisher reverses all of the replacements that it made since the command was last invoked.

Global deletion   If you leave the Replace With field empty, Publisher simply removes the text specified in the Find What field. This is a handy way to make global deletions.

Defaults   The default settings on the Replace dialog box are

Direction	Down
Whole Words	No
Case	None

Related Topics   Find

Keyboard Shortcuts   (ALT)-(E) (E)

Appendix A: *Menu Reference*   333

Page Menu

The Page menu controls certain page layout options, including the number of pages in a publication, the publication type, and the page size. The menu also gives you access to the background page for creating objects that repeat at the same location on every page in a publication. In addition you can select views of the screen with different levels of magnification.

Screen Views

Usage   Commands

Description   Publisher lets you choose from eight different levels of screen magnification, called views. Changing your view of the page has no effect on the publication. If you select an object before you switch to one of the more magnified views, Publisher centers the new view around the section of the page that contains the object. The following table describes which portion of the page Publisher displays for each view.

View	Displays
Full	Entire page
25%	3/4 page
33%	2/3 page
50%	1/2 page
66%	1/3 page
75%	1/4 page
Actual	In actual size
200%	Double the actual size

Procedure   If you're going to switch to more magnified views, select the object(s) you want to look at. Then select Page from the Menu bar and click on one of the eight views.

Special Cases   *Last view/actual view*   (F9) switches between Actual Size view and the last view you selected from the Page menu. If you haven't selected anything other than Full Page view during the current session, then that is the last view.

Scrolling   Use the vertical and horizontal scroll bars or the scroll boxes to move around the page. Use PGUP and PGDN to scroll up and down the page in Actual Size view.

Defaults   Full Page

Keyboard Shortcuts   To view the screen in different ways:

PGUP	Move up (actual view)
PGDN	Move down (actual view)
ALT-P F	Full page
ALT-P 2	25% page
ALT-P 3	33% page
ALT-P 5	50% page
ALT-P 6	66% page
ALT-P 7	75% page
ALT-P A	Actual page
ALT-P 0	200% page

Insert Pages

Usage   Dialog box

Description   The Insert Pages dialog box lets you add one or more pages at a time to a publication. Several options exist for the content and location of the pages, as shown in Figure A-17. New pages all take on the existing layout for the publication.

Procedure   Select Insert Pages from the Page menu. Change any of the options, if necessary, or accept the default values for inserting a single blank page after the current one.

Buttons and Fields   In the Insert Pages dialog box:

Appendix A: *Menu Reference* 335

Figure A-17.   *Insert Pages dialog box*

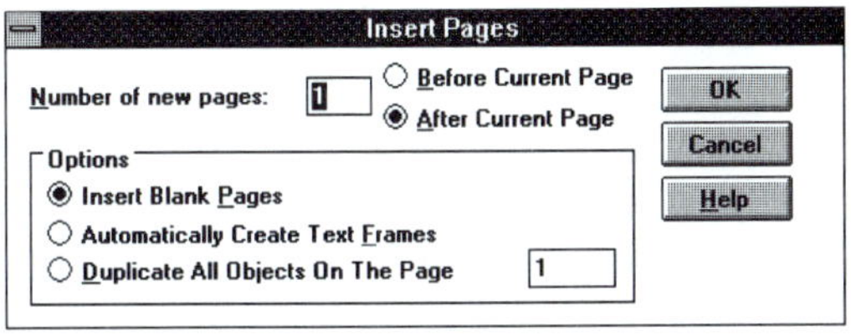

Number of new pages   Enter a value here to specify the number of new pages to add.

Before/After Current Page   You can insert new pages in front of or in back of the current page.

Insert Blank Pages   Select this option if you want Publisher to add empty pages.

Automatically Create Text Frames   Enable this option if you want Publisher to create pages with a single Text frame on each. The frame will conform to the margin guides for the publication.

Duplicate Objects On The Page   Click here, and Publisher copies all objects on the specified page onto each of the new pages in the same locations. Frames are copied *without* their content. The default source for the copies is the current page, but you can enter any other page number.

Defaults   The default settings on the Insert Pages dialog box are

Number	1
Location	After
Content	Blank

Keyboard Shortcuts   CTRL-N

Delete Page

Usage   Command

Description   Delete Page lets you remove one page at a time from a publication. This is always the current page. When you delete a page, all of the objects on the page are deleted as well.

Caution

Publisher does not display a warning or confirmation message when you select the Delete Page command! Make sure you want to delete a page, and that you are currently looking at the one you want to delete before executing the command. You may lose valuable information!

Procedure   Display the page that you want to delete. Then Select Delete Page from the Page menu.

Special Cases   *The scratch area*   The scratch area is common to all pages. Objects in the scratch area remain unaffected by page deletions. If you want to retain some or all of the objects on a page you're going to delete, move them into the scratch area before the deletion. They must be completely off the page area in order to avoid deletion. If they don't fit in the scratch area, use Cut from the Edit menu to move them to the Clipboard, and then paste them on another page or in another publication.

Connected frames   If the page you delete contains Text frames that are connected to Text frames on other pages, the frames on the deleted page are removed, but the flow of the text is maintained between the frames that still exist in the publication. If necessary, Publisher places excess text in the overflow area.

Undo   Undo works with the Delete Page command. If you Undo immediately after the deletion, it will restore a deleted page.

Related Topics   Delete Text Frame, Delete Object

Keyboard Shortcuts   [ALT]-[P] [D]

Insert Page Numbers

Usage   Command

Description   Insert Page Numbers lets you insert a page marker in a Text frame on the background page. When you insert a page marker in a publica-

Appendix A: *Menu Reference*

tion, Publisher automatically numbers pages and prints page numbers on foreground pages. This is the only way to print page numbers without creating them individually. The frame that contains the page marker can also contain other text, as shown here:

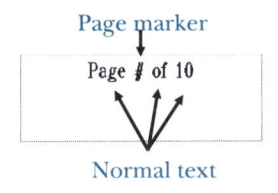

```
        Page marker
            ↓
    ┌─────────────────┐
    │  Page # of 10   │
    │    ↗  ↑  ↖     │
    └─────────────────┘
         Normal text
```

On the background, Publisher only displays the pound sign as the page marker. However, Publisher replaces the page marker with the correct page number on each foreground page. Page markers only display or print Arabic numerals. If you want additional text, such as the word "Page" or dashes around the number, you must enter it yourself. Text frames that contain page markers are no different from other Text frames in a publication. You can also treat the page marker itself just like any other text character for editing and formatting purposes.

Procedure   Follow these steps to insert page numbers:

1. Select Page from the Menu bar and select Go to Background from the Page menu.
2. Create a Text frame (or select an existing one) at the location where you want page numbers to print.
3. Select Page from the Menu bar and select Insert Page Numbers from the Page menu.
4. Add, edit, or format the page marker and any other text in the frame.

Special Cases   *Starting page number*   Publisher normally begins numbering the pages in a publication on page 1 with the number 1. You can, however, cause it to begin with a different starting number through the Settings dialog box on the Options menu.

Facing pages   If you create a frame with a page marker before activating the Mirrored Guides option, Publisher automatically copies it to the left background page in a mirrored location.

Defaults   Current character style

Related Topics   Editing text, Text frames, the background page, mirrored guides, options

Keyboard Shortcuts   `ALT`-`P` `N`

Ignore Background

Usage   Command

Description   Ignore Background lets you suppress the appearance of background material on any foreground page. You can toggle it on or off for an individual page at any time.

Procedure   Turn to the foreground page for which you want to override the background material and select Ignore Background from the Page menu.

Defaults   Use Background

Related Topics   Background page, page numbers

Keyboard Shortcuts   `ALT`-`P` `R`

Go to Background/Foreground

Usage   Command

Description   Go to Background/Foreground switches the Publisher display between the current foreground page and the background page. If the publication uses a layout with mirrored guides, the appropriate background page appears.

Procedure   Select Go to Background from a foreground page or Go to Foreground from a background page.

Related Topics   Facing pages

Appendix A: *Menu Reference*

Keyboard Shortcuts   CTRL-M

Page Setup

Usage   Dialog box

Description   The Page Setup dialog box lets you determine the publication type and page size, as shown in Figure A-18.

Procedure   Select Page Setup from the Page menu. Pick a publication type and adjust the page size, if necessary.

Buttons and Fields   In the Page Setup dialog box:

Full Page   This is the most common setting for publication type. All of the space on the paper constitutes a page, and the pages that appear on screen are exactly like those that you print. The paper size and page size are equal.

Book   Book publications are printed as spreads. Publisher assumes that you want the pages to face each other as they do in a book. Publisher divides the paper size equally from top to bottom to form two pages, assuming that a collection of these sheets will be bound together at the

Figure A-18.   *Page Setup dialog box*

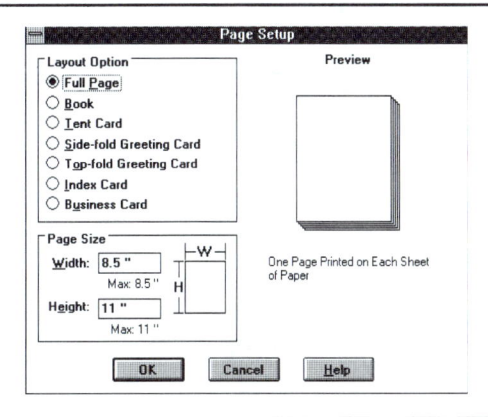

center line to produce a multipage book. When Publisher prints the publication, it pairs the pages on each piece of paper to facilitate book binding: the first with the last, the second with the second to last, and so on, as shown here:

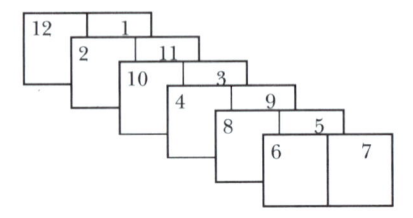

Tent Card Publisher assumes that you want to create a four-sided tent card using a single sheet of paper with a single fold and printing on two sides. The paper size is divided equally from left to right in order to form a page, as shown in Figure A-19. Since both pages will ultimately face outward, Publisher prints the text and graphics for the second page upside down. After you fold the paper, text will appear right side up on both pages.

Side-fold Greeting Card Publisher prints side- and top-fold cards with the assumption that a four-sided card with two folds will be produced from

Figure A-19.   *Tent card*

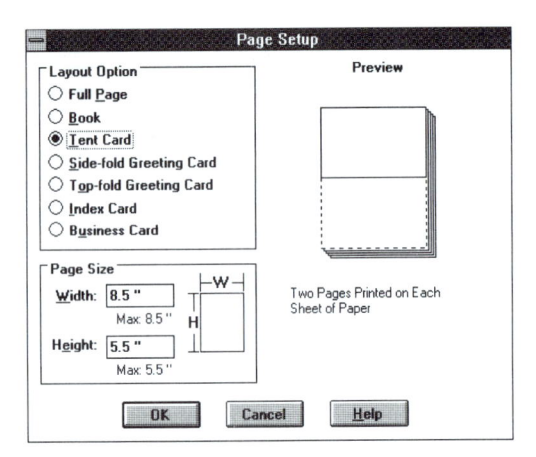

Appendix A: *Menu Reference* 341

a single sheet of paper with printing on all four sides. The paper size is divided equally from left to right and top to bottom in order to form four pages, as shown in Figure A-20. Publisher assumes that this sheet will be folded twice, once at each center line. After it is completely folded, text will appear right side up on all four sides.

Top-fold Greeting Card Top-fold cards are basically the same as side-fold cards in their construction. The difference between side- and top-fold cards is the order of the folds. This affects the sequence of the pages and the edge from which the card opens.

Index Card Index cards are approximately 3 by 5 inches and print on a single page, as shown in Figure A-21.

Since they use less than a full page, you should turn on Crop Marks when printing index cards.

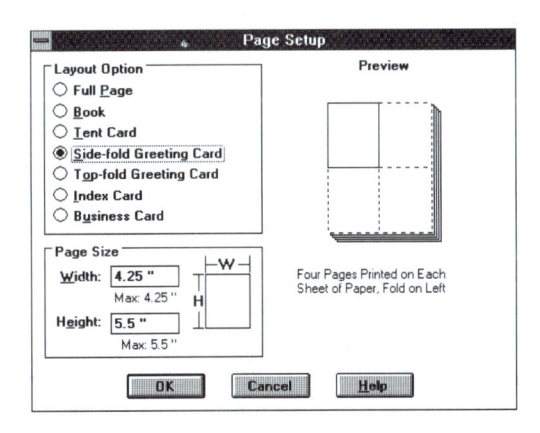

Business Card Business cards are approximately 3.3 by 2 inches and print on a single page, as shown in Figure A-21.

Since they use less than a full page, you should turn on Crop Marks when printing business cards.

Page Size Page size determines which part of the current paper size Publisher uses as an individual page and what the size of the page area

Figure A-20.   *Side-fold greeting card*

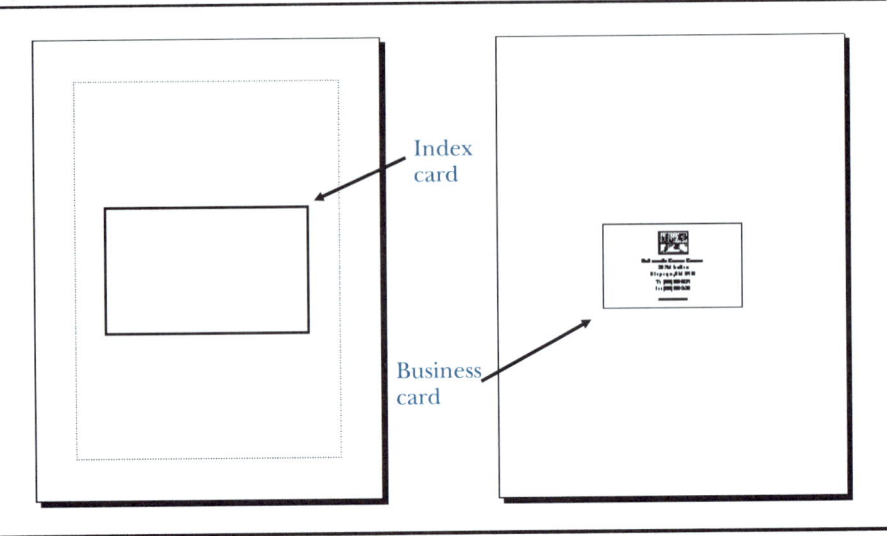

Figure A-21. *Index and business cards*

will be on screen. When you select a publication type, Publisher alters the page size automatically. The maximum dimensions that you can use for page size will always be governed by the orientation and paper size you have selected in Print Setup. However, you can make individual adjustments to the length or width within those constraints.

Special Cases *Adding pages for cards and books* Be sure to add additional pages to your publication if you select a card or book type. For example, selecting a tent card only causes Publisher to divide the paper size in half and print the second page upside down. It doesn't add the actual second page. You must select Insert Pages from the Page menu and explicitly add a second page for this publication type to print properly.

Nonletter-sized paper Publisher takes care of updating the page size when you change between orientations for letter-sized pages. However, this is not the case for other paper sizes including legal, A4, and B5. If the appearance of the page area does not change to reflect a new orientation or paper size, you may need to adjust the page size manually. Make sure that all three settings—paper size, orientation, and page dimensions—are correct before you start any detailed work on the publication.

Appendix A: *Menu Reference*

Special sizes   You must change the page size manually if you are using a size that Publisher does not list as a Paper Size or Publication type, such as an envelope or custom-sized business card.

Partial values   You can type partial values for measurements as decimal fractions. For example, 1.5 is a valid measurement for 1 1/2 inches.

Defaults   The default settings on the Page Setup dialog box are

Publication Type   Full Page
Dimensions   8 1/2 by 11 inches

Related Topics   Orientation, paper size, layout guides, margins

Keyboard Shortcuts   [ALT]-[P] [T]

The Layout Menu

The Layout menu controls the placement of layout guides and page margins for an entire publication. In addition, it lets you manipulate a number of object-related formatting options, including setting frame margins, columns for Text frames, and controlling borders and frame backgrounds. Many of the options for borders, backgrounds, and shadows, however, can be controlled from the Toolbar more easily.

Layout Guides

Usage   Dialog box

Description   Layout Guides let you establish an informal map for a publication's appearance. They provide an easy-to-use visual reference for positioning frames and graphics. Guides appear in the page area based on the margin, column, and row settings that you choose for the overall design of a page. All settings are established in the Layout Guides dialog box, shown in Figure A-22.

Procedure   Select Layout Guides from the Layout menu. Click on any of the fields that you want to change and enter new values as needed.

Buttons, Lists, and Fields   In the Layout Guides dialog box:

> *Margins*   All margin settings—Left, Right, Top, and Bottom—are based on the page size (not the paper size). Margins are measured inward from their respective edge of the page. Margin guides appear on the screen in red on a color monitor.
>
> *Number of Columns/Rows*   Columns divide the area inside the margins vertically into equal sections. Rows divide the area inside of the margins horizontally into equal sections. Column and row guides both appear on the screen in blue on a color monitor.
>
> *Create Two Backgrounds With Mirrored Guides*   Books and other publications where pages face each other often use mirrored layouts for the left and right pages, as shown in Figure A-23. This gives facing pages a symmetrical appearance and also allows extra room for binding in the middle of the inside margin (called the gutter).
>
> When you enable the Mirrored Guides button, Publisher automatically creates a mirrored layout like this based on a design you create for a single page. Publisher recognizes the original page you designed as the right side and the mirrored page it creates as the left side. In mirrored layouts,

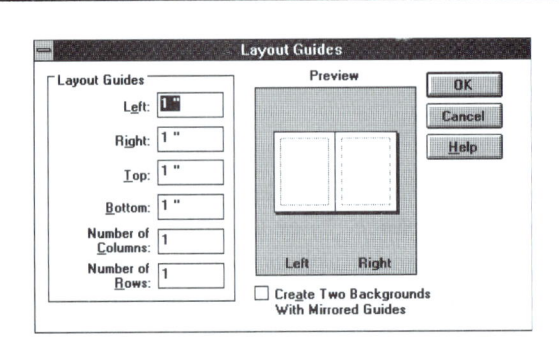

Figure A-22.   *Layout Guides dialog box*

Appendix A: *Menu Reference*

Figure A-23.   *Example of facing pages*

vertical margins for both the left and right pages are measured from the point at which the two pages are bound. The left margin of the right page and the right margin of the left page become the inside margins. The other sides of each page become the outside margins.

Special Cases   *Partial values*   You can type partial values for margins as decimal fractions. For example 1.5 is a valid measurement for 1 1/2 inches.

Canceling mirrored layout   If you cancel mirrored layout guides, the original design (the right page) becomes the design for all pages. You may need to adjust the location of objects that were located on left pages.

Background   When you enable Mirrored Guides, Publisher creates a separate background page for the left and right pages. Any objects that you place on the right (original) background page before implementing Mirrored Guides are automatically copied and mirrored to the background for the new left page layout.

Adding pages   Creating a mirrored layout does not automatically add any pages to a publication. You must add these explicitly from the Page menu.

Adding and deleting pages   When frames follow the layout of mirrored guides, they have symmetrical positions on left and right (even and odd) pages. In other words, their absolute location on each page—the distance between any two contiguous edges of the paper—will differ, depending on whether they are odd- or even-numbered. If you delete a single page, Publisher renumbers the pages that follow it in the publication. Odd-numbered pages become even, and even numbered become odd. As a result, objects may no longer appear at the proper location to maintain symmetry between facing pages. When you add or delete pages in a publication that uses mirrored guides, do so in multiples of two, in order to keep objects where you placed them on facing pages.

Defaults   The default settings on the Layout Guides dialog box are

Margins	1 inch
Columns	1
Rows	1
Mirrored Guides	No

Related Topics   Page size, paper size, orientation, publication type, the background page, page numbers

Keyboard Shortcuts   ALT-L G

Frame Columns and Margins

Usage   Dialog box

Description   Publisher lets you adjust the margins for all frame types. You can modify the setting for each pair of vertical or horizontal sides with a single value. In addition, you can change the number of columns and the space between columns in a Text frame. All of these settings can be altered in the Frame Columns and Margins dialog box, shown in Figure A-24.

Procedure   Select a frame and select Frame Columns and Margins from the Layout menu. Change any of the values for margins, columns, or the column gutter.

Buttons, Lists, and Fields   In the Frame Columns and Margins dialog box:

  Left and Right   Publisher applies this value to both the left and right margins in the frame.

  Top and Bottom   Publisher applies this value to both the top and bottom margins in the frame.

Appendix A: *Menu Reference*

Figure A-24.   Frame Margins dialog box

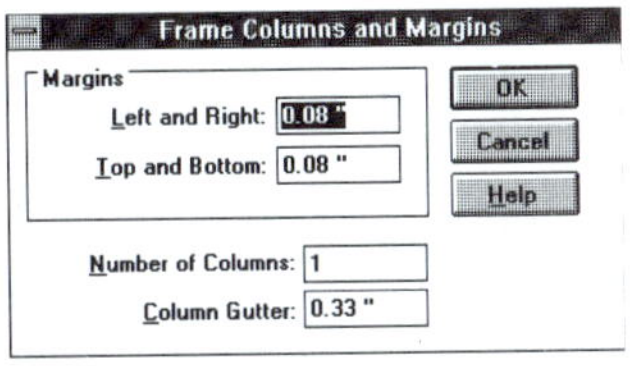

Number of Columns   This determines the number of columns into which Publisher will divide text for the frame.

Column Gutter   This determines the amount of space between each of the text columns.

Special Cases   *Hyphenation*   With multicolumn Text frames, text can appear choppy, or have rivers of white space running through the column. Having Publisher automatically hyphenate files can correct these visual problems by allowing more characters to fit on a line.

Forced Column Break   Within a multicolumn frame you can force a new column to begin to the right of the insertion point by pressing CTRL-ENTER.

Scaling Pictures   Publisher scales an image in a Picture frame when you add a margin setting. For example, if you increase the left and right margins, the image is squeezed from those sides.

Changing defaults   To alter the default margin or column settings for a particular frame type, make changes to the values in the Margins and Columns dialog box after you select the frame tool but before you draw the frame. All subsequent frames of that type will use the new settings.

Defaults   The default settings on the Frame Columns and Margins dialog box are

Text Margins	.08 inch on all sides
Columns	1
Gutter	.33 inch

Picture and WordArt Margins	0 on all sides

Related Topics   Page Margins, Hyphenation, run-arounds

Keyboard Shortcuts   `ALT`-`L` `M`

Send to Back/Bring to Front

Usage   Command

Description   Normally, objects that are created on top of or moved into an area already occupied by another object overlay the original object. This applies to all frame types and line art. However, objects can be shuffled in the visual plane much like playing cards. Objects in the foreground can be moved to the background, and vice versa. Interesting visual effects can be achieved with combinations of Picture frames and art objects in different visual planes, as shown in Figure A-25.

Procedure   Select the object to reposition and select Send to Back or Bring to Front from the Layout menu.

Related Topics   Backgrounds and shading

Keyboard Shortcuts   `CTRL`-`F`, Bring to Front and `CTRL`-`Z`, Send to Back

Borders

Usage   Dialog box

Description   You can surround any frame or piece of line art created with the box tool with a solid border of 1-, 2-, 4-, 8-, or 10-point thickness on any number of sides. You can also assign any one of eight colors to a border. All border options can be controlled from the Border dialog box, shown in Figure A-26. Borders automatically adjust when you resize a frame or object.

Appendix A: *Menu Reference* 349

Figure A-25. *Using the visual plane for different effects*

Procedure Click on the frame for which you want to add a border and then select Border from the Layout menu. Select individual sides and thicknesses

Figure A-26. *Border dialog box*

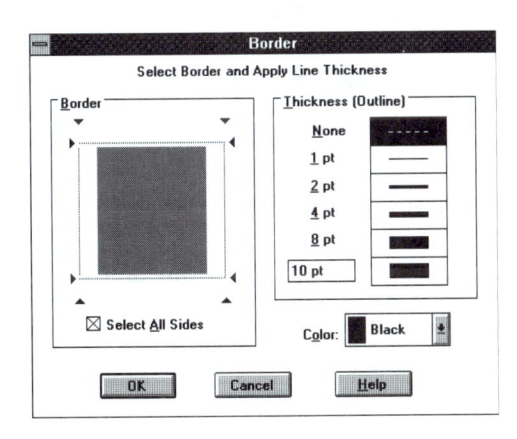

for each side of the frame, if necessary. To remove a border, click on **None** for any or all sides.

Buttons, Lists, and Fields   In the Border dialog box:

Border   The Border group on the left of the box lets you choose which sides of the frame will use a border. You can also specify a different thickness for each side. If you want to specify individual settings, click on the side you want to change in the border group on the left. Publisher identifies the selected side with the indication marks, as shown here:

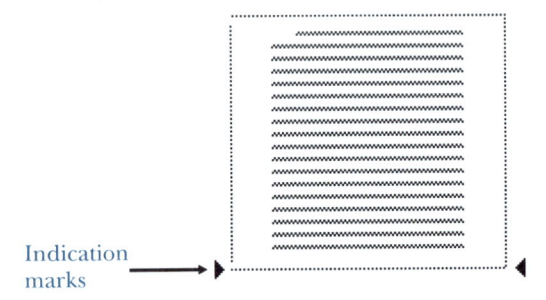

Indication marks

Thickness   Click on one of the thicknesses in the group on the right for each selected side or for all sides. To remove a border from a side, select the side and click on None for thickness.

Special Cases   *Changing defaults*   To alter the default border setting for a type of frame, select a Thickness button or make selections in the Border dialog box after you select a frame tool but before you draw the frame. All subsequent frames of that type will use the new settings.

Defaults   None

Related Topics   BorderArt

Keyboard Shortcuts   Thickness buttons on the Toolbar

Line

Usage   Dialog box

Appendix A: *Menu Reference*

Description   Publisher lets you format lines by adjusting their thickness and adding arrowheads or color, as shown in the Line dialog box in Figure A-27.

Procedure   Click on a line and select Line from the Layout menu. You can select the color or the thickness by choosing from the list or clicking on the appropriate button. All of the options from the Toolbar can also can be turned on or off here as well.

Buttons, Lists, and Fields   In the Line dialog box:

> *Thickness*   These buttons control the thickness of the selected line. You can select 1-, 2-, 4-, 8-, or 10-point thickness.
>
> *Arrowheads*   These buttons control the appearance of arrowheads on either or both ends of the line.
>
> *Color*   Choose from this list to add color to a line.

Defaults   The default settings on the Line dialog box are

Thickness	1 point
Color	Black
Arrowheads	None

Related Topics   Borders

Keyboard Shortcuts   Thickness and arrow buttons on the Toolbar

Figure A-27.   *Line dialog box*

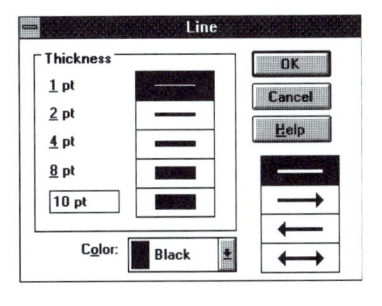

BorderArt

Usage   Dialog box

Description   You can apply BorderArt to any frame or line art created with the box tool. You can preview the entire selection of BorderArt in the dialog box shown in Figure A-28. Like simple borders, BorderArt automatically resizes when you adjust the dimensions of the frame to which it applies.

Procedure   Click on the frame for which you want to add BorderArt and select BorderArt from the Layout menu. Scroll through the list of patterns and use the Preview window to find the pattern you want to use. To remove BorderArt, select None from the list.

Buttons, Lists, and Fields   In the BorderArt dialog box:

Use Recommended Size   Disable this option if you want to create a custom size for the characters in the pattern.

Border Size   If you disable the Recommended Size button, you can enter a custom size in this field.

Special Cases   *Lines and Figures*   You can use BorderArt to create some novel thumbnail illustrations, or for horizontal and vertical lines composed

Figure A-28.   *BorderArt dialog box*

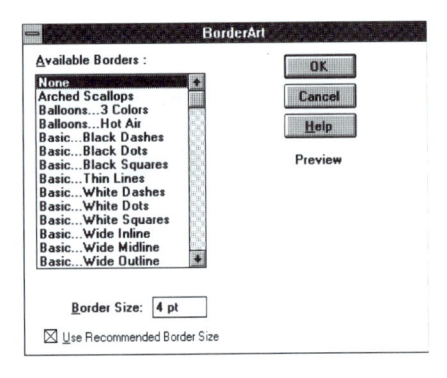

Appendix A: *Menu Reference* 353

of some of the more character-like BorderArt figures. Consider the following examples:

Adjust the point size for the BorderArt to an acceptable level. Then use the sizing icon to reduce the height of a frame to 0 for a horizontal line, or its width to 0 for a vertical line. Use one of the corner handles to reduce both the height and width to 0 in order to create an individual character.

Related Topics   Borders, Scaling

Keyboard Shortcuts   (ALT)-(L) (A)

Shading

Usage   Dialog box

Description   Publisher lets you add patterns and colors to a frame or line art. Each object has two visual planes, as shown in Figure A-29, although it's not necessary to use both of them. In addition, frames have a third plane. The lowest plane is the background. By default, the background of Picture frames, WordArt frames, and line art objects is transparent, whereas Text frames have a solid white background. The only way that Publisher lets you alter the background is by adding a color to it. The middle plane is the foreground (even though it's not the topmost layer for frames). For the foreground you can assign a pattern and a color. The foreground color is assigned to the lines or dots that compose the actual pattern. The background color, if any, appears through the open space between the lines and dots that form the pattern. The final plane contains the image, WordArt, or text that the frame was designed to display. This is truly transparent, and displays the foreground and background colors and patterns in any area that is not covered by the copy or image it contains.

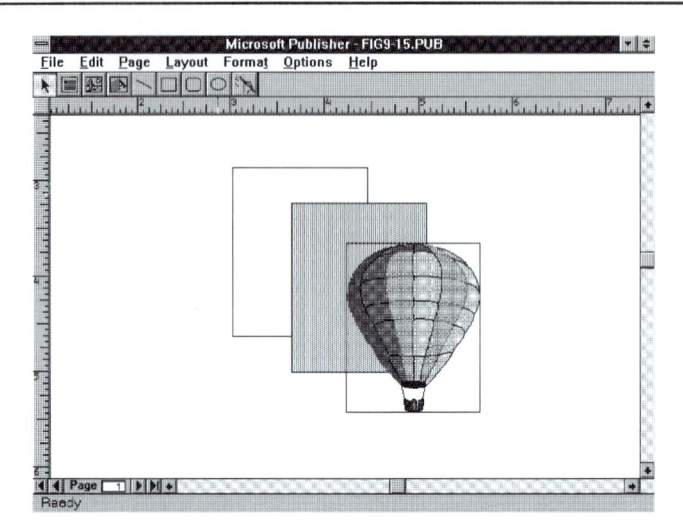

Figure A-29. Different visual planes in an object

To change the shading or colors for an object, use the Shading dialog box, shown in Figure A-30. Publisher offers a selection of 24 patterns and 8 colors.

Procedure Click on the object to which you want to add shading or color and select Shading from the Layout menu. Click on the Background or Foreground lists or on a pattern.

Buttons, Lists, and Fields In the Shading dialog box:

Preview The Preview window functions like a painter's palette in the Shading dialog box. You can mix colors and patterns in it until you find the combination you're looking for.

Background Open this list and select one of the colors for the background of the object.

Style Click on one of the patterns in this group to apply it to the foreground. Each pattern operates like an option button.

Appendix A: *Menu Reference* 355

Figure A-30.   *Shading dialog box*

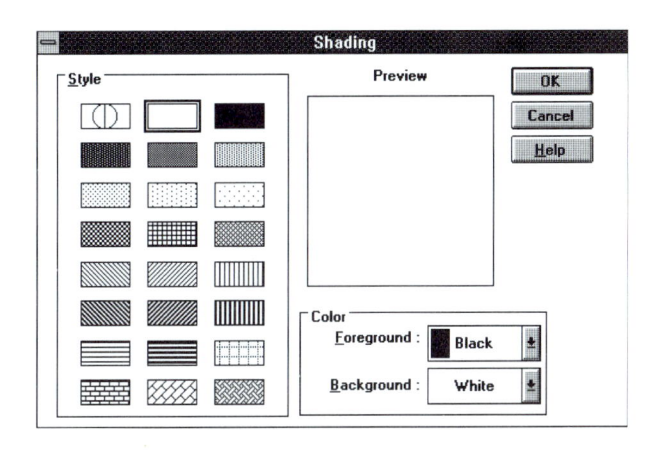

Foreground   Open the list and click on one of the colors for the pattern you selected. The foreground color does not appear unless you have selected a pattern.

Special Cases   *Color*   If you have a color printer, you can achieve subtle effects by using different colors for the pattern and background. Otherwise, colors print in black or not at all.

Defaults   The default settings on the Shading dialog box are

Background	Clear (pictures and WordArt), White (text)
Pattern	None
Foreground	Clear

Related Topics   Fill (WordArt), Color Background (WordArt), Send to Back/Bring to Front, Borders, Shadows, BorderArt

Keyboard Shortcuts   ALT-L H

Shadow

Usage   Command

Description   Drop shadows give a frame or line art objects a feeling of depth and perspective, as shown in the following illustration. Shadows are toggles: either on or off for any object.

Procedure   Select the object to which you want to assign a shadow. Then select Shadow from the Layout menu.

Defaults   None

Related Topics   Fill (WordArt), Color Background (WordArt), Send to Back/Bring to Front, Borders, Shadows, BorderArt

Keyboard Shortcuts   `CTRL`-`D` or the button on the Toolbar

Format Menu

The Format menu controls all aspects of text formatting, including font selection, paragraph alignment, and tab stop settings. You can also control some aspects of graphic images through scaling and cropping, although this is better done with the Toolbar and mouse.

Characters

Usage   Dialog box

Appendix A: *Menu Reference* 357

Description Publisher offers five groups of formatting options for characters: style, position, font, size, and color. Applying most character formats is easiest with the Toolbar; however, not all character formatting options are available there. You must use the Character dialog box, shown in Figure A-31, to access all options.

Procedure Select a Text frame and then select the characters in it that you want to change. Select Character from the Layout menu, and click on any of the options in the dialog box.

Buttons, Lists, and Fields In the Character dialog box:

> *Font* A font, or typeface, is a set of characters that all have the same design. In Publisher Text frames, the only fonts that you can print are the ones that have been installed for your copy of Windows. Any fonts that are available in your environment appear in the Font list. The content of this list may change if you select a different printer.
>
> *Point Size* Fonts are measured in points (1/72 inch). Font sizes, like fonts themselves, are printer dependant. Any sizes that are available in your environment appear in the Size list. The content of this list may change if you select a different printer.

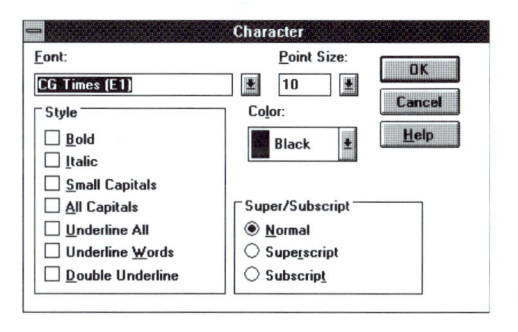

Figure A-31. Character dialog box

Bold   Boldface characters are thicker and more heavily inked than normal ones.

Italic   Italic characters lean to the right and give the impression of cursive handwriting.

Small Capitals   Lowercase characters formatted as small caps are all uppercase, but only a fraction of the height of full capital letters.

All Capitals   Characters formatted as all capital are converted to standard uppercase.

Underline All   If you enable this option, Publisher underlines the spaces between words as well as the words themselves.

Underline Words   This causes Publisher to underline only words, but not the spaces between them.

Double Underline   Publisher draws two underscores beneath words and the spaces between words.

Color   Colored characters appear on a color monitor, but will not print accurately without a color printer. The standard eight colors are available for text.

Normal   This option cancels superscripting and subscripting.

Superscript   Superscripted characters appear one-half line above normal characters.

Subscript   Subscripted characters appear one-half line below normal characters.

Special Cases   *Cancel Formatting*   To remove any character formats other than font, select the characters that you want to restore and press CTRL-SPACEBAR.

Defaults   The default font set is the default for the currently selected printer. All other styles are normal.

Related Topics   Kerning, fonts, Print Setup

Keyboard Shortcuts   ALT-T C and the text formatting buttons on the Toolbar.

Appendix A: *Menu Reference*

Spacing Between Characters

Usage   Dialog box

Description   Kerning lets you adjust the space between characters. Kerning is especially important in publications that use proportionally spaced fonts for headlines and other applications that require larger font sizes. Because proportional fonts allocate space differently to characters with different widths, unsightly gaps or jamming can sometimes occur between certain of them, as shown in Figure A-32. Kerning only operates with Text frames.

To adjust kerning, you must use the Spacing Between Characters dialog box, as shown in Figure A-33.

Procedure   Select the character immediately to the left of the space you want to adjust and select Spacing Between Characters from the Format menu. Click on the appropriate button to increase or decrease the amount of space

Figure A-32.   *The reason for kerning*

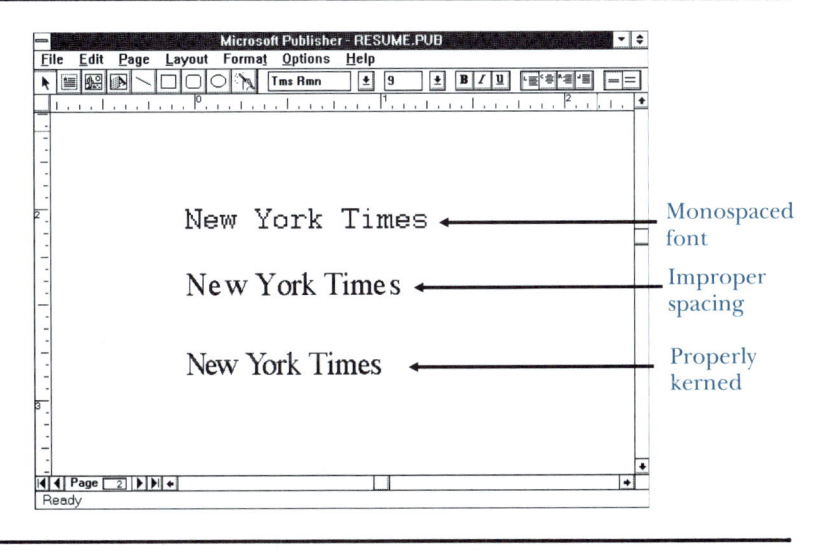

to the right of the selected character. Enter a new value for the distance, if necessary.

Buttons, Lists, and Fields   In the Spacing Between Characters dialog box:

Normal   This button restores the original spacing between characters.

Squeeze Letters Together   This button moves the selected characters together by the amount specified.

Move Letters Apart   This button spreads the selected characters apart by the amount specified.

By This Amount   This value determines the amount by which letters are squeezed together or spread apart.

Defaults   1 1/2 points

Related Topics   Formatting characters, Fonts

Keyboard Shortcuts   ALT-T B

Indents and Spacing

Usage   Dialog box

Figure A-33.   *Spacing Between Characters dialog box*

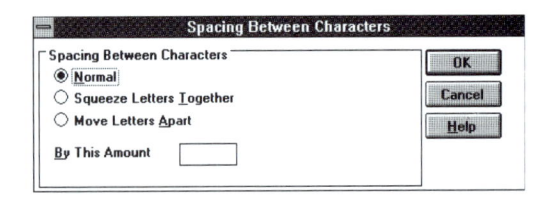

Appendix A: *Menu Reference*

Description   There are three groups of formatting options for text paragraphs in Publisher—alignment, indentation, and spacing. Applying paragraph formats is easiest with the Toolbar; however, not all options are available to you unless you use the Indents and Spacing dialog box, as shown in Figure A-34.

Procedure   Select the paragraphs that you want to change and select Indents and Spacing from the Layout menu.

Buttons, Lists, and Fields   In the Indents and Spacing dialog box:

> *Left Indent*   Indentation is space that you can add to each paragraph to increase the margins of that paragraph. The value you enter here adds space to the left margin of an individual paragraph.
>
> *First Line Indent*   The value that you enter here adds to or subtracts from the left indent for the first line of a paragraph.
>
> *Right Indent*   The value that you enter here adds space to the right margin of an individual paragraph.
>
> *Alignment*   Alignment defines the way that paragraphs position with respect to the boundaries and margins of a Text frame. The options for alignment are Left, Center, Right, and Justified.

Figure A-34.   *Indents and Spacing dialog box*

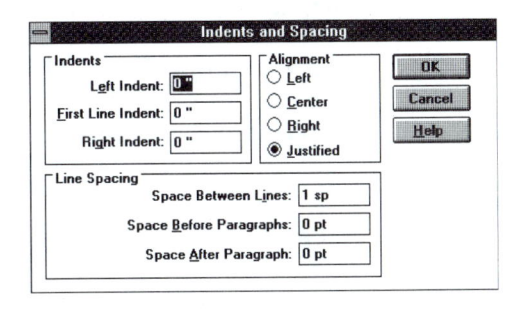

Left	Left-aligned copy is flush with the left margin of the page, and ragged on the right.
Right	Right-aligned copy is flush with the right side of the page and ragged on the left.
Centered	Centered copy is equidistant from both margins.
Justified	Justified copy spreads the words across each line so that both the left and right sides are aligned with their respective margins.

Space Between Lines   Publisher normally allocates 12 points (1/6 of an inch) to the height of a line. You can increase this value for multiline spacing, or decrease it to tighten the space between lines for small fonts.

Space Before Paragraphs   The value in this field adjusts the leading above a paragraph.

Space After Paragraphs   The value in this field adjusts the leading below a paragraph.

Special Cases   *Cancel Formatting*   To remove any paragraph formats that you may have assigned, select the paragraphs that you want to restore and press CTRL-Q.

Defaults   The default settings on the Indents and Spacing dialog box are

Indents	0 (All)
Alignment	Left
Spacing	1 space
Space Before	0 points
Space After	0 points

Related Topics   Character formatting, Frame Margins and Columns, Tabs

Keyboard Shortcuts   ALT-T-I or the buttons on the Toolbar

Tabs

Usage   Dialog box

Appendix A: Menu Reference

Description   The Tabs dialog box, shown in Figure A-35, lets you set locations for tab stops in a text paragraph. Tab stops are actually part of a paragraph's format. When you enter new tab stops, Publisher clears all of the default settings to the left of your entry. This only applies, however, to the current paragraph.

Procedure   To set and format a tab stop:

1. Select the Text frame in which you want to set tab stops.
2. Position the insertion point in the paragraph for which you want to set tab stops.
3. Select Tabs from the Format menu.
4. Enter the location for a tab stop and click on the desired tab formatting option for alignment or leader characters.
5. Click on Set to complete the individual setting.
6. Repeat steps 4 and 5 as many times as necessary for additional tab stops.
7. Click on OK.

To clear a tab stop:

1. Select the Text frame in which you want to clear tab stops.

Figure A-35.   *Tabs dialog box*

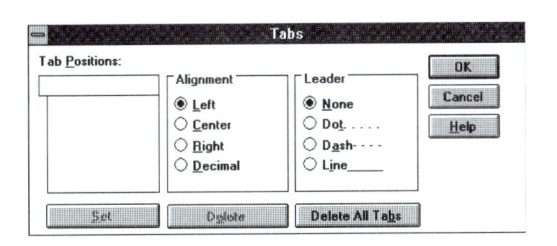

2. Position the insertion point in the paragraph for which you want to clear tab stops.

3. Select Tabs from the Format menu.

4. In the tab list, click on the location that you want to clear, or click on Delete All Tabs to clear them all.

5. Click on Delete to clear the individual setting.

6. Repeat steps 4 and 5 to clear additional tabs.

7. Click on OK.

Buttons, Lists, and Fields   In the Tabs dialog box:

Alignment   Publisher has four types of tab stops, as shown in **Figure A-36**.

Left	The text at left-aligned tab stops aligns to the right of the tab stop. All of Publisher's default tab stops are left-aligned.
Right	Right-aligned tab stops align on the right side, and text extends back toward the left.
Center	Center-aligned tab stops cause text to center around the tab stop.
Decimal	Decimal tab stops are for aligning columns of numbers. At decimal tab stops the first characters you type align to the right until you type a period. Subsequent characters align to the left.

Leader   Any of the four tab stop types can include a leader. A leader appears in Figure A-36 between the name of each accommodation type and the daily price. Leaders fill the space occupied by a tab with an appropriate number of characters to fill the gap. You can choose between dots, dashes, or underscores for Publisher to use as the leader character. Dots are shown in the figure.

Special Cases   *Moving tab stops*   To move or change a tab stop, you must first delete it and then enter a new setting in its place. The tab, however, remains in the paragraph. When you set a new location for the tab stop, the old tab moves the text that it supports to the new location.

Forced line breaks   By ending each line with a forced line break instead of a carriage return, you keep all of the lines for a table in a single paragraph

Appendix A: *Menu Reference* 365

Figure A-36.   *Different tab alignments and a dot leader*

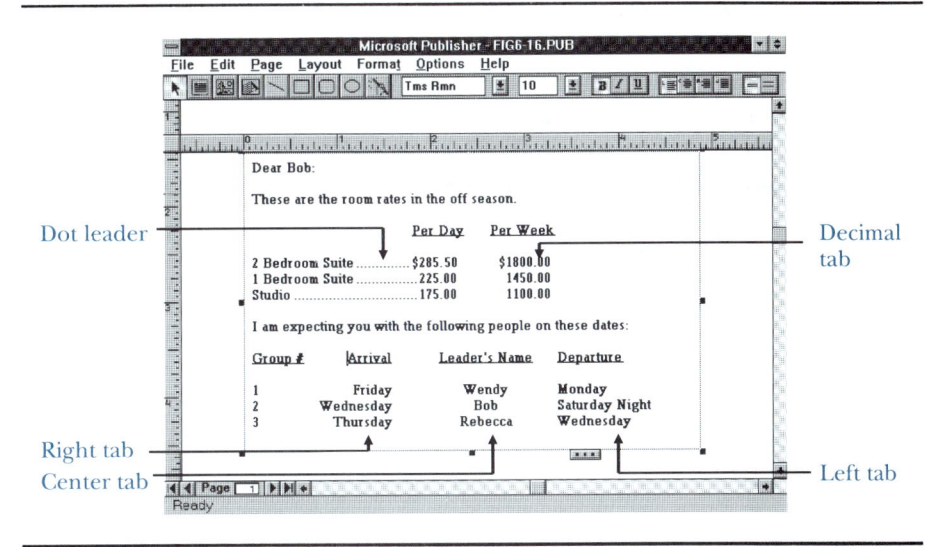

with the same tab stop settings. This makes editing much simpler if you decide to change a tab stop location, because you only need to make the change once for a single paragraph.

Defaults   Left aligned every 1/2 inch

Related Topics   Indents and spacing, Frame Margins, Fonts

Keyboard Shortcuts   ALT-T T

Scale Picture

Usage   Dialog box

Description   The easiest way to scale an image is by using the mouse to resize the frame that the picture appears in. Publisher automatically scales the image to the new dimensions of the frame. Using the Scale Picture dialog box, as shown in Figure A-37, presents you with two options, however, that are not available with the mouse alone. You can restore a picture to its original size, and you can scale the picture to exact proportions.

Procedure   Click on the frame that contains the picture and select Scale Picture from the Format menu.

Buttons, Lists, and Fields   In the Scale Picture dialog box:

Scale Height   This value is the percentage of vertical scaling currently used in the image.

Scale Width   This value is the percentage of horizontal scaling currently used in the image.

Original Size   Click this button to restore the original proportions of the image.

Special Cases   *Bitmapped and object-oriented graphics*   You can resize object-oriented graphics easily without distorting them. You can even distort them slightly without ruining their composition or the extent to which they can be recognized. Object-oriented graphics maintain the highest quality of resolution possible on your screen or printer, regardless of how they are scaled. Bitmapped images, on the other hand, can become faded or jagged when you enlarge them, and are easily distorted beyond recognition if you try to change their proportions. They are also device-dependent. In other words, their clarity and resolution are tied to the capabilities of the equipment that was used to create them, and you may not be able to take advantage of a high-resolution device, such as a laser printer, when you reproduce them.

Figure A-37.   *Scale Picture dialog box*

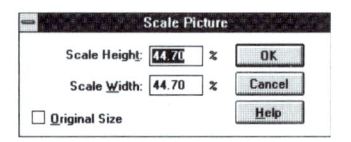

Appendix A: *Menu Reference* 367

Related Topics   Resizing, bitmap and object-oriented images, cropping, frame margins

Keyboard Shortcuts   (ALT)-(T) (S)

Crop Picture

Usage   Command

Description   Crop Picture turns the cropping tool on or off. This can also be done from the Toolbar. Cropping is the only way Publisher lets you alter the composition of an image. When you crop an image, you can cut sections off from or add blank space to any of its edges without affecting its scale.

Procedure   Select a Picture frame and select Crop Picture from the Format menu. Point to one of the handles of the Picture frame, and when you see the cropping icon appear, drag the handle in toward the center of the frame to trim the image or outward to add empty space (margin) to the frame.

Defaults   Off

Related Topics   Resizing, bitmap and object-oriented images, scaling, frame margins

Keyboard Shortcuts   (ALT)-(T) (P) or the Crop button on the Toolbar

Options Menu

The Options menu provides a number of toggles for screen appearance and program interaction. You can also run text utilities for spell checking and hyphenation.

Check Spelling

Usage   Dialog box

Description   Check Spelling lets you review the spelling of individual words, all words in a story, or all words for all stories in a publication. Publisher has a substantial dictionary, and can usually make good guesses for what you're trying to spell and how to spell it correctly. When you have spelled a word correctly but Publisher is not familiar with it, there is also an option for adding new words to the Publisher dictionary. The Check Spelling dialog box appears, as shown in Figure A-38.

Procedure   To check spelling:

1. Click on the Text frame that contains the story you want to check, or select the word for which you want to check spelling.
2. Select Options from the Menu bar and select Check Spelling from the Options menu.
3. Click on either of the option buttons to refine the settings for the spelling session, if necessary.
4. Click on one of the processing options described in the next section.
5. Click on Close to close the window and end the spell-checking session.

Figure A-38.   *Check Spelling dialog box*

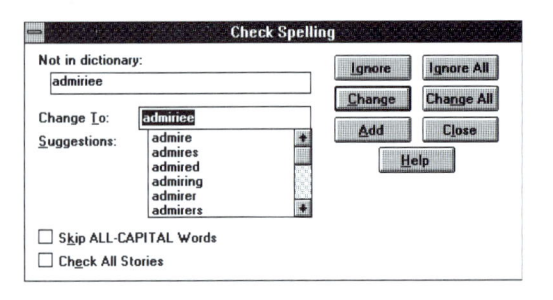

Appendix A: *Menu Reference* 369

Buttons, Lists, and Fields   In the Check Spelling dialog box:

Change To   If publisher has suggestions for the correct spelling, the most likely of them is displayed here. When Publisher doesn't offer the correct spelling in its list of suggestions, the misspelled word appears here, and you can correct the spelling yourself. Click on the word in the Change To field, and edit it as you would any other field in a Windows program.

Suggestions   These are the words that Publisher thinks you are trying to spell. If the correct one appear in the list, double-click on it.

Skip ALL-CAPITAL Words   Enable this option if you want Publisher not to check words that appear in all uppercase letters.

Check All Stories   Enable this option if you want Publisher to check the spelling in all stories in a publication.

Ignore   Click on this option if you want to retain the spelling for a word, even if Publisher doesn't recognize it.

Ignore All   Click on this option if you want to retain the spelling for all instances of a word in the current story, even if Publisher doesn't recognize it.

Change   Click on this option is you want Publisher to substitute the contents of the Change To field for the current spelling of the word.

Change All   Click on this option is you want Publisher to substitute the contents of the Change To field for all instances of the current spelling of the word in the story.

Add   Click on this option if you want Publisher to add the contents of the Change To field to its dictionary. Once you've added a word to the dictionary, Publisher recognizes it in future spelling sessions.

Close   Click on Close to close the window and end the spell-checking session.

Defaults   The default settings on the Check Spelling dialog box are

Skip ALL-CAPITAL Words	No
Check All Stories	No

Keyboard Shortcuts   `ALT`-`O` `S`

Hyphenate

Usage   Dialog box

Description   When Publisher hyphenates a story for you, it inserts optional hyphens at the correct location in words that can be hyphenated, based on the amount of space left on a line and the margin settings for the frame. By using optional hyphens, Publisher can decide to suppress hyphenation for a word if you edit text or resize a frame in such a way that hyphenation would no longer be useful. The Hyphenation dialog box is shown in Figure A-39. The word you select appears in the Hyphenate At field. Publisher inserts optional hyphens wherever the word can be hyphenated. Publisher selects the location that seems best, but you can click on any of the alternatives if you want to hyphenate somewhere else in the word.

Procedure   To apply hyphenation:

1. Click on the Text frame that contains the story you want to hyphenate, or select the word for which you want to check hyphenation.
2. Select Options from the Menu bar and select Hyphenation from the Options menu.
3. Adjust the hyphenation zone or click on any of the option buttons to refine the settings for the hyphenation session, if necessary.
4. Make any adjustments to Publisher's suggested hyphenation by clicking on one of the alternative optional hyphens, if necessary.

Figure A-39.   *Hyphenate dialog box*

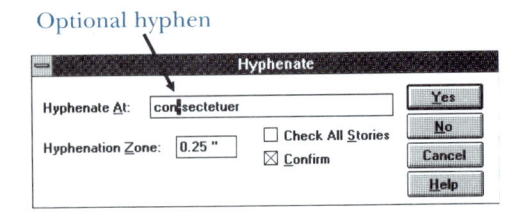

Appendix A: *Menu Reference*

5. Click on OK to accept hyphenation for the current word, or No to skip it.

Buttons, Lists, and Fields   Choose from the following options:

Hyphenate At   When Publisher suggests hyphenation, it provides choices whenever possible. Click on the location you want to use in this word.

Hyphenation Zone   The hyphenation zone determines when Publisher will attempt to hyphenate a word if at all. If the amount of space between the last character on a line and the right margin is less than the value set in the hyphenation zone, Publisher doesn't even attempt to hyphenate the next word, but rather places it on the next line. If the space remaining equals or exceeds the hyphenation zone, Publisher attempts to split the next word. You can adjust the hyphenation zone in order to tune the appearance of a frame. With a smaller zone, Publisher packs words more tightly on each line.

Check All Stories   Enable this option to have Publisher hyphenate all words for all stories in a publication. Publisher pauses at the beginning of each story and allows you to proceed with hyphenation for it, or skip to the next one in the publication.

Confirm   Enable this option to make Publisher display each word it intends to hyphenate, and let you inspect and modify the hyphen location in the same way that you do for individual words. Leave the option disabled to have Publisher hyphenate automatically.

Defaults   The default settings in the Hyphenation dialog box are

Confirm	Yes
Check All Stories	No
Hyphenation Zone	.25 inch

Related Topics   Justified alignment, Frame Margins

Keyboard Shortcuts   [ALT]-[O] [H]

Snap to Ruler Marks

Usage   Command

Description   Snap to Ruler Marks causes the tic marks on the rulers to become "sticky." If you're drawing a frame or a graphic object, the crosshair will tend to adhere slightly to them when passing over one slowly, or "jump" to the next mark. This makes it easy to align the starting and ending locations exactly with a mark on the ruler. If you're moving or resizing a frame, the same effect occurs when the boundaries of the frame encounter a guide: they pause.

Procedure   Select Snap to Ruler Marks from the Options menu.

Defaults   Off

Related Topics   Snap to Guides, resizing frames, moving objects, Views

Keyboard Shortcuts   [ALT]-[O] [M]

Snap to Guides

Usage   Command

Description   Snap to Guides causes the Layout Guides to become "sticky." If you're drawing a frame or a graphic object, the crosshair will tend to adhere slightly to any guide when passing over it slowly, or "jump" to the next guide. This makes it easy to align the starting and ending locations exactly with a set of guides. If you're moving or resizing a frame, the same effect occurs when the boundaries of the frame encounter a guide—they pause.

Procedure   Select Snap to Guides from the Options menu.

Defaults   On

Related Topics   Snap to Ruler Marks, resizing frames, moving objects, Views

Keyboard Shortcuts   [CTRL]-[W]

Appendix A: *Menu Reference* 373

Hide/Show Pictures

Usage Command

Description Select Hide Pictures to suppress the appearance of all pictures in the publication. They're still there and their frames are visible, but the actual pictures don't show up until you select Show Pictures from the same menu. The screen redraws much more quickly when pictures are hidden.

Procedure Select Hide Pictures from the Options menu.

Special Cases *WordArt* When pictures are hidden, so is WordArt.

Defaults Off

Keyboard Shortcuts ALT-O P

Hide/Show Rulers

Usage Command

Description Hide/Show Rulers turns their display on or off. Turning them off makes more display room available on the Publisher screen.

Procedure Select Hide/Show Rulers from the Options menu.

Defaults On

Related Topics Hide/Show Status Line

Keyboard Shortcuts CTRL-K

Hide/Show Status Line

Usage Command

Description　Hide/Show Status Line lets you control the appearance of the Status Line at the bottom of the screen. When the Status line is hidden, there is more space available on the Publisher screen.

Procedure　Select Hide/Show Status Line from the Options menu.

Defaults　On

Related Topics　Hide/Show Rulers

Keyboard Shortcuts　[ALT]-[O] [L]

Hide/Show Layout Guides

Usage　Command

Description　Hide/Show Layout Guides turns the display of the guides on or off. Since layout guides do not print, this can help you get a more accurate sense of how your publication will appear after it is printed. Hiding the guides has no effect on your layout or the position of objects on the page.

Procedure　Select Hide/Show Layout Guides from the Options menu.

Defaults　On

Related Topics　Hide/Show Object Boundaries

Keyboard Shortcuts　[CTRL]-[G]

Hide/Show Object Boundaries

Usage　Command

Description　Select Hide Object Boundaries from the Layout menu to suppress the appearance of frame outlines. You'll get a better sense of what the final piece will look like, since frame outlines don't print. Select Show Object Boundaries to make them appear again.

Appendix A: *Menu Reference*   375

Procedure   Select Hide/Show Object Boundaries from the Layout menu.

Defaults   On

Related Topics   Hide/Show Layout Guides

Keyboard Shortcuts   CTRL-Y

Settings

Usage   Dialog box

Description   The Settings dialog box, shown in Figure A-40 lets you control the appearance of certain screen details, the starting page number for a publication, and the status of overtype.

Procedure   Select Settings from the Options menu.

Buttons, Lists, and Fields   In the Settings dialog box:

> *Starting Page Number*   Publisher normally begins a publication on page 1, and numbers pages consecutively from that point. These are the numbers that the page marker uses. To begin at a number other than 1, enter it here. All subsequent pages will be numbered consecutively beginning with that number.

Figure A-40.   *Settings dialog box*

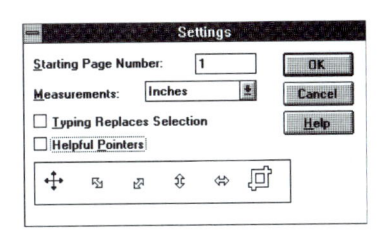

Measurements Publisher normally measures distance in inches. It will, however, accept measurements in centimeters (cm), points (pt), or picas (pi). Select a different unit of measure from this list to change the default for the editing session. The tic marks on the ruler, and all other displayed measurements in all fields are converted to the new scale.

Typing Replaces Selection When you enable this option, Publisher replaces selected text with pasted text. This option can be useful for deleting text quickly, but you should use it sparingly. When you work with this option enabled, you can lose text very easily.

Helpful Pointers This option changes the appearance of the icons for moving, cropping, and sizing (shown in the following illustration). Helpful Pointers operates as a toggle to change the icons' appearance between the two settings.

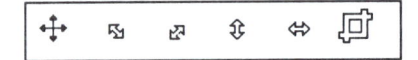

Helpful Pointers are elementary in their appearance; for example, a moving van is used for the mover, as opposed to the "unhelpful" alternative: a four-headed arrow.

Special Cases *Measurement* You can always use any unit of measurement regardless of the current default, as long as you follow it with the proper abbreviation. For example, to enter 2 centimeters when the Measurements setting is in inches, type **2 cm**.

Defaults The default settings in the Settings dialog box are

Starting Page Number	1
Measurements	Inches
Typing Replaces Selection	On
Helpful Pointers	On

Keyboard Shortcuts ALT-O T

B

Design Gallery

Lost Holdings

Page Size	5.75" x 8.75"
Margins	L/R - .75" T/B - 0"
Background Picture Frame	Full bleed Pattern taken from Windows wallpaper and pasted from Paintbrush; then scaled vertically
Text Frame	L/R .125" T/B 0"
Headline	48pt Palatino bold Centered 48pt internal leading 36pt above
Subhead	24pt Palatino bold italic 26pt internal leading 20pt above Lettering in the top 2 lines spread 3pt Words on last line have 2sp between
Author Line	18pt Palatino (plain) Lettering spread 3pt
Vertical Rules	1pt @ 1/8" indent

LOST HOLDINGS

THOUGHTS & RECOLLECTIONS OF MY PAST

JON ROSENSTEIN

Fifties

Page Size	5.75" x 8.75"
Margins	L/R - 0" T/B - 0"
Headline	WordArt 48pt Inglewood Fit horizontally Dropout
Subhead	WordArt Best fit Inglewood Fit horizontally Dropout
Collage	Clip art Photo - cropped and intentionally distorted Text - overlaying Text frame with clear background; 24pt New Century Schoolbook

FIFTIES

Lorem ipsum dolor sit amet, consectetuer adipiscing elit, sed diem nonummy nibh euismod tincidunt ut lacreet dolore magna aliguam erat volutpat. Ut wisis enim ad minim veniam, quis nostrud exerci tation ullamcorper suscipit lobortis nisl ut aliquip ex ea commodo consequat. Duis te feugifacilisi. Duis autem dolor in hendrerit in vulputate velit esse molestie consequat, vel illum dolore eu feugiat nulla facilisis at vero eos et accumsan et iusto odio dignissim qui blandit praesent luptatum zzril delenit augue duis dolore

Poems & Photos

Protection & Sense

Page Size	8.5" x 11" (landscape orientation)
Margins	L/R - .5" T/B - .5"
Front Cover Headline	New Century Schoolbook 40pt bold 40pt internal leading 60pt above
Subtitle	WordArt 48pt Marysville Color background White fill
Corner Squares	Box tool White background
Author	36pt New Century Schoolbook
Logo	Clip art (horse) Lines and ovals (tree in rear plane)
Back Cover	Title 18pt bold New Century Schoolbook
Copy	10pt Times Roman
Spine	WordArt (top to bottom style) 12pt Bellingham

PROTECTION & SENSE

Essays

Samuel Beck

PROTECTION & SENSE   Samuel Beck

PROTECTION & SENSE
Essays by Samuel Beck

"Lorem ipsum dolor sit amet, consectetuer adipiscing elit, sed diem nonummy nibh euismod tincidunt ut lacreet dolore magna aliguam erat volutpat. Ut wisis enim ad minim veniam, quis nostrud exerci tution ullamcorper suscipit lobortis nisl ut aliquip ex ea commodo consequat. Duis te feugifacilisi. Duis autem dolor in hendrerit in vulputate velit esse molestie consequat, vel illum dolore eu feugiat nulla facilisis at vero eros et accumsan et iusto odio dignissim qui blandit praesent luptatum zzril delenit au gue duis dolore te feugat nulla facilisi."

William Shakespeare
Dir Neuer Bard

"Ut wisi enim ad minim veniam, quis nostrud exerci taion ullamcorper suscipit lobortis nisl ut aliquip ex en commodo consequat. Duis te feugifacilisi."

Joe Johnson
Public Interest Magazine

"Lorem ipsum dolor sit amet, consectetuer adipiscing elit, sed diem nonummy nibh euismod tincidunt ut lacreet dolore magna aliguam erat volutpat. Ut wisis enim ad minim veniam, quis nostrud exerci tution ullamcorper suscipit lobortis nisl ut aliquip ex ea commodo consequat. Duis te feugifacilisi. Duis autem dolor in hendrerit in vulputate velit esse molestie consequat, vel illum dolore eu feugiat nulla facilisis at vero eros et accumsan et iusto odio dignissim qui blandit praesent luptatum zzril delenit au gue duis dolore te feugat nulla facilisi. Ut wisi enim ad minim veniam, quis nostrud exerci taion ullamcorper suscipit lobortis nisl ut aliquip ex en commodo consequat. Duis te feugifacilisi."

James Berry
The Shelby Journal

"Lorem ipsum dolor sit amet, consectetuer adipiscing elit, sed diem nonummy nibh euismod tincidunt ut lacreet dolore magna aliguam erat volutpat."

Christopher Calloway
English Country Life

Places, Spaces, and Things

Page Size	5.75" x 8.75"
Margins	L/R - 0" T/B - 0"
Background Picture Frame	Full bleed Dot pattern
Headline	Individual WordArt frames for each letter Sequim Best fit
Subheads	WordArt frames Langley White fill Color background Letter justify Blank space before first and after last letter

ROGER
places
BISONE
spaces
WRITINGS 1950 - 1960
things
EDITED BY SAM SPCE

Getting Started in Near East Philosophy

Page Size	5.75" x 8.75"
Margins	L/R - 0" T/B - 0"
Background Picture Frame	Full bleed Slanted brick pattern
Headline	Individual WordArt frames for each Bellingham Same height/differing lengths Best fit
Subheads	Text frame Palatino 14pt bold 6pt between letters 3sp between words

GETTING STARTED IN NEAR EAST PHILOSOPHY

A SEMINAR SERIES

Lingua Frenetica

Page Size	8.5" x 11"
Margins	All .5"
Frame	BorderArt Basic...wide outline
Feature Callouts	Separate text frames 10pt Helvetica bold 10pt Times Roman
Dotted Rule	BorderArt Box tool (reduced to a line) Basic black squares
Title	48pt Palatino
Picture	Clip art
Headline	36pt Helvetica narrow bold
Body Copy	10pt Times Roman
Initial Cap	WordArt Bellingham

TEN FEET UNDER
Some Men
do wear plaid
page 5

ACADEMIC LOVE
Trouble in the
sea of research
page 22

FUTURE STACKS
Librarians and the
book glut
page 41

Lingua*f*renetica

The Academic Social
Review
April/May

TALES FROM THE CLASS

A Lorem ipsum dolor sit amet, consectetuer adipiscing elit, sed diem nonummy nibh euismod tincidunt ut lacreet dolore magna aliguam erat volutpat. Ut wisis enim ad minim veniam, quis nostrud exerci tution ullamcorper suscipit lobortis nisl ut aliquip ex ea commodo consequat. Duis te feugifacilisi. Duis autem dolor in hendrerit in vulputate velit esse molestie consequat, vel illum dolore eu feugiat nulla facilisis at vero eros et accumsan et iusto odio dignissim qui blandit praesent luptatum zzril delenit au gue duis dolore te feugat nulla facilisi. Ut wisi enim ad minim veniam, quis nostrud exerci taion ullamcorper suscipit lobortis nisl ut aliquip ex en commodo consequat. Duis te feugifacilisi.

Lorem ipsum dolor sit amet, consectetuer adipiscing elit, sed diem nonummy nibh euismod tincidunt ut lacreet dolore magna aliguam erat volutpat. Ut wisis enim ad minim veniam, quis nostrud exerci tution ullamcorper suscipit lobortis nisl ut aliquip ex ea commodo consequat. Duis te feugifacilisi. Duis autem dolor in hendrerit in
Continued on Page 20

Leaving So Soon?

Page Size	8.5" x 11"
Margins	All .75"
Rules	Border 1pt above 3pt below Sides - none
Headline	WordArt Sequim Best fit Shadow
Subheads	14pt AvantGarde bold
Picture	Clip art Run around with 2 sets of overlaying frames for each "bulge" in the illustration
Coupon	PageWizard (coupon)

Leaving So Soon?

Lorem ipsum dolor sit amet, consectetuer adipiscing elit, sed diem nonummy nibh euismod tincidunt ut lacreet dolore magna aliguam erat volutpat. Ut wisis enim ad minim veniam, quis nostrud exerci tution ullamcorper suscipit lobortis nisl ut aliquip ex ea commodo consequat. Duis te feugifacilisi. Duis autem dolor in hendrerit in vulputate velit esse molestie consequat, vel illum dolore eu feugiat nulla facilisis at vero eros et accumsan et iusto odio dignissim qui blandit praesent luptatum zzril delenit au gue duis dolore te feugat nulla facilisi. Ut wisi enim ad minim veniam, quis nostrud exerci taion ullamcorper suscipit lobortis nisl ut aliquip ex en commodo consequat. Duis te feugifacilisi.

Consider This...

Lorem ipsum dolor sit amet, consectetuer adipiscing elit, sed diem nonummy nibh euismod tincidunt ut lacreet dolore magna aliguam erat volutpat. Ut wisis enim ad minim veniam, quis nostrud exerci tution ullamcorper suscipit lobortis nisl ut aliquip ex ea commodo consequat. Duis te feugifacilisi. Duis autem dolor in hendrerit in vulputate velit esse molestie consequat, vel illum dolore eu feugiat nulla facilisis at vero eros et accumsan et iusto odio dignissim qui blandit praesent luptatum zzril delenit au gue duis dolore te feugat nulla facilisi. Ut wisi enim ad minim veniam, quis nostrud exerci taion ullamcorper suscipit lobortis nisl ut aliquip ex en commodo consequat. Duis te feugifacilisi.

Why go now?

Lorem ipsum dolor sit amet, consectetuer adipiscing elit, sed diem nonummy nibh euismod tincidunt ut lacreet dolore magna aliguam erat volutpat. Ut wisis enim ad minim veniam, quis nostrud exerci tution ullamcorper suscipit lobortis nisl ut aliquip ex ea commodo consequat. Duis te feugifacilisi. Duis autem dolor in hendrerit in

vulputate velit esse molestie consequat, vel illum dolore eu feugiat nulla facilisis at vero eros et accumsan et iusto odio dignissim qui blandit praesent luptatum zzril delenit au gue duis dolore te feugat nulla facilisi. Ut wisi enim ad minim veniam, quis nostrud exerci taion ullamcorper suscipit lobortis nisl ut aliquip ex en commodo consequat. Duis te feugifacilisi.

Think about it.

Lorem ipsum dolor sit amet, consectetuer adipiscing elit, sed diem nonummy nibh euismod tincidunt ut lacreet dolore magna aliguam erat volutpat.Lorem ipsum dolor sit amet, consectetuer adipiscing elit, sed diem nonummy nibh euismod tincidunt ut lacreet dolore magna aliguam erat volutpat. Ut wisis enim ad minim veniam, quis nostrud exerci tution ullamcorper suscipit lobortis nisl ut aliquip ex ea commodo consequat. Duis te feugifacilisi. Duis autem dolor in hendrerit in vulputate velit esse molestie consequat, vel illum dolore eu feugiat nulla facilisis at vero eros et accumsan et iusto odio dignissim qui blandit praesent luptatum zzril delenit au gue duis dolore te feugat nulla facilisi. Ut wisi enim ad minim veniam, quis nostrud exerci taion ullamcorper suscipit lobortis nisl ut aliquip ex en commodo

Drop Us A Line

See what we can do to help you re-locate

☐ National ☐ International

Name _____
Address _____
_____
_____

Your comfort is Our Business

Politics

Page Size	6" x 9"
Margins	L/R - 0" T/B - 0"
Background Picture Frame	Full bleed Black
Headline	WordArt Vashon Best fit White fill
Subhead	WordArt Vashon Best fit White fill
Title	WordArt Longview Best fit White fill
Banner	WordArt Walla Walla Best fit Slant up (less) White fill Extended frame
Rules	3pt lines White
Letter Box	Box tool White

"Do all these examples mean that the President is thinking about war?" (see inside)

INSIDE: Your chance to receive a short-term subscription to

Politics
FREE

BULK RATE
U.S. POSTAGE
PAID
Politics

Politics
1600 Political Ave.
Capitol, Dist of Col

XYZ-11

Family Focus

Page Size	11" x 17" (magazine spread)
Margins	L/R - 0" T/B - 0"
Headline	WordArt Marysville 72pt
Subheads	WordArt Bellingham Best fit
Body Copy	10pt Times Roman
Pictures	Clip art Family drawing Head shots cropped and scaled from same picture

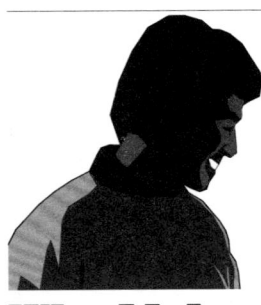

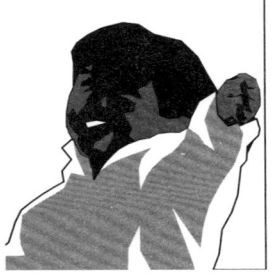

Family Focus

by lorne frenda
photos by snap shutter

March 15, 1990: Lorem ipsum dolor sit amet, consectetuer adipiscing elit, sed diem nonummy nibh euismod tincidunt ut lacreet dolore magna aliguam erat volutpat. Ut wisis enim ad minim veniam, quis nostrud exerci tution ullamcorper suscipit lobortis nisl ut aliquip ex ea commodo consequat. Duis te feugifacilisi. Duis autem dolor in hendrerit in vulputate velit esse molestie consequat, vel illum dolore eu feugiat nulla facilisis at vero eros et accumsan et iusto odio dignissim qui blandit praesent luptatum zzril delenit au gue duis dolore te feugat nulla facilsi. Ut wisi enim ad minim veniam, quis nostrud exerci taion ullamcorper suscipit lobortis nisl ut aliquip ex en commodo consequat. Duis te feugifacilisi.

Lorem ipsum dolor sit amet, consectetuer adipiscing elit, sed diem nonummy nibh euismod tincidunt ut lacreet dolore magna aliguam erat volutpat. Ut wisis enim ad minim veniam, quis nostrud exerci tution ullamcorper suscipti lobortis nisl ut aliquip ex ea commodo consequat. Duis te feugifacilisi. Duis autem dolor in hendrerit in vulputate velit esse molestie consequat, vel illum dolore eu feugiat nulla facilisis at vero eros et accumsan et iusto odio dignissim qui blandit praesent luptatum zzril delenit au gue duis dolore te feugat nulla facilisi. Ut wisi enim ad minim veniam, quis nostrud exerci taion ullamcorper suscipit lobortis nisl ut aliquip ex en commodo consequat. Duis te feugifacilisi.

Lorem ipsum dolor sit amet, consectetuer adipiscing elit, sed diem nonummy nibh euismod tincidunt ut lacreet dolore magna aliguam erat volutpat. Ut wisis enim ad minim veniam, quis nostrud exerci tution ullamcorper suscipti lobortis nisl ut aliquip ex ea commodo consequat. Duis te feugifacilisi. Duis autem dolor in hendrerit in vulputate velit esse molestie consequat, vel illum dolore eu feugiat nulla facilisis at vero eros et accumsan et iusto odio dignissim qui blandit praesent luptatum zzril delenit au gue duis dolore te feugat nulla facilisi. Ut wisi enim ad minim veniam, quis nostrud exerci taion ullamcorper suscipit lobortis nisl ut aliquip ex en commodo consequat. Duis te feugifacilisi.

Lorem ipsum dolor sit amet, consectetuer adipiscing elit, sed diem nonummy nibh euismod tincidunt ut lacreet dolore magna aliguam erat volutpat.Lorem ipsum dolor sit amet, consectetuer adipiscing elit, sed diem nonummy nibh cuismod tincidunt ut lacreet dolore magna aliguam erat volutpat.

Who Makes The Rules?

Who Makes The Dinner?

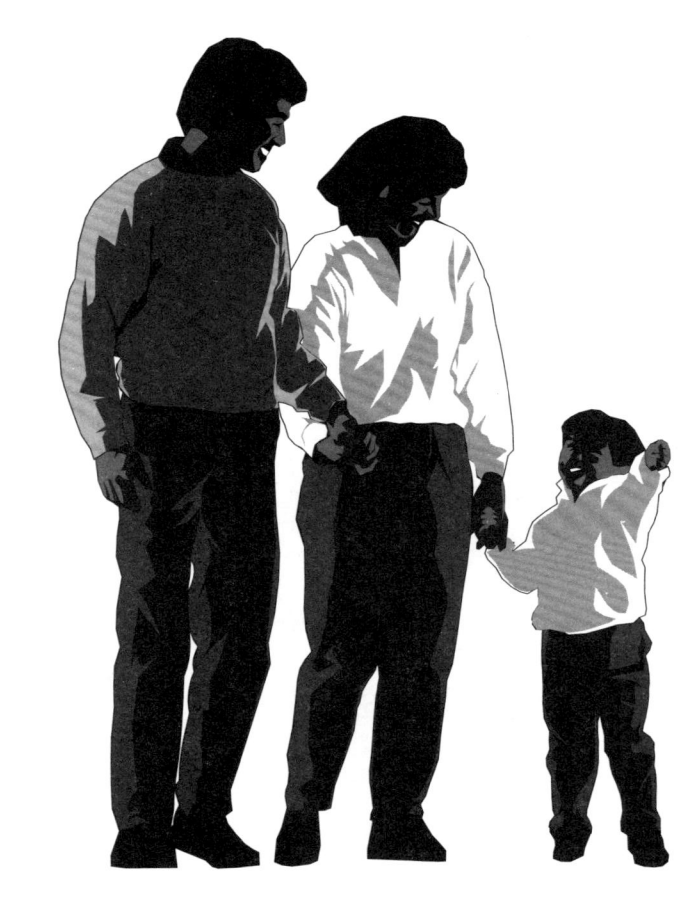

Beyond the America's Cup

Page Size	11" x 14"
Margins	L/R - 0" T/B - 0"
Headline	WordArt Inglewood Best fit Shadow
Subheads	WordArt Inglewood Best fit
Logo	WordArt Longview (2 frames) Best fit

BEYOND THE AMERICA'S CUP:

SAILBOATS, SAILORS & THE SEA

SC FORUM

Serious Authors

Page Size	8.5" x 11"
Margins	L/R - 0" T/B - 0"
Border	.5" Overlaying black/white box tool objects
Book Cover Title	Black box with 3 overlaying WordArt frames 1 and 3 - Vashon/white fill/best fit/fit horizontally 2 - Longview/white fill/best fit/fit horizontally
Subheads	14pt Helvetica bold italic
Bullets	10pt Helvetica
Review Section Headline	WordArt Vashon Best fit
Body Copy	14pt Times Roman bold
Bottom Logo	18pt and 24pt New Century Schoolbook (text) White fill/clear frame on a black box

HANDBOOK FOR SERIOUS AUTHORS

REVISED EDITION

- How to choose a publisher for your book
- Negotiating a contract
- Submitting journal articles
- Writing a manual
- Word processing

MARTIN ROGERS

REVISED AND UPDATED

"This should be a must for anyone starting out in the commercial writing field. It's simply priceless in terms of getting to know the ins and outs of succeeding in this difficult professional arena."

Modern Author

CRANBRIDGE UNIVERSITY PRESS

27 West 480th Street Manhatten, New Plaza 88774-1234
Call toll-free 100-400-7000

Finance & Greed

Page Size	5" x 5"
Margins	L/R - .25" T/B - .25
Border	4 WordArt frames Vashon / normal / upside down / top to bottom / bottom to top / fit horizontally
Headline	18pt AvantGarde
Body Copy	10pt AvantGarde

FINANCE GREED DECEPTION & LUCK

ECONOMICS ISN'T BORING ANYMORE!

Now the proven principles established by the giants of international finance come to life in torrid and romantic video featuring today's leading stars. And each is available for only $29.95!

Bill Smith	Cat# 1145	Mike Margin	Cat# 4462
Roger Marx	Cat# 1254	William Bluespan	Cat# 4421
Peter Ross	Cat# 6021	Ivan Rastar	Cat# 8894

To order call 1-100-FOR-MONY or send check including $29.95 for each title plus $4.50 (shipping & handling) to GREEDNET, 7979 Chapter 11 Blvd., Eugene, WA 88888

African Weaving

Page Size	8.5" x 11"
Margins	L/R - .0" T/B - 0"
Background Picture Frame	Full bleed Pattern
Title	WordArt Wenatchee Best fit Clear background
Subtitle	WordArt Wenatchee Best fit White background
Credit Lines	14pt Helvetica narrow bold Centered
Subhead	14pt Helvetica narrow bold Centered All letters spread by 3pt
Art	Oval tool - 4 overlaying circles with different fill patterns

AFRICAN WEAVING

Design & Origins

ALBERTO SORRENO, EDITOR
FERNANDO LANGUSTINO, PHOTOGRAPHER
ENGLISH LANGUAGE EDITION

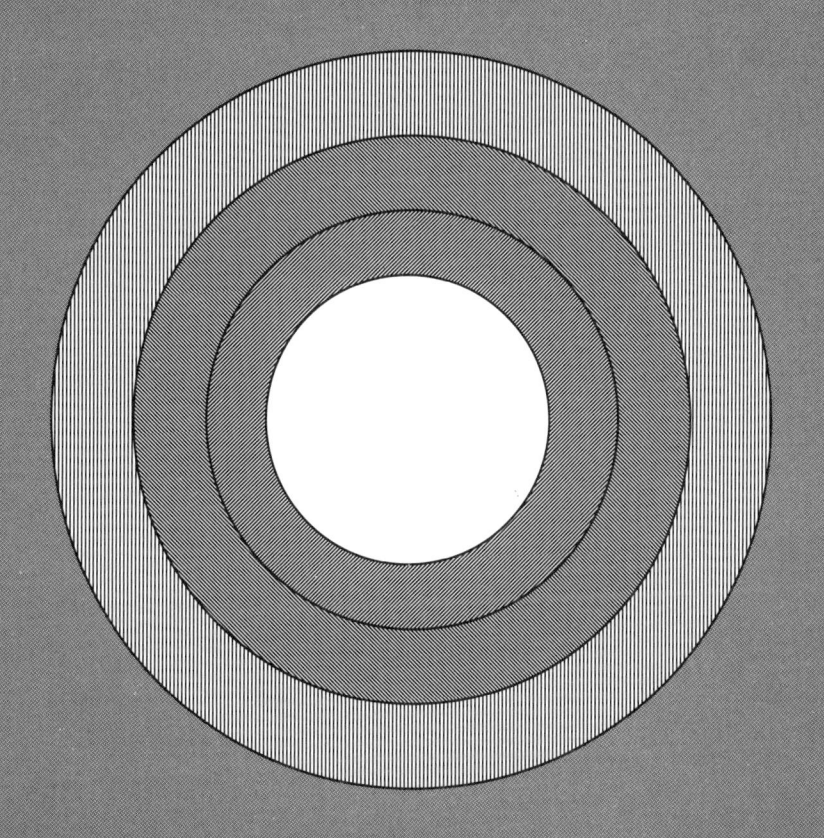

THE THIRD WORLD IN ITS CULTURE, VOLUME

Poetry & Literature

Page Size	8.5" x 11"
Margins	L/R - 1" T/B - .3"
Title	24pt Palatino bold plain
Subtitles	18pt Palatino bold
Body Copy	10pt Times Roman
Rules	1pt

HUMANITIES
POETRY & LITERATURE

MODERN AMERICAN POETS

A look at the greats of the 50's and 60's

James Tipton

Lorem ipsum dolor sit amet, consectetuer adipiscing elit, sed diem nonummy nibh euismod tincidunt ut lacreet dolore magna aliguam erat volutpat. Ut wisis enim ad minim veniam, quis nostrud exerci tution ullamcorper suscipit lobortis nisl ut aliquip ex ea commodo consequat. Duis te feugifacilisi. Duis autem dolor in hendrerit in vulputate velit esse molestie consequat, vel illum dolore eu feugiat nulla facilisis at vero eros et accumsan et iusto odio dignissim qui blandit praesent luptatum zzril delenit au gue duis dolore te feugat nulla facilisi. Ut wisi enim ad minim veniam, quis nostrud exerci taion ullamcorper suscipit lobortis nisl ut aliquip ex en commodo consequat. Duis te feugifacilisi.

Lorem ipsum dolor sit amet, consectetuer adipiscing elit, sed diem nonummy nibh euismod tincidunt ut lacreet dolore magna aliguam erat volutpat. Ut wisis enim ad minim veniam, quis nostrud exerci tution ullamcorper suscipit lobortis nisl ut aliquip ex ea commodo consequat. Duis te feugifacilisi. Duis autem dolor in hendrerit in vulputate velit esse molestie consequat, vel illum dolore eu feugiat nulla facilisis at vero eros et accumsan.
392 pp./bibliography/index
ISBM-56564
$9.50

WHERE DID THE WORD REVOLUTION START?

An investigation into the etymology of modern usage for the inquiring mind

Simon Marsalis

Lorem ipsum dolor sit amet, consectetuer adipiscing elit, sed diem nonummy nibh euismod tincidunt ut lacreet dolore magna aliguam erat volutpat. Ut wisis enim ad minim veniam, quis nostrud exerci tution ullamcorper suscipit lobortis nisl ut aliquip ex ea commodo consequat. Duis te feugifacilisi. Duis autem dolor in hendrerit in vulputate velit esse molestie consequat, vel illum dolore eu feugiat nulla facilisis at vero eros et accumsan et iusto odio dignissim qui blandit praesent luptatum zzril delenit au gue duis dolore te feugat nulla facilisi. Ut wisi enim ad minim veniam, quis nostrud exerci taion ullamcorper suscipit lobortis nisl ut aliquip ex en commodo consequat. Duis te feugifacilisi.

Lorem ipsum dolor sit amet, consectetuer adipiscing elit, sed diem nonummy nibh euismod tincidunt ut lacreet dolore magna aliguam erat volutpat.
300 pp/charts
ISBN 99-XOXOX
$15.50

THE POLITICS OF ECSTASY

Branton Wilson

Lorem ipsum dolor sit amet, consectetuer adipiscing elit, sed diem nonummy nibh euismod tincidunt ut lacreet dolore magna aliguam erat volutpat. Ut wisis enim ad minim veniam, quis nostrud exerci tution ullamcorper suscipit lobortis nisl ut aliquip ex ea commodo consequat. Duis te feugifacilisi. Duis autem dolor in hendrerit in vulputate velit esse molestie consequat, vel illum dolore eu feugiat nulla facilisis at vero eros et accumsan et iusto odio dignissim qui blandit praesent luptatum zzril delenit au gue duis dolore te feugat nulla facilisi. Ut wisi enim ad minim veniam, quis nostrud exerci taion ullamcorper suscipit lobortis nisl ut aliquip ex en commodo consequat. Duis te feugifacilisi.

Lorem ipsum dolor sit amet, consectetuer adipiscing elit, sed diem nonummy nibh euismod tincidunt ut lacreet dolore magna aliguam erat volutpat. Ut wisis enim ad minim veniam, quis nostrud exerci tution ullamcorper suscipit lobortis nisl ut aliquip ex ea commodo consequat. Duis te feugifacilisi. Duis autem dolor in hendrerit in vulputate velit esse molestie consequat, vel illum dolore eu feugiat nulla facilisis at vero eros et accumsan et iusto odio dignissim qui blandit praesent luptatum zzril delenit au gue duis dolore te feugat nulla facilisi.
229 pp/ bibliography/index/
ISBN 99-XXXX
$9.75

Delphi

Page Size	7" x 9"
Margins	All .35"
Title Series	WordArt 2 frames (1 for each word) Marysville Slant up (less) Best fit
Product	WordArt Touchet Best fit Fit horizontal
Art	Box tool squares with different patterns

Working With

DELPHI

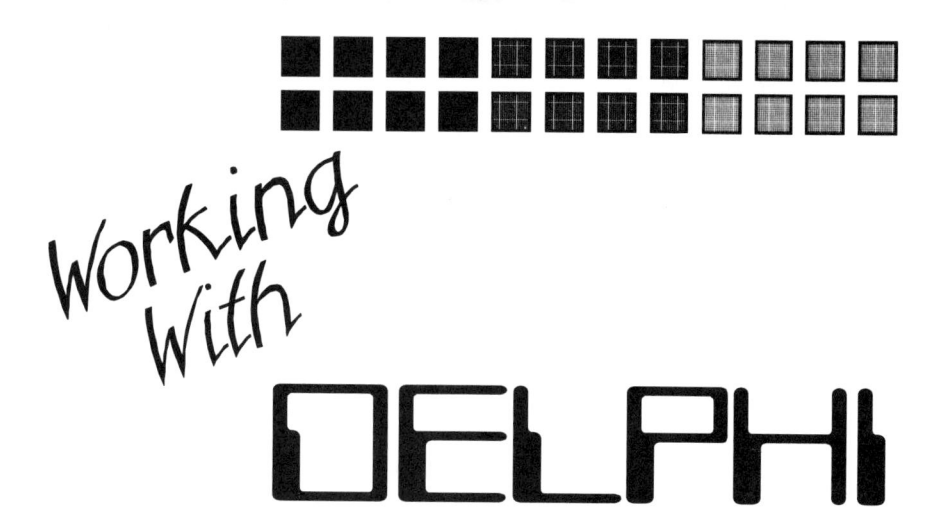

STRUCTURED QUERY TOOLS
Roger O'Neill

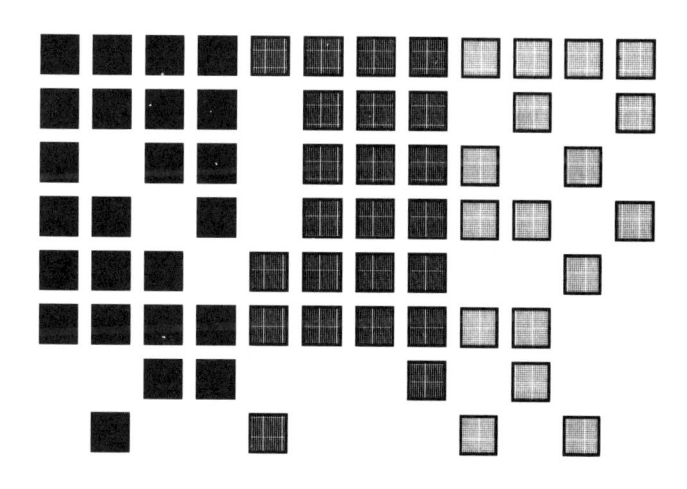

RushWIND

Page Size	8.5" x 11"
Margins	Mirrored backgrounds Inside .5" Outside 2.25" T/B .75"
Title	WordArt Longview Best fit Fit horizontally
Subtitle	Vashon Best fit Fit horizontally White fill Color background
Major Headlines	Vashon Best fit Fit horizontally
Minor Headlines	12pt Times Roman bold
Sidebars	10pt Times Roman bold
Body Copy	10pt Times Roman
Rules	1pt lines (background page)
Header	12pt AvantGarde bold (background page)
Coupon	PageWizard (coupon)

RushWIND
THE EAST-WEST HIGH-WIND BOARDSAILING REPORT

ANOTHER SEASON BEGINS

Lorem ipsum dolor sit amet, consectetuer adipiscing elit, sed diem nonummy nibh euismod tincidunt ut lacreet dolore magna aliguam erat volutpat. Ut wisis enim ad minim veniam, quis nostrud exerci tution ullamcorper suscipit lobortis nisl ut aliquip ex ea commodo consequat. Duis te feugifacilisi. Duis autem dolor in hendrerit in vulputate velit esse molestie consequat, vel illum dolore eu feugia nulla facilisis at vero eros et accumsan et iusto odio dignissim qui blandit praesent luptatum zzril delenit au gue duis dolore te feugat nulla facilisi. Ut wisi enim ad minim veniam, quis nostrud exerci taion ullamcorper suscipit lobortis nisl ut aliquip ex en commodo consequat. Duis te feugifacilisi.

Lorem ipsum dolor sit amet, consectetuer adipiscing elit, sed diem nonummy nibh euismod tincidunt ut lacreet dolore magna aliguam erat volutpat. Ut wisis enim ad minim veniam, quis nostrud exerci tution ullamcorper suscipit lobortis nisl ut aliquip ex ea commodo consequat. Duis te feugifacilisi. Duis autem dolor in hendrerit in vulputate velit esse molestie consequat, vel illum dolore eu feugia nulla facilisis at vero eros et accumsan et iusto odio dignissim qui blandit praesent luptatum zzril delenit au gue duis dolore te feugat nulla facilisi. Ut wisi enim ad minim veniam, quis nostrud exerci taion ullamcorper suscipit lobortis nisl ut aliquip ex en consequat. Duis et al ete feugifacilisi.**(Continued on Page 2)**

WHERE THE ACTION IS

Lorem ipsum dolor sit amet, consectetuer adipiscing elit, sed diem nonummy nibh euismod tincidunt ut lacreet dolore magna aliguam erat volutpat. Ut wisis enim ad minim veniam, quis nostrud exerci tution ullamcorper suscipit lobortis nisl ut aliquiprit in vulputate velit esse molestie consequat, vel illum dolore eu feugiat nulla facilisis at vero eros et accumsan et iusto odio dignissim qui blandit praesent luptatum zzril delenit au gue duis dolore te feugat nulla facilisi. Ut wisi enim ad minim veniam, quis nostrud exerci taion ullamcorper suscipit lobortis nisl ut aliquip ex en commodo consequat. Duis te feugifacilisi.

Lorem ipsum dolor sit amet, consectetuer adipiscing elit, sed diem nonummy nibh euismod tincidunt ut lacreet dolore magna aliguam erat volutpat.Lorem ipsum dolor sit amet, consectetuer adipiscing elit, sed diem nonummy nibh euismod tincidunt ut lacreet dolore magna aliguam erat volutpat. Ut wisis enim ad minim veniam, quis nostrud exerci tution ullamcorper suscipit lobortis nisl ut aliquip ex ea commodo consequat.

INSIDE

ON THE WIND 2
Lorem ipsum dolorsit amet, consectetuer adipiscing elit, sed diem nonummy nibh euismod tincidunt ut lacreet dolore magna aliguam erat volutpat. Ut wisis enim ad minim veniam, quis nostrud exerci tution ullamcorper suscipit lobortis nisl ut aliquip ex ea commodo consequat. Duis te feugifacilisi.

OFF SHORE 6
Duis autem dolor in hendrerit in vulputate velit esse molestie consequat, vel illum dolore eu feugiat nulla facilisis at vero eros et

NEW GEAR 9
cumsan et iusto odio dignissim qui blandit praesent luptatum zzril delenit au gue duis dolore te feugat nulla facilisi. Ut wisi enim ad minim veniam, quis nostrud exerci taion ullamcorper suscipit lobortis nisl ut aliquip ex en commodo consequat. Duis te feugifacilisi.

A publication of HighWind Holdings Inc., 4800 Baja Avenue Western Austrailia PT60K1 (222) 676-9099

lipsum dolor sit amet, consectetuer adipiscing elit, sed diem nonummy nibh euismod tincidunt ut lacreet dolore magna aliguam erat volutpat. Ut wisis enim ad minim veniam, quis nostrud exerci tution ullamcorper suscipit lobortis nisl ut aliquip ex ea commodo consequat.

Duis autem dolor in hendrerit in vulputate velit esse molestie consequat, vel illum dolore eu feugiat nulla facilisis at vero eros et accumsan et iusto odio dignissim qui blandit praesent luptatum zzril delenit au gue duis dolore te feugat nulla facilisi. Ut wisi enim ad minim veniam, quis nostrud exerci taion ullamcorper suscipit lobortis nisl ut aliquip ex en commodo consequat. Duis te feugifacilisi. orem ipsum dolor sit amet, consectetuer adipiscing elit, sed diem nonummy nibh euismod tincidunt ut lacreet dolore magna aliguam erat volutpat.

(Continued from Page 1) wisis enim ad minim veniam, quis nostrud exerci tution ullamcorper suscipit lobortis nisl ut aliquip ex ea commodo consequat. Duis te feugifacilisi. Duis autem dolor in hendrerit in vulputate velit esse molestie consequat, vel illum dolore eu feugiat nulla facilisis at vero eros et accumsan et iusto odio dignissim qui blandit praesent luptatum zzril delenit au gue duis dolore te feugat nulla facilisi.

Ut wisi enim ad minim veniam, quis nostrud exerci taion ullamcorper suscipit lobortis nisl ut aliquip ex en commodo consequat. Duis te feugifacilisi. Lorem ipsum dolor sit amet, consectetuer adipiscing elit, sed diem nonummy nibh euismod tincidunt ut lacreet dolore magna aliguam erat volutpat. Ut wisis enim ad minim veniam, quis nostrud exerci tution ullamcorper suscipit lobortis nisl ut aliquip ex ea commodo consequat. Duis te feugifacilisi.

Looking for conditions this fall

Duis autem dolor in hendrerit in vulputate velit esse molestie consequat, vel illum dolore eu feugiat nulla facilisis at vero eros et accumsan et iusto odio dignissim qui blandit praesent luptatum zzril delenit au gue duis dolore te feugat nulla facilisi. Ut wisi enim ad minim veniam, quis nostrud exerci taion ullamcorper suscipit lobortis nisl ut aliquip ex en commodo consequat. Duis te feugifacilisi.

Lorem ipsum dolor sit amet, consectetuer adipiscing elit, sed diem nonummy nibh euismod tincidunt ut lacreet dolore magna aliguam erat volutpat. Lorem ipsum dolor sit amet, consectetuer adipiscing elit, sed diem nonummy nibh euismod tincidunt ut lacreet dolore magna aliguam erat volutpat. Ut wisis enim ad minim veniam, quis nostrud exerci tution ullamcorper suscipit lobortis nisl ut aliquip ex ea commodo consequat. Duis te feugifacilisi. Duis autem dolor in hendrerit in vulputate velit esse molestie consequat, vel illum dolore eu feugiat nulla facilisis at vero eros et accumsan et iusto odio dignissim qui blandit praesent luptatum zzril delenit au gue duis dolore te feugat nulla facilisi. Ut wisi enim ad minim veniam, quis nostrud exerci taion ullamcorper suscipit lobortis nisl ut aliquip ex en commodo consequat. Duis te feugifacilisi.

Points to Remember on Rigging

- Lorem ipsum dolor sit amet, consectetuer adipiscing elit, sed diem nonummy nibh euismod tincidunt ut lacreet dolore magna aliguam erat volutpat.

- Ut wisis enim ad minim veniam, quis nostrud exerci tution ullamcorper suscipit lobortis nisl ut aliquip ex ea commodo consequat. Duis te feugifacilisi.

- Duis autem dolor in hendrerit in vulputate velit esse molestie consequat, vel illum dolore eu feugiat nulla facilisis at vero eros et accumsan et iusto odio dignissim qui blandit praesent luptatum zzril delenit au gue duis dolore te feugat nulla facilisi.

- Ut wisi enim ad minim veniam, quis nostrud exerci taion ullamcorper suscipit lobortis nisl ut aliquip ex en commodo consequat. Duis te feugifacilisi.

Lorem ipsum dolor sit amet, consectetuer adipiscing elit, sed diem nonummy nibh euismod tincidunt ut lacreet dolore magna aliguam erat volutpat. Ut wisis enim ad minim veniam, quis nostrud exerci tution ullamcorper suscipit lobortis nisl ut aliquip ex ea commodo consequat. Duis te feugifacilisi. Duis autem dolor in hendrerit in vulputate velit esse molestie consequat, vel illum dolore eu feugiat nulla facilisis at vero eros et accumsan et iusto odio dignissim qui blandit praesent luptatum zzril delenit au gue duis dolore te feugat nulla facilisi. Ut wisi enim ad minim veniam, quis nostrud exerci taion ullamcorper suscipit lobortis nisl ut aliquip ex en commodo consequat. Duis te feugifacilisi.

Coping With Big Surf

Lorem ipsum dolor sit amet, consectetuer adipiscing elit, sed diem nonummy nibh euismod tincidunt ut lacreet dolore magna aliguam erat volutpat.Lorem ipsum dolor sit amet, consectetuer adipiscing elit, sed diem nonummy nibh euismod tincidunt ut lacreet dolore magna aliguam erat volutpat. Ut wisis enim ad minim veniam, quis nostrud exerci tution ullamcorper suscipit lobortis nisl ut aliquip ex ea commodo consequat. Duis te feugifacilisi. Duis autem dolor in hendrerit in vulputate velit esse molestie consequat, vel illum dolore eu feugiat nulla facilisis at vero eros et accumsan et iusto odio dignissim qui blandit praesent luptatum zzril delenit au gue duis dolore te feugat nulla facilisi. Ut wisi enim ad minim veniam, quis nostrud exerci taion ullamcorper suscipit lobortis nisl ut aliquip ex en commodo consequat. Duis te feugifacilisi.

Lorem ipsum dolor sit amet, consectetuer adipiscing elit, sed diem nonummy nibh euismod tincidunt ut lacreet dolore magna aliguam erat volutpat. Ut wisis enim ad minim veniam, quis nostrud exerci tution ullamcorper suscipit lobortis nisl ut aliquip ex ea commodo consequat. Duis te feugifacilisi. Duis autem dolor in hendrerit in vulputate velit esse molestie consequat, vel illum dolore eu feugiat nulla facilisis at vero eros et accumsan et iusto odio dignissim qui blandit praesent luptatum zzril delenit au gue duis dolore te feugat nulla facilisi. Ut wisi enim ad minim veniam, quis nostrud exerci taion ullamcorper suscipit lobortis nisl ut aliquip ex en commodo consequat. Duis te feugifacilisi.

Coming Soon

Lorem ipsum dolor sit amet, consectetuer adipiscing elit, sed diem nonummy nibh euismod tincidunt ut lacreet dolore magna aliguam erat volutpat. Ut wisis enim ad minim veniam, quis nostrud exerci tution ullamcorper suscipit lobortis nisl ut aliquip ex ea commodo consequat. Duis te feugifacilisi. Duis autem dolor in hendrerit in vulputate velit esse molestie consequat, vel illum dolore eu feugiat nulla facilisis at vero eros et accumsan et iusto odio dignissim qui blandit praesent luptatum zzril delenit au gue duis dolore te feugat nulla facilisi. Ut wisi enim ad minim veniam, quis nostrud exerci taion ullamcorper suscipit lobortis nisl ut aliquip ex en commodo consequat. Duis te feugifacilisi.

RushWIND

Lorem ipsum dolor sit amet, consectetuer adipiscing elit, sed diem nonummy nibh euismod tincidunt ut lacreet dolore magna aliguam erat volutpat. Ut wisis enim ad minim veniam, quis nostrud exerci tution ullamcorper suscipit lobortis nisl ut aliquip ex ea commodo consequat. Duis te feugifacilisi. Duis autem dolor in hendrerit in vulputate velit esse molestie consequat, vel illum dolore eu feugiat nulla facilisis at vero eros et accumsan et iusto odio dignissim qui blandit praesent luptatum zzril delenit au gue duis dolore te feugat nulla facilisi. Ut wisi enim ad minim veniam, quis nostrud exerci taion ullamcorper suscipit lobortis nisl ut aliquip ex en commodo consequat. Duis te feugifacilisi.

Lorem ipsum dolor sit amet, consectetuer adipiscing elit, sed diem nonummy nibh euismod tincidunt ut lacreet dolore magna aliguam erat volutpat. Ut wisis enim ad minim veniam, quis nostrud exerci tution ullamcorper suscipit lobortis nisl ut aliquip ex ea commodo consequat. Duis te feugifacilisi. Duis autem dolor in hendrerit in vulputate velit esse molestie consequat, vel illum dolore eu feugiat nulla facilisis at vero eros et accumsan et iusto odio dignissim qui blandit praesent luptatum zzril delenit au gue duis dolore te feugat nulla facilisi. Ut wisi enim ad minim veniam, quis nostrud exerci taion ullamcorper suscipit lobortis nisl ut aliquip ex en commodo consequat. Duis te feugifacilisi.

Yes! I want to subscribe!

Sign me up for ☐ 1 Year ($24) ☐ 2 Years ($40)
Please bill my account: #_____
Payment Enclosed: $_____

Name_____
Address_____
City_____
State_____
Zip_____

☐ American Express
☐ Visa
☐ MasterCard
☐ Diners
☐ Carte Blanche

Be sure to attach postage
No Postage Guaranteed

C
WordArt Fonts

Anacortes

AaBbCcDdEeFfGgHhIiJjKkLlMmNn
OoPpQqRrSsTtUuVvWwXxYyZz
1234567890()!@#$%&()/|\{}[]?

Bellingham

AaBbCcDdEeFfGgHhIiJjKk
LlMmNnOoPpQqRrSsTtUu
VvwWxXyYzZ
1234567900!@#$%&()/|\{}[]?

Duvall

AaBbOcDdEeFfGgHhIiJjKkLlMmNn
OoPpQqRrSsTtUuVvWwXxYyZz
1234567890()!@#$%&()/|\{}[]?

Ellensburg

AaBbCcDdEeFfGgHhIiJjKkLlMmNn
OoPpQqRrSsTtUuVvWwXxYyZz
1234567890()!@#$%&()/|\{}[]?

Enumclaw

AaBbCcDdEeFfGgHhIiJjKkLlMmNn
OoPpQqRrSsTtUuVvWwXxYyZz
1234567890()!@#$%&()/|\{}[]?

Inglewood

AaBbCcDdEeFfGgHhIiJjKkLlMmNn
OoPpQqRrSsTtUuVvWwXxYyZz
1234567890()!@#$%&()/|\{}[]?

Appendix C: *WordArt Fonts* 415

Langley

AaBbCcDdEeFfGgHhIiJjKkLlMmNn
OoPpQqRrSsTtUuVvWwXxYyZz
1234567890()!@#$%&()/\[]?

Longview

AaBbCcDdEeFfGgHhIiJjKkLlMmNn
OoPpQqRrSsTtUuVvWwXxYyZz
1234567890()!@#$%&()/\[]?

Marysville

AaBbCcDdEeFfGgHhIiJjKkLlMmNn
OoPpQqRrSsTtUuVvWwXxYyZz
1234567890()!@#$%&()/\[]?

Mineral

AaBbCcDdEeFfGgHhIiJjKkLlMmNn
OoPpQqRrSsTtUuVvWwXxYyZz
1234567890()!@#$%&()/\[]?

C

Omak

AaBbCcDdEeFfGgHhIiJjKkLlMmNn
OoPpQqRrSsTtUuVvWwXxYyZz
1234567890()!@#$%&()/|\{}[]?

Sequim

AaBbCcDdEeFfGgHhIiJjKk
LlMmNnOoPpQqRrSsTtUu
VvWwXxYyZz
1234567890()!@#$%&()/|\{}[]?

Snohomish

AaBbCcDdEeFfGgHhIiJjKk
LlMmNnOoPpQqRrSsTtUuVv
WwXxYyZz
1234567890()!@#$%&()/|\{}[]?

Touchet

AaBbCcDdEeFfGgHhIiJjKkLlMmNn
OoPpQqRrSsTtUuVvWwXxYyZz
1234567890()!@#$%&()/|\{}[]?

Appendix C: *WordArt Fonts*

Tupelo

AaBbCcDdEeFfGgHhIiJjKkLlMmNn
OoPpQqRrSsTtUuVvWwXxYyZz
1234567890()!@#$%&()/|\{}[]?

Vancouver

AaBbCcDdEeFfGgHhIiJjKk
LlMmNnOoPpQqRrSsTtUuVv
WwXxYyZz
1234567890!@#$%&()/|\{}[]?

Vashon

AaBbCcDdEeFfGgHhIiJjKkLlMmNn
OoPpQqRrSsTtUuVvWwXxYyZz
1234567890()!@#$%&()/|\{}[]?

Walla Walla

AaBbCcDdEeFfGgHhIiJjKkLlMmNn
OoPpQqRrSsTtUuVvWwXxYyZz
1234567890()!@#$%&()/|\{}[]?

Wenatchee

AaBbCcDdEeFfGgHhIiJjKk
LlMmNnOoPpQqRrSsTtUuVv
WwXxYyZz
1234567890
()!@#$%&*()/|\<>?

D

Keyboard Shortcuts

Actual view	`F9`
Background/foreground	`CTRL`-`M`
Beginning of frame	`CTRL`-`HOME`
Boldface	`CTRL`-`B`
Bottom of frame	`CTRL`-`END`
Bring to front	`CTRL`-`F`
Center paragraph	`CTRL`-`E`
Copy	`CTRL`-`C`
Cut	`CTRL`-`X`
Delete	`DEL`
Delete Text frame	`CTRL`-`DEL`
Double-space paragraph	`CTRL`-`2`
Exit	`F3`
Help	`F1`
Hide/show layout guides	`CTRL`-`G`
Hide/show object boundaries	`CTRL`-`Y`

Hide/show rulers	CTRL-K
Hyphenate	CTRL-H
Insert page	CTRL-N
Italic	CTRL-I
Justify paragraph	CTRL-J
Left-align paragraph	CTRL-L
Next connected frame	CTRL-TAB
Next page	F5
Next paragraph	CTRL-DOWN
Next word	CTRL-RIGHT
New line	SHIFT-ENTER
New page	CTRL-ENTER
Paste	CTRL-V
Previous connected frame	CTRL-SHIFT-TAB
Previous page	CTRL-F5
Previous paragraph	CTRL-UP
Previous word	CTRL-LEFT
Print	CTRL-P
Remove character formatting	CTRL-SPACEBAR
Remove leading above paragraph	CTRL-O
Remove paragraph formatting	CTRL-Q
Right-align paragraph	CTRL-R
Save	CTRL-S
Select story	CTRL-A
Send to back	CTRL-Z
Shadow	CTRL-D
Single-space paragraph	CTRL-1
Snap to guides	CTRL-W
Underline	CTRL-U
Undo	ALT-BACKSPACE

E

PageWizards

PageWizards are like having a publishing consultant around all the time. One of the most outstanding features in Publisher, they turn everyone into a page designer with practically no training or startup time. A PageWizard lets you design any of about a dozen different kinds of objects and publications by asking you a series of questions on screen. Then the PageWizard uses your answers to have Publisher design the application for you.

If you were to depend on PageWizards exclusively for your publishing needs, you could become productive with the program after learning only two or three simple Publisher commands. PageWizards give Publisher tremendous scope—they completely facilitate publishing projects of almost any description.

On the other hand, PageWizards are helpful for tedious work, even if you are an experienced user. Consider the calendar or invoice in Figure E-1. Detail work of the type necessary to implement either of these publications—creating and precisely aligning numerous and identical frames and rules—is tiresome for users at all levels of expertise. PageWizards take care of it all for you. Much of this book is dedicated to showing you how to get the *most* out of Publisher's

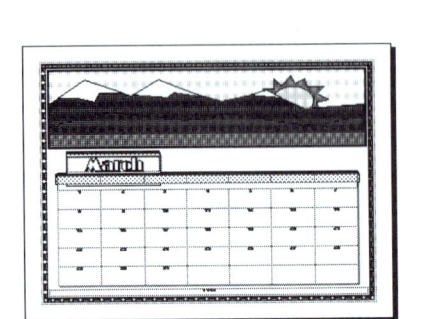

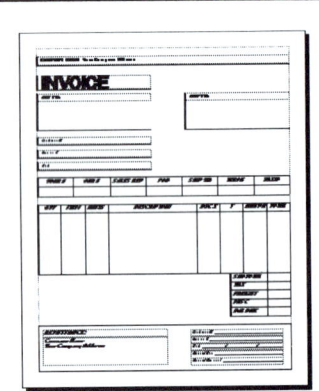

Figure E-1.   *Calendar and invoice created with PageWizards*

features. PageWizards let you get the most out of its human engineering by making everything easy to do.

There are 12 PageWizards in all. Each lets you create a publication for one of the applications shown in the following list. You can begin a new publication with a PageWizard, or use one to take care of some section of a piece you've created on your own. In either case, all you need to do is respond to a few simple on-screen questions about how you want the product to look. Then Publisher creates it for you. Afterward, you can use the result as is or make changes to parts of it.

Application	Full Publication	Frame
Advertisement		x
Calendar	x	x
Fancy First Letter		x
Newsletter Banner		x
Note-It		x
Paper Aeroplane	x	x
Table		x
Greeting Card	x	
Newsletter	x	
Business Form	x	
Brochure	x	

Appendix E: *PageWizards* 423

With a simple application such as a greeting card, the PageWizard prompts you for every part of the piece, from the greeting itself to the artwork you want to include. More sophisticated applications, such as the newsletter, require that you add text and pictures after the PageWizard finishes its work. If you are unfamiliar with working with text, information on getting text into a publication can be found in Chapter 6. Likewise, Chapter 9 details how to introduce graphics. In any case, you'll probably want to print the finished publication, and may want to keep it around for future use. Basic instructions for printing and saving publications can be found in Appendixes A and H.

How PageWizards Work

There are two ways to start a PageWizard: from the Publisher Start Up screen, or from the Toolbar, as shown here:

Whichever way you decide to begin, the method for making choices about how to design PageWizard material is identical. PageWizards present all of their questions in a series of dialog boxes. Each box presents you with questions in the form of option buttons, fields, and lists about different aspects of the publication, such as border style or picture size. In addition to these choices, each box contains four control buttons in the lower-right corner:

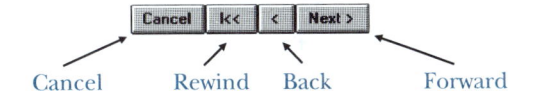

Cancel Rewind Back Forward

These buttons control the flow of the PageWizard questionnaire. The Next> button displays the next dialog box in the questionnaire. The < (Back) button displays the previous one. The |<< (Rewind) button returns to the initial dialog box, and Cancel terminates the PageWizard (a picture frame remains on screen with no contents). You can click on any of the control buttons at any time. This makes it easy to revise choices you have already made and return to the last screen you worked on.

Using the PageWizard Frame Tool

If you completed the tutorial in Chapter 3, you've used a PageWizard to create a calendar and are already familiar with the process. If you haven't used one before, follow this short tutorial to see how PageWizards work. The exercise lets you create a fancy first letter that you might use in a greeting card, invitation, or the beginning of a story or article.

1. Start a new publication using a blank page. Then click on the PageWizard tool and create a frame approximately 1 inch square. After you complete the frame, the PageWizard dialog box appears:

2. Click on Fancy First Letter and click on OK. The banner screen for this PageWizard appears.

3. Click on Next>. The first dialog box in this PageWizard appears, as shown in Figure E-2. This screen lets you decide on a type style and border for the letter.

4. Try clicking all of the option buttons on the screen. Each time you select a new style, Publisher displays a preview of what your choice will look like in the completed frame. Settle on a style you like and click on Next>.

5. The second dialog box lets you choose one of three locations for the accompanying border. Click on each of the option buttons to investigate all of the possibilities before proceeding to the following screen. Then click on Next>.

Appendix E: *PageWizards* 425

Figure E-2.   Fancy First Letter dialog box

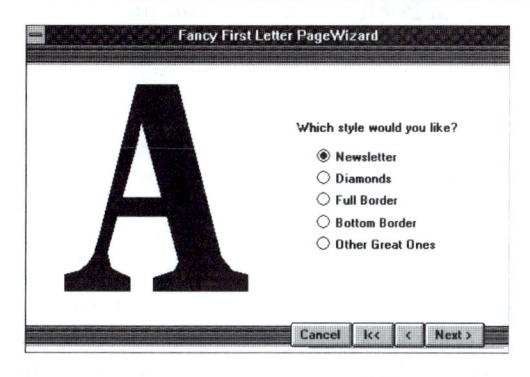

6. Just to see the effects, click on the |<< (Rewind) button. Click on Next> to review each of the screens you have already processed. Following the screen for border location, Publisher prompts you for the actual letter that you want to use in the PageWizard. Enter a single letter (or accept the default *A*) and click on Next>.

7. For each PageWizard, the final dialog box in the question-and-answer session ends with a button called Create It. At this point you can still return to any of the previous screens if you need to make revisions. Once you're satisfied with your choices, click on Create It. The Publisher screen returns, and the program begins to create your PageWizard. The dialog box shown here remains on the screen throughout the process:

8. In this box, Publisher describes each step in the process of building the object or publication you designed with the PageWizard. You can drag the box to different sections of the screen if it blocks the current activity, and you can control the overall speed of the procedure by sliding the control box to the right or left.

9. The final dialog box displays the checkered flag. Click on **OK**, and a normal Publisher session continues.

Starting a Document from Scratch

When you start a new publication, the startup screen appears. PageWizards are one of the three ways to proceed, as shown in Figure E-3. The list in the center of the dialog box displays all of the PageWizard choices for creating a complete publication. Just select one of the entries on this list and then click on **OK**. When creating a complete publication, Publisher presents you with a larger number of dialog boxes, but the process is the same as that described earlier for creating a PageWizard with the Frame tool.

Modifying PageWizard Material

PageWizards use only the standard Publisher tools to create publications. There is no difference between any object created by a PageWizard and one you create yourself. Any and all of the skills you have in working with

Figure E-3.   Create New Publication dialog box

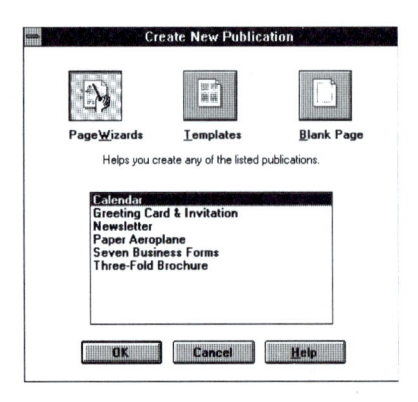

Appendix E: *PageWizards* 427

Publisher can be applied to modifying a PageWizard once it is completed, so the more familiar you are with the program, the more sophisticated the results you can obtain.

The material you create with a PageWizard is usually composed of many objects, even if you use only the Frame tool to start the PageWizard. Dissecting a PageWizard creation can be quite educational in learning how to use some of Publisher's special effects more dramatically. In general, however, you will need to replace text, pictures, or both in order to personalize the material. Publisher leaves instructions in the Text frames of a PageWizard creation, where it is assumed you will want to make replacements, as shown in Figure E-4.

Text

To change the text in a PageWizard, click on the frame containing the text and delete the instructions or marker material that the PageWizard automatically inserted. Then type your own text, or use one of the Publisher commands, Paste or Import, to fill the frame with your own material, and format the text as necessary.

Figure E-4. Completed PageWizard with text markers

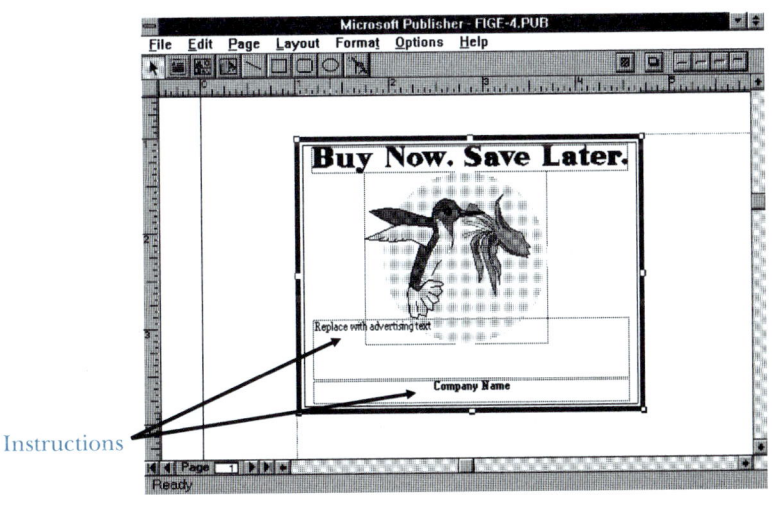

Pictures

To change the images in a PageWizard, click on the frame containing the image you want to change. If you are not concerned about scaling effects, use one of the Publisher commands, Paste or Import, to replace the contents of the frame with your own material. If you want to preserve accurate scaling, use Copy to duplicate the frame. Then import the image you want to use in its native dimensions. Use cropping and scaling to fit it to the copy. Finally, replace the original with the copy and delete the original.

WordArt, Line Art, BorderArt, and Shading

To change WordArt, line art, BorderArt, or shading, click on the object you want to modify and use standard Publisher editing procedures to alter it. For example, to change the copy in a WordArt frame, double-click on the frame and edit the copy field. Be aware, however, that Publisher often combines several objects to create an effect. If you inadvertently separate objects that should be together, use Undo to restore their original position. Then select them as a group.

Tip

If you want to move or copy a frame created with a PageWizard, the marquee is useful for selecting all of the objects at once.

F

Templates

Templates are completed publications that contain preconfigured page layouts, including frames and artwork. Microsoft Publisher comes with templates, and you can create your own. They are useful both for starting applications quickly and for learning more about the way Publisher puts objects together. In cases where expediency is paramount, you can load a template and simply substitute your own text and graphics for those in the template. You can practically go straight to press. Like PageWizards, templates are particularly effective with simple projects such as price lists or product rosters. In such applications unique or innovative design may not be of the greatest importance, but detailed work is required to create and position a large number of frames. A sample template is shown in Figure F-1.

    The templates contain so many good layouts that becoming familiar with them can only save you unnecessary work in the long run. Using or modifying the layout from an existing template for one of these applications, when appropriate, is always faster than designing a publication from scratch. You can, of course, use any of the standard Publisher editing techniques to modify a template and then save it as a new publication.

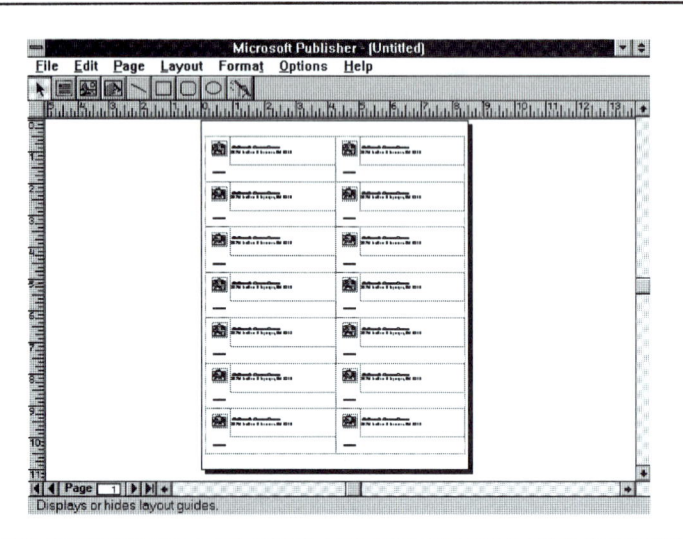

Figure F-1.   *Sample template*

A template is also a great place to store commonly used or difficult to develop publication *fragments*. If you do a lot of tabular work, for example, you might create a template that contains frames with frequently used tab stops. Similarly, you shouldn't need to repeat the chore of creating a neatly aligned column of identically sized bullets if you've already spent the time to do it once. By saving such objects as templates, you can use them in a new publication whenever you need them.

How Templates Work

Templates only differ from other publications in where Publisher stores them and how they are loaded. All templates are located in a directory called MSPUB\TEMPLATE on the drive where Publisher was installed on your system. Whenever you begin a publication using a template, Publisher displays all of the publications from that directory in the list on the Create New Publication dialog box, as shown in Figure F-2.

Appendix F: *Templates*

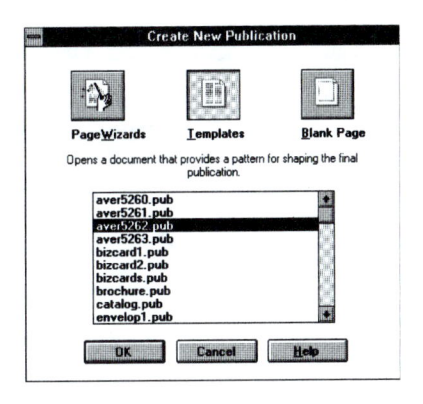

Figure F-2.   List of templates shown at startup

To use one of the templates in the list, click on it and click on OK. Publisher opens a new publication (untitled) using a copy of the template. When you save the new publication, provide an original name, and the file becomes a standard publication. The template, however, remains unchanged in the \MSPUB\TEMPLATE directory.

Note: All of the original Publisher templates are stored with Hide Object Boundaries and Hide Layout Guides turned on. You'll probably want to change those settings before you begin to alter it in a new publication.

Creating a Template of Your Own

Creating a template is as easy as saving a file. First design a publication that contains the material you want to save in the template. This process is no different from creating a standard publication. Then select Save As from the File menu. The Save As dialog box appears, as shown in Figure F-3.

Click on the Template button to enable it if you want to save the publication as a template. Publisher automatically stores the file in the \MSPUB\TEMPLATE directory. In the future, the file will automatically

Figure F-3.   Save As dialog box

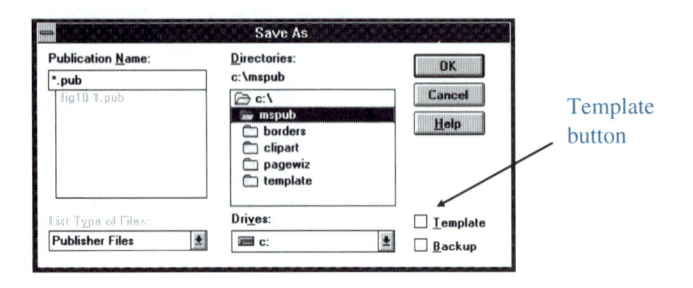

Template button

appear on the list of templates in the Create New Publication dialog box, and will load as a template when you select it.

Modifying a Template

Templates use only the standard Publisher objects. When you open a template as a publication, the actual file is loaded into Publisher. Any and all of the skills you have in working with Publisher can be applied to modifying a template.

1. To change the contents of a template, use Open Existing Publication from the File menu.
2. Select the TEMPLATE directory in the directory tree, and select the template publication that you want to change.
3. Make any of the changes that you want to the file.
4. Save the publication. The next time you use the template to start a new publication, it will contain the changes you made.

Appendix F: *Templates*

Template Types

Publisher contains approximately two dozen templates. Since they only have DOS filenames to identify them, use the following table as a reference for the contents of the files. The rattlesnake picture and letter Z are used as dummy material in several of the templates to demonstrate different design styles. The templates that use each of these styles are noted in the list.

Filename	Description
AVER5260	Three-up labels, four lines each
AVER5261	Two-up labels, four lines each
AVER5262	Two-up labels, two lines each with picture
AVER5263	Two-up business cards
BIZCARD1	Mechanical for landscape business card (rattlesnake)
BIZCARD2	Mechanical for portrait business card (Z)
BIZCARDS	Eight different business card designs
BROCHURE	Landscape brochure, letter-sized paper
CATALOG	Portrait catalog, letter-sized paper
ENVELOPE1	Envelope with picture (rattlesnake)
ENVELOPE2	Standard envelope (Z)
FLYER	Letter-sized handout
LABEL1	Mechanical for 3-by-5-inch label (rattlesnake)
LABEL2	Mechanical for 3-by-5-inch label (Z)
LTRHEAD1	Letterhead design, letter-sized paper (rattlesnake)
LTRHEAD2	Letterhead design, letter-sized paper (Z)
MEMO	Centered memo heading, letter-sized paper
MEMOZ	Left-aligned memo heading (Z)
PRICELST	Catalog page, letter-sized, ten items with **pictures**
PRODINFO	Catalog page, letter-sized, single product
REPORT	Newsletter, letter-sized paper
REPORTZ	Report Form, letter-sized (Z)
RESUME	Resume
ROSTER	Sign-in sheet/directory 28 lines, 4 columns

G

Installing Dover Clip Art

In addition to the clip art that comes with Publisher, the supplementary disk included with this book contains approximately 100 illustrations from the Dover Publications Pictorial Archive Series. The disk includes a varied selection of Dover clip art that is easy to load into your computer and place in your documents. Dover has been an outstanding name in clip art since long before the advent of desktop publishing, and is extremely well known throughout the fields of commercial graphics and art direction for the quality and scope of its material.

The illustrations on the disk were designed especially to work with Publisher. They use the same Computer Graphics Metafile format (CGM) as the clip art that comes with Publisher, and will work easily in a picture frame from any publication. Like all object-oriented files, they can be easily scaled without losing resolution.

The Dover clip art requires 900K of disk space. To make easiest use of the material—assuming that you have sufficient disk space—you'll probably want to install the illustrations on your system. The following instructions copy all of the Dover files into the directory \MSPUB\CLIPART, which is where the original Publisher clip art files are stored. The Dover files all begin with *D_*, so none of the original clip art is in danger of being overwritten. In addition, the instructions assume that the floppy drive on your system is drive A. If the drive you are using has another designation, substitute it in the instructions.

Windows Installation

1. Insert the disk into drive A.
2. Select Run from the File menu in the Windows Program Manager.
3. Type **a:install** (or substitute the appropriate drive letter).
4. Use the cursor keys to move to the fields for source drive or destination drive or directory, and adjust any of the field values.
5. Press (F10) to continue.
6. At the next screen press (ENTER) to continue, and then type **Y**.
7. Press (ESC) to return to Windows.

Manual Installation

1. Insert the disk into drive A.
2. Copy the file DOVERART.EXE into the directory in which you want to install the files.
3. Type **DOVERART**. This is a self-extracting file that will simply unpack the files in the current directory.
4. Delete the file DOVERART.EXE.

H

Printers and Printing

The subject of printers and printing in the desktop environment could, by itself, easily fill several books the size of this one. In addition, the Publisher *User's Guide* has a helpful section on troubleshooting common printing problems. This appendix is intended only to describe the basic print options available to you in Publisher.

Most printing options and some of the important page setup and formatting options available in Publisher are printer dependent. The selection of fonts and font sizes, for example, or the page size and paper source, all depend on the type of printer you use and how the printer is configured. Publisher can make use of only those printers you have installed under Windows. To use a new printer with Publisher, you must first install it in Windows.

Since publications are printer dependent, it is important to select the printer you want to use for a publication before starting the work. That way, you will know the scope of options before you begin. Just as important, don't switch printers once a publication is underway. For example, if you were to design a newsletter with 11-point CG Times for body copy, and then open the publication using a printer that supports only 12-point Courier, you would get surprising results. Since the larger nonproportional font (Courier) requires substantially more space to display characters, it is more than likely that all of the stories in the publication would spill into the overflow area. In addition, the piece would almost certainly lose its professional look. You can remedy the situation by selecting the printer that was used to create the piece originally. All should return to normal.

Installing Other Printers

Installing another printer is necessary if you acquire a new printer at your own location, but can also be useful if you plan to print at another location. If you add a printer to Windows, you don't necessarily need to have the physical printer connected to your system to design a publication using its features, but rather only to print it. If you know in advance, for example, that you will ultimately print a publication on an Apple LaserWriter or Linotronic 500, install those printers in Windows and select them in Publisher before designing the publication. Then send the print job to a file, as described later in this section, and carry or send the file to the location where the device exists.

Print Options

You can control most aspects of a Publisher print job from the Print and Print Setup dialog boxes. Print, shown in Figure H-1, contains different options for printing an individual publication. Print Setup is geared more to modifying settings for the current printer itself.

Print Range

The Print Range group of options lets you indicate which part of a publication to print. The All and Pages choices are mutually exclusive—by

Appendix H: *Printers and Printing*

Figure H-1.   *Print dialog box*

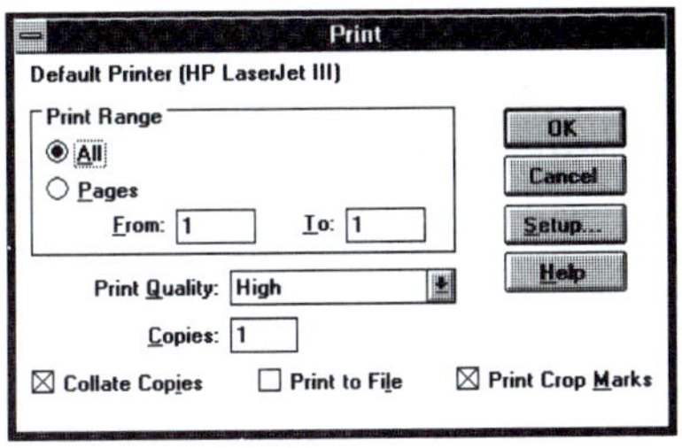

---

selecting All, you decide to print an entire publication and cannot enter a specific sequence of pages. If you select Pages, All is automatically deselected, and you can enter beginning and ending page numbers for the print job in the From and To fields. The default value is All.

Print Quality

The choices on the Print Quality list affect the speed and resolution at which a publication prints. In general, higher quality means slower speeds, and lower quality means faster ones. However, this will also depend on your printer. Some lasers, for example, print at the same speed, regardless of the resolution you select in Publisher. The Draft option prints a publication without printing its pictures. Since graphics require more computation, this almost always speeds up the print job, regardless of which printer you're using. The default value is High.

Copies

The Copies field determines the number of copies of the publication that print. Publisher will print any number of originals. This can be handy if you don't have a copier nearby. The default value is 1.

Collate Copies

When you print multiple copies of a multipage publication, enable the Collate Copies option to have Publisher print the pages of each copy in sequence. The default for this setting is off.

Print to File

The Print to File option lets you create a disk file of the print job. A disk file is useful if you plan to print the final copy of a publication on an output device that is somewhere other than your current location. By sending the publication to a file, it becomes portable. You can send the completed print job to another location by modem, or copy it to disk. If you select this option, Publisher prompts you for a filename before completing the job. The default for this option is off.

Print Crop Marks

Crop marks are used when the size of the pages in a publication will ultimately be smaller than the physical page on which they are printed. These are commonly found, for example, on a mechanical for business cards. Crop marks indicate where a page should be cut to make a final publication. They appear as small corner-shaped lines that frame the final page area as shown in the following illustration. The default for this setting is on.

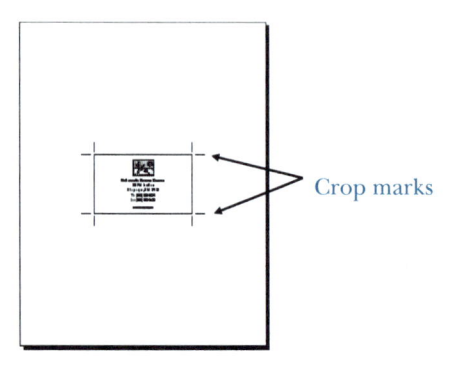

Crop marks

Appendix H: *Printers and Printing*

Figure H-2. *Print Setup dialog box*

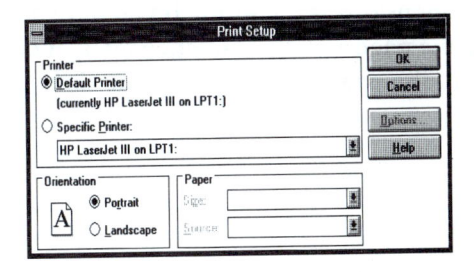

Print Setup Options

The Print Setup dialog box lets you change printers and settings for paper size, feed, and orientation as shown in Figure H-2. The choices available here are closely related to the printers you have installed under Windows.

Printer

The options in the Printer group control which printer Publisher uses to output publications. The Default printer is the current default printer installed for Windows. The selections in the Specific Printer list are the other printers you have installed under Windows. If you select one of these, Publisher will use the alternative printer, regardless of what is currently selected under Windows (provided that the printer is online). This is simply a method of overriding the printer selection in the Windows Control Panel.

Orientation

Page orientation lets you control the direction that Publisher prints in—left to right or bottom to top. In portrait orientation, printing occurs from left to right. Portrait is the more standard of the two orientations; it's always available and usually the default setting for most printers. In landscape orientation, printing occurs from bottom to top in order to use the larger of a page's two dimensions as the width. If you were using a typewriter, you could simply rotate the page 90 degrees. Since many modern printers do not allow you to reorient the page in its carriage, the direction of the printing itself is reoriented.

Paper

The Paper options let you choose the size of the paper and its source. The Size list lets you select one of the standard American (letter/legal) or European (A4/B5) paper sizes. When you select other than letter-size paper, you must enter the new dimensions for the page size in the Page Setup dialog box manually. Publisher does not automatically update these settings.

The Source list lets you select from different paper feeds. For example, some printers have two paper trays, each for a different size of paper. In such a case, you can select one of the two trays to draw paper from for a particular print job. If the printer you're using has only a single source, the list is inactive.

Options

The selections available from the Options dialog box vary, depending on the printer you are using. It may be inactive if the currently selected printer has no special options.

Index

A

Absolute location, 142
Active frame, 54
Actual Size view, 333, (illus., 63)
    page in, (illus., 154)
Actual view, 201, 206
Alignment, 9
    justified, 361, 362
    spacing buttons and, 37
    tab stop, 364
    in WordArt, 324-325
Anacortes font, 413
ANSI format for Windows, 308
Application icons, for Windows screen, 23
Application program, starting from Picture Frame, 327
Apply button, 231
Arch style, 245
Arrowheads, adding to lines, 351

Art. *See also* Graphics
    additional line, (illus., 80)
ASCII
    converting to, 173
    converting text to, 307-308
    exporting, 176
    importing, 176
Autoflow, 59, 180-182
    working with, (illus., 182)
Autoflow dialog box, (illus., 59)
Autoflow messages, (illus., 181)
    displaying, 182
Automatically create text frames option, 335

B

Back button, 32
Background button, 36
Background, ignore, 338
Background page, 82-83, 147-153

mirrored guides and, 150-151
objects created on, (illus., 149)
Backup button, 305
Bellingham font, 413
Best Fit, 238, 241
font scaling, 324
template, 244
Bitmap option, 264
in Paste Special dialog box, 320
Bitmapped images, 270-271, 366
Blank pages, inserting, 335
Blends, 86
Boldface type, 358
Book publications, 129-130
Books
page printing order in, (illus., 129)
pages as spreads in, 339
BorderArt, 13, 295-297
adding, 297
automatic resizing of, 296
dialog box, (illus., 296, 352)
modifying, 428
removing, 297, 352
samples, (illus., 14, 296)
usage and description of, 352-353
Borders, 115, 251
automatic adjustment of, 348
and BorderArt, 293-297
creating, 71
dialog box, (illus., 349)
partial, (illus., 295)
removing, 350
simple, 293-294
thickness, 293
usage and description of, 348-350
Browse buttons, 32-33
Bullets
creating, 286
handling, (illus., 286)
Business cards, 132-134
creating sheet of, (illus., 134)
dimensions of, (illus., 342)
format of, 341
sample, (illus., 87)
screen page and printed page for, (illus., 128)
Button
back, 32

background, 36
connect, 60
crop, 37
cropping, 112
index, 32
search, 33-34
shadow, 36
style, 245
Buttons, 28-29
alignment and spacing, 37
browse, 32-33
command, 28
help, 31-34
line, 37-38
line width, 37
minimize/maximize, 25
option, 28
toolbar and, 36-38

C

Calendar, creating with PageWizards, 421, (illus., 422)
Capital letters, 358
Cards
business, 132-134. *See also* Business cards
index, 132-134. *See also* Index cards
side- and top-fold, 131-132
tent, 130-131
Carriage returns, 188
finding, 213
Catalog, creating, 275-277
Centering frames, 91-93
Character dialog box, 66, 205, (illus., 66, 206)
toolbar and, 205
Character formats, toolbar and, 204
Character formatting, 201
position, 202
style, 202
Characters
bold, 367
dialog box, (illus., 357)
formatting, 202-211, 235-247
formatting options for, 357
italic, 358
usage and description, 356-358
Chart, editing, 327

Index 445

Check spelling
    dialog box, (illus., 368)
    usage and description, 368-369
Clicking, 20-21
Clip art, 252. *See also* Art, Graphics
    installing, 435-436
    residing in a directory, 254
    samples, (illus., 11)
Clipboard
    copying and cutting a frame in, 257
    Windows, 107
Cloning objects, with Paste command, 318-319
Close publication, usage and description, 303
Collate copies option, 311
Color
    background, 290
    foreground, 290
    selecting background, 326
Color shading, 355
Colors
    accenting frames with, 289
    adding to lines, 351
Column gutter, 222-223, 225
    creating, (illus., 225)
    determining, 347
Columns
    definition of, 4
    page divided into, (illus., 5)
    picture placed between, (illus., 7)
    at right of insertion point, 225
Columns/rows, setting numbers of, 344
Command buttons, 28
Commands. *See* specific command
Computer Graphics Metafile (CGM), 252, 310, 435
    clip art and, 253
Connect button, 179-180, 183
    appearance of, (illus., 180)
    changes when text flows, (illus., 60)
    definition of, 60
Connect frames, text flows and, (illus., 179)
Connecting frames, 182-185
    and Autoflow, 180-182
    story between frames, 185
Connecting text, 178-185
Connection arrows, 180
Control menu, box for Windows screen, 24

Copies
    collating, 440
    number of printed, 311
    printing number of, 439
Copy, 168-171
    Cut, Paste, and, 107-111
    definition of, 161
    format, 164
    getting the, 163-164
    refining, 164
    and work files, 162-164
Copy command, 317-318
Copy field, 232
Copy sheet, definition of, 178
Copying
    block of text, (illus., 169)
    to Clipboard, 168, 172
Correcting, with Undo command, 208
Create New Publication
    dialog box, (illus., 426)
    usage and description, 300-301
Crop button, 37
Crop marks, printing, 311-312, 440
Crop picture command, 367
Cropping, 240
    image, 274-278, (illus., 274)
    explanation of, 10
    with handles, 275
Cropping button, 112
Cropping icon, 278
Cut command, 185, 317
Cut, copy, paste, and move pictures, 266
Cut, paste, and copy, 107-111, 168-171
    described, 111
    options, 172

D

Decimal tab stops, setting, 364
Default margins, text frames and, 218
Default selection, 49
Defaults, changing, 347
Delete, 171
    global, 332
    pages, 146
Delete command, 321
Delete Page command, 335-336
Delete text, 166, 167

Delete Text Frame command, 321-322
Design gallery, 377-409
Desktop publishing, defined, 2
Desktop, for Windows screen, 23
Dialog box, typical, (illus., 26). *See also* specific type
    appearing when page is too large, (illus., 136)
    use of, 27-29, 42-43
Dictionary, Publisher, 368
Directory tree, 302
    in file importing, 307
    in Import Picture dialog box, 309
Disconnect, story between frames, 185
Display, normal, 302
Display options
    to change rulers, 159
    for layout guides, 139-140
    for pictures, 269-270
    for rulers, 158-159
Documents, creating from scratch, 426
DOS formats, reading files in various, 307-308
Dot leader, 365, (illus., 365)
Double-clicking, definition of, 21-22
Dover clip art, installing, 435-436
Dover Publications Pictorial Archive Series, 250
Draft option, in printing, 311, 439
Dragging
    definition of, 22-23
    window, (illus., 22)
Drawing tools, 13
Drives
    list of in Open Existing Publications dialog box, 302
    list of in Save As dialog box, 305
Drop shadows, 115, 292
Dropout letters, 243
Dummy text, 175
Duplicate objects, on the Page option, 335
Duplicating frames, 109-111
Duvall font, 414

E

Edit menu, 39, 171, 315-332
Edit WordArt object, 232
    dialog box, (illus., 323, 325)

    usage and description, 322-327
Editing
    and formatting pictures, 265-278
    text, 165-171
Ellensburg font, 414
Ellipses, 179
Embedding
    considerations in, 320
    files, 263-265
    material from a Microsoft application, 265
    picture frame with files, 263-264
Encapsulated PostScript, 252, 310
Endmark, 180
Entering
    and formatting text, 61-66
    text, 165-171
Enumclaw font, 414
Envelopes, manual sizing of, 343
Errors
    correcting, 169
    correcting with Undo, 316
Excel spreadsheet, embedding an, 259
Exchanging texts
    with non-Windows programs, 173-178
    with Windows applications, 172-173
Exit Publisher command, 315
Exporting ASCII, 176
Exporting text
    to a non-Windows program, 178
    to a Windows application, 172
    to a word processor, 178

F

Facing pages, 344-345, (illus., 345)
Fancy first letter, 424-425, (illus., 425)
Fields, definition of, 27-28
File extensions, automatic, 306
File format, converting, 178
File menu, 38, 300-315
    in Program Manager, (illus., 26)
File Type list, 175
Filename, providing a, 304
Files. *See also* Text
    recently accessed, 300
    text added, (illus., 62)
    types of in importing, 307

Index 447

Fill option, adding color with, 324
Find, 186-189. *See also* Searching
    dialog box, (illus., 329)
    and overflow area, 186
    usage and description, 328-331
Find and Replace, 186-191
    text, 191
Find dialog box, 187
Find Next, 187, 190
Find options
    practicing with, 186-188
    selecting, 187
Find Text, 189
Fit horizontally, 247
Float, definition of, 89
Flowing text, 60-61
Flyer, example of, (illus., 91)
Font, 357. *See also* Fonts
    list, 205
    selection for printing, 437
    size, 205, 357
    stretched vertically, 241
Font window, definition of, 37
Fonts
    definition of, 9
    and font sizes, 213, (illus., 203)
    monospaced, 237
    nonproportional, 437
    proportionally spaced, 237
    sans serif, 237
    scalable, 324
    serif, 237
    and shadows, 243
    substituting, 204
    WordArt, 323, 413-418, (listed, 324)
Forced column break, 347
Forced line breaks, 364-365
Format menu, 40, 205, 356-367
Formats
    copy, 164
    removing style and position, 205
Formatting
    characters, 202-211
    entering text and, 61-66
    page, 122-143
    paragraphs, 211-222
    text, 199-226
    text in PRODINFO.PUB, (illus., 204)

    text selection techniques and, 201
    WordArt, 234-247
Frame
    active, 54
    completed text, (illus., 53)
    formatting, 201, 222-227
    graphics, 115-119
    layout, (illus., 100)
    three levels of, (illus., 290)
    tools, 7, 86
Frame Columns and Margins
    changing, 225
    dialog box, 223, 224, (illus., 347)
    setting, 95-97
    usage and description, 346-348
Frame tool, using PageWizard, 424-426
Frames, 54-56, 85-119
    adding, 7-8, (illus., 8)
    adding graphics quickly to, 118
    adding picture, 66-69
    adding text, 52-54
    from another publication, 257
    centering, 91-93
    completed text, 89
    connecting several, 185
    creating, 86-97, 163
    customizing, 9-12
    deleting, 184
    deleting connected, 321-322
    disconnecting, 182, 184
    duplicating, 109-111
    explained, 3
    empty, 181
    filling, 8-9
    formatting, 247
    moving, 103-107
    moving connected, 184
    moving group of between pages, 104-107
    moving to scratch area, 268
    multiple, 99-101
    on a page, (illus., 163)
    picture, 10-11
    publication after adding text, (illus., 56)
    resized picture, (illus., 70)
    resizing, 69-71, 112-115, 240
    review for, 119
    selecting, 97-102

selecting and moving, (illus., 267)
selecting multiple, 99-102
squaring, 93-94
text, 9-10
with text, (illus., 81)
tracking the sequence of, 184
WordArt, 11-12
Full page, 127-128

G

Geometric shapes, 283
Global deletion, 332
Go to Background/Foreground command, 338-339
Graphics. *See also* Art
    adding, 77-79
    adding to frame quickly, 118
    adding spice with, 12-13
    bitmapped, 366
    frame, 115-119
    object-oriented, 366
    options to create letterheads, (illus., 116)
    repeated in multipage project, 285
    and work flow, 250-251
Graphics accents
    adding, 282
    using, 281, (illus., 282)
Graphics file formats, 252
    supported by Publisher, (list, 309-310)
Greek, definition of, 58
Greeting cards
    formats of, 340-341, (illus., 341)
    in PageWizards, 423
Gutter, definition of, 141

H

Handles, 88
Headings, in mirrored layout, (illus., 151)
Headlines, completed for second article, (illus., 67)
Help, 29-34, 66
    buttons, 31-34
    indexes, 30
    menu, 41
    screen, (illus., 67)

Hide Boundaries option, 270
Hide Object Boundaries, 270
    templates sorted with, 431
Hide Pictures option, 270
Hide/Show and Snap tools, 139
Hide/Show Layout Guides command, 374
Hide/Show Object Boundaries command, 374-375
Hide/Show Pictures command, 373
Hide/Show Rulers command, 373
Hide/Show Status Line command, 373-374
Highlight Story command, 321
Highlighting story, 167-168, 185, 207
HiJaak file conversion program, 309
Horizontal alignment, 326
Horizontal rules, 79
Hyphen
    modifying location of, 193
    non-breaking, 192
    optional, 192
    suppressing, 192
Hyphenate At field, 192
Hyphenate dialog box, (illus., 370)
Hyphenation, 193, 194, 370-371
    automatic, 13, 224, 347
    and check all stories, 193
    checking correct, 192
    confirming, 193
    in next story, 193
    skipping, 193
    and white space, (illus., 192)
    zone, 193, 371

I

Icons, sizing, 112-113
Ignore Background command, 338
Illustrations, creating with BorderArt, 352-353
Images, 249-279. *See also* Pictures
    copied to Windows Clipboard, 256
    cropping, 274-278
    importing, 252-255
    loading, 251
    object-oriented, 271
    pasted between Windows applications, 256-257
    pasting, 257
    scaling and cropping, 251

Index 449

storing, 252
working with, 249-279
Import for Windows file conversion
 program, 309
Import picture, 308-310
 dialog box, (illus., 69, 253, 308)
Import pictures, 255
Import text, 176, 306-308
 dialog box, (illus., 59, 174, 307)
 in recognized format, 174
Import warning message, (illus., 257)
Imported PROFILE.TXT, (illus., 175)
Imported text, combined with other material, 175
Importing
 ASCII, 176
 different results, (illus., 254)
 images, 252-255
 text, 58-59, 224
 text from non-Windows programs, 176
Indent, 213-215
 alignment, 361
 first line, 361
 left, 361
 right, 361
Indents and Spacing, 360-362
 dialog box, (illus., 215, 361)
Index button, 32
Index cards, 132-134
 format, 341, (illus., 342)
Indexed and context-sensitive systems, 30
Indexes, help, 30
Indication marks, border, 350
Inglewood font, 414
Insert mode, 165
Insert Object, 327-328
 dialog box, 233, (illus., 259, 328)
 object from Microsoft application, 261
Insert Pages, 145, 334-335
 dialog box, (illus., 335)
Insert Page Numbers command, 336-338
 procedure, 337
Inserting
 and embedding objects, 258-265
 in a native environment, 259
 objects, 259-260
 pages, 143-145
Insertion point, 27

Inspection, of work, 13-14
Installation, Dover clip art, 435
 manually, 436
 in Windows, 436
Italic characters, 358

J

Justification
 definition of, 10
 letter, 247
 text in WordArt, 325
 word, 246

K

Kerning, 209-211, 359-360, (illus., 359). *See also* Spacing
 characters, 211
 definition of, 210-211
 and large font sizes, 211
 proportional spacing after, (illus., 210)
Keyboard equivalents, 41
 to editing commands, 171
Keyboard shortcuts, 41-42, 419-420

L

Labels, creating page of, (illus., 110)
Landscape orientation, 123
 screen display for letter-sized paper in, (illus., 126)
Langley font, 415
Laser printer, 366
Layout, 121-160
 from different templates, (illus., 122)
 mirrored, 141, (illus., 141)
 options, (illus., 6)
 page, 160
 sample, (illus., 137)
 selecting, 51-52
Layout Guides, 54, 343-346
 dialog box, (illus., 138, 344)
 Hide/Show, 374
 page margins and, 136-143
 to set Hide/Show or Snap for, 140
Layout menu, 39-40, 343-356
Leader character, 364

Leading, 216
    adjusting, (illus., 216)
    and indents and spacing, 216
    and space after paragraph, 216
    and space before paragraph, 216
Line art, 251, 283-289. *See also* Art, Graphics
    adding borders and shading, 251
    additional, (illus., 80)
    applications of, (illus., 283)
    BorderArt and shading, 281-298
    combining, (illus., 285)
    creating, 285
    definition of, 284
    modifying, 428
    object handles, 284
Line buttons, 37-38
Line dialog box, (illus., 288)
Line spacing, 362
Line width buttons, definition of, 37
Lines, 287, 350-351
    adjusting thickness of, 351
    dialog box, (illus., 351)
    inserting new, 232
    resizing, 287
    rotating, 287
Link, between programs, 264-265
Lists, definition of, 29
Longview font, 415

M

Magnification screen, 333
Margins
    adjusting for frame types, 346-348
    changing layout guides and, 139
    definition of, 4
    frame and page, (illus., 223)
    page, 136-143
    picture frame, 266-268
    in run-arounds, (illus., 268)
    setting, 97, 344
    setting frame, 95-97
Marquee, 101-102
    selecting whole column with, (illus., 102)
Marysville font, 415
Match case option
    in Replace, 332
    in Search, 329-330
Match Whole Word Only option
    in Replace, 332
    in Search, 329
Measurements, typing, 215, 376
Mechanicals, definition of, 133
Menu, 25-27. *See also* specific types
    bar, 25
    Edit, 39
    File, 38
    Format, 40
    Help, 41
    Layout, 39-40
    Options, 40
    Page, 39, (illus., 63)
    Publisher, 38-42
    reference, 299-376
Message line, 36
Metafile option, 264
    in Paste Special dialog box, 320
Micrografx Designer, 252
Mineral font, 415
Minimize/Maximize buttons, 25
Mirrored Guides
    background pages and, 150-151
    facing pages and, 141-142
    implementing, 143
    pagination and, 337
Mirrored layouts, (illus., 141)
    in books, 344-346, (illus., 345)
    headings in, (illus., 151)
Mistakes, correcting, 43-44
Modem, 440
Monospaced fonts, 209. *See also* Fonts
Mouse, 20-23
    moves in Undo, 316-317
Mover, definition of, 103
Moving
    frames, 103-107
    objects, (illus., 145)
MS Works, converting text from, 308
Multiple pages, using, 143-147

N

Naming files, 304
Native option, in Paste Special dialog box, 320

Index

Network environment, working in, 262
Newsletter
    completed sample, (illus., 48)
    in PageWizards, 423
Next button, in PageWizards, 423
Note, size of, 263
Note-It, 261-263
    in action, (illus., 262)
    creating, 263
    definition of, 261
    dialog box, (illus., 262)
    editing, 261
    text of, 261
Notepad
    accessory, and Windows, 172
    embedding and, 320

O

Object boundaries, Hide/Show, 374-375
Object linking, 259, 320, 328
Objects, 3
    fitting on page, (illus., 4)
    manipulating in Edit menu, 315
    repeating on every page, 150
Omak font, 416
Open Existing Publication, 301-303
    dialog box, (illus., 302)
Option buttons, 28
Optional hyphen, 190
Options
    dialog box, 442
    display for layout guides, 139-140
    display for rulers, 158-159
    layout, (illus., 6)
    menu, 40, 367-376
    other screen display, 159
Orientation
    business card, (illus., 124)
    changing page, 126
    landscape, 123, 313, 441-442, (illus., 124, 314)
    page, 123-126
    portrait, 123, 313, 441-442, (illus., 124, 314)
    screen display for letter-sized paper, (illus., 126)
Overflow area, 58, 182, 184

Find command and, 330
Overflow message, (illus., 170)

P

Page
    area, 34
    creating label, (illus., 110)
    creating three-up label, (illus., 110)
    design with PageWizards, 421-428
    divided into four columns, (illus., 5)
    divided into six rows, (illus., 5)
    formatting, 122-143
    indicator and controls, 36
    margins and layout guides, 136-143
    marker, 336, 337
    menu, 39, 333-343, (illus., 53)
    repeating objects on every, 150
Page layout, 3, 121-160
    controlling with Page menu, 333
    creating, 3-7
    review for, 160
Page numbers, 151-153, 375
    changing, 337
    creating, 153
    inserting, 336-338
Page orientation, 123-126, 441-442. *See also* Orientation
    changing, 126
    setting for, 312, 313
Page Setup, 339-343
    dialog box, (illus., 128, 339)
Page size, 135-136
    changing, 136
    checking, 342
    determining in page setup, 339
    inserting, 143-145
    settings for, 312
Pages, 3
    adding, 79-82
    applying different text formats to, 10
    background, 82-83, 147-153
    changing, 147
    deleting, 146
    fitting objects on, (illus., 4)
    frames added to, (illus., 8)
    inserting, 145
    reformatted, (illus., 106)

using multiple, 143-147, (illus., 108)
PageWizards, 74-77, 300, 421-428
    applications, (list, 422)
    calendar, (illus., 77)
    control buttons, 423
    dialog box, (illus., 75)
    icon, 301
    modifying material in, 426-427
    questionnaire sample page in, (illus., 16)
    starting, 423
    templates and, 14-17
Pagination, 147
Paintbrush accessories, 256
Paper options, 442
Paper sizes, 442, (list, 313)
    changing page orientation for, 126
    page orientation and, 123-126
Paragraph alignment, 212
Paragraph formatting, 201, 211-222
    and lines, 212
    options, 214
    removing, 214
Paragraph spacing, 362
Paragraphs
    carriage returns for, 212
    formatting, 211-222
    indents, alignment and spacing of, 213-215
    leading, 216
    selecting, 212-213
    tabs and, 217-222
Paste, 168-171
    between Windows applications, 256-258
    image from Paintbrush, (illus., 256)
Paste command, 318-319
Paste, Copy, and Cut, 107-111
Paste Special command 319-321
    dialog box, (illus., 320)
    inactive, 264
PC Paintbrush, 252, 309
Pictorial Archive Series, 435. *See also* Dover
Picture Frame tool, 252
Picture frames, 10-11, 250-251
    adding, 66-69
    creating, 251
    margins on, 266-268
    placed on background, 269

resizing, 271-273, (illus., 70)
    transparent, 289
    tutorial publication with, (illus., 68)
Pictures
    changing in PageWizards, 428
    creating, 252-265
    cropping, 367
    Cut, Copy, Paste, and Move, 266
    display option for, 269-270
    editing, 265-278
    formatting, 265-278
    importing, 308-310
    linking, 233
    repeating and replacing, 269
    restoring the size of, 273
    scaling, 270-273, 309, 347, 365-366
    text flowing around, 267
Plain style, 244
Plain text, 175. *See also* ASCII
Pointing, 20
Portrait orientation, 123. *See also* Orientation
Preview, in Import Pictures dialog box, 309
Print, 310-312
    dialog box, (illus., 43, 310, 439)
    options, 438-440
    quality, 439
    quality options, 311
    range options, 311, 438-439
Print Setup, 312-314
    dialog box, (illus., 125, 313, 441)
    options, 441-442
Print to File option, 311, 440
Printers, 44-45, 437-442
    changing, 312
    default, 441
    installing, 437, 438
    options, 312-313
    switching, 437
Printing, 83-84, 437-442
    color, 203-204
Proportional scaling, 275
Proportionally spaced fonts, 209, 210. *See also* Fonts
.PUB file extension, automatic appending of, 304
Publication type, 127-134
    selecting, 134
Publications, 2

Index 453

    books, 129-130
    close, 303
    creating new, 300
    opening existing, 301-303
    putting together, 1-17
    types of, 127
Publisher, 34-45
    concepts, 2-3
    dialog boxes, 42-43
    menus, 38-42
    operation, 19-45
    screen, 153-160, (illus., 35, 50)
    starting, 49-50
    template, 208
    window features, 34-36

Q

Questionnaires
    control buttons, 423

R

README.TXT file, location of, 187
Redo, 316
Reformatted pages, (illus., 106)
Repeating and replacing pictures, 269
Replace, 189-191, 331-332. *See also* Find and Replace
    dialog box, (illus., 190, 331)
    in PageWizards, 423
    Undo and, 189
Replace All, 190
Replace and Find, 186-191
    text, 191
Replace options, 189-190
Resizing, frame, 69-71, 112-115
RESUME.PUB, using, 213, (illus., 214)
Review. *See* ends of chapters
Rewind button, in PageWizards, 423
Rich Text Format (RTF), converting, 308
Ripple effect, in deleting connected frames, 321-322
Rows, 4
    page divided into, (illus., 5)
RTF (Rich Text Format), converting, 308
Ruler tick marks
    resetting, 157-158
    setting, 158
Rulers, 35, 155-159
    display options for, 158-159
    moving, 155-156, (illus., 156)
    repositioning vertical, (illus., 52)
Rules, 13
    horizontal, 78-79
    vertical, 78-79
Run-arounds, 267, 268

S

Sans serif fonts, 209
Save As command, 304-306
    dialog box, (illus., 42, 57, 177, 305)
Save command, 304
Save feature, warning message, 303, (illus., 303)
Save Selection As button, 305-306
Saving, 56-58
    before exiting, 315
Scale and crop, using rulers to, (illus., 276)
Scale picture, 365-367
    dialog box, (illus., 366)
Scaling, 10
    revising effects of, 273
Scaling effects, on images, (illus., 272)
Scaling pictures, 270-273
Scanned, 252
Scratch area, 35
    in delete, 336
Screen, (illus., 35, 50)
    display options, 159
    help, (illus., 67)
    Start Up, (illus., 50)
    working with Publisher, 153-160
Screen views, 333-334
    keyboard shortcuts, (list, 334)
Scrolling, in Actual Size view, 334
Search. *See also* Find
    button, 33-34
    dialog box from help system, (illus., 33)
    directional, 330
Searching
    back up the page, 188
    from the beginning, 187
    block of text, 180
    carriage returns, 188

    with forced line breaks, 188
    match case button, 188
    match whole words only in, 188
    nonprinting characters, 188
    question mark and, 188
    skipping words and, 188
    with tabs, 188
    white space and, 188
    wildcard character, 188
Selecting
    frames, 97-102
    multiple frames, 99-102
    text, 166-168
Send to Back/Bring to Front command, 348
Sequim font, 416
Series, deleting with Highlight Story, 322
Serif fonts, 209
Settings, 375-376
    dialog box, (illus., 375)
Shading, 115, 353-355
    adding color and to frame, 291
    colors and, 289-292
    dialog box, (illus., 117, 291, 355)
    modifying, 423
    shadows and, 289-292, (illus., 292)
Shadow, 243-244, 292
    alignment, 326
    button, 36, 292
    color and, 292
    command, 356
Side-fold cards, 131-132, (illus., 132)
Size
    list, 205
    page, 135-136
    reduction, 232
    resetting text problems with, 208
    window, 37, 208
Sizing icon, 112-113
Slant Down style, 244
Slant Up style, 244
Snap to guides, 140
    command, 372
Snap to Ruler Marks command, 372
Snohomish font, 416
Solid shapes, 285-286
Source list, 442
Spacing, 213-215
Spacing Between Characters, 359-360

    dialog box, (illus., 360)
Spell checking, 13, 194-196, 368
    and Change All, 195
    and Change To Field, 195
    and Ignore All, 195
    and Skip All-Capital Word, 195
Spelling dialog box, (illus., 195)
Spreads, 129
Squaring frames, 93-94
Start Up
    dialog box, (illus., 301)
    screen, 423
Status line, Hide/Show, 373-374
Stretch, 241
    vertical, 241, 242
    vertical font scaling, 326
Style list, 230
Subscript, 358
Superscript, 358

T

Tab character, 218
Tab dialog box, (illus., 220)
Tab stops, 218. *See also* Tabs
    aligning, 364
    center-aligned, 219
    changing, 222
    clearing, 221, 222
    copying, 221
    copying a text frame and, 221
    copying paragraphs, 221
    decimal, 219
    deleting text, 221
    entering new, 220
    formatting, 221
    leader and, 219
    left-aligned, 218-219
    moving, 222, 364
    right-aligned, 219
    setting, 219, 363-364
    templates and, 221
    WordArt and, 232
Tabs, 217-222, 362-365. *See also* Tab stops
    dialog box, (illus., 363)
    text alignment and, 218
    used in copy, (illus., 217)
Templates, 4, 429-433, (illus., 431)

Index 455

    creating, 431-432
    creating new publication with, 300
    layouts from different, (illus., 122)
    modifying, 432
    PageWizards and, 14-17
    price list, (illus., 15, 98)
    sample, (illus., 430)
    saving publication as, 304-305
    storing fragments in, 430
    types, (listed, 433)
Tent card, 130-131, (illus., 131)
    format of, 340, (illus., 340)
Text
    other applications and, 171-178
    blending graphics with, (illus., 249)
    changing in PageWizards, 427
    connecting, 178-185
    creating, 161-197
    deleting, 166-167
    dummy, 175
    entering and editing, 165-171
    entering and formatting, 61-66
    exchanging, 172-175
    exporting, 172, 178
    finding, 189
    finding and replacing, 191
    flowing, 60-61
    highlighting, 167-168
    importing, 58-59, 174, 176, 306-308
    modifying in WordArt frame, 323
    non-Windows programs and, 173-178
    placing in overflow area, 180
    selecting larger blocks of, 166
    shortcut for selecting, 167
    transferring, 171
    Windows applications and, 172-175
    WordArt applications for, (illus., 200)
Text correction tools, 185-196
Text files, added, (illus., 62)
Text flows, changes in Connect button when, (illus., 60)
Text formatting, 199-226
    effects of, (illus., 202)
    types of, 201
Text frames, 9-10, 161, (illus., 81)
    adding, 52-54
    completed, (illus., 53, 89)
    connecting, 179

    deleting, 321-322
    empty, 165, (illus., 165)
    pasting text into, 172
    publication after four added, (illus., 56)
    Undo, 54
Text markers, with PageWizard, (illus., 427)
Text-oriented frames, 162. *See also* Text frames
Text selection, clearing, 167
Title bar, Windows screen, 24
Toggles, 139
Toolbar, 36-38
    buttons and, 36-38
    definition of, 36
    formatting with, 204-205
    indents, 214
    starting PageWizards from, 423
    type size and, 209
Tools
    drawing, 13
    frame, 86
    Hide/Show and Snap, 139
    PageWizard, 15
Touchet font, 416
Tupelo font, 417
Tutorial publication, (illus., 68)
Type. *See also* Fonts
    applications for, (illus., 207)
    of file list, 309
    publication, 127-134
    scaling. *See* Fonts
    size, 200
Type Style buttons, 37
Typefaces, 212. *See also* Fonts, Type

U

Underlining, 358
Undo command, 43, 169, 316-317
    for text frame, 54
    working with Replace, 332
Upside Down style, 245

V

Vancouver font, 417
Vashon font, 417
Vector graphics, 271

Vertical rule, (illus., 78)
Vertical scroll bars, 34-35
Views, 153
    switching, 153-155
Visual effects, creating unusual, 348, (illus., 349)
Visual plane, (illus., 288)
    shading along, 353, (illus., 354)
    switching, 287-289
    switching object, 289

W

Walla Walla font, 417
Warning message, save, 303
Wenatchee font, 418
Wildcard character, 188
    Find command and, 330
Window
    font, 37
    size, 37
Window features, 34-36
Windows, 23-34
    dragging, (illus., 22)
    screen, 23-25, (illus., 24)
Windows Bitmap, 252, 309
Windows Clipboard, 107
    Cut command in, 317
    Paste command in, 318-319
    sending copy to, 317-318
Windows Help Index, (illus., 31)
Windows Metafile, 252, 310
Windows Notepad, embedding and, 259
Word for DOS, converting text from, 308
Word for Windows, embedding, 259
Word wrap, 165, 232
    margins and, 232
WordArt, 71-73, 227-250
    added for headline and Fancy First letter, (illus., 73)
    aligned copy and, 246
    alignment, 246-247
    applications, 227
    Clipboard and, 229
    color background option, 247
    combining styles and alignments in, 244
    creating a border with, 236-237
    creating a button with, (illus., 246)
    creating a logo with, 236
    dialog box, 234
    effects, 234
    entering and editing, 229-233
    fill option, 242-243
    fixed sizes for, (illus., 239)
    fonts, 228-229, 235-237, 413-418, (illus., 235)
    fonts in color in, 235
    formatting, 234-247
    formatting characters, 235-244
    formatting frames, 247
    formatting paragraphs, 244-247
    importing texts, 229
    letter justified, 247
    modifying, 428
    multiple frames and, 234
    paragraph alignment, 234
    paragraph styles, 234
    samples of, (illus., 12)
    scalable fonts, 238
    shadow, 243-244
    size, 238-241
    stretch vertical and, 234, 241-242
    style, 244-246
    uses of, (illus., 228)
    vertical stretching and, (illus., 242)
    Word justified copy and, 246
WordArt dialog box, (illus., 72, 230)
    copying text into, 229
    displaying, 232
    dragging the, (illus., 231)
WordArt frames, 11-12, 161, 163, 233, 242
    changing contents of, 229
    changing margins of, 247
    creating, 230
    color characters and, 242
    definition of, 161
    reducing the size of, 240
    transparent, 240
WordArt styles, 244, (illus., 245), (table, 237)
    arch, 245
    button, 245
    plain, 244
    slant down, 244
    slant up, 244
    upside down, 245
WordPerfect, converting text from, 308

Index

Words, into text frame, 164-185
WordStar, converting text from, 308
Write accessory, 172

Osborne McGraw-Hill

Computer Books

(800) 227-0900

Bookmarker Design — Lance Ravella

Tear off for Bookmark

You're important to us...

We'd like to know what you're interested in, what kinds of books you're looking for, and what you thought about this book in particular.

Please fill out the attached card and mail it in. We'll do our best to keep you informed about Osborne's newest books and special offers.

▶ *YES, Send Me a FREE Color Catalog of all Osborne computer books*
To Receive Catalog, Fill in Last 4 Digits of ISBN Number from Back of Book (see below bar code) 0-07-881_ _ _ – _

Name: _____ Title: _____

Company: _____

Address: _____

City: _____ State: _____ Zip: _____

I'M PARTICULARLY INTERESTED IN THE FOLLOWING *(Check all that apply)*

I use this software
- ☐ WordPerfect
- ☐ Microsoft Word
- ☐ WordStar
- ☐ Lotus 1-2-3
- ☐ Quattro
- ☐ Others _____

I use this operating system
- ☐ DOS
- ☐ Windows
- ☐ UNIX
- ☐ Macintosh
- ☐ Others _____

I rate this book:
- ☐ Excellent ☐ Good ☐ Poor

I program in
- ☐ C or C++
- ☐ Pascal
- ☐ BASIC
- ☐ Others _____

I chose this book because
- ☐ Recognized author's name
- ☐ Osborne/McGraw-Hill's reputation
- ☐ Read book review
- ☐ Read Osborne catalog
- ☐ Saw advertisement in store
- ☐ Found/recommended in library
- ☐ Required textbook
- ☐ Price
- ☐ Other _____

Comments _____

Topics I would like to see covered in future books by Osborne/McGraw-Hill include:
_____

IMPORTANT REMINDER
To get your FREE catalog, write in the last 4 digits of the ISBN number printed on the back cover (see below bar code) 0-07-881 _ _ _ – _

NO POSTAGE
NECESSARY
IF MAILED
IN THE
UNITED STATES

BUSINESS REPLY MAIL
First Class   Permit NO. 3111   Berkeley, CA

Postage will be paid by addressee

Osborne McGraw-Hill
2600 Tenth Street
Berkeley, California 94710-9938

Osborne McGraw-Hill

Computer Books

(800) 227-0900